The Big Problem of Small Change

THE PRINCETON ECONOMIC HISTORY
OF THE WESTERN WORLD

Joel Mokyr, Editor

The Big Problem of Small Change, by Thomas J. Sargent
and François R. Velde

*Growth in a Traditional Society: The French Countryside,
1450–1815*, by Philip T. Hoffman

*The Vanishing Irish: Households, Migration, and
the Rural Economy in Ireland, 1850–1914*,
by Timothy W. Guinnane

*Black '47 and Beyond: The Great Irish Famine in
History, Economy, and Memory*, by Cormac Ó Gráda

*The Great Divergence: China, Europe, and The Making
of the Modern World Economy*, by Kenneth Pomeranz

The Big Problem of Small Change

Thomas J. Sargent

François R. Velde

Princeton University Press   Princeton and Oxford

© 2002 by Princeton University Press
Published by Princeton University Press, 41 William Street,
Princeton, New Jersey 08540
In the United Kingdom: Princeton University Press, 3 Market Place,
Woodstock, Oxfordshire, OX20 1SY

All Rights Reserved

ISBN 0–691–02932–6

This book has been composed in Adobe Garamond by the authors,
using TEX and the TEXsis 2.16 macros.

Printed on acid-free paper. ∞

www.pup.princeton.edu

Printed in the United States of America

10 9 8 7 6 5 4 3 2 1

In memoriam
Carlo Maria Cipolla
(August 15, 1922–September 5, 2000)

Contents

Part I: A Problem and Its Cure

1. Introduction   3

Paper and gold. The enduring problem of small change. A model. Supply side: the mint. Demand side: the coin owner. Shortages. Price level determination. Remedies. A history. Structure of subsequent chapters.

2. A Theory   15

Valuation by weight or tale. A basic one-denomination theory. Multiple denominations. Supply. Demand. Interactions of supply and demand. Economics of interval alignments. Perverse dynamics. Spontaneous debasements: invasions of foreign coins. Costs and Temptations. Opportunity cost. An open market operation from Castile. An open market operation for the standard formula. Transparency of opportunity cost. Trusting the government with $b_i = 0$.

3. Our Philosophy of History   37

History and theory. Clues identified by our model. Cures. Our history.

Part II: Ideas and Technologies

4. Technology   45

Small coins in the Middle Ages. The purchasing power of a small coin. The medieval technology: hammer and pile. Production costs and seigniorage. Mechanization. The screw press. The cylinder press. Other inventions. The steam engine. Counterfeiting, duplicating, imitating. Technologies and ideas.

5. Medieval Ideas about Coins and Money

Medieval jurists as advocates of Arrow-Debreu. Romanists and Canonists. Construction of the medieval common doctrine. Sources and methods of the romanists. Money in a legal doctrine of loans. Tests in a one-coin environment. Multiple currencies and denominations. Multiple denominations. Multiple metals. Fluctuating exchange rates: the stationary case. Multiple units of accounts. Demonetization. Overdue payments and extrinsic value. Trends in exchange rates. Debasements and currency reforms. A question from public law: setting seigniorage rates. Sources of the canonists. Debasements and seigniorage rates. Qualifications, exceptions, and discoveries. Early statement of double coincidence. Romanists repair the breach. Canonists versus romanists on seigniorage. Another breach. Philosophers help. The cracks widen: debasements and deficit financing. Concluding remarks.

6. Monetary Theory in the Renaissance

Precursors of Adam Smith. Debt repayment, legal tender, and nominalism. Dumoulin the revolutionary. Dumoulin's impact. Dumoulin the conservative. Fiat money. Fiat money in theory: Butigella. Double coincidence of wants revisited. Other formulations. Fiat money in practice. The conditions for valued fiat money. Restrictions on fiat money. Limited legal tender. Quantity theory. Lessons from the Castilian experience: fiat money. In Spain: Juan de Mariana (1609). Forecasting inflation. In France: Henri Poullain (1612). Concluding remarks.

Part III: Endemic Shortages and "Natural Experiments"

7. Clues

Shortages of small change and bullion famine. Shortages and invasions of coins. Ghost monies and units of account. Free minting. The evidence.

8. Medieval Coin Shortages

England. France. Shortages elsewhere. Concluding remarks.

9. Medieval Florence

Turbulent debut of large coins in Tuscany. The Quattrini affair. Ghost monies as legal tender and unit of account. Florentine ghost monies: details. Concluding remarks. Appendix A: mint equivalents and mint prices. Minting. Appendix B: a price index for fourteenth-century Florence.

Illustrations

Tables

Preface

This book describes our efforts to discover the origins of a principle that central banks now routinely use to manage a country's supplies of coins and notes. Because that principle cured what had been widespread and enduring problems of monetary management, our search revealed much about broader historical monetary and fiscal problems and about the origins of the general principles that most experts now think should govern monetary policy.

Today almost all governments use a "standard formula" for supplying and pricing coins and currency. A government's monetary authority sets prices; the public chooses the quantities. The monetary authority sets the prices by offering to convert unlimited quantities of different denominations of currency and coins at fixed exchange rates (e.g., the U.S. government stands ready to buy or sell a quarter for five nickels). With an eye toward controlling an overall index of the price of goods and services, the monetary authority also sets the total quantity of government currency and coins (the supply of "base money"), but it does not choose its composition across denominations. The public determines the composition of base money by exchanging coins and currency with the government. Today coins and currency of all denominations are "tokens": they are valued not because of their constituent paper or metal, but because of the goods that people can exchange for them.

This standard formula for determining the relative prices and quantities of denominations of coins and currency has worked well for over a century. But for hundreds of years before 1850, other and less reliable principles regulated the denomination structure of coins. Governments did not offer to convert one denomination for others at fixed prices. Instead the market set those prices, but in ways that troubled monetary authorities. For centuries, monetary authorities and traders complained about undesirable fluctuations in both the quantities and the relative prices of coins of different denominations.

Monetary policy experts struggled with these problems for a long time before they eventually adopted the modern standard formula in the mid-nineteenth century. That put in place an essential piece of our modern fiat money system, as well as of the gold standard that preceded it.

Work on this book began after a conversation between the authors in August 1996 about the discovery of the modern standard formula. Carlo Cipolla told how centuries of monetary problems and trials and errors in monetary policy preceded the standard formula, but did not reveal how it was discovered. Sargent conjectured that before the standard formula, public policies for supplying small change were flawed because policy makers had the wrong model; the inventors of the standard formula revealed a better model and thereby made better policy possible. Citing Redish (1990), Velde countered that to implement the standard formula requires a reliable technology for making coins that are difficult to counterfeit, and that technological limitations, not ignorance of good monetary theory, could just as well have been responsible for the monetary difficulties that were observed before policy makers implemented the standard formula.

So this book began with the question: Was it poor economic theory or inadequate technology that long delayed the proper implementation of the standard formula? We now think that it was both. We eventually identified an early proponent of the standard formula, Sir Henry Slingsby in 1661. But we also found that Slingsby did not work in a vacuum, that he must have learned from earlier theorists and monetary experiments, and that there were formidable technological impediments to implementing Slingsby's policy recommendations. We discovered how ideas about supplying small change contributed much to the development of modern monetary doctrines.

We came to this project as modern monetary economists whose curiosity was aroused by reading Carlo Cipolla's (1956) account of monetary puzzles from the fourteenth and fifteenth centuries. We sought to understand Cipolla's observations about renaissance Florence with monetary theories constructed mostly during the 1980s. As we returned to Cipolla's account during the process of building our model, and as we listened to what our model told us, we came more and more to respect and appreciate Cipolla's account, and how his selection of facts and his interpretations reflected modern monetary theories. But Cipolla wrote before modern theories were developed. Late in our research, we recognized the likely identity of Cipolla's teachers: the commentators and discoverers from long ago, some of whose works we cite in this book. Much of the novelty of the monetary theory of the 1980s is in its formal style, not the ideas that it represents, which were created partly through the process to be described in this book.

August 2001

Acknowledgments

We thank the following people for their criticisms and comments: Whitney Bagnall, Jodi Beder, Michael Bordo, Marcelle Chauvet, John Cochrane, Paul David, George Essig, José García de Paso, Avner Greif, Philip Hoffman, Kenneth Kasa, Guido Menzio, Joel Mokyr, Beatrix Paal, Angela Redish, William Roberds, Martin Schneider, George Selgin, Bruce Smith, Richard Sutch, Richard Sylla, Aaron Tornell, Gabriel Verd SJ, Juerg Weber, and Warren Weber. We thank our editor, Peter Dougherty, who has encouraged us and offered wise suggestions, and Carolyn Sargent for advice in artistic matters. We also thank seminar participants at the California Institute of Technology, the University of California at Los Angeles, the University of Chicago, the University of Illinois at Urbana-Champaign, Ohio State University, Rutgers University, Stanford University, and the Stockholm School of Economics. Although we are both affiliated with Federal Reserve Banks, the views expressed herein are not necessarily those of the Federal Reserve Banks or the Federal Reserve System.

Thomas Sargent
François Velde

I thank the National Science Foundation for supporting my research on this book through a grant to the National Bureau of Economic Research. I also thank the Hoover Institution for supplying wonderful research support. Part of my work was completed when I was a Moore Distinguished Scholar at the California Institute of Technology.

Thomas Sargent

Part I

A Problem and Its Cure

CHAPTER I

Introduction

Paper and gold

A century ago few would have foretold the kind of money we use today. In 1873, the U.S. Congress had passed a law, section 14 of which states: "the gold coins of the U.S. shall be a one-dollar piece, which, at the standard weight of 25.8 grains, shall be the unit of value" (*Statutes at Large of USA* 17:427). Section 14 thus defined the American unit of account,[1] the dollar, as a specified quantity of a particular metal. In doing so, it embodied a shared wisdom accumulated from centuries of experience. And, while some countries did not adhere to the gold standard in 1900, relying instead on some type of inconvertible paper money, they were regarded as backward by the "advanced nations." Today, the definition of the dollar as an amount of gold is gone and long forgotten. The "advanced nations" now all rely on inconvertible paper money.[2]

A remarkable switch in monetary standards

How can we explain this remarkable reversal? With hindsight, can we detect groundwork laid in earlier times for the universal replacement of gold by fiat?

On closer inspection, ancillary sections of the 1873 U.S. law portend the monetary developments of the twentieth century. Sections 15 and 16 prescribed that smaller denominations, from 50¢ to 1¢, were to be made in metals *other than gold*. An act of 1879 (*Statutes at Large* 1879, 7) made these subsidiary coins convertible, in sums of $20 or more, into "lawful money" (i.e., gold) on demand at the Treasury. Subsidiary coins were tokens: their value came not from metal within but from trust in the government's promise to convert them into gold (dollars) upon demand.

The 1873 arrangement for small coins prefigured a new monetary standard.

---

[1] This and other terms are defined in the glossary.

[2] Few countries even define their unit of value as a particular quantity of another country's paper money, i.e., peg exchange rates.

— 3 —

In 1900, sections 15 and 16 were thought unremarkable, dealing as they did with a matter of subsidiary importance, a technical issue much like minting charges or employee salaries. Indeed, similar provisions for small change could be found in the monetary laws of other advanced countries, and monetary textbooks of the time routinely described what had become by then a "standard formula" for managing the supply of small change.

Yet it took centuries to devise the formula. And until it was devised, the supply of small change was an important and persistent problem. Furthermore, from our vantage one hundred and twenty-five years later, the more enduring features of the act of 1873 are sections 15 and 16: for today *all* parts of our money, not just small change, have now become "tokens," convertible only into other tokens.

This book is about the "big problem of small change": what the problem was, how it was solved and why it took so long, and what was learned in the process about broader monetary and fiscal affairs. A long struggle with the problem of small change eventually produced a practical solution. It also produced a monetary theory that was able to extend token coinage to the entire denomination structure and found the comprehensive fiat money system that prevails today.[3]

The enduring problem of small change

Western Europeans long struggled to sustain a proper mix of large and small denomination coins, and to free themselves of the belief that coins of *all* denominations should be full-bodied.

Commodity money prevailed. The monetary system begun by Charlemagne about A.D. 800 had only one coin, the silver penny. From the end of the twelfth century, various states introduced larger denominations. To do so, they established a monetary system that embodied the prevailing views about money. At the time, European monetary authorities

---

[3] The gold standard finally ended when President Nixon closed the gold window on August 15, 1971.

did not think of money as something whose value emerges from its role as medium of exchange. Instead, they shared a conception of money that ignored its moneyness and focused solely on the substance it contained, namely silver. Therefore, in their view, coins of all denominations should be full-bodied, and rates of exchange of coins of different denominations should reflect their relative metal contents. They understood how a commodity money anchored nominal prices, and they sought to maintain that anchor throughout the denomination structure. So they set up a system in which supplies of coins of all denominations were chosen by private citizens, who decided if and when to use metal to purchase new coins from the mint at prices set by the government.

In the following centuries, that system produced intermittent shortages of small denomination coins, persistent depreciations of small coins relative to large ones, and recurrent debasements of the small coins. Cipolla (1956, 31) stated that "Mediterranean Europe failed to discover a good and automatic device to control the quantity of petty coins to be left in circulation," a failure that extended across Europe. He called this failure the "big problem of small change." *Shortages and depreciations*

By the middle of the nineteenth century, the mechanics of a sound system were well understood, thoroughly accepted, and widely implemented. According to Cipolla (1956, 27): *A standard formula*

> Every elementary textbook of economics gives the standard formula for maintaining a sound system of fractional money: to issue on government account small coins having a commodity value lower than their monetary value; to limit the quantity of these small coins in circulation; to provide convertibility with unit money. . . . Simple as this formula may seem, it took centuries to work it out. In England it was not applied until 1816, and in the United States it was not accepted before 1853.

The standard formula avoided shortages and depreciations of small denomination coins without causing inflation. It retained a commodity money anchor but did not impose it coin by coin.

Instead, it made the smaller denominations into token coins, convertible into gold.

In 1900, J. Laurence Laughlin (1900, 113–14) described the standard formula and added: "As a matter of course, countries have not always had clear conceptions regarding this kind of money, so that the principles just enumerated have come forth only by a process of evolution out of experience."

The standard formula evolved from experience.

Thus, Cipolla, Laughlin, and others[4] have highlighted the discrepancy between the formula's simplicity and the time required to devise it. The aim of our book is to understand the sources of this discrepancy. We retrace events from 1200 to 1850, following three strands.

First, important ideas about money had to be discovered and others discarded. It took a long time before theorists recognized the superiority of tokens over full bodied coins.[5] Second, technologies that made it possible to issue token coinage had to be developed. Third, by trial and error, policy makers had to learn the properties of new institutions.

The long process of evolution out of experience provides a fascinating perspective on the growth of monetary theories and institutions, with many interactions among the three strands of theories, technologies, and experiments. Commentators tried to make sense of their observations, building monetary theory in the process. Governments ran diverse experiments, sometimes in response to commentators' advice. Technical innovations in metal working altered the relative costs of legal and illegal suppliers of small change, and

---

[4] Feavearyear (1963, 169–70) writes of England in the eighteenth century: "The failure for the better part of a century to make adequate provision for fractional payments in spite of all the profound discussion of economic matters which went on may seem to us somewhat remarkable, accustomed as we are to a well-managed token currency which, while being useful, and indeed indispensable, to the public, brings in the long run a good profit to the state. From the earliest times there had been great difficulty in getting an adequate supply of small coins into circulation."

[5] "Monetary policy would have faced fewer difficulties if the commodity money concept of money had commanded less respect. Its persistence as an ideal obstructed and delayed the development of a workable system of redeemable token money" (Usher 1943, 196).

made new monetary policies feasible.

Governments had long experimented with issuing token coinage themselves and sometimes allowed private agents to issue it, before they discovered, or accepted, that, as in Cipolla's standard formula, small change should be tokens backed by a government standing ready to exchange them for full-bodied large denomination coins or currency. In the process, they discovered the two main ideas that underlie the twentieth century concept of a "well-managed fiat" system: the quantity theory of money, and the need to restrain the suppliers of token money from creating inflation.

A model

We use a model to guide our narrative. The "big problem of small change" took a long time to solve, in part because it is in truth technically complicated. The only way we have been able to understand the problem, as well as the decisions made over the centuries by monetary authorities, is to construct a model that highlights the problem and that isolates alternative potential solutions, including, among others, the standard formula. We created our model by modifying and extending a more or less standard model of fiat money that does not differentiate the supply or demand for money by denominations.[6] While that model has performed well in describing various twentieth-century experiences with fiat money, we have to modify the demand side to accommodate diverse denominations of coins and the supply side to account both for different denominations and the fact that money was based on a commodity, not on government fiat. We believe that our model illuminates a variety of problems that stalked monetary authorities for centuries.

We need a model because the facts don't speak for themselves. To understand economic phenomena we have to appreciate the views that guided historical decision makers, that is, their models. To

---

[6] Versions of this model appear in Lucas (1982) and Sargent and Wallace (1973) and are used in Sargent (1993, ch. 3).

judge when they chose well and when they chose poorly, we measure their models against ours.

Our model explains why the medieval money supply mechanism was prone to shortages of small coins. It shows why debasements or reinforcements of parts of the denomination structure would temporarily cure those shortages. The model also explains why shortages and depreciations of small coins happened *simultaneously*.

Our model uses the concepts of supply and demand to sort the forces operating on the market for coins of different denominations into two mutually exclusive categories. The supply and demand sides of the model both have unusual features designed to focus on the denomination structure of money.

Supply side: the mint

The supply side of our model represents the arrangements by which coins were provided in medieval times. The mint stands ready to convert gold or silver into specified coins at fixed prices. People choose the quantities of coins to be produced at any point in time. If they want to convert coins into silver or gold, people can either melt them or use them to purchase silver or gold from metal merchants. The supply side determines intervals bounded by "silver points," one interval for each denomination of coin, within which the price level (the price of goods in terms of coins) must reside if coins of all denominations are to circulate. Were the price level to fall below the lower bound of the interval for a particular coin, that coin would be minted; were it to exceed the upper bound, the coin would be melted. Thus, whether a particular coin exists depends on the position of the price level with respect to that coin's interval. The size of the interval for each coin depends on the production costs and the seigniorage taxes (or subsidies) for that coin. The model asserts that coin shortages can be avoided only if costs and seigniorage rates imply a nonempty intersection of all of the intervals.

In the model, the government sets the limits of the intervals, the silver points. The lower limit is called the "mint equivalent" and the upper limit is called the "mint price." The government sets these limits by choosing the metal content of each coin and the price that the mint will pay, in each coin, for gold or silver. In making these choices, the government is constrained by its own production costs and those of its competitors, counterfeiters and foreign mints. Technological developments in the minting process can provide the government with a cost advantage over its competitors and give it more freedom to adjust the intervals, at least for a while. But even if a government finds it feasible initially to set the intervals properly, the demand side can separately generate shortages.

Demand side: the coin owner

To understand shortages of small coins, we need a model that grants them a special role in transactions. The standard model of the demand for money, for example Lucas (1982), assigns a special transactions role to the aggregate stock of currency, but does not distinguish among denominations. The special role assigned to the aggregate stock of currency permits nominal interest rates to be positive, thereby letting currency, which bears no interest, be dominated in rate of return by other assets. The positive nominal interest rate reflects the extra "liquidity services" provided only by currency.

A demand for making change

The demand side of our model extends the standard model by distinguishing among denominations and assigning to small denominations a further special role. This allows small coins to be dominated in rate of return by large coins during shortages of small coins. At such times, small coins render more liquidity services than large coins. Then large coins appreciate relative to small coins, so that the resulting capital loss on small coins exactly offsets their special liquidity services, and equalizes the total yield of large and small coins, inclusive of liquidity services.

Our model extends Lucas's model to incorporate two cash-in-advance constraints, one like Lucas's that constrains all consumption purchases, and a second that constrains only small purchases. These constraints represent the idea that small denomination coins can be used to purchase expensive items, but large denomination coins cannot be used to buy cheap items. The second cash-in-advance constraint (denoted the penny-in-advance or p.i.a. constraint) embodies a demand for small change and adds an *occasionally* binding constraint and an associated Lagrange multiplier that plays a decisive role in characterizing "shortages" of small change. The Lagrange multiplier measures the extra liquidity services of small denomination coins. When the p.i.a. constraint is not binding, the model exhibits a version of penny-versus-dollar exchange rate indeterminacy, a feature of many models with inconvertible currencies.[7] So long as pennies and dollars bear the same rates of return, holders of currency are indifferent to the ratio in which they hold pennies and dollars. Exchange rate indeterminacy stops during small change shortages, manifested in a binding p.i.a. constraint and a rate of return on dollars that exceeds that on pennies. This rate of return dominance manifests itself in an *appreciation* of dollars when measured in pennies. It is the market signal that causes money holders to conserve pennies.

Shortages

Incentives that created shortages

How can shortages occur when people can always use silver to purchase new coins from the mint? The answer is that people want to convert metal into coins only if it is profitable to do so. Whether it is depends on the price level. Most of the time, movements in the price level are determined by the aggregate stock of currency, not just the stock of small denominations.

A novel prediction of our model is that, within the medieval system, shortages can occur away from the bounds of the intervals constraining the price level, and that a shortage may fail to induce the price level movements necessary to trigger production of more coins. Moreover, the price signals induced by shortages of small change perversely hasten the day when small coins will eventually be melted. Since they depreciate as currency, they ultimately become more valuable as metal than as coins, unless the government makes appropriate adjustments in the parameters governing the melting point for small coins. This feature of the model explains the widely

---

[7] See Kareken and Wallace (1981).

observed persistent depreciation of small coins, inspires our interpretation of debasements of small coins as a cure for shortages of small change within the medieval money supply mechanism, and suggests how that mechanism needed to be reformed.[8]

Price level determination

An ideal commodity money system is designed to equate the price level to a relative price of a metal for consumption goods, and, by making stocks of coins endogenous, to prevent effects on the price level coming from exogenous fluctuations in the quantities of coins. As in the medieval monetary system, that ideal is imperfectly realized in our model because seigniorage and other production costs induce a spread between the minting and melting points. Within those silver points, there is scope for exogenous movements in the quantities of coins to influence the price level. The interval between the silver points thus makes room for influences on the price level conforming to the quantity theory of money.[9]

Because there are silver points for each denomination of coin, our model embodies various forms of the quantity theory of money, depending on how those different silver points are aligned and on whether the penny-in-advance constraint is binding. The intervals between the minting and melting points for large and small denomination coins identify a price level band within which the ordinary quantity theory operates, cast in terms of the *total* quantity of coins. The price level is inside this band during periods in which coins of both denominations circulate and neither is being melted or minted. However, when the p.i.a. constraint binds but neither coin is melted or minted and both circulate, the quantity theory breaks in two, with one holding for "dollars," another for "pennies." Yet another more standard version of the quantity theory holds in a regime in which the

---

[8] See also Sargent and Smith (1997). Glassman and Redish (1988) also interpret debasements in early modern Europe as a cure.

[9] See Sargent and Wallace (1983, 172) for a similar result. If our model abstracted from seigniorage, the silver points would coincide and no such room would be left for the quantity theory (as in Niehans 1978, 147–48).

parameters of supply have been set to cause large denomination coins to disappear because they have been expelled by token small coins.

These features of the model explain how a system designed to anchor the price level to the value of gold or silver nevertheless allowed observers to learn about the quantity theory. The intervals between minting and melting points could be wide enough occasionally to provide a glimpse of the quantity theoretic mechanism for price level determination that controls the price level under today's pure fiat money regime.

Remedies

The model formalizes the contributions of various parts of Cipolla's standard formula, including the roles of token coinage, costless to produce upon demand; of convertibility at a pegged exchange rate between large and small coins; of limited legal tender for smaller coins, to modify the cash-in-advance constraints. The model produces elements to seek in the historical record. Was a technology available to produce a token coinage? Could institutions be trusted to guarantee convertibility? When and how was the belief discarded that coins of all denominations should be full-bodied?[10]

A history

A model as a guide to history Armed with our model, we sift through the historical record. Our story begins in Carolingian times,[11] when money came in one simple form: a coin called the penny, produced by a crude technology,

---

[10] Though sophisticated analysts had long before articulated a coherent theory of convertible token subsidiary coins, John Locke's position in 1695 was that full-bodied coins should be maintained throughout the denomination structure. His views prevailed in Parliament. Even *after* England had embraced the standard formula, Macaulay ([1855] 1967, ch. 22) lauded Locke's analysis and belittled Locke's opponents for advocating token small coins (see chapter 16).

[11] Further back, Burns (1927, ch. 12) found evidence of token coinage for small denominations in Greek and Roman times, and Reekmans (1949) discussed copper inflation in Ptolemaic Egypt.

and thought of as a commodity like wheat or wine. The growing needs of trade led to the introduction of larger denominations, silver and gold coins. From then on, a variety of puzzling phenomena occurred, including chronic coin shortages, flows of small coins across borders, varying exchange rates between coins, and correlations between the quantity of coins and the price level, suggesting a "quantity theory." Governments sometimes used debasements to alleviate these problems. Lawyers grappled with these observations as they confronted related legal issues, refined their views of money as a commodity, and ultimately recognized the concept of fiat money. In the late fifteenth century, isolated experiments with convertible token coinage were carried out, but they floundered on technological constraints and undisciplined governments.[12]

The sixteenth century brought mechanization of minting. Coins of higher quality, more immune to counterfeiting, could be produced, but at a high fixed cost. This tempted Castile into an experiment to reap some of the efficiency gains from a well-managed fiat currency system based on token copper coins. But deficit finance ultimately created unprecedented inflation. Other countries across seventeenth-century Europe confronted the same temptation, with a range of outcomes. Monetary doctrine responded to these experiments with an understanding of when fiat money might be desirable, how to manage it, and why the quantity theory of money might recommend limiting the role of small coins as legal tender. In England in 1661, Sir Henry Slingsby proposed a version of the standard formula.

It took another century and a half before England implemented Slingsby's recommendations. We close our story by endorsing Angela Redish's (1990) account of how the application of the steam engine opened the way for the first de facto implementation of the

---

[12] See Kohn (2001, ch. 7) for another account of coin shortages during medieval times. Kohn alludes to some of the same mechanisms that are captured in our model. Schmoller (1900) briefly surveys the development of monetary policy with respect to small coins from the Middle Ages to the early 19th century, with emphasis on the emergence of overvalued small denominations with limited legal tender; he does not, however, mention convertibility.

standard formula in Britain in 1816. It took more decades before the formula was to be adopted in the United States, France, and Germany, providing an important element of the Classical Gold Standard.

After this long learning process, societies emerged with a well-functioning commodity money system, and also with the theoretical tools and the collective experience to prepare a fiat money system with stable prices. Nevertheless, the twentieth century brought many prolonged inflation experiments with fiat money that resemble ones described in this book, with paper replacing copper as the handmaiden of inflation. So learning continued well into the last quarter of the twentieth century.

Structure of subsequent chapters

We have used our model to organize our history of doctrines, technologies, and experiments. Our historical account refers to our model so often that sometimes we may seem to be writing a history of how past monetary experts learned our model, piece by piece through a long process of trial and error.

We have structured our exposition as follows. The remainder of part I describes our model in an informal way, and conveys enough intuition about its workings to guide the reader as the model has guided us. Part II presents histories of technologies and ideas, while parts III and IV describe shortages and experiments. Chapter 19 summarizes and interprets our historical observations. Finally, part V presents our model formally. Mutual influences among technologies, ideas, and events will prompt frequent references across parts.

ℰᴑ

CHAPTER 2

A Theory

That eternal want of pence,
Which vexes public men.
— Alfred, Lord Tennyson

This chapter presents the main elements and outcomes of our model. The exposition here contains enough to reveal the features that we watched in history. A complete account of the model appears in part V.

Our theory allows us to interpret a pervasive and persistent depreciation of small denomination coins, exhibited for example in the data shown in figure 2.1. The six panels record estimates of the (inverse of the) silver content of small denomination coins from 1200 to 1800 for six countries. Increases in exchange rates of large for small coins and recurrent shortages of small coins accompanied these persistent depreciations in the silver content of small coins. Our theory identifies the source of the upward drifts in figure 2.1 and explains how they related to the concurrent shortages.[1]

How can something in short supply have its price *fall* over time? The demand side of our model gives our answer.[2] The appropriate market signal for agents to economize on small denomination coins is a reduction in the rate of return on those coins relative to rates of return on other coins. A lower rate of return on small denomination coins occurs when those coins depreciate relative to large denomination ones. Depreciating exchange rates for small denomination coins are thus symptomatic

---

[1] In chapter 16, we describe how William Lowndes collected the English data in figure 2.1 for the purposes of establishing a precedent behind the debasement that he was proposing to cure a shortage of small change in 1695.

[2] We must remember that we are in the domain of monetary and financial theory: lower rates of return on an asset are what make people want to diminish their holdings of it.

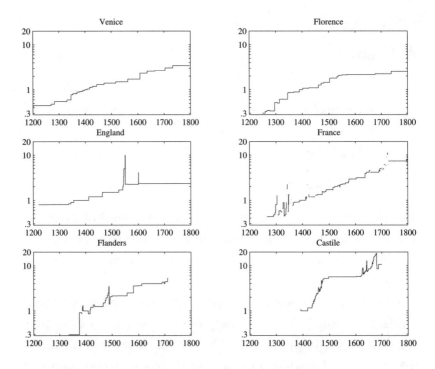

Figure 2.1 Indices of the mint equivalent of small coinage (number of small coins produced from a given weight of silver) in various countries, 1200 to 1800. All indices are set to 1 in 1400. *Sources*: Bernocchi (1976) and Galeotti ([1930] 1971) for Florence, Papadopoli (1893–1909) for Venice, Wailly (1857) for France, Challis (1992a) for England, Munro (1988), Van Gelder and Hoc (1960) for Flanders, García de Paso (2000b) for Castile.

of times when small coins render especially high "liquidity services."

Valuation by weight or tale

In a commodity money system, coins might exchange "by weight" or "by tale." In the former case, the exchange value of a collection of similar coins (say, pennies) would be determined by their aggregate weight; in the latter, by their aggregate number, one coin counting the same as another. For multiple denominations, circulation "by

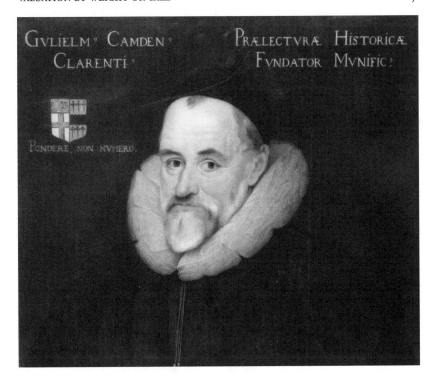

Figure 2.2 Portrait of Sir William Camden (1551–1623) by Marcus Gheeraerts (detail). Camden was a historian and antiquarian, headmaster of Westminster School, and Clarenceux king of arms. He endowed a chair in History at Oxford. His Latin motto, shown here beneath his coat of arms, was "pondere, non numero": by weight, not by tale. (Bodleian Library, Oxford University).

weight" refers by analogy to exchanges where the intrinsic content of a coin determines its value relative to coins of other denominations; when it doesn't, the coin is said to circulate "by tale."[3]

A fiat money *ipso facto* exchanges by tale. Circulation by tale was common for commodity money systems too, despite the preference of Sir William Camden, a seventeenth-century gentleman, shown in figure 2.2, whose personal motto was "pondere, non numero"

---

[3] Our model assumes circulation by tale in the first sense, as it applies to coins of a given denomination. The exchange rate between multiple denominations is determined by the market, so that coins may or may not circulate by tale in the latter sense.

("by weight, not by tale").[4]   We shall focus on observations that
seem explicable only if coins are at least sometimes valued by tale.[5]
Adam Smith ([1776] 1937, book I, ch. 5, 44; book IV, ch. 6, 517)
and many other theorists of commodity money systems also noted
that coins often circulate by tale.[6]

A basic one-denomination theory

We use and extend a theory of commodity money that describes the
demand and supply for coins made of a precious metal that we shall
call silver. Ultimately, we shall use a multiple-coin version of the
theory, but it is helpful to begin with a more standard version of the
theory cast in terms of a single denomination, which we take to be
the penny.

Elements of a
commodity money
system

    The basic one-denomination theory has the following features:
(a) coins are made of valuable metal; (b) coins circulate by tale, not
by weight; (c) the metal content of coins puts an *upper* bound on the
price level (expressed in number of coins per consumption good).
There are two methods for setting the quantity of new coins: (d)
the government can instruct the mint to make coins on government
account; alternatively, (e) the government can set up a system of
unlimited minting in which citizens are free to purchase coins for
silver at the mint at a set price of coins per unit of metal. An
unlimited coinage regime puts a *lower* bound on the price level. The
ideal single-commodity money system of the nineteenth century
puts the upper and lower bounds close together, thereby tying the
price level to the relative price of the metal in the coinage. We briefly
describe each of these important features in turn.

b is ounces of silver
per penny.

a. The government specifies that each penny contains b ounces of

---

[4] John Locke agreed (see chapter 16).

[5] Sargent and Smith (1997) let coins differ by weight and assume circulation by
tale.

[6] Also see Bernstein (2000, 83).

silver.[7]

b. As in modern fiat money systems (in which b equals zero), the theory assumes that coins exchange for goods by tale, not by weight. This means that the prices of goods are posted in *number* of coins per good, rather than ounces of silver per good. Whenever a coin buys more consumption goods than would the silver within the coin, the value by tale exceeds the value by weight, so that there is a fiat component to the tale value of the coin.

Number not weight

c. The metal content of coins puts an upper bound on the price level because, although circulation by tale lets coins be worth more than the intrinsic value of the silver they contain, they cannot be worth less, provided that people can without cost melt the coins to retrieve the silver. Let ϕ be the relative price of consumption goods in terms of silver, measured in ounces of silver per good. The price level p_t must obey

ϕ is ounces of silver per consumption good, the world price of consumption goods in silver.

$$p_t \leq \frac{\phi}{b} \equiv \bar{p}, \qquad (2.1)$$

where p_t has the units of pennies per good. If the price level were ever to exceed $\frac{\phi}{b}$, people would have the incentive to melt coins. That would drive the price level down, by diminishing the quantity of coins. The upper bound (2.1) is attained when the value by tale equals the value by weight.

One component of the theory of commodity money is the quantity theory of money, as encapsulated in a demand function for money or coins. Assume a demand function for coins of the simple form

$$\frac{m_t}{p_t} = k_t, \qquad (2.2)$$

where m_t is the stock of coins measured in pennies, and k_t is the demand for real balances at time t, measured in consumption goods. Through equation (2.2), the stock of coins m_t determines the price level, subject to the upper bound expressed in the inequality (2.1).

---

[7] In chapter 16, we describe a version of our model that allows underweight pennies that contain b/δ units of silver, where $\delta \in (0,1)$. The existence of underweight coins widens the silver points described below.

Equation (2.2) and inequality (2.1) determine a maximum stock of
coins:

$$m_t \leq k_t \overline{p} \equiv \overline{m}_t. \tag{2.3}$$

People have the incentive to melt into silver stocks of coins exceeding
the bound in (2.3). The upper bounds (2.1) and (2.3) embody the
discipline on the issuers of coins provided by the commodity content
of the coins.

In practice, there were two ways of determining the stock of coins
m_t in commodity money systems.

Minting on government account   d. The government could set m_t directly by making the mint a
monopoly and by using government-owned silver to create new
coins on government account. The government could set m_t to
any quantity less than $\overline{m}_t$, provided it had the required amount
of silver bm_t. In this system, the price level varied with m_t as
predicted by the quantity theory, up to $p_t \leq \overline{p}$.[8]

Free minting   e. The government could surrender direct control over the quantity
of coins. In this system, the government set a percentage $\sigma \in
(0, 1)$ that covered production costs and profits for the mint, as
well as any seigniorage tax on minting. It instructed the mint
to coin unlimited quantities of pennies for citizens who brought
silver to the mint, in other words, to buy unlimited amounts of
silver for a set price paid in pennies. For each ounce of silver, the
mint offered $\frac{(1-\sigma)}{b}$ pennies. The government shared net proceeds
of $\frac{\sigma}{b}$ per penny with the mint. A system of unlimited or "free"
minting gives rise to a lower bound on the price level:

$$\underline{p} = \frac{(1 - \sigma)\phi}{b} \leq p_t. \tag{2.4}$$

If the price level were to fall below $\underline{p}$, people would have the
incentive to bring silver to the mint to purchase coins, which

---

[8] Notice that so long as $p_t \leq \overline{p}$, the government collects seigniorage revenues
when it creates new coins. The seigniorage revenues generated at time t equal
$\frac{m_t - m_{t-1}}{p_t}$ *minus* the value in terms of consumption goods of the quantity of silver
put in the new money, $\frac{(m_t - m_{t-1})b}{\phi}$. These revenues are positive whenever $p_t < \overline{p}$.

would increase the stock of coins. The upper and lower limits on the price level in (2.1) and (2.4) are the "silver points" associated with a system of commodity money in which there is unlimited minting. These are the counterparts of the "gold points" for the nineteenth-century gold standard.

Feavearyear (1963, 2) summarized the conditions underlying a pure commodity money system:[9]

> The efficiency of a metallic standard for controlling the value of money, given reasonable stability of value in the metal itself, depends upon the monetary regulations in force. To secure the maximum efficiency there must be complete freedom to exchange metal for money and money for metal at a fixed rate. There must be freedom of trade in the metal, with liberty to export and import it. If coins circulate, they must be issued by the Mint of accurate weight and fineness, in exchange for bullion in unlimited quantities and without charge; and they must be protected from clipping and from counterfeiting. Steps must be taken to replace regularly worn pieces, and there must be liberty to melt the coins if it pays to do so.

Multiple denominations

The basic theory is cast in terms of a single coin, the "penny." Because this book is about repeated depreciations and shortages of small denomination coins, we must somehow put multiple denominations of coins into the theory. To do this, we modify both the demand and supply sides of the theory. Each side contributes to our explanation. Under a regime of unlimited coinage, the supply side of our model implies a multiple-coin version of the silver points: for each denomination of coin there are price levels that determine the minting and melting points, respectively, for that coin. A big part

---

[9] He proceeded to discuss deviations from these conditions in England in the form of mint charges, laws against export, and others.

of our story will be about society's long process of learning how to align the intervals for coins of different denominations to prevent shortages or surpluses of small denomination coins. We modify the demand side of the model to permit occasions when coins of different denominations are not perfect substitutes for one another, so that there can be shortages of small denomination coins. To capture the notion that it is difficult to make change, the demand side of our theory assigns small coins a special role in some transactions. Our theory of demand predicts that shortages of small coins will coincide with depreciations in the rate at which they exchange for large coins, contributing the key to understanding the trends observed in figure 2.1. Subsequent sections of this chapter describe the multiple denomination version of our theory.

Supply

Our supply theory gives gold or silver "points" for coins of each denomination and lets in the possibility that some denominations may disappear. For reference, table 2.1 catalogs symbols. To illustrate the supply mechanism, let all coins be silver. Let the relative price of consumption goods in terms of silver be ϕ, measured in ounces of silver per units of consumption good. An ideal commodity money makes the price level proportional to ϕ, where the factor of proportionality b_i^{-1} is the number of coins of type i per ounce of silver, a parameter set by the government. The value by weight of coin i is $\gamma_i \equiv \phi/b_i$ measured in coins per unit of the consumption good. A coin is valued by weight when the price level denominated in that coin is γ_i. When coins are valued by tale, γ_i serves as an upper bound on the price level.

For most of the remainder of this chapter, we assume two denominations, so that $i = 1, 2$. Let coin 1 be the unit of account (the penny) and let e_i be the market exchange rate of coin i, in units of coin 1 per coin i (e.g., pence per coin i), with $e_1 = 1$. To facilitate the historical comparisons to follow, we choose pence to be the unit

Table 2.1 Symbols.

Variable	Meaning	Units
ϕ	world price of silver	oz silver / cons good
b_1	intrinsic content of penny	oz silver / penny
b_2	intrinsic content of dollar	oz silver / dollar
γ_1	melting point of penny	pence / cons good
γ_2	melting point of dollar	dollars / cons good
σ_i	seigniorage rate	(none)
b_1^{-1}	mint equivalent of penny	pence / oz silver
b_2^{-1}	mint equivalent of dollar	dollars / oz silver
m_1	stock of pennies	pence
m_2	stock of dollars	dollars
e	exchange rate	pence / dollar
p	price of cons goods	pence / cons good

of account.[10] The penny was the first and only coin for a long time in medieval Europe, and for much longer it served as the unit of account. Let p be the price level, in pence per unit consumption good. If all coins are full-weight, then $p = e_i \gamma_i$ for all i.

Operating rules for the mint

The government charters a mint and instructs it to sell newly minted coins to anyone offering to pay silver. The mint is not required to buy coins for silver. The government sets two parameters b_i, σ_i for each coin i. For each ounce of silver brought to it, the mint must pay $e_i(1 - \sigma_i)/b_i$ pence worth of coin i. Here $\sigma_i \geq 0$ is a parameter to capture all costs that the mint incurs manufacturing coin i, including a seigniorage tax and a brassage fee. Angela Redish calls $e_i(1 - \sigma_i)/b_i$ the mint price and e_i/b_i the mint equivalent for coin i.

Melting and minting points

If the price level were ever to fall below $e_i(1 - \sigma_i)\gamma_i$, arbitrage profits would accrue to anyone taking silver to the mint and asking for coin i. A surge of minting would extinguish those profits by pushing the price level up. If the price level were ever to rise above

---

[10] We use the English word "penny" to translate the Latin *denarius*, Italian *denaro*, French *denier*, as coin and as unit of account. The plural of the coin is "pennies," that of the unit is "pence."

$e_i \gamma_i$, arbitrage profits would accrue to people melting coins of type i, and such coins would all disappear. Therefore, as long as coin i is in circulation, the absence of arbitrage profits on that coin requires that the price level must satisfy[11]

$$e_i \left(1 - \sigma_i\right) \gamma_i \leq p \leq e_i \gamma_i. \tag{2.5}$$

The left side of this inequality gives the rate at which consumption goods can be exchanged for silver and then taken to the mint to get coins of denomination i. The right side gives the rate at which coins of denomination i can be converted to consumption goods by melting the coins and then exchanging the silver for consumption goods. Notice that the transformations from consumption goods to pennies (on the left, by minting) and from pennies to consumption goods (on the right, by melting) are irreversible.

Coin by coin, (2.5) identifies silver points for melting (the right endpoint) or coining (the left endpoint) a commodity money. By making the range narrow, a commodity money system links the price level to ϕ, the relative price of consumption goods in terms of the metal.

Equation (2.5) imposes silver points throughout the denomination structure. The medieval monetary authority intended that coins of all denominations should be full-bodied. Cipolla's standard formula suspends (2.5) for all but one standard coin, and makes all other coins tokens that the government promises to convert into the standard coin on demand.

We complete our model of supply with identities that track stocks of coins:

$$m_{it} = m_{it-1} + n_{it} - \mu_{it}, \tag{2.6}$$

---

[11] Our specification of supply is consistent with the reasoning of Adam Smith ([1776] 1937, book I, ch. 5, 44). Smith described how coins must be valued more than by weight if citizens are ever voluntarily to use metal to buy coins at a price that covers the mint's costs of production and seigniorage fees. Smith pointed out that if there were a delay in delivering the coins after the metal was paid to the mint, an interest factor would contribute an additional wedge beyond the seigniorage fee and production costs. Smith presumed valuation by tale, and considered the interval of values above their values by weight that is created by seigniorage fees, production costs, and delivery delays.

where m_{it} is the stock of coin i carried from time t to time $t + 1$, $n_{it} \geq 0$ is the quantity of coins of type i newly minted at time t, and μ_{it} is the quantity of coins of denomination i melted at time t, which must satisfy $m_{it-1} \geq \mu_{it} \geq 0$. The no-arbitrage requirements imply $n_{it} = \mu_{it} = 0$ if $e_i(1 - \sigma_i)\gamma_i < p < e_i\gamma_i$; $e_i(1 - \sigma_i)\gamma_i = p$ if $n_{it} > 0$; and $e_i\gamma_i = p$ if $\mu_{it} > 0$. That is, there is neither melting nor minting of coin i if the price level is strictly between its silver points. There is melting only if the price level is at or above the upper limit, the melting point. There is minting only if the price level is at or below the lower limit, the minting point. Later we shall modify (2.6) to incorporate open market operations.

Demand

The quantity theory of money rests on a demand function for an aggregate $M = \sum_i e_i m_i$, where m_i is the number of coins or notes of denomination i. Aggregation assumes that different denominations are perfect substitutes. The perfect substitutes assumption is justified when (1) different denominations bear identical rates of return, presenting no advantage to holding one denomination rather than another, and (2) it is costless to make change. But shortages of some denominations are symptomatic of distinct demand functions for different coins because somehow feature (1) has broken down.

Shortages and rates of return

Because coins and notes do not pay nominal interest, denominations have identical rates of return if and only if the exchange rates e_i are constant over time. Consider the case of two coins, with coin 1 the penny and coin 2 the dollar. When pennies depreciate relative to the dollar, dollars have a rate of return greater than pennies by a factor of $\frac{e_{2,t+1}}{e_{2,t}} > 1$. This signals a shortage of *pennies* and makes people economize on them.

We require a theory of demand that lets different denominations be perfect substitutes, but that occasionally permits shortages of some denominations. Our theory identifies one class of transactions to be made by any and all denominations and another class that

requires specific small denominations.[12]   In particular, we allow
small denomination coins to make all types of transactions but let
large denomination coins make only some.

Standard models have one demand function for money and one
quantity theory equation. This can be true of our theory too,
but only sometimes. At other times, our model has two or more
demand functions for money and two or more quantity theory equations. During shortages, one quantity theory equation holds for real
balances aggregated over all of the nonscarce currencies, and others
hold for each of the scarce coins.

A demand for
making change   We illustrate the demand side of our model with the special case of
two denominations. Let m_1 be the supply of the small denomination
and m_2 be the supply of the large one; e_t is the exchange rate of
small for large denominations (pence per dollar). Parameterizing
the demand for money in terms of the "Cambridge k" gives the
following theory. During times without currency shortages,

$$\frac{m_{1t-1} + e_t m_{2t-1}}{p_t} = k_{1t} + k_{2t}, \qquad (2.7a)$$

$$\frac{m_{1t-1}}{p_t} \geq k_{1t}, \qquad (2.7b)$$

$$e_t = e_{t-1}. \qquad (2.7c)$$

During shortages of small denominations,

$$\frac{m_{1t-1}}{p_t} = k_{1t}, \qquad (2.8a)$$

$$\frac{e_t m_{2t-1}}{p_t} = k_{2t}, \qquad (2.8b)$$

$$e_t > e_{t-1}. \qquad (2.8c)$$

Here the k_{it}'s sum to the Cambridge k and measure purchases of
different sizes. The k_{it}'s express demands for stocks of coins m_{it-1}
carried over from time $t-1$ to t. System (2.7)–(2.8) expresses
that small denomination coins can be used for all transactions and
that *only* they can be used for some transactions. The variable
k_{1t} measures transactions that require small change. We refer to

---

[12] A shortage indicates an additional component of value beyond the explicit rate
of return. The Lagrange multiplier on our additional restriction on transactions
contributes this additional component of value (see chapter 21).

constraint (2.7*b*) as the penny-in-advance constraint. It is slack in regime (2.7) but binding in regime (2.8). Equations (2.7) prevail during normal times when all denominations are perfect substitutes and equations (2.8) prevail during shortages. When $e_t = e_{t-1}$, large and small denomination coins are perfect substitutes. But strict inequality (2.8*c*) induces holders of small coins to economize and makes constraint (2.7*b*) hold with equality.

Movements in the variables k_{1t}, k_{2t} reflect changes in preferences and growth or contraction in income. The formal presentation in part V links these parameters explicitly to the endowment and preference structure of the model.

Equations (2.7*c*)–(2.8*c*) make e_t a nondecreasing sequence. This prediction lets the model match the upward drift indicated, for example, in figure 2.1. The model predicts that shortages will coincide with periods when rates of return are less on small denomination coins than on large ones, dissolving people's indifference about denominations. The price that signals shortages is the rate of return e_t/e_{t-1}, not the *level* e_t. The market manages a shortage by temporarily giving a low return to small coins: (2.7*c*)–(2.8*c*) translate this into a *permanent* effect on e. This feature of demand creates problems in conjunction with the supply mechanism.

Interactions of supply and demand

If the operation of (2.5) coin by coin is to be consistent with positive amounts of each type of coin, intervals must be aligned to let the price level satisfy

$$\max_i \left(e_i \gamma_i \left(1 - \sigma_i \right) \right) \le p \le \min_i \left(e_i \gamma_i \right). \tag{2.9}$$

If the price level exceeded the right limit of (2.9), coins of all denominations for which $p > e_i \gamma_i$ would have been melted.

Demand specification (2.7)–(2.8) makes the price level satisfy

$$\max_i \left(e_i \gamma_i \left(1 - \sigma_i \right) \right) \le p \le \gamma_1.$$

The right inequality allows $e_i \gamma_i < p$ for $i = 2, \ldots$ and consequently allows melting of all but the small coins. The aspect of our theory that opens this possibility is the asymmetry in the uses of large and small denomination coins incorporated in (2.7)–(2.8) (small denomination coins can be used for all transactions, but large coins cannot). In the two-coin case, when $e\gamma_2 < p$ and $m_{2t} = 0$, the quantity theory prevails in terms of small denomination coins:

$$\frac{m_{1t}}{p_t} = k_{1t} + k_{2t}. \tag{2.10}$$

Chapter 14 tells how this possibility was to be realized in a seventeenth-century Castilian experiment that aligned intervals so that

$$\gamma_1 (1 - \sigma_1) < e (1 - \sigma_2) \gamma_2 < e\gamma_2 < \gamma_1, \tag{2.11}$$

and that augmented the sources of supply in (2.6) to allow government purchases of coin 2 with coin 1, an open market operation. The Castilian open market purchases of silver coins were originally intended to keep $m_{2t} > 0$, implying that $p \leq e\gamma_2$ and thereby retaining the upper bound on the price level associated with the melting point for silver large denomination coins. Such operations would raise silver revenues for the government without causing inflation. But there is a bound on the amount of silver that can be raised with open market operations: the initial total stock of silver coins. Beyond the bound, more revenues can be raised only if the government engages in inflationary finance. To accommodate that, (2.6) must be modified to include a term for deficit finance, as was discovered in Castile in the late 1620s. Chapter 14 studies the Castilian episode in detail.

Economics of interval alignments

Misalignments of intervals   Various alignments across coins of the minting and melting intervals are possible, depending on the settings for σ_i, the per coin sums of production costs and seigniorage taxes. It is difficult to avoid misalignments. Consider the following cases.

1. If $\sigma_1 = \sigma_2$, the intervals can be aligned by setting the b_i's so that $\frac{\gamma_1}{\gamma_2} = e$.

2. Per coin cost differences create problems in aligning the intervals, and present a choice about whether to equalize the mint prices $(e_i(1 - \sigma_i)/b_i)$ or the mint equivalents (e_i/b_i). Evidently, if $\sigma_1 > \sigma_2$, the intervals cannot coincide. The case $\sigma_1 > \sigma_2$ is realistic because it embodies the notion that per unit value, small coins are more expensive to manufacture than large coins. (It takes as much labor to strike a small coin as a large one.) When $\sigma_1 > \sigma_2$, we can align the *right* limits by setting $e\gamma_2 = \gamma_1$, which implies $e\gamma_2(1 - \sigma_2) > \gamma_1(1 - \sigma_1)$. This inequality implies that the small denomination coin 1 won't be minted. Alternatively, when $\sigma_1 > \sigma_2$, we can align the *left* limits, but then $e\gamma_2 < \gamma_1$, which sets the melting point for large coins below that for small, allowing price levels that cause large coins to disappear.

3. The σ_i's determine the widths of the bands. Small σ_i's produce small bands, but require small or possibly negative seigniorage taxes, negative if the government subsidizes the minting of a coin to offset part or all of the production costs.

4. Consider a period in which e_t drifts upward, causing the interval for dollars to drift rightward relative to the interval for pennies. Suppose that the price level expressed in pence also drifts up, always remaining within the interval for dollars. Eventually, the price level can reach the melting point for pennies, threatening to eradicate the stock of pennies. This situation can be remedied by debasing pennies, that is, reducing b_1, thereby raising γ_1, and shifting the interval for pennies to the right.

5. A situation when the large coin has disappeared because $e\gamma_2 < p$ can be remedied by shifting the interval for coin 2 (the dollar) to the right by increasing e or by increasing γ_2 through a decrease in b_2, a debasement of the large coins. In seventeenth-century Castile, the market and the monetary authorities repeatedly devalued small coins, in effect resetting e.[13]

---

[13] In our discussion of the Castilian episode, we shall add a parameter x that the government can manipulate to alter the exchange rate.

6. The government can push σ_i above production costs if it can monopolize the best technologies for producing coins and can detect and punish counterfeiters.[14]

Perverse dynamics

The dynamics in case 4 are perverse because they are self-aggravating. The demand specification makes e_t a monotone nondecreasing sequence, e_t rising during periods of shortages. The response to shortages that arise even while the price level is in the interior of all intervals is to shift the interval for coins not in short supply to the right relative to intervals for coins experiencing shortages. The rise in e_t thus hastens the day when the price level will give incentives to traders eventually to *melt* the coin in short supply. Unless a policy intervention changes some of the parameters, say through a debasement or an exogenous resetting of the exchange rate, the mechanism cannot give the signal for minting. This perversity was one of the main problems that was to be cured by Cipolla's standard formula.

Spontaneous debasements: invasions of foreign coins

The monetary authorities could remedy a shortage by debasing the smaller coin, that is, raising b_1 to match the rightward shift in the large coin's interval. Even without such measures by the policy authorities, the market sometimes produced another remedy with the "spontaneous debasements" that occurred with "invasions" of foreign currencies (for example, see chapter 9). Those invasions happened when a nearby sovereign minted coins roughly similar to the domestic small coins, but at a mint price sufficiently higher

---

[14] Concern about counterfeiting is a continuing theme in our narrative. Feavearyear (1963, 171) writes the following about the temptation to counterfeit in Britain in the eighteenth century: "Here we have a picture of the difficulty which persisted almost down to modern times. So long as the coins contained much less than their face value of metal, there was a great temptation to copy them. The technique of coining was still not sufficiently good to give to the money a stamp which it was beyond the skill of the forger to imitate even upon a scale large enough to make it worth while in the case of halfpennies and farthings, and the machinery for the detection of crime was bad."

than the domestic mint price to make minting worthwhile. Instead of exporting goods and importing silver to be coined by the domestic mint, residents chose to export goods and import foreign coins. [15]

Having access to foreign mints thus offered traders choices among mints. When domestic pennies were scarce, traders could sell domestic dollars to the foreign mint and receive foreign pennies to augment the domestic pennies.

The choice among mints and systems of coinage opens possible indeterminacies sparked by indifference among alternative types of pennies. Laws forbidding the use of foreign currencies appear frequently in the historical record. In situations of indifference, the laws can be regarded as a "tie-breaking" device. So long as there were enough domestic pennies, the laws could be obeyed costlessly. During shortages, the laws were often disobeyed or resisted. In 1339, the king of England prohibited certain foreign coins in Ireland, but rescinded his order shortly after protests by the people suffering from a shortage of small denominations (Ruding 1840, 1:212).

Cipolla (1956, 64), Lane and Mueller (1985, 267), Glassman and Redish (1988, 82) and others have interpreted these invasions of foreign coins as reflecting the operation of Gresham's law. In our model, there is no need to appeal to that ambiguous law. [16] Indeed, it was not a case of one coin chasing another, but one coin supplementing the other. An invasion of foreign pennies was a consequence, not a cause, of a shortage of domestic pennies.

---

[15] In a similar vein, Feavearyear (1963, 169) wrote that in the eighteenth century, "Considerable quantities of foreign and counterfeit pieces were imported and passed off as English. In point of fact, so long as the Government was unable to find a method of providing the country with a sound and adequate coinage, the importation and issue of counterfeit or light silver was a good thing. The coins in circulation were now definitely tokens, and the only disadvantage of the Mint's neglect to produce them was that it created a shortage. The counterfeiter tended to fill up the void, and he could do no harm to the standard."

[16] The entry on Gresham's law in the index of Friedman and Schwartz (1963) is "Gresham's law, misapplication of." Also see Rolnick and Weber (1986). Sargent and Smith (1997) describe various senses of Gresham's law, and some situations where a version of the law applies and others where it does not.

Costs and Temptations

We have identified inherent weaknesses in the way multiple denominations were supplied in many early commodity money systems.
The standard formula remedies these weaknesses by prescribing particular open market operations. In doing so, it draws attention to the
opportunity cost of commodity money and puts before governments
the temptation to overissue token coins or currencies. Learning to use
the standard formula involved learning to to resist that temptation.

Opportunity cost

A commodity money absorbs resources. In the special case of two denominations, the stock of silver in the
money supply is $m_1 b_1 + m_2 b_2$. The silver money stock is worth

$$\frac{m_1 b_1 + m_2 b_2}{\phi} \leq \frac{m_1 + e m_2}{p} \qquad (2.12)$$

units of consumption good, where the inequality follows from
(2.5).[17] The left side of (2.12) measures the capital cost of maintaining a commodity money system. This cost can be saved under
a well-managed fiat money system. If $m_1 + e m_2$ can be limited
without the automatic supply mechanism, silver can be conserved
by driving both b_i's toward 0. Setting b_i's equal to 0 for all coins
would implement a pure fiat standard.

An open market operation from Castile

In the 1590s, economists in Castile recommended that the supply
mechanism be altered to permit the government to exchange one
coin for another at the prevailing exchange rate. When there are

---

[17] See Friedman (1951) who estimates the right side of (2.12) for the United
States as a measure of the waste in a commodity money system. The advisors of
the king of Castile in 1596 may also have done such a calculation (see chapter
14). See Sargent and Wallace (1983) for an argument that Friedman's calculation
overstates the cost of maintaining a commodity money system. Friedman (1951)
remarked that in terms of their values in consumption goods, the resources tied
up as a commodity money don't depend on the particular commodity used. This
is true in our model.

no shortages of particular denominations, the perfect substitutes assumption makes private parties willing to accept such open market operations at the prevailing p and e.

Suppose that $\gamma_1 > e\gamma_2$, so that the intervals are aligned as in the Castilian case (2.11). This inequality implies that $b_2 > eb_1$. Consider a government purchase of dollars for pennies. This open market operation is constrained by

Using tokens economizes on the resource costs of a commodity money system.

$$(m_{1t} - m_{1t-1}) = -e_t(m_{2t} - m_{2t-1}) > 0. \qquad (2.13)$$

Through this operation the government acquires $-(m_{2t} - m_{2t-1})\,b_2$ units of silver at the cost of $(m_{1t} - m_{1t-1})\,b_1$ units of silver required to produce the pennies. Taking the difference and using (2.13) shows that the government's net proceeds in silver are

$$\text{Profits} = \left(\frac{b_2}{e} - b_1\right)(m_{1t} - m_{1t-1}). \qquad (2.14)$$

These are positive whenever $\gamma_1 > e\gamma_2$. They are larger when b_1 is *smaller* (i.e., when γ_1 is higher).

Such calculations lay beneath a seventeenth-century Castilian experiment to be studied in chapter 14. The calculations identify an open market operation that is not inflationary and that substitutes a cheap money for an expensive one, leaving the total quantity of money unaltered. The silver that the government can obtain by such an operation is bounded by $(b_2 - b_1 e)\,m_{2t-1}$, the amount raised by setting $m_{2t} = 0$ in (2.13), thereby making the entire stock of money into pennies.

An open market operation for the standard formula

The standard formula eliminated possible misalignments of the intervals (2.5). It altered the supply arrangement by doing away with all of the intervals except for one dominant coin. It made subsidiary coins into tokens. Tokens are created not by coining precious metals but by promising to conduct open market purchases and sales of intrinsically valueless tokens for a coin of precious metal.

In the two-coin case, form the exchange rate weighted sum of (2.6) across coins to get

$$(m_{1t} + em_{2t}) = (m_{1t-1} + em_{2t-1})$$
$$+ (n_{1t} + en_{2t}) - (\mu_{1t} + e\mu_{2t}). \qquad (2.15)$$

The standard formula disposes of all pairs of silver and gold points except that for the standard coin.

The standard formula suspends the supply arrangement (2.6) for all coins except the last ($i = n$, where we have taken $n = 2$ in most of this chapter). Other coins $i < n$ are to be tokens with no valuable metal ($b_i = 0$ for all $i < n$). The mint is told to supply only the nth coin in exchange for silver. The mint is also told to stand ready to buy *and sell* token coins for the dollar at a fixed exchange rate e.[18] In (2.15) we set $\mu_{1t} = n_{1t} = 0$, because token coins are not created or destroyed by minting or melting precious metal ($b_i = 0$ for a token coin) but by being exchanged for dollars. Token coins are warehouse certificates for metal coins, printed on cheap metal.[19]

The supply of token coins satisfies

$$m_{1t} = eR_t \geq 0, \qquad (2.16)$$

where R_t is the stock of reserves in dollars that the mint holds to "back" pennies. Equation (2.16) implies

$$m_{1t} - m_{1t-1} = e(R_t - R_{t-1}).$$

This states that token coins m_{1t} are created only through open market operations. These specifications let us write (2.15) as

$$m_{2t} + R_t = m_{2t-1} + R_{t-1} + n_{2t} - \mu_{2t}. \qquad (2.17)$$

Now (2.5) applies only for coin $n = 2$ with e being the penny-dollar exchange rate. This is a Gordian knot solution to the enduring problem of aligning the intervals: the standard formula aligns the intervals by eliminating all intervals but one.

---

[18] Remember that the mint had earlier been told only to *buy* coins for silver, and not to sell. Now it is told both to buy and to sell at a fixed price.

[19] For convenience, we assume that token coins are stamped on intrinsically valueless metal.

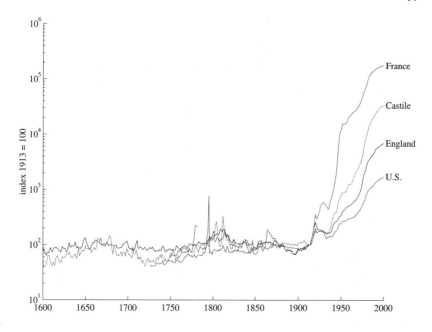

Figure 2.3 Indices of prices in terms of the unit of account in England, the United States, France, Spain. *Sources*: United Kingdom, Schumpeter-Gilboy index from 1661 to 1799 and Rousseaux index from 1800 to 1913, both in Mitchell (1988), Twigger (1999) after 1913. France: price index computed by David Weir from 1726 to 1860, Singer-Kerel cost-of-living index for Paris from 1861 to 1913, Insee consumer price index after 1913. United States: index of wholesale prices from 1749 to 1913 in Warren and Pearson (1933, 10), consumer price index after 1913. Spain, García de Paso (2000b) from 1600 to 1700, Reher and Ballesteros (1993) after 1701.

Transparency of opportunity cost

The standard formula regime makes part of the opportunity cost of the commodity money regime more evident. The reserves R_t backing the tokens lie in vaults. It would be profitable to lend the reserves at interest and thereby convert the backing for the tokens from metal to credit. Lending those reserves is one step toward a fiat money system.

Trusting the government with $b_i = 0$

The waste from keeping those reserves may have been one of the factors that prompted Keynes to call a commodity standard a "barbarous relic." A fiat money system disposes of all reserves behind a currency. In doing so, it also eliminates the automatic supply mechanism constraining the price level. A low-inflation fiat money system replaces that automatic mechanism with an enlightened government that commits itself to limit the quantity of a pure token, no-cost currency.

Because most nineteenth-century proponents of a commodity money system did not trust governments properly to manage a fiat money system, they were willing to pay the resource costs associated with setting up and maintaining a commodity money system. In light of the high inflation episodes that many countries experienced in the twentieth century after they abandoned commodity monies,[20] it is difficult to criticize them for that. See figure 2.3, which records price levels in Castile, France, England, and the United States. The inflationary experience of the twentieth century, the century of paper money, is unprecedented.

☙

---

[20] See Rolnick and Weber (1997).

CHAPTER 3

Our Philosophy of History

History and theory

Subsequent chapters contain selective histories of thoughts and events that pertain to managing the coinage. We present only a sample from a vast record of thoughts and events. Our model helped us select it, so our sample is biased. Because we are prejudiced observers, we tell the reader what we watched for in the historical record and how our model directed our search.

Clues identified by our model

Our model assumes that coins of a given denomination circulate by tale. The intervals between the minting points and melting points permit gaps between valuations by tale and by weight. That feature of our model implies a range of indeterminacy for the initial exchange rate e, the price of large denomination coins in terms of small denomination coins. Thus, recall our finding that if both coins are to circulate in a two-coin world, the price level p must satisfy

Melting and minting points limit the exchange rate.

$$\max \left\{ e\gamma_2 \left(1 - \sigma_2\right), \gamma_1 \left(1 - \sigma_1\right) \right\} \leq p \leq \min \left\{ e\gamma_2, \gamma_1 \right\}. \qquad (3.1)$$

It follows that if both coins are to circulate, the exchange rate must satisfy

$$\underline{e} = \frac{\gamma_1 \left(1 - \sigma_1\right)}{\gamma_2} \leq e \leq \frac{\gamma_1}{\gamma_2 \left(1 - \sigma_2\right)} = \overline{e}. \qquad (3.2)$$

The bound on the right side of (3.2) is attained if the exchange rate aligns the melting point for dollars with the minting point for pennies. The bound on the left side is attained if the exchange rate is set to align the minting point of dollars with the melting point of pennies.

There is a corresponding range of indeterminacy for the initial price level. In the notation of chapter 2, when there are no "within the interval" shortages of small coins, the price level must satisfy

$$\underline{p} = \frac{m_1 + \underline{e}m_2}{k} \leq p \leq \frac{m_1 + \overline{e}m_2}{k} = \overline{p}. \qquad (3.3)$$

These indeterminacies concern the initial exchange rate and price level. Given an initial e, our model determines the exchange rate and price level over time.

At given settings for the γ_i's and σ_i's, inequalities (3.2) limit the increases that can occur in the exchange rate due to "within the interval" shortages caused by a binding penny-in-advance constraint. Once the exchange rate is at the upper bound, the only way that further increases in the exchange rate can occur is through an increase in γ_1 (a debasement of the penny) or a decrease in γ_2 (an enhancement of the dollar).

Changes in the price level and exchange rates can misalign the intervals.
The theoretical model of chapters 2 and 21 describes how movements in endowments or preferences can cause shortages of small coins even when the price level is within the distinct intervals bracketed by the minting points and melting points for all coins. The consequence of a shortage is to drive both the exchange rate and the price level upward. But in general, the price level may rise more or less than proportionately with the exchange rate. This opens two possibilities, each of which exacerbate the basic problem, but in different ways:

1. If the price level rises less than proportionately with the exchange rate, it brings the price level closer to the point at which dollars will be *minted*. When that happens, it makes the small change shortage worse by raising m_2, which raises the ratio of $\frac{m_2}{m_1}$. In chapter 22, we make precise how an increase in this ratio worsens the shortage problem.

2. If the price level rises more than proportionately with the exchange rate, it makes it more likely that pennies will soon be *melted*, because the price level is brought relatively closer to the melting point for pennies. That will obviously exacerbate the shortage.

Cures

In addition to identifying the cause of shortages of small change, the model identifies cures.

1. Debase the small coins. For fixed parameters σ_1, σ_2 controlling the lengths of the intervals, a debasement of pennies and a simultaneous resetting of the exchange rate shifts the interval for pennies to the left, promoting minting and inhibiting melting.

Cures for shortages included debasements and coining on government account.

   Cure 1 repairs a shortage by shifting an interval of fixed size for the small coin to the right. But when σ_1 and σ_2 are kept small to insure narrow intervals, movements in endowments and other exogenous variables that influence the demand for the quantity of real balances and its composition by denomination, the k_{it}'s from chapter 2, will eventually cause shortages of small coins to recur under the item 1 solution. Maintaining narrow intervals exposes the system to threats of recurrent shortages of either large or small denomination coins. Our model points to a longer lasting but risky cure:

2. Widen the intervals. Debase the small denomination coin (by raising γ_1) to move its melting point far to the right, and widen its interval by raising σ_1, moving the minting point far to the left. Then mint the small denomination coin on government account in limited amounts to forestall shortages.

   Cure 2 proposes to diminish the standing of the small coin as a commodity money, and to use some method other than a narrow interval to regulate its supply. A wide interval creates two sorts of problems. First, a low value of the minting point $\gamma_1(1 - \sigma_1)$ means that people might rarely have an incentive to bring metal to the mint to buy coins. Second, a high value of the melting point means that the automatic upper limit on the price level coming from the money supply mechanism is lost. A government could solve the first problem by minting coins on its own account. But to solve the second problem requires that the government restrain itself not to issue too much on its own account.

Our history

The remaining chapters of this book contain our history of how technologies and prevailing ideas for a long time combined to forestall the standard formula; and then how during the Renaissance improvements in the machines for making coins and more sophistication in monetary theory led to policy experiments that sharpened theorists' understanding of the elements of the standard formula.

Scholars debated.   We begin in early medieval times and describe how scholastics, secular lawyers, and eventually economists discussed whether coins should be exchanged by weight or by tale, and how a widespread preference for valuation by weight eroded slowly over the centuries. The strength of a writer's preference for circulation by weight influenced whether he thought that the seigniorage rate σ_i should be set above or below production costs. Some wrote that a narrow band was just. Others said that what counted was price level stability, which they said could be achieved with valuation by tale. Their discussions clarified the distinction between value by weight and value by tale. Authorities recognized that narrow bands deterred counterfeiters but that they also limited the government's seigniorage.

Depreciations, shortages, and debasements   We recount many examples in which the exchange rate (the price of large coins in units of small coins) sporadically drifted upward over time (see fig. 2.1). During periods of rapid increases in the exchange rate there were also often shortages of the small coins. The authorities often responded to those shortages by debasing the small coins, a remedy that our model identifies. When the domestic authorities were slow to debase, the market sometimes accomplished an "endogenous debasement" by importing lighter small denomination coins that were being minted by neighboring states.

Tokens as cures for shortages   In time the monetary authorities learned that if a government could monopolize a superior technology for making token coins, it could deter counterfeiting, widen the bands, and increase seigniorage. An important instance occurred when advisors to the king of Castile recommended using the open market operation described by

(2.13) to generate royal revenues like (2.14). The king did. But eventually discipline broke: the authorities stopped open market operations in silver and replaced them with pure deficits financed by token coins. The price level rose, and the experiment was abandoned when Castile returned to a full-bodied coinage. From the wreckage of that experiment and other similar ones, theorists later constructed the quantity theory of money, cast in terms of subsidiary coins.

Especially in England, private enterprises again discovered the profitability of open market operations like (2.13) and (2.16). Private citizens could obtain interest-free loans by issuing convertible tokens. Private tokens flourished until the government reclaimed the monopoly for coin issue. The British government implemented the standard formula during the nineteenth century. Later in the nineteenth century, the standard formula triumphed completely when France and the United States adopted it at nearly the same time that they abandoned bimetallism.

Private firms issued convertible tokens.

This book blends histories of ideas, technologies, and monetary policies. Our theoretical model supplies us a glue that we use to bind together these different aspects of the problem of small change and its solution. In the following three chapters, which compose part II of this book, we describe the technologies and theoretical ideas that were available to guide historical monetary authorities as they encountered and struggled to manage the problem of small change. Part III will then describe in detail how those monetary authorities put these technologies and ideas to work.

Ͼᴐ

Part II

Ideas and Technologies

CHAPTER 4

Technology

Our model identifies economically significant features of the technology of coin production, including ones that govern the costs of entering the business of producing counterfeits. This chapter is about technologies for producing coins. We describe the constituent metals of coins and the methods and machines available for making them. Three major technologies produced coins: (1) the hammer and pile, which prevailed from the beginning until at least 1550; (2) the screw press and the cylinder press, which were available after 1550; and (3) Boulton's steam press, which became available after 1787. Later chapters describe how technological innovations joined with advances in monetary theory to inspire new policies for supplying coins.

Small coins in the Middle Ages

We begin our story around A.D. 800, when Charlemagne claimed the title of "Emperor" for himself.[1] Among his many reforms was establishing a uniform coinage throughout his vast dominions in 794. The silver penny was the only coin minted. It was made of 96% silver and contained about 1.7g of pure metal (see fig. 4.1).

From 794 to about 1200, western Europe relied on the penny as its only denomination of coin. However, the rapid disintegration of central authority during that time let feudal lords, bishops, and cities assume the right to mint coins without oversight. Each fief or city had its own penny, and these coins were minted with progressively less silver, at rates that varied from place to place. By 1160, European pennies contained anywhere from England's 1.3g to Venice's 0.05g

At first, a sparse denomination structure prevailed.

---

[1] See Spufford (1988a) for medieval monetary history.

Figure 4.1 A penny of Charlemagne, minted in Melle. (Author's collection). Photograph: Robert Lifson.

of fine silver, with fineness ranging from 92.5% in England to 20% in Barcelona (Spufford 1988a, 102–3).

Yet everywhere in Europe the penny was the only coin at any given location; large quantities of pennies were counted in dozens, called "shillings," and sets of twenty dozens, called "pounds."[2]

Then more denominations were issued.

For the following four hundred years, from 1200 to 1600, European monetary systems consisted of multiple denominations, with the penny (1d.) as the lowest, or one of the lowest.[3] Larger silver coins and gold coins, introduced in the mid-thirteenth century, formed the large denominations.

Medieval small change consisted mostly of a copper-silver alloy.

In medieval times, small change was made from a mixture of silver and copper. When the share of silver, or fineness, was low (markedly less than 50%), it was called *billon*. In England, the small change was made from sterling silver (92.5%), the same standard as larger denominations. The royal mint never minted below sterling (92.5%) until 1672.[4]

---

[2] We abbreviate the medieval system of units as follows: penny, denier, denaro = 1d.; shilling, sou, soldo = 1s. = 12d.; pound, livre, lira = £1 = 20s. = 240d.

[3] France and the Low Countries minted halfpennies (½d), England also minted farthings (¼d).

[4] With the exception of the Great Debasement of 1540 to 1550.

In other countries, silver was mixed with copper to create larger, more convenient coins, but the silver content of the lower denominations was nevertheless proportional to their face value, as compared to larger coins. This was true in France until the mid-sixteenth century. When debasements occurred in medieval times, the entire denomination structure was debased simultaneously. During periods of intense debasement (1340–60, 1417–29) no small coins were minted. Originally, small coins were under the same free minting regime as larger coins, but by the 1480s, small denominations were minted only on government orders, and sometimes in specific regions, prohibitions were even placed on minting.

In addition to silver and full-bodied billon coins, other coins were "light" relative to higher denominations, usually by no more than 10 or 20%. Examples are found in Spain, the Low Countries, and Italy. When the *quattrino* (4d.) was first minted in Florence in 1332, it was lighter than the *grosso* (30d.), in the sense that it contained less than ⁴⁄₃₀ of a grosso's silver, by about 17%. During debasements, relative contents could change. In fourteenth- and fifteenth-century Florence, the three silver coins were the grosso, the quattrino, and the *picciolo* (1d.). In 1366, only the picciolo was debased; in 1371, the quattrino was debased; in 1385 and in 1461, the grosso was debased; in 1472 the quattrino and the picciolo were both debased.[5]

Coins were close to full-bodied. Private traders chose the quantities.

The purchasing power of a small coin

What was small change as a fraction of income? Munro (1988, 393) provides detailed information on the purchasing power of the Flemish penny, and concludes that "small silver and petty coins played a far greater role in medieval society than they do in today's economy. For most people, such coins were then certainly the principal means, for many the only means, of transacting retail trade, in buying and selling daily necessities."

The purchasing power of small change was substantial.

---

[5] Curiously, from 1461 to 1471 the quattrino was actually the heaviest coin, and the grosso (worth 80d.) was 14% lighter. See Bernocchi (1976, 302–8), Cipolla (1990, 191–209), and chapter 9 for details.

Table 4.1 Daily wage for unskilled labor and denomination structure of coinage in late medieval Europe. Denominations of billon coins are in smaller font, those of silver coins in normal font, those of gold coins in italics. Units are the local pence (deniers parisis for Flanders; maravedis for Castile).

Place and time	Daily wage	Existing denominations
Paris, 1402	30d.	½, 1, 2, 5, 10, *270*
Paris, 1460	35d.	1, 3, 10, 30, *330*
Florence, 1347	30d.	1, 4, 32, 48, *744*
Flanders, 1389	48d.	½, 1, 24, *528*
Low Countries, 1433	60d.	½, 1, 3, 6, 12, 24, *288, 576*
England, 1349	2.2d.	¼, ½, 1, *20, 40, 80*
England, 1467	5d.	¼, ½, 1, 2, 4, *30, 60, 120*
Castile, 1471	25mr	¼, ½, 2, 31, *420*

Sources: France: Baulant (1971). Florence: La Roncière (1982, 326). Flanders, Low Countries: Verlinden (1959–73, 2:95, 4:325). England: Postan (1973, 199). Castile: MacKay (1981, 76–77, 151).

Table 4.1 compares the denomination structure with the daily wage of unskilled labor at various dates in western Europe. Typically, the daily wage represented 1 to 3 silver coins, and thus daily necessities required smaller coins. Another way to appreciate its role is to estimate what the smallest silver coin could purchase. In Florence, in the second half of the fourteenth century, the smallest silver coin was the grosso (5s.): it could purchase 5 liters of the cheapest wine, 1 kg of mutton, 20 eggs, or 1 kg of olive oil; or pay a month's rent for an unmarried manual laborer (La Roncière 1982, 394–95).

The medieval technology: hammer and pile

Most mints were contracted out to private entrepreneurs who were usually allowed different charges for different denominations.[6]

---

[6] See Mayhew (1992, 99–103, 114–21, 140, 148, 152–58, 166–71) for the English mints, Blanchet and Dieudonné (1916) for the French mints. Spufford (1988b) confirms that similar arrangements prevailed in the Low Countries and elsewhere. The cities of Florence and Venice managed their mints directly; but,

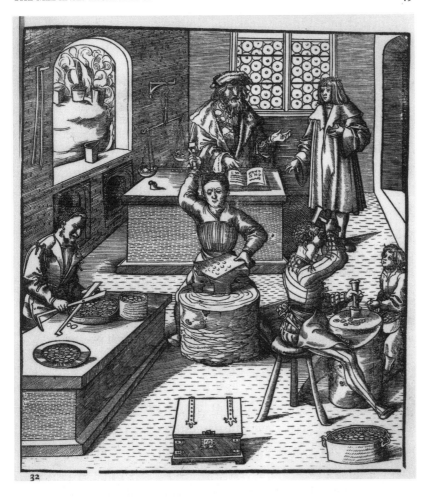

Figure 4.2 A late medieval mint, engraving by Leonard Beck (1516). *Source*: Hans Burgkmair, *der WeißKunig*, reprint Vienna 1775. (Photograph courtesy of the John M. Wing foundation, the Newberry Library, Chicago.)

After melting and refining the metal, the technology for making coins involved three main steps: preparing sheets of metal, cutting the sheets into blanks, and striking the blanks. Figure 4.2 represents the future German emperor Maximilian observing a technology that

---

as elsewhere, the mint merely posted prices and let the private sector choose quantities.

The technology for minting coins remained unchanged from ancient times until the sixteenth century. It produced imperfect coins.

was little changed from Greek and Roman times.[7] The metal, once brought to the desired standard in the furnaces (at top left of fig. 4.2), was hammered into a sheet (at center). A sizer cut the sheet into squares with shears, then beat the squares to a round shape and adjusted the weight (at left). The resulting blanks were blanched to remove tarnish, and then struck by the moneyers (at right). To do this, the lower die or pile, whose other end was shaped like a spike, was driven into a wooden block. The moneyer put the block between his legs, placed a blank on the pile, placed the upper die or trussell on top of the blank, and struck the top of the trussell several times with a hammer.

The dies were made locally by the mint's engraver on a pattern provided by the central government. The engraver prepared a collection of punches, each bearing in relief one of the elements of the coin's design. He then used the punches to engrave the dies with the design, replacing them as they wore out.

The technology required specialized labor: each step was performed by different laborers, usually members of privileged (and hereditary) corporations. The tools were simple, the plant was of limited size (furnaces were the largest piece of equipment), and minting could be carried out in a decentralized fashion. But this technology had serious drawbacks. Since dies were produced locally, with common goldsmith's tools, there was considerable variation in the style and quality of the imprints on the coins. The process produced imperfect coins of varying size and weight, with a poorly centered imprint, making it difficult to spot an altered coin. An imitation could pass as genuine. The coins were thus subject to falsification and clipping.

Production costs and seigniorage

Per unit of value, the production process made small coins more expensive to produce than larger ones, since the same effort was

---

[7] This account is based on Blanchet and Dieudonné (1916), Wedel (1960), and Cooper (1988). The technology in Roman times is charmingly illustrated by a Pompei fresco (Paolozzi Strozzi et al. 1992, 44–45).

Table 4.2 Production costs (brassage) of coinage in late medieval Europe. Gold coins are in italics. Legal values are in local pence (maravedis in Castile).

	name of coin	legal value	silver/gold content (mg)	brassage (%)
Florence, 1347	picciolo	1d.	52	15.65
	quattrino	4d.	217	6.22
	grosso	32d.	1960	1.20
	fiorino	744d.	3537	0.14
England, 1349	farthing	¼d.	283	3.64
	halfpenny	½d.	570	2.96
	penny	1d.	1178	1.94
	noble	80d.	8188	0.42
Flanders, 1389	double mite	¹⁄₁₂ d.	53	43.71
	gros	1d.	1018	9.73
	noble	72d.	7649	1.58
France, 1402	denier	1d.	145	10.67
	blanc	10d.	1448	6.46
	écu	270d.	3948	0.72
Low Countries, 1433	double mite	¹⁄₁₂ d.	45	36.34
	gros	1d.	814	4.51
	philippus	48d.	3598	0.94
Milan, 1447	denaro	1d.	37	20.50
	sesino	6d.	272	8.56
	grosso	24d.	1175	2.25
France, 1460	denier	1d.	109	12.50
	blanc	10d.	1086	4.94
	gros	30d.	3258	2.32
	écu	300d.	3321	0.56
England, 1467	penny	1d.	707	3.11
	groat	4d.	2828	3.11
	ryal	120d.	7643	0.55
Castile, 1471	blanca	½mr	39	24.39
	real	31mr	3195	1.49
	enrique	420mr	4553	0.50

Sources: Milan: Cipolla (1990, 111–23). Florence: Bernocchi (1976, 33–44). Castile: Pérez García (1990, 83–86) and MacKay (1981, 76). France: Saulcy (1879–92, 2:117, 3:226). England: Challis (1992a, 703, 713). Low Countries: Munro (1972, 202–5) and Munro (1988, table 5).

Minting costs were higher for small coins. They were born by the mint or the sovereign out of seigniorage or by the private sector.

required to strike a coin of any size, and not much less to prepare smaller blanks than larger blanks. Table 4.2 presents data on production costs from a variety of western European countries in the Middle Ages.[8] Who paid those costs varied by country, depending on mint prices set for each denomination.

The difference between the mint price and the mint equivalent of each denomination constituted gross seigniorage. Production costs were called brassage. Given that brassage varied by denomination, an identical mint price across denominations required either cross-subsidization of lower denominations by higher ones, or subsidization of the mint by the government.

The public and the mintmaster decided the mix of denominations.

In Florence, whose mint was run directly by the city, the opposite tack was taken, namely, charging private parties for costs by paying different mint prices for different denominations. In 1347 (the period for which the figures in table 4.2 apply), the seigniorage rate was 0.6% for the gold *fiorino* or florin, 4.6% for the grosso, 6.6% for the quattrino and 17.8% for the picciolo (Bernocchi 1976, 38–40).

In France and the Netherlands, the mint price was the same regardless of denomination, but the mintmaster was permitted to deduct different production costs from gross seigniorage.[9] Thus the net seigniorage on the larger coins was used to subsidize the production costs of the smaller coins. Furthermore, the output mix between gold and silver was often part of the mint's contract, but only the aggregate value actually mattered, and quantities of small currency were never specified, leaving them to be determined by public demand and the mintmaster's decisions. The mintmaster's only obligation was to provide a minimal amount of net seigniorage during his lease. Since he could meet his obligation with any mix of coins, he preferred to mint larger denomination silver coins, unless ordered to do otherwise.

---

[8] Sprenger (1991, 83) only gives rates for Germany: 2% for Florins, 7% for Schillings and 15% for Hellers, in line with our figures for other countries. Plotting the numbers in table 4.2 suggests that costs were inversely related to the square root of the intrinsic content.

[9] The mint price for low-grade silver was usually lower, by as much as 10%; but the mint price does not seem to have depended on the coins in which it was paid.

In England, after 1351, the mint price did not depend on denomination, but the mintmaster was allowed a flat rate for all coins of the same metal. This gave the mintmaster an incentive to produce only the largest coins. Occasionally, the proportions of various coins were specified in the contract, but the king could not force a competitive bidder to assume such costs. In 1461, the mix of denominations was left to the discretion of the comptroller, a government official, who should consult "the desire, ease, and content of the People." Production remained strongly biased toward large coins until a complete scale of differential payments across denominations was adopted in 1770.[10]

Mechanization

Innovations came from the art of medal making, which began in Italy in the 1430s.[11] Often much larger than coins, medals were usually cast and eventually chiseled, but around the turn of the sixteenth century the demand for high-quality medals increased and people sought new ways to strike medals.[12] This required a mechanized technology both to prepare the larger flanks and to strike them with sufficient force and accuracy. Ultimately, the key innovations occurred among goldsmiths of southern Germany and Switzerland around 1550. They quickly disseminated throughout Europe.[13] Two methods of striking the coins developed: one using a screw press as in figure 4.3, the other using two cylinders on which the dies were engraved, thus laminating and striking at the same time. The screw press came to be adopted in France and England in the seventeenth century, while the cylinder press was adopted earlier

---

[10] Craig (1953, 75), Mayhew (1992, 168).

[11] This account is based on Wedel (1960) and Cooper (1988).

[12] Some medals were cast and then struck over. This method was imported from Venice to produce groschen in Tirol in 1484 (Wedel 1960, 103).

[13] Earlier developments in Italy by Bramante, Leonardo da Vinci, and Benvenuto Cellini (who directed the Rome mint from 1529 to 1534) were not pursued.

in Austria, Germany, Spain, Italy, and Sweden. In the eighteenth century, the screw press overtook the cylinder press as the main minting apparatus.

The next sections discuss the diffusion of the two technologies across Europe. Some countries experimented with both. In the following chapters, we examine the impact made by both methods on governments' policies regarding small coinage, and the experiments that were undertaken in the seventeenth century.

The screw press

The screw press appeared around 1550 but met resistance. It did not come into widespread use until the mid-seventeenth century.

In 1547, the French king Henri II decided to reform coinage in his realm. He appointed an engraver-general to produce all the punches for making dies in all mints and so brought greater uniformity to realizations of the designs. He also asked his envoys in all countries to report new technologies that could be put to use to produce better coinage. In 1550, he learned from his ambassador in Germany that an Augsburg goldsmith had perfected equipment to produce high-quality coins.[14] The ambassador's brother was sent along with an engineer named Aubin Olivier to Germany. They negotiated the rights to the machines and had them built in Augsburg and brought to Paris. The machinery was set up in a building on the Île de la Cité in Paris, where a water mill had been installed in the 1530s for gem polishing.[15] The Mill Mint (*Monnaie du Moulin des Étuves*) began producing gold coins in 1551, and Olivier became its director in 1556. A rolling mill (powered by the water mill) created smooth strips of metal or fillets; a drawing bench brought them to the exact width; a hand-activated cutter or punch press perforated the strips into blanks; and a press struck the blanks on both sides. By 1555, Olivier had improved the press by adding a segmented collar to hold the blank in place. During the strike, the collar impressed on the edge of the coin a design or a motto (the collar had to be segmented so as to remove the coin after the strike). The new machines thus mechanized each

---

[14] The details are in Vaissière (1892).

[15] Hocking (1909), Mazerolle (1907, 26–31).

step in coin making, and also marked the edges to prevent clipping.

We do not know whether the original Augsburg machinery used
a traditional drop press, where a weight falls vertically on top of the
blank, or a real screw press like the one depicted in figure 4.3.[16] But
by the mid-seventeenth century, the screw press was well developed:
its first known depiction is on a painted window in the Constanz mint
in 1624. It gained its force from the momentum of two large lead
balls (weighing 40 to 150 lb each) at the extremities of a horizontal
bar. At the time of its installation in London in 1662, it could strike
30 coins per minute. By the late eighteenth century, the removal
of struck coins and feeding of new blanks had been automated; the
Paris press took 16 men to operate and could produce 60 coins per
minute.[17]

The new mint set up at the Mill Mint did not long function as
coinage mint, however, because of the high costs of operation, and
perhaps some initial mismanagement. In 1563, the Mill Mint was
restricted to making medals and tokens. In 1575, its mandate was
extended to pure copper coinage. It continued to function in that
capacity, producing high-quality medals and small copper coins in
limited quantities, until 1625.[18] Historians usually attribute the
failure to use the mint for coins to the resistance of entrenched interests among mint workers and monetary officials, although problems
such as those to be encountered England in the late seventeenth
century may have been foreseen.

England became interested in the new process early on, and in
1554 attempted to imitate the French press. In 1561, a former

---

[16] It is usually assumed that the stamping was originally done by a screw press, but
there is solid evidence for its use in Paris only after 1600. It is rather unlikely that
an Augsburg goldsmith would have had an operating screw press in his workshop,
and more plausibly some kind of drop press was involved (Wedel 1960, 130).
A 1676 depiction of the Paris Mint machinery shows both a drop press and a
screw press. Which mintmaster introduced the screw press is unknown, and no
connection with the earlier advances in Italy has ever been found.

[17] Cooper (1988, 59), Craig (1953, 164), Wedel (1960, 158).

[18] Mazerolle (1907, 26–34), Blanchet and Dieudonné (1916, 192–95).

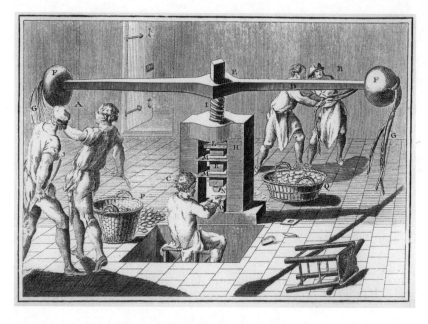

Figure 4.3 A screw press, engraving by Robert Benard, 1771. *Source*: *Encyclopédie, ou Dictionnaire raisonné des arts, des sciences et des métiers*, plates, vol. 8. (Photograph courtesy of the Newberry Library, Chicago.)

employee of the French mint named Eloi Mestrell came to England and introduced the new technology at the Tower Mint. The machines were ten times slower than the hammering process and the experiment terminated after 11 years.[19]

In 1630, an engraver from Liège named Jean Warin became director of the Mill Mint, now called the Medal Mint and located in the Louvre Palace. On the occasion of a general overhaul of the French coinage in 1640, he was allowed to try again to use screw presses for minting coins, and in 1645 he succeeded in having the mechanized process used in every French mint. The old technology subsisted only in the coat of arms of the corporation of moneyers (fig. 4.4).

England followed within a few years. In 1649, the Frenchman

---

[19] Craig (1953, 118–23), Borden and Brown (1984). Mestrell was terminated in 1578 for counterfeiting.

Figure 4.4 Silver token issued by the mint of Rouen, 1787. The center depicts a screw press. The two hammers in the small oval below recall the previous technology. The Latin motto at the top means "hence weight and value." (Author's collection). Photograph: Robert Lifson.

Pierre Blondeau was invited to England to bring with him the technology: his sample coins were approved in 1651, but the first coins produced with the new method did not appear until 1658. The method was extended to the whole English coinage in 1662. The rolling mills were driven by horses. In his diary for 1663, Samuel Pepys noted that the machinery made coinage more expensive for the king.[20] In England, however, no recoinage occurred, and the "milled" money circulated along with the older, hammered money. Chapter 16 describes how England ultimately recoined all of its silver money in 1696.

---

[20] Pepys (1970–83, 4:147).

The screw press did not diffuse widely until after its nearly simultaneous adoption in England and France. It was adopted in Bran-
denburg soon after the peace of Westphalia in 1648, and by the
Netherlands in 1671. Spain, where the grandson of the king of
France came to the throne in 1700, switched to the screw press
in 1728; his son introduced it in Parma, from where it passed to
Venice in 1755.[21] Though it ultimately proved to be the superior
technology, reluctance to make the associated large investments in
human and physical capital delayed adoption of the screw press for
a hundred years after it first appeared.

The cylinder press

By 1600 the cylinder press was accepted in Germany and southern Europe. While Henri II of France was actively searching for a new technology,
so also was Charles V, German emperor and king of Spain. In 1551,
one of his advisors, Count zu Solm-Lich, recommended mechanization to reduce minting costs. He proposed the principle of a cylinder
press, similar to the rolling presses already used by goldsmiths, to
produce flat strips of metal. The cylinders themselves would be engraved with the coin die (see fig. 4.5). Horses or waterwheels would
provide power. The Emperor's brother Ferdinand, count of Tirol,
showed interest and asked his mint officers in the city of Hall to
investigate the possibilities.

In the end, the first working cylinder press was set up in Zürich
in the early 1550s, by two goldsmiths.[22] The mechanism had the
advantage of simultaneously laminating and stamping the metal, but
punching out the coins after impression was laborious. A variant
method fed cut blanks through the cylinder press, but the unequal
stretching of the blank as it passed between the rolls resulted in oval
and sometimes warped coins, making it impossible to serrate the
edges. This could be corrected by cutting oval blanks and engraving

---

[21] Walther (1939), Majer (1953). The screw press technology is also known
to have been transferred to the small kingdom of Navarre (soon to be united to
France), where a similar mint was set up by a former engraver of the Paris mint in
1556.

[22] See Hahn (1915, 19) and Newald (1885) for the early development of the
cylinder press.

Figure 4.5 Cylinder used in the Segovia mint, 1620. This trial cylinder is engraved with six different designs and was used to produce pattern coins (Museo Casa de la Moneda, Madrid).

oval dies, resulting in round coins. In spite of these drawbacks, the process proved very popular. The Swiss inventors set up a partnership to develop the new invention commercially and export it abroad; they obtained a patent for all of Germany. Ferdinand bought it for Tirol and it was installed in Innsbruck in 1568. Austria would remain faithful to the cylinder press until 1765.

The cylinder press was soon adopted throughout Germany and beyond: Heidelberg in 1567, Cologne in 1568, Augsburg in 1572, Dresden in 1574, Danzig in 1577, Nyköping (Sweden) in 1580, Madgeburg in 1582, Hamburg in 1591, Saalfeldt in 1593, Rostock in 1594, Osnabrück in 1597, Münster in 1599. It reached Poland in the late sixteenth century, where the Göbel brothers secured a patent and exported it to Königsberg, Riga, Denmark. Before 1600 it had also reached Clausthal-Zellerfeld in Hannover near the mines of the Harz, Berlin, and Strasbourg. Sweden began using cylinder presses in 1625 in Kopparberg, near its large copper mines.[23]

A variant of the cylinder press was developed in the seventeenth

---

[23] Walther (1939), Wedel (1960, 134).

century. Instead of engraving a whole cylinder, two mushroom-shaped pieces were engraved and inserted in slots of rotating axles. This design, known as *Taschenwerk*, required precut oval-shaped blanks. Passing them between the dies made them round. The design was introduced in the early seventeenth century in France and England, but did not take root. Nicolas Briot, a mintmaster in northern France and Lorraine, traveled extensively to Germany, where he learned of the various techniques used there. He became engraver of the mint in 1606, and in 1620 obtained the lease for the Paris mint. In 1617, a trial of his proposed minting device was carried out before French officials, but ended in failure: wastage was high and the coins were not of good quality.[24] In 1625, he left for England where he became chief engraver of the mint. In 1629, he was allowed to experiment with machinery which he had been using to strike medals. He was also put in charge of producing pure copper coinage at the mint in Edinburgh, but neither attempt proved conclusive. In 1639, he tried again in Scotland with silver coinage. He used a Taschenwerk for large denominations and a screw press for small denominations. The machinery was partly powered by horses. The costs were substantial, and the machines apparently remained experimental. Later, during the Civil War, Briot minted coins for the Royalists using cylinder presses.[25]

From Germany, the cylinder press technology quickly spread to southern Europe. Venice's ambassador to the German emperor persuaded the authorities to import it in 1575 (Majer 1953). The following year, Florence installed it in the new Zecca (mint) on the banks of the Arno, near Santa Croce. The machinery was imported from Germany, and operated by German engineers who proved to be excellent workers and consumers of Chianti wine.[26] Rome had similar equipment by 1581. That year, Philip II of Spain asked his

---

[24] See Poullain (1709) for the minutes of the trial.

[25] Craig (1953, 147–50), Challis (1992b).

[26] Cipolla (1990, 233). Only silver coinage was produced in the new mint; gold was produced in the old Zecca. Cipolla does not specify the method used, but Wedel (1960, 134) states that it was a cylinder press.

cousin the archduke Ferdinand, count of Tirol, to send him a copy
of the Innsbruck machines, and the archduke obliged by sending six
German craftsmen, who built them in the Segovia mint, henceforth
known as the *Ingenio*.[27] The first coins, silver reales, were issued
in 1586. The installation of this machine in Spain had important
consequences which we will trace in chapter 14.

Other inventions

An important innovation during the seventeenth century was the
marking of edges of coins with the Castaing machine (invented in
England and adopted in France in 1685), a process by which a coin
was rolled on a horizontal surface between two steel bars, one of
which bore a motto or serrated design in relief.[28]

Several innovations occurred in the late eighteenth and early nineteenth centuries. The portrait lathe and hubbing were invented by
the Swiss Jean-Pierre Droz around 1780. They allowed coin dies to
be identically reproduced, and eliminated one of the last sources of
variation from one coin to the next. They were adopted by Dupré,
engraver of the French mint, in 1791, and Boulton in Birmingham.

The steam engine

In 1786, Matthew Boulton of Birmingham, partner of James Watt,
adapted steampower to the minting press. Private minters first took
advantage of the new technology, the Anglesey Copper Company in
1787 soon being followed by many others. Boulton's main ambition,
however, was to win a contract from the government, which he
obtained in 1797. From 1797 to 1807, he produced copper coins

*Using steam power
to drive presses
presented a new
opportunity for
token coinage.*

---

[27] The story of the Segovia Ingenio is told in Del Rivero (1918–19).

[28] Because this innovation was introduced in England at the same as mechanization, and therefore the first marked edges appeared on coins produced in a mill,
such edges came to be called "milled."

Figure 4.6 A press at the Paris mint, *L'Illustration*, December 28, 1895. (Photograph courtesy of the Newberry Library, Chicago.)

for the government. But so strong was the attachment to full-bodied coinage that the 1797 pennies weighed 1 ounce each. Rising copper prices during the Napoleonic wars forced the reduction in weight to

Figure 4.7 5s. copper coin issued by the Monneron Frères firm, Paris, 1792. The coin was redeemable in assignats in quantities of 50F or more, as stated on the reverse. The scene on the obverse is the oath to the constitution of the French taken during a ceremony on July 14, 1790. (Author's collection.)

⅔ ounce in 1798 and to ½ ounce in 1805. Royal coinage stopped in 1807, but private coinage continued to be issued. Meanwhile, the royal Mint was rebuilt and fitted with Boulton's machines in 1810, which were by then capable of striking 70 to 80 coins per minute.

Boulton's new technology immediately attracted attention abroad. As early as 1791, the firm of Monneron frères in Paris contracted with Boulton to produce private copper coinage in France (see fig. 4.7). The issuers of these coins were soon put out of business when the government monopolized the issue of small denominations and put out its own paper currency. The revolutionary government's nationalization of private small denomination tokens in France prefigured the British government's way of adopting the standard formula (see chapter 17). Russia was the first government to buy Boulton's presses in 1799, followed later by Denmark and Spain (Craig 1953, 264). Steam engines were not, however, easily adapted to the old screw press, and there were technical problems in accommodating the rotation and recoil of the screw. In 1817, Dietrich Uhlhorn, a German engineer in Grevenbroich near Cologne, invented a lever or knuckle-action press which could more easily be driven by steam.

His machine could strike 30 to 60 coins per minute, depending on the size of the coin. By 1840, Uhlhorn had built presses for mints in Düsseldorf, Berlin, Utrecht, Vienna, Munich, Karlsruhe, Schwerin, Stockholm, Wiesbaden, and Naples; Uhlhorn machines were also in use in Australia starting in 1853 (Meyer 1840–55, s.v. "Münze"). The method was adapted by Pierre-Antoine Thonnelier in France in 1834. Striking 40 coins per minute, the Thonnelier press came into use in Philadelphia in 1836 and Paris in 1845.[29] By the late nineteenth century, when it was used throughout Europe, the Thonnelier press could strike 60 to 120 coins per minute (fig. 4.6).[30]

Counterfeiting, duplicating, imitating

We now discuss an ever-present aspect of all arrangements for supplying societies with coins: counterfeiting. A counterfeit coin belies either its content or its origin.[31] With false content, the counterfeiter cheats the recipient of the coin, who receives less than he thought. With false origin, the counterfeiter cheats the monetary authority of its seigniorage.[32] A counterfeiter might be the mint itself (a case we set aside),[33] a private party, or a foreign mint.

The technologies for counterfeiting and for deterring counterfeiters

Sometimes the term "counterfeiting" is reserved for the production of a coin that contained less than its appearance suggested, while "duplicating" means producing a coin substantially identical

---

[29] Blanchet and Dieudonné (1916).

[30] *Encyclopaedia Britannica*, 9th ed., s.v. "mint." The London mint began to use lever presses in 1872, which produced 90 coins per minute.

[31] Luschin von Ebengreuth (1926, 145) distinguishes between "falsch" and "unecht." Carothers (1930, 128) uses the terms counterfeits and duplicates.

[32] He may also be cheating the recipient, if the coin's value depends on it being authentic.

[33] When the mint itself counterfeits, the coin's origin is what it seems, but its content is not: such are coins produced by corrupt mint officials or a monetary authority secretly debasing its currency. Thus Dante accused King Philip IV of France of being a counterfeiter. See Velde, Weber, and Wright (1999) for a model of debasement based on asymmetric information about the content of coins.

to the mint's by someone else. While counterfeiting in the restricted sense was always a problem for monetary authorities, the possibility of duplication also had important consequences for monetary policy. It meant that the mint faced potential competitors, domestic or foreign. The mint's ability to collect gross seigniorage on any denomination was restrained by the counterfeiter's production costs (and transportation costs in the case of foreign mints).

The mint could mitigate the problem of duplication by raising its competitors' production costs above its own, or by depriving them of the coin making technology. Its ability to do so differed for its domestic and foreign competitors.

The production costs of domestic competitors were large because counterfeiting was illegal and severely punished, and because no distinction was made between counterfeiting and duplication (see, for example, Grimaudet 1576, 147). The tradition of Roman law saw the right to mint as a royal prerogative and treated any infringement of this regalian privilege as a form of lese majesty or high treason. The punishment in Roman law and in early German law was the loss of one or both hands, but by the fourteenth century some form of gruesome death was the norm: hanging in England (Ruding 1840, 1:81), burning in Venice (Stahl 2000, 235), boiling in France (Saulcy 1879–92, 1:180).

The force of law could thus be brought to bear on domestic competitors. Punishment required detection, which was uncertain. But even a small probability of dying a gruesome death increased counterfeiters' labor costs. This argument was made by the Italian Montanari: "those who work at the public mint do not risk their lives, and receive only the price of their labor; but if a worker has to make coin dies in secret, at the risk of his whole being, he will be persuaded to do so only with a lot of gold." He cited an example of this risk premium, a counterfeiter who paid ten times more for his dies than did the public mint (Montanari [1683] 1804, 104, 115).

Innovations in minting technology afforded the mint some means of restricting access. Mechanization during the Renaissance and the development of the steam engine during the Industrial Revolution initially gave the mint exclusive ownership of the technology. Even after the technology had diffused, the mint could still try to maintain a cost advantage and make the new technology too expensive for competitors. The medieval technology was easy to hide in a goldsmith's shop, where the tools and equipment were the same as those of the mint. But a screw press was more difficult to conceal and justify, a steam-driven press even more so. The risk of detection might restrict counterfeiters to scales of operation too small to recover high fixed costs.

Foreign competitors were harder to suppress, short of military action. In medieval times, most states were small and no place was far removed from neighboring states. Governments had limited enforcement resources and could not patrol borders. England, being an island, sometimes intercepted foreign imports. The Statute of Money of 1335 prescribed that intensive searches of incoming vessels for counterfeit money be carried out in all ports, and hostelers were ordered to search their guests as well. A few years later, diligent searchers were promised a third of their finds, and lax ones were threatened with fines and imprisonment.[34] The evidence reviewed in chapter 8 indicates that these efforts were not successful.

One episode illustrates how foreign competitors were poised to exploit any profitable opportunity. In 1577, France began to mint pure copper pennies using the screw press technology. A few decades later, the technology had spread far enough that a number of small states along France's borders found it profitable to produce imitations of French pennies. Figure 4.8 shows the French 2d. coin and its imitations in Dombes, Château Renaud, Sedan, and Charleville.[35]

These foreign coins were not duplicates, since they were clearly distinguishable from the originals. The obverse bore the profile and

---

[34] Ruding (1840, 1:211, 215). How the inspectors could dispose of their reward is not explained.

[35] In the case of Dombes and Château Renaud, the issuers were brother and first cousin of the king, respectively.

Figure 4.8 Seventeenth–century copper coins from France and nearby areas. *Top:* double tournois, France, 1642; double tournois, Dombes, 1641. *Bottom:* double tournois, Sedan, 1633; double tournois, Château Renaud, 1603–05; denier tournois, Charleville, 1653. (Author's collection.) Photograph: Robert Lifson.

name of their respective issuers rather than that of the French king, and the reverse, shown in figure 4.8, display recognizable variations on the French royal arms. But the overall design was similar, and they were clearly intended to pass for French pennies. These coins are best described as imitations rather than duplications.

Official attitudes toward duplication softened in eighteenth-century Britain. Imitations of the official copper coinage were produced on a large scale, Manchester being one of the main centers. While counterfeiting the king's coinage had been made an act of treason by a statute of 1351, imitating the coinage was not held by the courts to be illegal, so long as the coins were sufficiently different from the official ones (see page 270). Parliament could have passed laws against imitations, but did not.

Public policies toward counterfeiting evolved.

Technologies and ideas

A technology is a collection of ideas about how to do something. This chapter has summarized the history of technologies for making coins: before 1550, the ancient hammer and pile; after 1550, the screw press and the cylinder press; and after 1787, Matthew Boulton's steam press. At any moment, the leading technology determined the best possible quality of coins as well as the fixed and variable costs for all potential suppliers of coins. The available technology influenced the contest between public monetary authorities and counterfeiters, and placed constraints on what policy makers could attempt.

Against this background, in the next two chapters we shall describe the evolution of another kind of technology, namely the prevailing monetary theory, seen as a more or less coherent set of ideas about what money is and how to supply enough for the needs of trade without causing inflation. We shall document advances in monetary theory that were at least as important as those for making coins from metal that we have studied in this chapter.

એ

CHAPTER 5

Medieval Ideas about Coins and Money

Implementing the standard formula required both a theory of convertible tokens and a technology for producing counterfeit-proof small denomination coins. Having described the history of the relevant technology, we now recount theoretical developments that culminated in the discovery of the standard formula. This chapter summarizes the contributions of medieval jurists and how they constructed and then gradually qualified a money-as-commodity view. The next chapter then tells about the fresh approach and new findings about monetary theory brought by the Renaissance. In both chapters, we can't help seeing theorists discovering features of our model and arguing about its parameters.

Theory and technology for making token coins

Our story begins in 1100, when pious lawyers and monks trusted God for many things, but not to support the values of coins. For that they trusted only silver and gold. It ends near 1900, when philosophers proclaimed that "God is dead," but monetary theorists had discovered how a limited supply of currency saying "in God we trust" could be better than gold. Theorizing about small denomination coins contributed in many ways to that discovery.

Medieval jurists as advocates of Arrow-Debreu

All modern theories of money begin by observing, as Hahn (1965) did, that the competitive equilibrium model of Arrow (1951) and Debreu (1954) has no role for fiat money, an asset that is valued only because it facilitates exchange. In the Arrow-Debreu model, all exchanges occur through a frictionless credit system. Credit works so well that no coins or notes are ever required for exchange. The Arrow-Debreu model would make coins worth the metal they contain.

Valuation by weight

Modern theories of money try to explain how intrinsically useless

Valuation by number (or tale)

fiat money can have value. All such theories point to frictions in the environment that inhibit credit.[1] When theories of fiat money are applied to coins, they explain how a coin can have a market value that exceeds that of its metal content. In our model, this happens any time the price level is lower than the melting point of a coin.[2]

We begin our account of monetary theory with the medieval jurists, who wrestled with a range of legal problems related to money. Remarkably, their starting point was the coins-as-commodity view of Arrow and Debreu. The jurists applied a type of linear pricing argument now common in finance, valuing a coin by unbundling it and additively pricing its constituent elements. We describe how they originally came to this view, how they applied and then slowly modified it as they confronted practical problems created by an increasingly diverse set of coins.

Romanists and Canonists

We trace the evolution of thought through two groups of jurists: the romanists, who specialized in Roman law, and the canonists, who studied the law of the Church.

Romanists theorized about commodity money in the context of contract law.

Romanists developed their view of money in the context of a doctrine to handle disputes about repaying money loans. Roman law classified contracts according to the nature of the object lent. When disputes about money loans first arose, romanists classified money as a fungible, then applied the rules governing consumption loans. They settled on the principle that money should be valued by weight.

When they adopted this principle, the romanists chose from among several relevant but conflicting passages of Roman law. Parts of Roman law viewed money as deriving its value from government authority, or from its usefulness in overcoming the difficulties of barter. The romanists downplayed and distorted such passages to minimize possible conflict with the principle of valuation by weight.

---

[1] For example, see the contributions in Kareken and Wallace (1980).

[2] Of course, if a theory predicts that a coin with some intrinsic value can exchange for more, it might also predict that a "coin" with no intrinsic value can exchange for a positive value.

They went so far as to prescribe that minting should be subsidized by the government, by setting the seigniorage plus the brassage rate to 0. In our model, that collapses the interval bounding the price level to a point, and makes valuation by tale identical with valuation by weight.

Valuation by weight applied easily enough to the relatively simple cases that arose in the single denomination coin system that prevailed before 1200 based on the Carolingian penny. But after 1200, more difficult cases arose because monetary systems grew more complex with the appearance of multiple denominations (large and small silver coins); coins of different metals with fluctuating relative prices; debasements, enhancements, and demonetizations; and units of account based on different coins. For a long time, valuation by weight survived these tests. In the early sixteenth century it was still called the "communis opinio." But over time various jurists allowed qualifications and exceptions, some of which were seeds for later ideas about token and fiat currencies. Some of these, such as legal tender laws, or the liquidity value of an object that solves the double coincidence of wants problem, are central to modern theories of money. Thus, here and there individual authors carved out exceptions and introduced nuances, making the commodity-based view of money increasingly difficult to apply, beset by special cases, and less and less based on a universal principle.

Meanwhile canonists developed their own views of money. On the subject of loan repayments, they were content to adopt the romanists' doctrine. But as students of church law, they approached money from other points of view, closer to public law than to private law. They thought about the morality of debasements, the conditions under which governments could and should levy a positive seigniorage rate, and what seigniorate rate to set.

Canonists theorized about money from the perspective of public policy.

The next chapter describes how the Renaissance brought an attempt to break away from the traditional interpretation of Roman law. Money then became a subject of its own, not merely an incidental to the law of contracts. More intent on basing law on reason than

rationalizing existing law, humanists returned to the texts of Aristotle
and also drew on monetary experiences recounted by historians and
travelers. They considered the validity of valuation by tale. Coincidence or not, the Renaissance also witnessed a new technology that
made it possible to experiment with a new idea: money worth more
than its weight in silver.

The remainder of this chapter is organized as follows. In the
next section, we recount the construction of a common doctrine
on debt repayment based on valuation by intrinsic value or weight,
and we describe how well the doctrine handled the practical cases
presented to it before 1200. The following section describes a series of questions that arose to challenge the common doctrine along
with the monetary complications following 1200. These included
the following questions: How should pennies issued by different
states be valued? If a state redefines a penny, how should it be
valued? How should metal bullion be valued in terms of coin?
How should demonetized coins be valued by creditors? Should
valuations be aligned with observed market exchange rates? How
should settlements of debt contracts respond to debasements, currency reforms, and the spread of alternative "units of account"?[3]
And how could debts owed in units of one currency be repaid in
coins of another? The common doctrine of valuation by weight
tried to provide a workable unified framework that answered these
questions. We then describe how a question arose from public law:
What should the seigniorage rate be? Divergent answers to this question further undermined the common doctrine. Finally, we show
how important elements underlying the concept of fiat money were
discovered, preparing the way for the replacement of the common
doctrine.

---

[3] Feavearyear (1963, 2) writes: "To measure prices in terms of a unit of account
is not the same as to measure prices in terms of a certain weight of metal. A unit
of account begins to be used as soon as coins are accepted in payment by tale and
not by weight."

Construction of the medieval common doctrine

The shape of the common doctrine owes much to the way in which medieval jurists worked. It was created neither by legislatures nor by judges, but by scholars who tried to make a long-forgotten text relevant to the world in which they lived.

Sources and methods of the romanists

In the High Middle Ages, western societies were governed mostly by customary law imported by the German tribes who had invaded the Roman empire. In the late eleventh century, some Italians rediscovered the law of the Roman empire in books written under the emperor Justinian in the sixth century: the Code; the Institutions, a first-year textbook for law students; and the Digest, a compilation of the works of Roman jurists. These three books, collectively known as the Corpus, represented an enormous body of material (rules in the Code, explanations of the rules and legal reasoning in the Digest and the Institutions) to apply to the new commercial situations encountered during the economic expansion fueled by Italian traders. Traders needed rules for contracts. Roman law provided them. People in Italy, Germany, southern France, regions nominally part of the Holy Roman Empire, progressively adopted Roman law.

The Roman Law codified by Justinian was rediscovered in the late 11th c. and was soon applied to questions about contracts and money.

In the late eleventh century, Roman law was just a collection of books. To bring it to life required judges and lawyers who thought in terms of this law. So people devoted themselves to reading and applying the Code and the Digest of Justinian. They told other people about it. They started universities where they read the law.

Romanists were jurists who specialized in Roman law. They read, compared, synthesized, and refined the Corpus. Reading a passage of the Corpus made them recall another passage connected by similarity or contradiction. They made notes (glosses) in the margins of the manuscript, at first merely references or grammatical clarification, later discussions of the similarities or contradictions. They distilled similarities to derive general principles. They used contradictions to refine these principles.

Glossators read each other's glosses, cited them, and commented on them. The work of the glossators continued from 1090 to 1260. By then Azo (d. c1220) and Accursius (d. 1260) had completed their Glosses, critical compilations of existing glosses. The Gloss of Accursius, called the Ordinary Gloss, became a standard part of Roman law and was studied along with the Digest.[4]

After Accursius, romanists continued to study and comment on the Corpus of Roman law. These later romanists are known as the post-glossators or commentators. Their works are usually presented as Commentaries on the Code or the Digest, in which case they follow the arrangement of the original text closely, or as "Summae," organized thematically.

Money in a legal doctrine of loans

The romanists took some doctrines from Roman law and invented others. From Roman law, they classified money loans to be of the mutuum *kind. To the Romans, money was to be counted. To the romanists, it was to be weighed.*

Romanists focused on questions of private law. Their monetary doctrines emerged from contractual issues involving monetary obligations, mainly loan repayments but also debts arising from rents, fees, and fines.[5] Romanists' view of money developed in the context of a particular loan contract called the *mutuum*.

The *mutuum* applied to loans of fungibles, as opposed to a deposit (*depositum*) or a loan of an asset such as a house or a plot of land (*commodatio*). Unlike the latter two, the mutuum contract did not prescribe that the borrower return the very same object that had been provided by the lender.

The Digest explains that "the mutuum loan consists of things that are dealt in by weight, tale (number) or measure" (Dig. 12.1.2.1). The Institutes gives examples: "such are coins (*pecunia numerata*), wine, oil, wheat, bronze, silver, gold. Those things we give out by

---

[4] We have used *Corpus Juris Civilis* (1598) for the text of the Gloss. All Roman law and canon law citations will follow the conventions described in Brundage (1995).

[5] Täuber (1933), Stampe (1928), and Dupuy (1989) have studied Roman and canon law as a source on monetary doctrines. See Trifone (1962) on Bartolo.

counting, or measuring, or weighing them, so that they be received and that at some time, not the same things but others of the same nature be returned to us" (Inst. 3.14). The text suggests that the Romans considered coins as subject to the mutuum contract. But it also suggests that they viewed coins as objects that were counted, not weighed; other passages in the Digest and the Code confirm this. Of course, the Roman monetary system had coins of different denominations, and ratings of the coins were set by law, so it was natural for the Romans to evaluate coins by counting them. But the glossators' world was limited to the single penny (Täuber 1933, 209, 338).

One could not expect the exact same fungible object to be returned, since it could be of value to the borrower only by his consuming it. So an equivalent object should be returned. The glossators considered money to be a fungible because the actual coins had to be spent by the borrower to be of any use.[6] Thus, they naturally included money loans under the mutuum class, but treated them as commodities that are measured and weighed.[7]

The main rule governing repayment of loans in the mutuum class came from the Digest (12.1.3): "the debtor is not allowed to return a worse object of the same nature, such as new wine for old wine" and, even in the absence of an explicit clause to that effect, "the thing paid back must be of the same kind (*genus*) and quality (*bonitas*) as the thing given."[8]

The glossators took the example of wine literally, and decided

---

[6] Viewing money as a fungible rather than as a productive asset helped rationalize the medieval prohibition on usury: one could charge a rent for the loan of a productive asset such as a plot of land or a house, because there was a stream of returns from which to collect the rent. Money, however, was spent and gone, and could not be said to bear any fruit. In Aristotle's words, "money does not beget children."

[7] Post-glossators did note that, although coins could be weighed as well as counted, money had been invented for counting (Dig. 18.1.1) (see page 93 regarding how romanists handled the problem).

[8] This requirement is still present in modern civil codes grounded in Roman law: French Code §1892, Italian Code §1813, German Code §607. But note that §1893 of the French Code excludes money from this requirement!

An
Arrow-Debreu
view of coins

that in the case of coins, "same kind" meant silver for silver, and "same quality" meant the same fineness. Thus coins were merely metal objects (Täuber 1933, 196), to be treated as commodities like wine or wheat. The shape or imprint of the coin was irrelevant. Some applications refined this doctrine.

Tests in a one-coin environment

The coin-as-commodity doctrine served well in the first practical cases faced by romanists. Until the thirteenth century, the simplicity of the monetary system limited the range of cases. A single answer to fit all cases prevailed, summarized in a slogan known as Azo's brocard: "the same money (*moneta*) or measure (*mensura*) is owed that existed at the time of the contract" (*eadem moneta vel mensura debetur, quod erat tempore contractus*, Täuber 1933, 328). Azo's brocard made money a commodity.

Exchange rates for
pennies from
different issuers

The penny was the only coin locally, but after the breakdown of the Carolingian empire the content of the penny varied from one location to another. Could one penny be repaid for another?

A passage of the Digest (46.3.99) stated: "a creditor cannot be compelled to accept coins in another form, if he is to suffer some loss by it." Likewise, Digest 12.1.2.1 stated that the creditor cannot be repaid something for something else against his will. Glossators decided that different pennies were merely the same thing in another form, and therefore not "something else" (Täuber 1933, 196–97). Thus, Accursius's gloss (to Dig. 46.3.99; cited in Täuber 1933, 197) cited as allowable the repayment of pennies of Bologna for Milan's *denari imperiali*, at a rate of 3 for 1 .[9]

Similar decisions were reached by popes in disputes about the unit of measure or the coin in 1185, 1200, and 1206, and included in the parts of canon law called the *Compilationes* and the *Liber Extra* (2 Comp. 3.25.3, X 3.39.20, X 3.39.18, respectively; see Täuber 1933, 85, 105–13). These decisions were incorporated into canon

---

[9] The imperiali had been first issued around 1160 by the emperor Frederic I from the mint in Milan, and the rate reflected their content (Spufford 1988a, 225; 1986, 102).

law. The glossator Azo spotted the pattern and generalized these decisions into the brocard mentioned earlier, which gained wide acceptance among romanists as well as canonists.

What if the units of measure changed over time? Early on, jurists considered the following hypothetical question. A field had been rented in exchange for an annual payment of ten Bolognese bushels of wheat, and later Bologna had reduced the size of its bushel. Which bushel should be used to mete out the rent? Bulgarus (d. 1166) argued for the original bushel, and later glossators agreed (Täuber 1933, 219–20, 225–28). [10]

Policies toward debasements of pennies

The question of repayment of money by weight or by tale first arises in a text from around 1180 by Pillius, who taught in Bologna. The text is a collection of question-and-answer sessions that Pillius held with his students on Saturdays. Pillius's hypothetical question was inspired by the recent 50% debasement of the penny of Lucca: one man lends pennies of Lucca to another for five years, during which time the penny of Lucca is unexpectedly debased. [11] Should the creditor accept repayment in the new, debased pennies, or may he insist on the original pennies? Pillius applied the rule in Digest 12.1.3, requiring repayment of the same kind of object, in this case coins, and the same quality, in this instance the same intrinsic content. Therefore, only the original pennies would free the debtor, and not the debased pennies.

Exchange rates of bullion for coins

The last test to arise in a single-coin environment was the payment of bullion for coin. Hugolinus (early 13th c.) thought that because bullion was weighed and coins were counted, bullion represented a different *genus*. Therefore he said repayment of bullion debts in coin would violate the standard rule. But Azo and Accursius said coins are the same *genus* as bullion so long as they have the same fineness (Täuber 1933, 163–64, 195–201, 315). This position fit other

---

[10] Some early glossator tentatively argued otherwise on the basis of Saint Jerome, quoted in Gratian's Decretum (D C. 32 q. 4 c. 6): "As Abraham found favor with God in marriage, so today virgins find favor in chastity. He was observing his law and his time, let us observe ours."

[11] See page 139 for the circumstances.

aspects of the glossators' doctrine. Writing in Dig. 32.78.4, Rogerius (mid-12th c.) argued that the term "gold" or "silver" included coins as well as bullion: "wool and cypress-wood and similar things lose their name when they are given form. But metals even when they are shaped can return to their raw mass and do not lose their name. For a ring is no less called 'gold' than 'golden'; but clothes are never called 'wool,' but 'woollen,' and a ship is called 'wooden,' not 'wood'" (Täuber 1933, 337). Later jurists noted that flour could not be converted into wheat, but coins could be converted into bullion, and were therefore of similar type (Täuber 1933, 196).

Multiple currencies and denominations

The prevailing view in 1200 of money as metal commodity had evolved when monetized exchanges were only one and not necessarily the predominant form of exchange, and when only one form of coinage existed, the silver penny. We have seen how the commodity-based view of money view readily handled disputes arising from the debasement of a penny and from the repayment of pennies of one location with pennies from another location.

Then more complications arose. One came from the appearance of different denominations of coins, and coins of different metals, after 1200. That raised the issue of how to treat market exchange rates between those coins. Another complication arose after debasements, when governments attempted to fix exchange rates between various coins, or to make particular coins illegal to use altogether.

In this section, we review some of these complications and challenges, in the face of which romanists upheld the doctrine of Pillius and Azo with such consistency that as late as the fifteenth and sixteenth centuries, it was still called the "communis opinio." Bartolo da Sassoferrato (1313–57), the greatest of the post-glossators, represented this opinion. But the consensus wore at the edges; a new complication often led some jurist to explore a different approach or to voice a doubt. Over time, these voices grew louder.

Multiple denominations

During the thirteenth century, Western societies began to issue more than one denomination of coin. Should these different denominations be valued by weight?

Large silver coins were introduced first. Around 1200, Venice and other major cities of northern Italy issued high-grade silver coins of about 2g. The new coins, usually called *grosso* (groat, groschen) because of their size, were not intended to replace pennies, whose value they far exceeded, but to circulate concurrently. By the end of the thirteenth century, every area of western Europe (except England) had larger denomination silver coins circulating alongside the traditional pennies.

Because the penny was the original money, the larger coin's value was expressed in pence. When the grossi were first issued, they were assigned silver contents that made them exact multiples of the existing penny. Thus, the Venetian grosso (1201) was probably intended to be worth 24 pence, or 2 shillings. The silver *fiorino* of Florence (1237) and the *sou* of France (1266) contained the silver equivalent of 12 pence, or one shilling. But authorities in Venice and elsewhere soon found that it was not easy to maintain a fixed parity between the two coins, as we shall see in chapter 10.

Romanists covered the cases of multiple denominations and of multiple currencies with the passage of the Digest protecting creditors from incurring a loss upon repayment (Dig. 46.3.99). The condition was open to interpretation: must actual damage be proven for the creditor to refuse the tender, or does this clause give the creditor the option to refuse any tender other than the original coins? Pursuing this question and examining possible forms of "loss" to the creditor led some jurists to think of coins in terms of other than their metal content. For example, Jacopo de Arena (d. c1296) considered the following case: "I lent English sterlings to you, you want to repay me with other pennies, and it is not in my interest to accept them, because I want to go to England and they are not worth as much there as they are here—and I

Exchange rates for diverse denominations

am not obliged to accept them, because it is my interest to have them in the form I lent them" (in Inst. 4.6.28; Täuber 1933, 197).

Valuation by weight prevails.

The majority opinion adhered to intrinsic content: silver was silver, in whatever shape, and the creditor was only entitled to receive silver for silver. Most romanists required that the alloy be of the same grade (Bartolo, to Dig. 46.3.99, §4; 1570–71, 6:103r). But some, such as Paulo de Castro (d. 1441), even accepted tender of coins of different alloy, as long as the requisite amount of pure silver was tendered (Täuber 1933, 199). The spirit of Pillius's solution remained, however.

Multiple metals

Another tier was added to the denomination structure around 1250. Although gold coins had been in use in previously Muslim areas such as Sicily and Spain, the nearly-identical gold coins of Florence and Genoa (1252), and Venice (1284) and their imitations in the rest of western Europe in the fourteenth century were new. As with the large silver coins, the gold coins were often issued to represent, initially at least, a round number of the local silver pence (8 shillings in Genoa, 20 shillings or 1 pound in Florence).

Exchange rates of coins of silver and gold

Could a loan of gold florins be repaid with silver *soldi*? Baldus (1327–1400) asked the question (to Dig. 12.1.2.1; cited in Täuber 1933, 273–74):

Is it possible to repay number for number in different material, such as the number of soldi that a florin is worth in repayment of a florin? The gloss says no, because the difference in matter is seen as a difference in kind (*genus*). I respond that they are to be interpreted as being the same, because all quantities fall under the category of things that are dealt in with number, so that number as category (*genus*) encompasses quantity of any matter and form and the congruence in category alone suffices. And in coins it is not the intrinsic quality that is considered, but the value, as with other things.

The last sentence opens the door to valuation by tale. Nevertheless, Baldus concluded by stating the point of view of the gloss, and in other places he also sides with the majority opinion.

Fluctuating exchange rates: the stationary case

Although the larger denomination coins were issued initially at some convenient multiple of existing pennies, over time the actual exchange rate varied. Large coins were quoted on a daily basis in terms of small coins (Bernocchi 1978).

The standard view recommended ignoring those variations and treating the large coins as any other commodity. Commenting on feudal law (see page 97), the Neapolitan jurist Andrea d'Isernia (1220–1316) wrote: "If I lend you a measure of wheat in May when it is expensive and is worth perhaps 3 tarini, and I reclaim it in July after the harvest when it is worth perhaps 1 tarino, it is enough to return the measure of the same wheat in kind, even though it is worth less; likewise if it is worth more, for example if I lent it in July and demanded it in the following May . . . the same reasoning applies for money as it does for wheat and wine" (to *Usus Feudorum*, 2.F.56; 1541, 98). Similarly, Bartolo wrote: "Whenever the intrinsic quality is unchanged, but its value varies: as when the florin is worth more or less than it was, that is not taken into account, except in case of overdue payment" (Bartolo, to Dig. 12.1.3, §17; 1570–71, 2:7r).

However, the canonist Panormitanus (1386–1445) argued that if *ex ante* the creditor's expected loss was zero, then no adjustment should be made *ex post*: "when the alteration [in value] is not permanent, but for a time, as it happens everyday, when a florin is worth more one day than another, that is, when its value rises and falls according to circumstances, it is commonly held that no attention should be paid to this variation. Just as the creditor would want to be repaid if the coin was worth more, so he should receive the same money if it is worth less, since he can expect an increase" (Panormitanus, to X 2.24.18, §12; 1617, 4:141r).

Multiple units of accounts

*Conventional units
of account denoted
a given number of
a particular coin.*
Even though "pound" initially meant 240 pennies, the word took on
additional meanings in the Middle Ages, particularly in Italy. When
coins other than the penny appeared, it was natural to count them
in pounds as well, so that "a pound of X" meant 240 coins of type X.
In Venice, a *lira di piccoli* contained 240 *piccoli denari* or pennies, a
lira di grossi contained 240 grossi.

When the exchange rate e between two coins X and Y (where
e represents coins X per coin Y) remained stable for some period
of time, the two coins were treated equivalently in payments, and a
pound of X could be paid with $240/e$ coins of type Y. Thus came
about another use of the word "pound" in the form "pound of X in
Y."

In Venice, in 1250 a *lira [di piccoli] a grossi* was worth 240 piccoli
but contained 9 grossi and 5 piccoli, reflecting an exchange rate of
26 $\frac{1}{9}$ piccoli per grosso. In 1328, a *lira di grossi a oro* was worth 240
grossi, but contained 10 gold ducats, reflecting the rate of 24 grossi
to the ducat. In 1350, a *lira di grossi a monete* contained 640 *soldini*
(which had replaced the piccolo as small coin or moneta), reflecting
a rate of $\frac{32}{12}$ soldini per grosso.

Similarly, in Florence, the *lira [di denari] a oro* equaled 1 gold
florin, reflecting the florin's original valuation at 240d. per florin.
After 1279, the *lira [di denari] affiorino* consisted of $\frac{20}{29}$ florin, reflecting a florin at 29s. Each of these "pounds" was then subdivided
into its own shillings and pence: the Venetian *grosso* was the *denaro*
of the *lira di grossi*, and the Florentine *denaro a oro* was $\frac{1}{240}$ of a gold
florin, a unit without any corresponding coin.

Units of account of the form "pounds of X in Y at e" sometimes
survived even after the exchange rate between X and Y had long
since deviated from e.[12] The lira affiorino, for example, was used
in Florence well into the fifteenth century when the florin was worth
80s. or more, rather than the original 29s. The lira a grossi was

---

[12] Indeed, the persistent movement in the exchange rate probably caused these
units of account to arise: see chapter 7.

still used in Venice in the 1330s, when the grosso had reached 44d. rather than 26 ⅑d.

In this way, the expression "one pound" represented different amounts of silver or gold at different times and in terms of different coins. Nevertheless debts were expressed in such units of account as pound, not always accompanied by an explicit reference to a specific coin.

Different meanings of a unit of account

When a debt was expressed in such a unit of account, the meaning of "pound" was in most cases resolved by an appeal to local custom. Bartolo (Bartolo 1570–71, to Dig. 46.3.99, §1; 1570–71, 6:102v) wrote:

> When I promise £100, in what coin do I make this promise? In that money that is current in the city, with respect to which the shilling and the pound are determined. What if in a city there are two monies, with respect to which the shilling and the pound are given, as is the case in Florence? Indeed, sometimes shilling and pound are determined with respect to the small old florins, in which the gold florin is worth 29s. But there is a new money of theirs, the new florins, in which the gold florin is worth £3.[13] If I promise you £100, which is understood? This will be decided according to the custom of the city, and the likelihood of the situation. When I say "custom," I mean this: here it is the custom that, for fabrics and silk, "soldi" and "lire" refer to old florins, and in other matters they are understood to mean new florins. And when I said "likelihood" I mean this: if we were to interpret [a sum] in old coin, it would happen that a thing of small price would be given for a large price. Therefore we must always consider the likelihood based on the nature of the thing.

---

[13] The "small old florins" are probably the grossi of 1318 and the associated unit of account, the lira affiorino, while the "new florins" are the silver guelfi of 1347; see table 9.3.

Demonetization

Occasionally states demonetized coins, making them into pieces of metal. How should debts denominated in a demonetized coin be repaid?

For such cases, jurists sought whether to apply a passage of the Digest that incidentally states: "false coins do not absolve the debtor" (*reproba pecunia non liberat solventem*, Dig. 13.7.24.1). In medieval Latin, demonetizing or decrying a coin was called *reprobare*, so that a demonetized coin was *reprobata pecunia*, and the passage appeared applicable to cases of legal manipulation of the coinage. Pillius had invoked it when he classified debased coins as "partially" *reprobata*, and thus not acceptable tender. But what of the case of a complete repudiation of a coin? This passage seemed to contradict Digest 12.1.3 and the doctrine of exclusive consideration of intrinsic content, since a demonetized coin is unchanged with respect to its intrinsic content.

An exception to valuation by weight

Two romanists, Odofredo de Denari (d. 1265) and Jacopo de Belvisio (1270–1335), held that the debt must be discharged in coin current at the time of repayment, instead of the decried coins. A later jurist (Cino da Pistoia, to Cod. 2.40.3; [1578] 1964, 1:104v). reported their opinion as follows:

> Some, like Ja[copo de Belvisio] and Odofredo, hold the con-
> trary opinion, that is, that I must pay in deniers or money
> now current, and I will not be quit otherwise; because there
> are things whose quality (*bonitas*) is considered with respect
> to matter (*penes materiam*), and the debtor will be quit by
> repaying those in the same amount, and by taking into ac-
> count the intrinsic quality with respect to the matter. But
> there are things in which quality is considered with respect
> to use (*penes usum*). Suppose indeed that first, for a de-
> nier tournois now current I can have one measure, or one
> weight of something, but now I cannot have as much for
> a tournois. Certainly, having considered the extrinsic qual-
> ity with respect to use (*bonitas extrinseca penes usum*), I will

not be quit when repaying this money which is not current now.

But that remained a minority opinion. Pierre de Belleperche (d. 1308), Cino da Pistoia (1270–1336), and Bartolo ruled on the basis of Digest 12.1.3 that the debtor was discharged by tendering the decried coins. In Bartolo's words, "the debtor is freed from providing that coin in its shape (*forma*), but at least he must provide it in material. For in coin and in any kind of metal, the material is considered directly, and it draws the shape to itself more than the shape draws the material to itself" (to Dig. 12.1.5, §6; 1570–71, 2:8r). As a practical matter, Bartolo accepted that "if [the coin] cannot be found, or its circulation is totally forbidden, the estimation (*aestimatio*) of this old coin must be repaid" (to Dig. 46.3.99, §6; 1570–71, 6:103r). In 1328, the Parlement of Paris handed down a judgment conforming to this principle (Stampe 1930, 7).

Demonetized coins upheld

Overdue payments and extrinsic value

The notion that there is more to a coin than its intrinsic value had, in fact, already been developed in the context of overdue payments, as a result of a misunderstanding.

Medieval doctrine distinguished between repayments made on time and those overdue (*in mora*). An overdue debtor had to compensate a creditor for any losses suffered because of the delay. When it came to monetary debts, romanists misinterpreted a passage of the Digest and unwittingly opened the door to the concept of extrinsic value (Täuber 1933, 177–93).

Roman law prescribed that any payment or fine ordered by a court be in monetary form, even in the case of a commodity loan. Thus, if a debtor failed to return a loan of wheat or wine, the creditor could sue and secure a judgment against him, but would receive money instead of wheat or wine. A passage of the Digest (12.1.22) dealt with the question of converting the original commodity loan into monetary value, that is, determining an assessed value (*aestimatio*).

Glossators were unaware of the procedural aspect underlying the passage in Digest 12.1.22, and they interpreted it as referring to the

"Extrinsic" or exchange value

case of *mora* or negligent delay in repayment.[14] They nevertheless had to reconcile the consideration of the *aestimatio* of a good, which clearly depended on time and place, with the fact that repayment was due in a very specific form. They thus arrived at the concepts of intrinsic and extrinsic quality, *bonitas intrinseca* and *bonitas extrinseca*, which became part of the Ordinary Gloss (*to* Dig. .12.1.3, v. *bonitate*, and Dig. 12.1.22, v. *cum petitum esset*; *Corpus juris civilis*, 1598, 1:1423, 1444). Bartolo (to Dig. 12.1.3, §16; 1570–71, 2:7r) wrote: "You must know that there is something called the intrinsic quality of a thing: in the case of wine, what its taste is, and color, and such characteristics. There is the extrinsic quality: for wine, how much it is worth. This comes from outside: because it is the same wine and of same quality, when it is worth more as when it is worth less: but that, by which it is worth more or less, comes from accident. That extrinsic quality is not taken into account, except from the inception of a delay (*a tempore morae*)."

Adjusting overdue payments for exchange rate changes

Romanists applied Digest 12.1.22 by saying that, in case of overdue payment, the extrinsic value of a debt must be taken into account. Bartolo reinterpreted this requirement as a measure designed to compensate the creditor for a loss suffered because of the delay.[15] The question was how to measure this loss: his answer was to look at the value of the coins in terms of pennies. In his words: "if you suppose that I owed you 100 gold florins on January 1, and the florin was worth £4, and now that you are repaid it is worth less, I say that from the time you became overdue the risk is on the debtor. The reason is, that since the florin is estimated by small coins, and the estimation of the florin has changed, it appears that the florin is degraded in estimation, as we say for wine or other goods. Likewise

---

[14] Their puzzlement is expressed by Odofredo de Denari's remark to his students: "Signori, if the jurisconsult had sworn to write worse Latin he could not have done so."

[15] Medieval jurists made a curious distinction between *damnum emergens*, capital loss, and *lucrum cessans*, opportunity cost, and countenanced compensation for the former but not the latter. Canonists and romanists debated at great length whether depreciation of a coin fell in the first or second category (Stampe 1928, 123–26).

I say for any large coin which is estimated by small coins" (Bartolo, to Dig. 46.3.99, §8; 1570–71, 6:103r). But since the penny could not depreciate in terms of pennies, debts expressed in pence (units of account based on the pennies) were repaid penny for penny.

Followed by many romanists, Bartolo's theory was an attempt to remedy the glossators' misreading of the Digest. It was inconsistent with his attachment to the intrinsic content when the debt was not overdue. It thus introduced more difficulties in the doctrine, and opened the door to valuation of coins by standards other than content.[16]

Trends in exchange rates

Repeated depreciation of pennies, debasements of large silver coins, introductions of other coins, and changes in the relative price of gold and silver all meant that changes in exchange rates could have permanent components. Permanent changes in the market value of a coin, without any attending change in its intrinsic content, posed a serious challenge to jurists. The commodity-based view of money came into conflict with their strong interest in preserving contracts and protecting creditors (Dig. 46.3.99).

Jacopo de Arena was the first to distinguish between a fall in value due to a change in the intrinsic content, in which case the debtor must deliver more coins, and a change in the external valuation of the coin, in which case the debtor must deliver the same number of coins as owed (Cino da Pistoia, to Dig. 12.1.3, §9; cited in Täuber 1933, 324–27). Jacopo's solution remained based on sole consideration of the intrinsic content. But other writers saw a permanent loss in the external valuation of the coin as analogous to a partial demonetization. Thus, the canonist Antonio de Butrio (1338–1408) and his student Panormitanus sided with Odofredo in considering the purchasing power of the coins: if it had been permanently lowered,

Consequences of exchange rate fluctuations versus depreciations or debasements

---

[16] Bartolo's gesture toward making all coins equivalent moved him closer to our model. Although our specification allows for the exchange rate between coins to vary endogenously over time, reflecting the reality of medieval money markets, the main cash-in-advance constraint treats large and small coins as equivalent for purchases of large goods.

the debtor should be obliged to repay a larger number of the same coins (Butrio, to X 2.24.18; 1578, 3:78–80).

Debasements and currency reforms

The king should not tamper with the unit of account.
Could the king alter the prevailing unit of account? The common doctrine said not. Events in France under King Philip IV the Fair provided a test of these views. Starting in 1290, the French penny was debased so that by 1302 its silver content had fallen by two thirds. In 1306, the king decided to return to the old standard and minted new "strong" pennies that were officially rated at 3d. (in the debased pennies). Then it was announced that, as of October 1, 1306 the "strong" penny was to be the standard of account, and that all sums expressed in pounds, shillings and pence should be understood in terms of the strong money. An ordinance of Oct. 4, 1306 prescribed that "All rents shall be paid in good money. Transactions will be settled in the coins current at the date of the transaction. If contracts were written such that payments were to be made over several years, each payment will be made in the coins current in that year. Housing rents will be paid in current money, but if the rent was so high that the tenant would be burdened, it will be paid in the coins current at the time of the rental contract" (Saulcy 1879–92, 1:165). At Christmas 1306, when landlords in Paris demanded their rent payment in strong money, riots erupted, and the king passed another ordinance allowing for payments of the next three quarters' rents in weak money.

Romanists unanimously accepted that a contract that called for repayment of specific coins should be honored. Cino da Pistoia cited the French episodes we have just described and adhered to the intrinsic-content view. Oldrado da Ponte wrote a brief based on the same view in a particular court case between two French abbeys in 1320. It was repeatedly cited by later jurists of canon law.[17]

But when repayment was specified in units of account, or in the

---

[17] Remarkably, courts of the French king upheld repayment in the original currency, at least in the case where the obligation arose from a single transaction. Although the French king repeatedly outlawed contracts denominated in specific domestic or even foreign coins, the courts consistently upheld them (Timbal 1973,

cases of fines or dues set by laws without explicit reference to a coin, what coin should be used? Guillaume Durant (1231–96) argued that fines, salaries, and other sums set by law in units of account should be interpreted in terms of the money current at the time of payment (*Speculum Judiciale* lib. 4, §3, n. 9; Durant 1574, 361–62; cited in Stampe 1928, 28). Thus, although he adhered to the intrinsic content doctrine in matters of debt contracts, here he departed from it. His opinion, which Bartolo did not follow, was often cited but sometimes disputed by other canonists (Stampe 1928, 66–67, 113).

Jean Faure (d. 1340), who taught in Montpellier, extended Durant's position. "If you contracted with me in a time of strong money, which the king then altered and replaced with a weaker money, will you be quit by tendering this weaker money? It seems that no, and that you must repay such value as there was at the time of the contract, as noted by Durant. I believe that if the prince has decreed the latter currency should circulate for the former, although it were weaker in value, the debtor is freed by tendering it, if he had contracted in pounds and shillings. Certainly the king has powers in such matters, and he is competent to set the rate (*cursus*) and value of money" (Stampe 1928, 52–53).

Faure proposed a role for State fiat.

Faure was not cited much by other jurists until the sixteenth century (see chapter 6 for a revival of his ideas). Not even the French kings tried to implement his views. The legislation in matters of debt repayments (studied exhaustively in Stampe 1930) was built up during the several monetary reforms that followed debasements, from 1306 to 1358. Small denomination coins were not legal tender for debts contracted in silver or gold coins. For most debt contracts, and after the reform of 1421, for almost all contracts, the law required repayment of the original coins. If the original coins no longer existed, the debt was to be converted into current coins using the ratio of the original and current mint prices (not the mint equivalents). The law also gave parties to a contract the freedom to denominate the debt as they wished, and courts steadfastly enforced such clauses (Timbal 1973, 331–91).

1:331–91; see also Stampe 1930).

Thus, Durant and Faure contributed to the penumbra of qualification that by 1500 came to surround the "communis opinio."

A question from public law: setting seigniorage rates

Money and   Another body of doctrine about debasements came from canon law,
morality   which governed the Church. The subject of money appeared in
canon law, sometimes in cases of contracts or debts between ecclesiastical bodies. The cases resembled those examined by romanists,
and canonists mostly shared their romanist colleagues' views on standards of deferred payment. But, fortuitously, the canonists were led
to think about money in a broader context, that of public policy.
Their contribution played a key role in the later evolution of jurists'
thinking about money.

Sources of the canonists
A canon was a decision made either by a council or by an individual
bishop to govern the behavior of members of the Church. As the
Church grew in size and complexity, so did the body of canons.
Around 1140, the monk Gratian produced a compilation of canons
called Gratian's *Decretum*, thematically arranged. Further papal de-
crees appeared in new collections (in particular the Liber Extra of
1234) until 1315.

Canon law dealt with clerics or with lay persons in their relation
to religious matters (such as marriage). Jurists were usually trained
in both laws, Roman and canon, but tended to specialize afterward
in one or the other. Because of this shared training, romanists and
canonists used similar methods, and cited one another.

Debasements and seigniorage rates
An important case and the papal decree it prompted became the
locus classicus for canonist doctrine on debasements. It dealt with a
king's oath to uphold a debased currency.

In 1196, Pedro I succeeded his father as king of Aragon and
swore to maintain the currency. The oath was required of the kings
upon their accession. Pedro then discovered that the currency had
been secretly debased shortly before his father's death. Pedro asked
the pope to be relieved of his oath in 1199. The pope accepted
his request, and the resulting decree or canon was included in the
Liber Extra (2.24.18) in the chapter on oaths. The canon caused
canonists to discuss money. Because the context was not contract
law, but rather a sovereign's monetary policy, their attention was
drawn to a question that the romanists had ignored, the desirability
or morality of debasements.

A promise to maintain the value of the currency, made with incomplete information

The pope had allowed the king to break his solemn oath because
the currency he had sworn to maintain was "false." Canonists sought
to understand what was so wrong about a debased currency that it
conflicted with the duty to uphold a solemn oath. And what was a
false or defrauded coin?

Innocent IV (1195–1254), another pope and himself a canonist,
was the first to comment on this decree. He said that a debased coin
was fraudulent: "Money is said to be deprived (*defraudata*) of its
legitimate weight when it has been initially ordered that a specific
weight of gold or silver be put in any money, but later it has been
ordered that less gold or silver be put, and that this money be spent as
if it were of the same weight." But is any initial content acceptable?
He continued: "and the same is said if the money has been made
from the beginning of much greater weight or value (*valor*) than the
metal or material from which it is made is worth, with necessary
and useful expenses deducted therefrom" (cited by Hostiensis, to
X 2.24.18, [1581] 1965, 2:130). Thus, Innocent IV observed that,
in practice, sovereigns were able to levy positive gross seigniorage,
but determined that seigniorage net of production costs should be
zero.

Debasement as fraud

Canonists disapproved of currency manipulations. Hostiensis
(1190–1271) wrote: "There is also fraud by those who hold lordship
over a land and rule it, when they make a money of lesser weight and
force it to be received at par with a money of greater weight, or when

they decry a good money and approve an equivalent money of lesser weight, so as to have the decried money at a good price, and then have it melted and coined at the same weight or even lighter weight, with the same imprint as the approved money" (Hostiensis, in X 2.24.18, [1581] 1965, 2:130). Canonists condemned debasements in the sphere of public law, and, drawing on the romanists' doctrine of monetary debts, tried to undo its effects in the sphere of private law by disregarding currency manipulations driven by greed. Thus Hostiensis added: "if money is not diminished but is decried solely out of greed so that it may be collected and melted and afterwards minted at the same weight, as frequently happens . . . if the debtor is in no fault, it suffices that he return money of the same kind and weight, and the same value in weight, even if the coin is current for less (*diminuta quo ad cursum*), unless specified otherwise, because contracts have force of law out of convention."

As of 1250, then, canonists shared the romanists' approach, but they had introduced new avenues of thought. In terms of our model, they had recognized the existence of an interval within which the price level could move, and, although they preferred it when kings kept the interval narrow, they realized that they could make it wide.

Qualifications, exceptions, and discoveries

Though they failed to overturn the dominant commodity-based doctrine at the time, various writers before 1500 set out elements that would later subvert it. We mention three related such sets of ideas: (1) that money helps overcome the absence of double coincidence of wants; (2) that in emergencies, money should exchange for more than its value as metal; and (3) that fiat money is feasible. Idea (1) points to a feature of the environment that goes far in giving coins more value as money than as metal. Discussion of idea (2) led to early versions of backed or token monies, where the backing was a more or less explicit promise to convert the money into metal sometime in the future. Idea (3) is the possibility of a valued unbacked money.

Early statement of double coincidence

The Corpus of Roman law had offered the romanists another view of money, but they disregarded it. Book 18 of the Digest is devoted to purchase contracts, and the first title, the *lex origo* (Dig. 18.1.1), begins with a philosophical discussion on the origin of money as a remedy to barter. The passage was due to the Roman jurist Paulus (d. A.D. 235), and contains the earliest known exposition of the double coincidence of wants problem:

> *Paulus stated that helping to avoid a double coincidence of wants could be a source of value for coins beyond their weight.*

> All buying and selling has its origin in exchange or barter. For in times past money was not so, nor was one thing called "merchandise" and the other "price"; rather did every man barter what was useless to him for that which was useful, according to the exigencies of his current needs; for it often happens that what one man has in plenty another lacks. But since it did not always and easily happen that when you had something which I wanted, I, for my part, had something that you were willing to accept, a material was selected which, being given a stable value (*aestimatio*) by the state, avoided the problems of barter by providing an equality of quantity (*aequalitas quantitatis*). That material, struck with a public design (*forma*), offers use (*usus*) and ownership (*dominium*) not so much by its substance (*ex substantia*) as by its quantity (*ex quantitate*), so that no longer are the things exchanged both called wares but one of them is termed the price (*pretium*).

The text is obscure, as this literal translation shows. Moreover, Paulus's explanation, that sums of money are useful and command ownership over other things by their quantity rather than their substance, seemed to conflict with romanists' view of money. Glossators were puzzled, and probably sensed the contradiction with the doctrine they were elaborating in Digest 12.1.2. They tried to make sense of the text while glossing the phrase "not so much by its substance as by its quantity" (Täuber 1933, 332–34).

Romanists repair the breach

*Romanists
explained away
Paulus's insight.*
How the glossators dealt with the troublesome issue Paulus had raised
provides a good illustration of how the glossators worked. They
resolved contradictions among different passages to bring them into
line with the money-as-commodity view that had been developed
elsewhere. The dual value of money, intrinsic and as a liquid medium
of exchange, threatened the simple doctrine of debt repayments.
The glossators neutralized the threat by requiring the two values to
coincide.

Thus, Paulus's statement that money has value from quantity
(A) rather than substance (B), was read as "more A than B." The
glossators analyzed A and B separately and perceived A and B to be
the same under the appropriate conditions. The statement was then
read as "A, and also B" and then "B, which is the same as A."

Irnerius (early 12th c.) correctly glossed "by its quantity" as "by
number" (*ex numero*) and made a reference to "things dealt in by tale"
cited in Digest 12.1.2.1. Placentinus (d. 1192) and, after him, all
glossators understood "not so much . . . as" in a comparative sense
(A more than B), not an elective sense (A instead of B): he glossed
the passage as "by both, but more by quantity than by substance, and
in exchange, only the quality or equality of quality was considered."
Hugolinus analyzed the two elements A and B separately, explaining
how each was a source of value. He wrote: "substance: just as it
is useful to have gold or silver in bullion form, so it is useful to
have it in coined form; quantity: it is useful to have money which
it is possible to use in buying, renting, or otherwise contracting."
Azo then incorporated Hugolinus's glosses into his, and refined the
explanation of the liquidity value of money: money, he wrote, "offers
the usefulness of possessing it in two ways. One is the substance itself,
because the gold or silver in the coin can be as valuable to you as if
it were in bullion (*in massa*). Also, it can be valuable, because with
coins it is easy to find everything."

At this point both sources of value A and B are identified and
ranked equally in importance in the glosses. Accursius made the

final step when he wrote: "note that money offers its usefulness in two ways, the usefulness of its use and of its possession. First, from its substance, one coin is worth as much as the silver in its mass; second, from its quantity, because the quantity of the coin is equated with the value of the object, and so by the coin equality in quantity occurs." In other words: first, a coin is worth the silver in it, say, x; second, a quantity N of coins can equate the value p of an object, so that by the coin $Nx = p$.

Accursius's gloss became the standard reference for romanists arguing that a coin should be worth as much coined as uncoined. They cited the gloss on Digest 18.1.1 to assert that the seigniorage rate should be set to 0. As a typical example, Bartolo wrote (to Dig. 12.1.2.1, §6; 1570–71, 2:4r): "you must know that by common law coin must be made such that it brings as much usefulness in coin (*in forma*) as in kind (*in materia*), and as much in kind as in coin, as said in the gloss on the word *praebet*, Dig. 18.1.1. And thus the expenses of minting must be borne by the public." In the elegant formulation of Bernardo Davanzati ([1588] 1807, 155), "metal should be worth as much in bullion as in coin, and be able to change from metal to money and money to metal without loss, like an amphibious animal."

Canonists versus romanists on seigniorage

Canonists differed from romanists on seigniorage. When Innocent IV said a coin defrauded if the seigniorage rate was higher than production costs, he accepted a positive seigniorage (see page 91). Romanists took note of this disagreement. They conceded that everyone levied positive seigniorage.[18] Bartolo himself, in the passage just quoted, recognized that "today, we observe that by custom there is less in coin than in kind, because of the expenses of minting." Acknowledging a component of value from the costs of minting opens cracks in the doctrine that coins are just pieces of metal.

---

[18] England was the first to fully subsidize minting costs as a matter of policy, starting in 1666 (see chapter 16).

Another breach

Legitimizing a king's manipulation of the value of coins

But canonists went further. Innocent IV wrote (to X 2.24.18; 1570, 285v):

> We believe, however, that the king, by his right, and by the fact that money receives authority and general acceptance (*authoritatem et communionem*) from his effigy or mark, can make money of somewhat less, but not much less value than the metal or matter from which it is made. Therefore, in the first case, when he wants to diminish a money already made, we do not believe he can do so without the consent of the people, but with its consent we believe that he can, just as anyone is allowed to renounce his right, D C. 7 q. 1 c. 8. And because the business of the king is considered to be the business of all, for this reason the consent of the majority of the notables of the kingdom suffices, Dig. 35.1.97; Dig. 50.1.19. Likewise we do not believe that the consent of the people suffices for that money to be circulated (*communiter expendatur*) outside of the realm.

This important passage, which was frequently reproduced by canonists over the following two hundred years, allowed substantial seigniorage rates to be levied, so long as the consent of the people was secured.[19] The passage comes close to viewing seigniorage as a tax. At the time, kings were expected to live from the revenues of their own lands, and taxes could only be levied with the consent of the people. The treatise on money by the German scholar Gabriel Biel (c1430–95) repeats this doctrine and adds arguments that debasement is a relatively efficient and fair form of taxation, falling on all classes alike (Biel 1930).

History offers examples of king and governed bargaining over seigniorage rates and debasements. In 1355, Jean II of France struck a bargain with the Estates of southern France, receiving tax revenues

---

[19] Note that the restriction to domestically circulating coinage practically excluded large denominations.

in exchange for a promise not to debase the currency; the Estates of northern France did not reach a similar agreement, and as a consequence the currency was repeatedly debased in the North but remained intact in the South.

Philosophers help

On the basis of moral considerations, canonists placed upper bounds on the seigniorage rate (and therefore on the width of the interval in our model). In this attempt at reducing the deviation of the price level p from the metal anchor γ, they were helped by philosophers.

Philosophers (theologians, moralists, logicians) took their theory of money mainly from specific passages of Aristotle (*Politics* 1257b–1258a, *Ethics* 1133a–b). The main contributors were Saint Thomas Aquinas (1224–74), Jean Buridan (c1290–c1360), and Nicole Oresme (c1320–82).[20] Aquinas was inclined to view money as a human institution and under the authority of the prince. Buridan and after him Oresme agreed, but viewed money as belonging to the community; thus, the common good was to be the guiding principle of monetary policy. By that criterion, they placed strong moral restrictions on the prince's ability to debase the currency. Buridan wrote (1637, 432, in *Ethics* q. 17 a. 2) that "if [a coin] were not worth as much, or nearly as much, according to the relation of its intrinsic content to human need, the king would be committing a sin, and unfairly profiting from the common people; unless he were excused of sinning because of a war involving the people, or some other public necessity."

The cracks widen: debasements and deficit financing

The idea of high seigniorage as a form of emergency financing was developed further by a line of Neapolitan jurists, Andrea d'Isernia and Matteo d'Afflitto (1443–1523), in their commentaries on the *Libri Usus Feudorum*. This collection of feudal laws formed in the eleventh and twelfth centuries. It included a section on the

---

[20] See Lapidus (1997) and references therein. Oresme's treatise on money was translated into English by Johnson (1956).

rights of the king (*quae sunt regaliae*, 2.F.56), probably written in
the mid-twelfth century, where the right to mint was cited. The
Neapolitan jurists glossed the word "moneta" and discussed money
from a public law point of view.

*Punishment
(damnation) for
damaging the
value of the
currency through
deficit finance*
Isernia (to 2.F.56, s.v. "moneta"; 1541, 98) stated that kings in
emergencies often make money from base material such as iron or
leather and order it to be accepted as if it were good money, because "the common good is preferred to the private good." Once
the emergency has passed, the king must compensate the holders of
the vile money, and accept it in exchange for good money (Isernia
pointed out that the current holders of the money need to be compensated, not the original recipients). Matteo d'Afflitto, who wrote
two centuries later, repeated Isernia's arguments but also suggested
that deficit financing had not been implemented successfully: "Alas!
How many princes have been damned because of this, and indeed we
have seen in past wars many men destroyed because they sold their
goods for vile money, namely the new copper pennies; and after the
peace was made those pennies were worth nothing, and men were
left with them" (to 2.F.56, s.v. "moneta"; 1598, 770–71).

Oresme's opposition to debasements was also rooted in personal
experience. He had witnessed first-hand the many debasements of
mid-fourteenth century France and was convinced of their ill effects.
He also had little trust in sovereigns (1956, 42, 44):

> A tyrant loves and pursues his own good more than the com-
> mon advantage of his subjects, and aims at keeping his people
> in slavery; a king, on the contrary, prefers the public good
> to his own and loves above all things, after God and his own
> soul, the good and public freedom of his subjects. . . . Be-
> cause the king's power commonly and easily tends to increase,
> the greatest care and constant watchfulness must be used, in-
> deed extreme and supreme prudence is needed, to keep it from
> degenerating into tyranny.

Thus, he conceded that the community could in principle decide
to debase its currency for emergency reasons, and recognized that
debasements could be a quick and fair form of emergency taxation.

But he did not trust the sovereign to be honest in determining when a true emergency had occurred, and he was concerned that the sovereign would ultimately assume the power to debase the currency at will (1956, 34–7). The very fact that the burden would be spread broadly made debasement particularly insidious, because "an exaction is the more dangerous the less obvious it is" (1956, 32). There were other ways to finance emergencies, such as loans (1956, 39).

Concluding remarks

In chapter 1 we observed that it took centuries to understand and implement the modern standard formula that uses convertible tokens as small change. Medieval monetary theory renounced tokens. Its "communis opinio" held that valuation by weight should prevail throughout the denomination structure of coins. This chapter has described the origins of that opinion in Roman and canon law, how durable it was, and how lawyers consistently and cleverly applied it to a range of practical problems. The valuation of all coins by weight that the medieval monetary authorities regarded as ideal excluded tokens whose value in exchange far exceeds that of their constituent metals. Thus, for medieval monetary theorists, the standard formula would have been wrong and unthinkable. However, in the next chapter, we shall see how Renaissance thinkers would modify old ideas and advance a recommendation for token small coinage with enough force to persuade the monarchs of Castile to embark on a long experiment with tokens.

℘

Chapter 6
Monetary Theory in the Renaissance

Renaissance writers divorced the value of a coin from that of its intrinsic content.

Renaissance writers dismantled the medieval "communis opinio" that ideally coins should be valued according to their intrinsic metallic content. They discovered three important and enduring ideas in monetary theory that undermined the "communis opinio." The first is that the value of a coin could exceed that of its constituent metal. A related second idea is that intrinsically worthless objects can function as money and displace full-bodied specie. A third idea is that using an intrinsically worthless object as money might generate inflation, but that whether it does depends on various circumstances, including the amount issued. Episodes with token coins that had produced inflation led some writers to approach a quantity theory of money.

Although these ideas seemed to emerge abruptly, earlier refinements of the "communis opinio" had prepared the way. But Renaissance writers reasoned in new ways. During the Renaissance, jurists became humanists. The advent of printing let non-jurists, particularly mint officials, debate monetary policy in public. Some of these writers drew evidence from historical chronicles and the accounts of travelers.

The three main ideas of Renaissance monetary theory are incorporated into our model and were used by post-Renaissance monetary theorists, including John Law and Adam Smith. Because they reflect ideas to be discussed in this chapter as well as policies and events in later chapters, it is useful to begin this chapter by briefly describing some of Adam Smith's ideas about money. We shall encounter the origins of some of Smith's ideas among Renaissance writers later in this chapter.

Precursors of Adam Smith

Our model embodies a feature of commodity money systems that
was the focus of a notable mental experiment of Adam Smith ([1776]
1937, book II, ch. 2, 276–81). Smith evaluated the effect on consumption and the price level of relaxing a prohibition on issuing
banknotes in a small country initially on a specie standard. Smith
predicted that if the country were to allow banks to issue paper
banknotes (i.e., intermediated evidences of safe private indebtedness
that he called "real bills"), there would result a one-time boom in
national consumption. Specie would leave the country in exchange
for a one-time importation of consumption goods because the banknotes would displace specie. So long as the notes were backed
by safe private IOUs, Smith predicted that the price level would
not be affected.[1] Smith's experiment highlights that a commodity money system is wasteful because there are better uses for the
resources absorbed by a commodity money. In various forms, calculations based on Smith's experiment form the backbone of the case
that a well-managed fiat money can dominate a commodity money
(see for example Ricardo 1817, ch. 27, Friedman 1959, 5, Fisher
1920).[2]

Smith's thought experiment represents the culmination of various experiments—in thought and fact—that began during the late
Renaissance and in the context of small change. In the remainder
of this chapter, we describe some writings about these experiments,
postponing detailed descriptions of the actual experiments until later
chapters.

Adam Smith's mental experiment substituted convertible paper tokens (banknotes) for gold and silver coins.

---

[1] He also predicted that domestic interest rates would fall. See Sargent and
Wallace (1982) for a representation of Smith's experiment.

[2] Fisher (in Fisher and Cohrssen 1934, 382) admitted that he had not dared
to propose going off gold completely in 1920, as such a plan would have been
"lampooned and hooted down" at the time.

Debt repayment, legal tender, and nominalism

Dumoulin's "nominalism" separated exchange value from weight.

The sixteenth century brought new ways of thinking about money. We begin by describing ideas of the influential French jurist Charles Dumoulin (1500–1566).[3] He was a transitional figure who struggled to move beyond the medieval theory of money. A man of the Renaissance, he dismissed the centuries of dissecting and commenting upon the same text as wrongheaded. He criticized many parts of the prevailing medieval monetary theory, proposed a nominalism that divorced exchange values from weight of metal, and had insights that might have led him—and indeed soon led others—to appreciate token money. But Dumoulin retreated from the more radical implications of some of this arguments, and reaffirmed circulation by weight. We credit his role as progressive before recounting some of Dumoulin's conservative recommendations.

Dumoulin the revolutionary

Dumoulin's treatise on usury[4] was a frontal attack on the medieval prohibition on interest. As he declared in his very first sentence, justice in contracts and trade is to be sought "not in fabricated constructions but in the things themselves." He discussed the standard of deferred payment, and, more abstractly, the value of money. He sought to base his legal opinions about these age-old issues on a rational understanding of money derived from its actual use in exchange.[5]

To understand money, Dumoulin returned to Aristotle's passage on barter and money in *Politics*. He also read Paulus's exposition

---

[3] See Stampe (1926), Täuber (1928), and particularly, Thireau (1980, 401–31).

[4] The *Tractatus contractuum et usurarum, redituumque pecunia constitutorum,* first published in 1546; Dumoulin published an abridgment in French, the *Sommaire du livre analytique des contrats, usures, rentes constituées, interests et monnoyes,* in 1547. References are to section numbers of the *Tractatus* (Dumoulin 1681, 2:1–332).

[5] Täuber (1928, 23–24) cites Conrad Summenhart's dictum that "lex ex ratione, non ratio ex lege": law should proceed from reason, not reason from the law.

of the double coincidence of wants in Digest 18.1.1, ignoring the glosses. He concluded that because it had a particular purpose, money was not a traded good like any other. Money is made of metal, but is distinct from uncoined metal: "the form and substance of money, as money, is not the matter or the physical appearance of the money, but its assigned value (*valor imposititius*): hence any money, as such, is not brought into a contract or clause other than from the point of view of its current assigned value or quantity (*quantitas*)" (§ 694; 1681, 2:285). Dumoulin identified the *quantitas* in Paulus's text with the exchange value of the coin, not its intrinsic content.

Dumoulin inverted terminology that had prevailed for three centuries.[6] He said that the intrinsic value of a coin *is* its *aestimatio*, its value in exchange. Therefore he said that the Roman law on repayment of commodity loans should be applied to values in exchange, not value by weight. The counterpart of wine's quality is the value of the coin, not its metal content, and its value at the time of the contract is the sum due. Thus, if N coins were lent when they were worth e_1 each, then Ne_1 is the sum that is owed. If the contract specified repayment in the same coins, and the coins are worth e_2 at the time of repayment, then Ne_1/e_2 coins are sufficient tender. This doctrine is usually called "nominalism."

Nominalism had important implications for disputes about debt repayment. In a loan, "it was both parties' intention that a certain number of coins be given for immediate use in trade, and to be soon spent in exchange, which can only happen from the point of view of the current value at the time the coins are counted." In this, Dumoulin anticipated Adam Smith's comment that "what the borrower really wants, and what the lender really supplies him with, is not the money, but the money's worth, or the goods which it can purchase" ([1776] 1937, book II, ch. 4, 334). It follows that "any subsequent increase or decrease of the same coins is completely irrelevant; because it does not make the quantity counted out earlier

Nominalism asserted the primacy of exchange value, not weight.

------

6 He was well aware that he was contradicting the "communis opinio" and cited Jean Faure as his only precursor in dissent (§749; 1681, 2:306).

any larger or smaller, nor does it make its value in trade any stronger or weaker" (§ 688; 1681, 2:283).

One motivation for Dumoulin's nominalism was no doubt its simplicity. Accepting that a franc is a franc and letting the king define the franc precluded protracted litigation over old debts and preserved the sanity of the legal system. Dumoulin cited, among many other "miserable entanglements of lawsuits on these matters," one court ruling that remained unenforced after thirteen appeals. Contemporary legislation in the Low Countries underscores this point. A law of 1571 required revaluation of long-term debts when repaid, but the resulting flood of litigation led to a 1601 law that allowed repayment at face value instead (Stampe 1928, 74–75).

Dumoulin's impact

The influence of nominalism spread. Leading French jurists quickly adopted Dumoulin's ideas. Although Denis Godefroy (1549–1621) remained attached to the medieval doctrine (to Dig. 12.1.3; 1688, col. 331), he stood apart. François Hotman (1524–90) distinguished debasements *per se* from changes in the official value of a coin. In the first case, so long as the new coin is rated at the same value as the old coin, repaying one for the other does not violate the Roman law rule against "aliud pro alio," because the purchasing power is the same. In the second case, it is not the coin itself that is owed but the number of units of account it is worth: if a creditor demanded the same number of coins after an increase in the value of the coin, he would be demanding more than he is truly owed ([1573] 1610, 127–28). Hugues Doneau (1527–91), citing Hotman, agreed that the official rate of a coin was its true "intrinsic quality" and that the rules of Roman law should be interpreted on that basis (to Dig. 12.1.3: 1847, 10:109–26).

French jurisprudence followed, albeit prudently.[7] Dumoulin was a lawyer and championed his ideas in court. His first important legal victory occurred on appeal in 1535. In the case, a loan had been made in 1505 of £2,400 in the form of 1,332 écus (at 36s. each) and 8s. In 1535, the debtor tendered 1,066 écus (then worth 45s.

---

[7] See Szlechter (1951, 1952) and Schnapper (1957, 184–96).

each) and 30s. in change. The creditor refused, the debtor sued and lost, but, with Dumoulin as counsel, won on appeal. The case has not been found, but a very similar case dated 1539 has been identified, in which the court ruled that when gold or silver coins had been explicitly valued in terms of units of account, the debtor had to repay the debt in the same coins, but at their current value. Thus, if the value of gold coins in units of account had increased, the debtor could tender fewer coins. The only thing the creditor could demand was to be paid in the same metal, but a ruling of 1569 made it possible to tender any coin for another.[8] A ruling of 1560 allowed courts to require repayment of the same number of coins in one case only: when the coins had not been explicitly quoted in units of account in the original contract. This exception suggests that the aim was to enforce the contract as written, without having to resort to outside information.

French law eventually assimilated Dumoulin's theory so thoroughly that, in the eighteenth century, the great jurist Pothier (1699–1772) could write that repayment on the basis of the value at the time of repayment is "constant practice in our jurisprudence; our jurisprudence is based on this principle that, in money, one does not consider the substance and the actual coins, but only the value attached to it by the prince" (Pothier 1824, 68). The authors of Napoleon's Civil Code followed Pothier on this point, as on so many others, and incorporated the same-quality prescription of Digest 12.1.3 in article 1892, while exempting money in article 1893.

Dumoulin's influence extended beyond France. In England, the ground-breaking decision on debt repayment was the "Mixt Moneys Case" of 1604 (*Brett v Gilbert*, 80 Eng. Rep. 507), which established nominalism in matters of debt payments in England (Nussbaum 1950, 177). The court's decision cited both Aristotle and Dumoulin, and defended the king's right to give value to base money with his stamp, just as he could make honorable a "mean person."

Nevertheless, the progression of nominalism was not uniform.

---

[8] The legal tender of the smallest denominations was limited in 1577, but the limit was implicitly removed in 1602.

Discussions over the standard of payment continued in law books
in Spain, Italy, and Germany (see, respectively, González Téllez, to
X 2.24.18, 1715, 2:550–54; Costa 1603, 266–71; and Glück, to
Dig. 12.1.3, 1841, 63–91). In Germany, the big inflation of 1622–
23 prompted legislation prescribing debt repayment on the basis of
an adjusted value, thus delaying the adoption of nominalism until
the nineteenth century.

Dumoulin the conservative

Dumoulin qualified his advocacy of nominalism.

Despite implications that others would soon extend, Dumoulin's
advocacy of nominalism was qualified and restrained. Some passages
suggest that Dumoulin's doctrine of debt repayment depended on
the ruler's absolute authority to set the legal value of coins. To the
question, who assigns the "assigned value?" he answered, the ruler,
but not arbitrarily. Dumoulin followed Bartolo in placing money in
the domain of international law, *jus gentium* rather than domestic
law. The ruler assigned value to coins, but only as a kind of notary:
"This public estimation and current value depends not only on the
prince in a monarchy or the leaders in a Republic, but also on the
consent and usage of the people, and the practice of trade" (§797;
1681, 2:322). More generally, as asserted by Aristotle, money serves
a purpose, and the object chosen as money should fulfill that purpose.
It cannot be made of inappropriate material, and there must be a just
proportion between the official rate and the intrinsic content. If the
official valuation departed too much from the intrinsic content, or if
it changed so frequently that it became useless as a standard of value,
then money ceased to be money and should be treated as bullion. In
that case, Dumoulin allowed a return to the medieval rules on debt
repayment.

Dumoulin thus saw the king's power to set legal rates as properly
exercised only when it ratified market-driven changes in exchange
rates between coins. He disapproved of monetary policies intended
to place a currency at a competitive advantage, a policy that some
merchants occasionally recommended.[9] Dumoulin also condemned

---

[9] For similar pressures in Saxony, see the three pamphlets published in 1530 and

debasements designed to collect seigniorage. But he did not think that the king's subjects should ignore the king's decisions when they were wrong. The law remained the law, except in the most extreme circumstances such as the extraordinary debasements in France during the Hundred Years War.

Changes in legal rates in sixteenth century France were mainly of the sort that Dumoulin approved (see chapter 11). But legal theory and monetary policy were soon to interact in an unexpected way. Shortages of small change developed in the 1570s, soon after Dumoulin's doctrine on debt repayment had prevailed. France experienced sharp increases in the exchange rate of large coins denominated in pence. When pennies were made essentially unlimited legal tender, creditors began to suffer large and unexpected losses. They pressed for a reform to make debts be denominated in the largest coin rather than the smallest. We shall study that reform in chapter 11. It implemented some features of the standard formula.

Fiat money

While promoting nominalism in the matter of debt repayment, Dumoulin continued to believe that the market value of a coin should be closely related to its intrinsic content. But if Dumoulin was unwilling to pursue nominalism to its logical conclusion, other writers would.

Dumoulin commented on these other writers. In the course of discussing debt repayment, he reviewed three existing theories about the value of money. The first was the romanist preference for zero seigniorage, which he endorsed, and the second was the canonist acceptance of a moderate seigniorage. The third, proposed "very recently," rejected the relevance of the money's content altogether, and accepted that money could be made of lead or leather and be tendered for a debt of gold or silver. Dumoulin dismissed it as "irrational and ridiculous: why, by the same token, it would be possible

Dumoulin foresaw and denounced paper money.

---

reprinted in Lotz (1893).

to make money out of printed paper, and that is just as ludicrous and ridiculous as a children's game, and not only contradicts the origin and definition of money, but also experience and common sense" (§798; 1681, 2:322).

Fiat money in theory: Butigella

Butigella theorized about fiat money.

Dumoulin attributed that third theory to the Italian jurist Girolamo Butigella (1470–1515, fig. 6.1), who was apparently the first to divorce money's value from its content. In his commentary on Digest 12.1.3, Butigella criticized Bartolo's view that the same money must be repaid, drawing on a variety of places in the Digest to assert that no attention should be paid to the quality of the material of a coin, and only to its estimation. If coins of a different material have the same value, the creditor cannot suffer a loss when he is repaid in a different coin. But Butigella went further, invoking Digest 18.1.1 as "a text that cannot be clearer." Money does not derive its use from its substance, that is, its material content, so much as from its quantity, that is, its value. He rejected the comparative interpretation of "so much as" as "nonsense," and concluded: "even if a coin were made of lead, indeed even of wood or leather, as long as it is publicly approved, it would be possible to repay it for another coin, because form rather than matter is taken into account." That any coin "publicly approved" was legal tender was not just a matter of practice, as Bartolo had conceded, but a matter of law (Butigella, to Dig. 12.1.3, §32; 1608, 2:86).

Butigella enunciated the concept of fiat money, referring to a passage of Roman law that posited the origin of money in overcoming barter, as Dumoulin had done. The same passage played a crucial role in the Renaissance as Roman law underwent a transformation at the hands of the humanists, who examined the text of Roman law with the same critical eye they had trained on the received text of the Bible. They used their tools of textual criticism and their growing knowledge of antiquity to purge the medieval vulgate. They also dared to criticize the Roman text itself, and assess its validity and logical coherence.

Figure 6.1 Portrait of Girolamo Butigella on his tomb in Santa Maria sopra Minerva, Rome.

Double coincidence of wants revisited

To the extent that Roman law continued to influence monetary thinking, it did not do so through the doctrine of debt repayment. Instead, the focus turned to Paulus's exposition of the origin of money and the double coincidence of wants (Dig. 18.1.1). Textual criticism of this passage fostered the propagation of ideas similar to those of Butigella. [10]

Discussions of fiat money spread.

In the late fifteenth century, a group of scholars led by Giasone del Maino had revised the Roman law corpus based on a better manuscript (the "Florentine" edition). Giasone had derided as

---

[10] Some modern economic theories of fiat money (e.g., Kiyotaki and Wright 1989) are similarly grounded in the double coincidence of wants problem.

"ridiculous" the statement by Paulus that "in times past money was not as it is now," since that implied that it could be other than it is, as if money could be made of something else than gold, silver, or copper. But others, such as Étienne Forcadel (1534–74), pointed out that money did not consist in its material content, and could be made of worthless material like leather (in *Nekyomantia*, dialogue 48, §2; 1595, 1:117).

In the same spirit, the scholar Guillaume Budé had proposed to revise the passage in Digest 18.1.1 that derives the power of money "not so much by its substance as by its quantity," and to replace "quantity" with "quality." Such a reading was actually consistent with the spin put on the text by the glossators (see page 94). But Budé's proposal elicited protests from other jurists, who insisted that the reading "quantity" was correct. François Duaren (1509–59) rejected the reading, and interpreted "quantity" to mean "value and estimation," adding that this was the amount due by the debtor, and if the coins had increased or decreased in value, the loss was suffered alternatively by the debtor or the creditor (in *Disputationum anniversariarum*, lib. 1, cap. 6; 1598, 1032).

Other formulations

Analogies between bonds and money

The notion that money did not derive its value from its content gained widespread acceptance. Its exposition became increasingly sophisticated, even among jurists steeped in the medieval tradition.

For example, the jurist François Hotman wrote in 1573: "it must be understood that coins are valued not by their content, but by the custom of men and public laws; and for this reason they are commonly made not only of gold and silver, but also of lead and sometimes even leather. . . . Money has the same principle as a written bond; for a bond is not valued for its content, which are tablets, wax, parchment, but from law and from its power" (in *Liber quaestionum illustrium*, qu. 15; [1573] 1610, 121–23).

The Spanish theologian Gregorio de Valencia (1549–1603) asked the moral question, How could public authority augment the value of an item? The answer was that, by designating money as the medium of exchange to be used by all, public authority turned it into something useful, just as an artisan turned a useless piece of wood into a useful box. Money, being useful, could be exchanged for other useful things (Valencia 1598, 1095; disp. 5 qu. 20 punct. 2).

Fiat money in practice

Fiat money was studied not only as a theoretical possibility but also as a practical reality. In the second half of the sixteenth century, writers paid increasing attention to examples of fiat money, drawn either from the past or from distant places.

Empirical examples provoked theorists' curiosity about fiat money.

Some examples came from antiquity. Forcadel (dialogue 48, §2; 1595, 1:117) cited a passage in Seneca's *De Beneficis* (5:14) that mentions leather money. Other examples came from more recent times. Hotman (in *Liber quaestionum illustrium*, qu. 15; [1573] 1610, 122) cited the episode of Frederic II during the siege of Faenza in 1241, and the fact that the Slavs of the island of Rügen off the coast of Germany used linens as currency. Pierre Grégoire (1540–1617) (in *De Republica*, lib. 3, cap. 6, n. 26; 1609, 43) cited two examples of obsidional monies: the episode of the count of Tendilla in 1483, and the use of siege money by Venetians in 1124 while they were besieging Tyre, an episode now considered apocryphal (see chapter 12). Grimaudet (d. 1580) learned from the reports of travelers that in China "they use a money that is made of paper, square-shaped and imprinted on one side with the image of the king" (1576, 20).

The synthesis of the two traditions, one showing the theoretical *possibility* of fiat money, the other pointing to its documented use as a means of raising revenues, was made by René Budel (1530–91), a jurist by training who worked as diplomat for the archbishop of Cologne, and later as mintmaster in Westphalia for the duke of Bavaria.

Budel was well aware of siege monies (see chapter 12). After reviewing several examples, and even providing pictures of these coins made of copper, lead, tin, and paper, he concluded (1591, 7): "I hold this to be indubitable that a Prince in the midst of costly wars, and therefore in great necessity, can order that money be made out of leather, bark, salt, or any material he wants, if he is careful to repair the loss inflicted thereby on the community with good and better money (see Andrea d'Isernia and Matteo d'Afflitto). This is what Girolamo Butigella says, that money can be made of lead or leather, provided that it is publicly approved, and it can be paid out instead of any other money, gold or silver."

The conditions for valued fiat money

The role of convertibility in imparting value

As the idea of fiat money progressed, writers sought to understand how it could acquire value. The historical examples of obsidional currencies, as well as the legal tradition stemming from the canon *Quanto*, promoted an understanding of the role of the convertibility of a token currency. For example, the Spanish canonist González Téllez (d. 1649) returned to the traditional canonist doctrine and its prohibition of excessive seigniorage, which "necessarily increases the price of goods and makes everything more expensive, as we have experienced more than once in our times" (a clear allusion to the Spanish vellón; see chapter 14). He rejected the "examples of various nations among whom we read that money has been made of diverse materials like wood and leather; for it will be answered that the monies of such peoples, and those made in times of pressing necessity, are not by right money but a pledge until a legitimate and rightful coin be made and exchanged for the wrongful one" (1715, 554).

Jakob Bornitz (1608), a German jurist, defined money not by its observable characteristics, but by its function as medium of exchange, following Aristotle. This inevitably led him to recognize the siege monies as "quasi-money," similar to money but lacking its form or content. He insisted, however, that they needed to be redeemed after the emergency.

Fiat money in a closed economy

Scaccia's influential legal treatise of foreign exchange includes a theoretical discussion of money (1619, §II, glos. III, 323). He repeated the romanist doctrine that metal should be worth no more coined than uncoined, justifying it with three arguments: (a) money is traded internationally, (b) it is threatened by counterfeiting, and (c) deviations from the bullion value occasion variations in the value of money. But, he added, in a closed economy that does not trade abroad, that has eliminated the risk of counterfeiting, and that has means to maintain the constancy of money, money could be made in whatever material and issued at whatever price the ruler wishes. Although the use of money belongs to natural law, as Bartolo had stated (to Dig. 18.1.1; 1570–71, 2:120), the precise monetary arrangements are a matter of positive law. Scaccia does not say how the invariability of the value of money is to be achieved.

The Frenchman Henri Poullain, writing in 1612, expressed the idea with a metaphor. "Within the state [bad coins] stand in for, and serve just as well as, the good ones; no more or less than in a card game, where various individuals play, one avails oneself of tokens, to which a certain value is assigned, and they are used by the winners to receive, and by the losers to pay what they owe. Whether instead of coins one were to use dried beans and give them the same value, the game would be no less enjoyable or perfect" (Poullain 1709, 67).

Geminiano Montanari, a mathematician and astronomer, wrote (Montanari [1683] 1804, 104): "If a state had no commerce with the other states and lived solely on its own productions, as China and a few others have done for so long, the prince could set the value of money as he pleased, and make it of whatever content he wished." He cited the case of Chinese paper money described by Marco Polo. "But if a prince wants his own coins of gold and silver to be accepted by foreigners, so that his subjects can trade with them, he cannot value them if he does not set the right content."

Both Poullain and Montanari drew the inference that, as small change was needed only for domestic transactions, it could be made of overvalued or fiat money. Montanari even made a comparison with deposit banking: the sovereign could make small change of any value he wanted, without prejudice to anyone, just as merchants use book transfers to clear their debts and the banks keep a fixed quantity of cash that "remains so to speak dead," and that the sovereign could use himself.

Small change circulating domestically as fiat money

The Neapolitan Antonio Serra ([1613] 1804, 147–48) highlighted the same temptation of token money when he advocated that
small money be issued "in quantities sufficient for making change
depending on the size of the state, and I say it should be made not
of alloyed silver but of pure copper, in which only the form and not
matter gives value, because this would result in a considerable profit
for the prince without generating any of the said inconveniences, and
in any case it will be very easy to determine the quantity which does
not generate them." He did not say how to compute that quantity.

Restrictions on fiat money

Writers drew   This leads us to the third idea discovered by Renaissance monetary
lessons from   theorists, namely, that inflation would occur if the quantity of token
contemporary   coins were not controlled, a form of the quantity theory of money.
experiences.

Limited legal tender

Limiting the demand for, rather than the supply of, small change
is an idea that appeared early. Whereas medieval jurists had not
allowed repayment of one coin for another without the creditor's
consent, Renaissance law had made all debts equivalent and payable
in pennies. Yet, at the same time, legal tender limitations on small
change, whether full-bodied or not, were becoming more common.
Venice limited its mainland petty coinage to tenders of 5s. in 1463
(see page 179). In 1462 and 1464, Florence tried to restrict silver
coinage to small payments, based on the nature of the transaction
(see chapter 9). Aragon limited legal tender in 1497 soon after the
introduction of convertible token coinage. In Germany, the Imperial
ordinances of 1559 and 1576 limited small change to 25 florins in
legal tender. In the United Provinces, in 1622, it was limited to ¼4
of sums over 100 guilders (Monroe 1923, 97). In France, the pure
copper coins issued in 1577 were legal tender up to 100s., and billon
coins for a third of a debt. In England between 1613 and 1644, the
copper coinage made under license was not legal tender. In 1672,

royal farthings were limited to 6d. (Carothers 1930, 12).

Gasparo Tesauro (1609) rationalized these legal restrictions as *Pecunia rerum* means to prevent fluctuations in the value of the small denomina- *omnium mensura.* tions. In his view, the goal of monetary policy should be price level stability. Money "is everlasting, and should have a fixed proportion, since it is used to value all things, and not be valued by others: the measure of all things."[11]

In his analysis, exchange rates between coins varied for three reasons: (a) changes in relative prices of different metals, (b) debasements of the small coins, (c) excessive issue of petty coins, even when it is full-bodied. In the last case, "when too much copper coinage is issued or imported from elsewhere, the price of the better coin is always altered, and this variation is detrimental to the creditor if he is repaid in that money; for, even if the quantity of copper coinage corresponds to the correct valuation in gold or silver, because of the tediousness of counting, the inconvenience of storage and the cost of transportation, some loss results for the creditor, and therefore it is thought that good coins of gold and silver correspond to a larger quantity of copper coins than the exact valuation requires, and thus their value changes."

Tesauro cited approvingly the limited legal tender provisions of Portugal and Germany. But his prescriptions went beyond: "to avoid this alteration it is good that an insufficient amount of small and copper coinage be made, since it is customarily made for small purchases of food and to supplement large coins, not to repay creditors."

Quantity theory

Restricting the quantity of small change to the needs of trade is an idea that recurs in the seventeenth century. Montanari's statement that small change can be overvalued or fiat money, which we read earlier, was accompanied by a major qualification: "it is clear enough that it is not necessary for a prince to strike petty coins having metallic content equal to their face value, provided he does not strike more of them than is sufficient for the use of his people, sooner striking

---

[11] Tesauro (1609, 629–33), partially quoted in Cipolla (1956, 30).

too few than striking too many. If the prince strikes only as many as the people need, he may strike of whatever metallic content he wishes" (Montanari [1683] 1804, 109; quoted in Cipolla 1956, 29). In case of over-issue, the small coins will replace the large ones, and merchants dealing with foreigners will need large coins, for which they will have to pay a premium, and prices will increase.

The Englishman William Petty (1899, 2:445) tried in 1682 to estimate the quantity to which small change should be restricted, by positing an appropriate per household figure of 12d. and multiplying by his estimate of total population. In an earlier work, published in 1662, he expressed general opposition to "debased" (that is, partly fiduciary or overvalued) coinage, he accepted that coins could be debased to a limited extent, with the seigniorage accruing to the king. Concerning privately issued money, he added: "nor are such tokens base as are coined for exchange in retailing by particular men (if such men be responsible and able to take them back, and give silver for them)" (1899, 1:85). He did not propose that state-issued small change be convertible, however.

Lessons from the Castilian experience: fiat money

The Castilian experiment (1596–1660) led writers to theorize about the possibility of fiat money as domestic currency.

These and other discussions about restrictions on quantities of small coins to be issued emerged largely in response to evidence from an experiment in Castile that involved large issues of overvalued copper coins called vellón (see chapter 14). That experiment prompted theoretical reactions. We survey reactions in Spain and France.

In Spain: Juan de Mariana (1609)

Mariana set out arguments for and against token copper small denomination coins.

Spaniards were among the first to draw lessons from the Castilian vellón experiment. The most famous was the Jesuit Juan de Mariana (1536–1624), whose *De Monetae Mutatione* was written between 1603 and 1606 and published in Cologne in 1609 to avoid royal censure (the Spanish Inquisition nevertheless paid him a visit).[12]

---

12 See Mariana ([1609] 1994) for a modern critical edition of the Latin text with

Though he disapproved of the vellón experiment, in the careful manner of the Jesuits, Mariana set out arguments in favor of the vellón experiment as well as against; he even refuted what he regarded to be weak reasons against the experiment. In doing so, he was probably describing the controversies between the advisors who pushed the kings of Spain toward that policy, and their adversaries. Among the advantages he cited were that silver would no longer be wasted in making coins; that instead of being absorbed within the money stock, silver from the Indies could be spent by the king for his wartime supplies;[13] that without a stock of silver coins as a potential reserve to settle the balance of trade, trade and production would eventually have had to adjust to make deficits less likely, thereby turning the balance of trade in Spain's favor and stimulating production; that the copper money was lighter and easier to transport, and that its cheap provision would lower the rate of interest and stimulate agriculture and industry.

Mariana rejected some arguments against the vellón. For example, he admitted that the over-valuation of copper coins would increase incentives for counterfeiting, but said that the new technology could resolve the problem. He recommended that coins only be made in the Ingenio of Segovia. He noted that effects on the balance of trade and aggregate demand were ambiguous, and "since they can go in either direction, they have force in neither" ([1609] 1994, 80).[14]

Forecasting inflation

Among his own main objections against the policy was his belief that small change should only be used for small transactions; he approved of laws that limited the acceptable amounts of small change in trade. While acknowledging that copper coinage was necessary in limited

Mariana predicted consequences of the vellón experiment.

German translation, and Laures (1928) for an English summary and analysis. A contemporary Spanish version has also been republished recently (Mariana [1609] 1987). García de Paso (1999a) analyzes Mariana's text in the framework of a trimetallic version of our model (with gold, silver, and copper). See Grice-Hutchison (1978, 1993) for contemporary Spanish economic thought.

[13] Compare this argument with the one of Adam Smith cited on page 101.

[14] Mariana claimed to prefer historical examples to a priori theorizing.

quantities, he wrote that an excess would lead to a disappearance of silver. He also alluded to historical observations that debasements always led to a rise in prices: he regarded the issue of vellón as a debasement and predicted that excessive quantities of copper coins would make them worthless. He noted that in some places a premium of 10% was already observed on silver coins, and elsewhere 5%. He predicted that price controls would be set by the king, but that individuals would either ignore them or abstain from trade. Ultimately, the king would be forced to demonetize the coins, or else devalue them, so that "overnight, as if in a dream, the owner of 300 ducats in this money will have 100 or 150" ([1609] 1994, 100). He saw the projected sequence of inflation and deflation as disruptive to trade and contracts, and therefore to the king's tax revenues. He regarded the high seigniorage rates of 50% in the restamping operations as immoral, because in his view the king had no right to tax his subjects without their explicit consent, and noted that such high tax rates would not be tolerated on any other tax base. The worst consequence would be general hatred of the king: quoting Tacitus, he recalled that "everyone claims prosperity for himself, but adversity is blamed on the leader" ([1609] 1994, 104).

In France: Henri Poullain (1612)

Poullain analyzed proposals for making copper token coins in France. As a member of the Cour des Monnaies, the Frenchman Henri Poullain advised the government on monetary policy.[15] He read Mariana and observed the unfolding events in Spain. In the course of his duties, he dealt with proposals by private individuals to mint copper coins under license in France (as was done at the same time in England), and made predictions about the likely consequences.

In a 1612 memorandum on one such proposal, he wrote: "In any state, depending on its size, productivity and endowment in things useful to human life, there must also be a proportionate and definite quantity of coins, for the needs of the trade and commerce which takes place within it." He estimated the quantity of money in France

---

[15] Some of Poullain's writings have been published (Poullain 1709), others are discussed by Harsin (1928). See page 204 on the Cour des Monnaies.

and the quantity of copper coins recently minted, and noted that in 1596 tax collectors were receiving large amounts of small coins, from which he concluded that the quantity of small coins in circulation was more than sufficient for trade. He then distinguished between foreign trade and domestic trade, and supposed that the total money supply was used half in one and half in the other.

He asserted that copper could displace large coins in domestic trade: "When the prince mints quantities of billon or copper coins, such bad coins remain in his state for the domestic trade, and the good silver and gold coins are taken out of the kingdom by its residents to purchase foreign goods. Thus bad coins hide and expel good coins" because, as we noted earlier, bad coins can just as well perform the function of money for domestic trade.

Poullain explained how copper coins were more expensive to make, and could not contain more than a third of their face value in metal: "they cannot pay or receive any price alongside the good coins of gold and silver without resulting in (leaving aside all other problems) an increase in the prices of all sorts of commodities, as it always happens with such devaluations" (Poullain 1709, 90), and he cited the example of Spain's vellón coinage.

In a separate memorandum on the Castilian "monetary disorder" in 1612, he explained the mechanism by which prices increase. As shown in figure 14.4, the "monetary disorder" to which he referred was not inflation but the substitution of light copper coins for full-bodied coins; in 1612, vellón coins were not yet going at discount. "Any state is always in need of a moderate quantity of billon or copper coinage." But an excess of such coins brings about a general rise in the price level: as gold and silver coins become rarer in proportion with the production of bad coins, so the price of imports rises. Eventually domestic goods also rise in prices, because "in any state there are always foreign goods of the same kind as the ones made within it."

Concluding remarks

By the late Renaissance, leading monetary theorists understood all elements of the standard formula.

By 1661, monetary theorists had done much to overturn or at least to amend the medieval money-as-commodity view. We have documented how writers understood various of the elements that would eventually come together to form Cipolla's standard formula; these included the theoretical possibility of token money and the role of convertibility for full-bodied money in supporting the value of tokens. In 1661, Sir Henry Slingsby (1621–90) proposed a complete version of the standard formula incorporating a government monopoly of convertible token coins. See page 268 for details. However, another century and a half would pass before Slingsby's recommendation became public policy.

Renaissance writers had also put forward the quantity theory of money and the ingredients of Adam Smith's 1776 "real bills" mental experiment (see page 101). Though he did not cite him, Adam Smith may have been influenced by the proposals of John Law ([c1704] 1994), originally written in 1703 or 1704 and recently published. Yet both Law and Smith can be seen mostly as reworking ideas from 1661 and earlier. They applied earlier analyses of the effects of substituting cheap metal coins for more expensive ones to substituting cheap paper notes for more expensive metal coins.

This completes our review of the thoughts of monetary theorists as they pertained to the policy problem of regulating the supply of small coins. These ideas were not created in a vacuum, but were influenced by contemporary policy discussions and experiments. Part III describes a variety of experiments that show the influence of ideas and technologies on events, as well as the influence of events on ideas.

‿

Part III

Endemic Shortages and "Natural Experiments"

CHAPTER 7

Clues

*Let experience, the least fallible guide of human opinions, be
appealed to for an answer to these inquiries.*
— *Alexander Hamilton, The Federalist Papers, No 6.*

In parts III and IV, we read history in the light of our model. Part III
describes events before and part IV events after the technological and
theoretical innovations of the Renaissance.

In part III, we document the recurrent shortages and debasements
that were symptomatic of the medieval money supply system. We
first provide a sample of problems from various parts of Europe, then
focus in more detail on evidence from three places where documentation is relatively abundant: Florence, Venice, and sixteenth-century
France. We close with some early experiments with convertible
coinage that emerged under special circumstances. We find evidence of shortages of small change and of authorities groping for
solutions. The authorities were confined by the technology, institutions, and theories of their times; in part III, we see them mostly as
adjusting the parameters of our model, especially those that influence the positions of the intervals, while living within the medieval
monetary mechanism. But at times, we see them pushed by the
problem of small change to strain against the constraints imposed
by the monetary mechanism and existing monetary theories. Some
early experiments in part III foreshadow later ones to be seen in
part IV.

Part IV describes monetary experiments of the seventeenth and
eighteenth centuries, which were influenced by a new technology and
new ideas that opened the realm of large-scale fiat monies. The seventeenth century witnessed unprecedented bursts of inflation. We
document an influential experiment carried out in Castile and its
echoes throughout Europe. One country, England, steered clear of

government-produced token coinage and experimented with alternate ways to provide small denominations, none of them satisfactory. We study the repercussions of one particular shortage-induced crisis, the Great Recoinage of 1696, and its consequences for England's subsequent move toward the gold standard. All in all, these experiments taught later monetary authorities much both about the difficulty of implementing a system with token coins and about more general aspects of monetary theory.

The remainder of this chapter presents some themes that will recur elsewhere in part III. We see some recurring syndromes as tell tale signs of particular forces that our model has isolated.

Shortages of small change and bullion famine

There were recurrent shortages of small change and public policies to cure them. Chapter 8 will review some of the evidence for shortages in medieval Europe. The evidence reveals a recurrent syndrome with the following symptoms. People grumbled that they lacked coins, particularly small ones. They complained about the poor condition of the money stock, with many coins being clipped and worn. There were reports of invasions of foreign coins, which, in spite of being obviously distinct and often of weaker intrinsic content, circulated widely. The monetary authorities responded with various actions. They prohibited the circulating of foreign coins, the melting of domestic coins (particularly small ones), and the export of bullion. Sometimes they minted small coins at a mint price that the government or the mintmasters topped off, or with silver compulsorily purchased. Often they used debasements and increases in the mint price to attract bullion.

A "bullion famine" did not cause shortages of small change. Such symptoms of coin shortages helped spawn a literature on an alleged "bullion famine" (Day 1987; Spufford 1988a, ch. 15). That literature interpreted the coin shortages as indicating that western Europe suffered from a shortage of bullion, that is, mintable metal. The cause was said to be an adverse balance of trade with the East, which resulted in a permanent drain of silver from Europe. The literature interpreted debasements as ways to make a dwindling amount of silver go farther by increasing the nominal stock. The monetary contraction has also been said to have helped cause economic depression during the late Middle Ages.

The "bullion famine" argument does not distinguish among denominations of coins, and so seems to use a one-coin model. But it would be difficult to rationalize the bullion famine story within a single-coin version of our model.[1] In that model, a permanent drain of silver resulting from "excessive" imports would raise the price of silver in Europe, change the terms of trade, and thereby end the imports. It is difficult to imagine how such a drain could persist for prolonged periods (Sussman 1998). Debasements would have distributional consequences, with ambiguous effects on macroeconomic aggregates. Even if the money stock had been shrinking due to imports, the welfare consequences would not be obvious, and it would be difficult to interpret the persistent complaints and the authorities' concern. Finally, the coexistence of complaints of currency shortage with local reports of repeated invasions of neighboring currency make it difficult to see a shortage at the aggregate level of western Europe, or even at the local level: how can one speak of currency shortages and invasions of currency at the same time?

Reports of shortages and policy makers' responses to them make more sense within our multiple-coin model, with its distinct demand for small change. Subsequent chapters use the model to interpret various aspects of those shortages and the policy responses.

Shortages and invasions of coins

Among the recurrent symptoms in periods of shortages are simultaneous complaints about the state of the domestic currency and about invasions of foreign coins. In chapter 2, we told how such invasions could be regarded as an endogenous or market-determined debasement that occurred when citizens decided to use the small

---

[1] See chapter 2 or Sargent and Smith (1997).

change offered by a foreign government whose melting and minting points for small coins bracketed the current domestic price level
when those for domestic small coins did not.

Ghost monies and units of account

Ghost monies
emerged after
exchange rate
fluctuations.
An enchanting passage in Cipolla (1956) is about "ghost monies":
at various times and places transactions came to be denominated
in units of coins whose physical manifestation had disappeared.
Cipolla presents the persistence of ghost monies as a mystery, but
our model makes us think that they are natural outcomes of the
medieval monetary mechanism.

Medieval units of account have long been a subject of debate.[2]
Understanding those units of account is important for historians because prices and values (including income and wealth) are expressed
with units of account in the original documents. We believe that
in medieval account books, the phrases that are generally classified
as "units of account" referred to the types of coins in which sums
had been or should be paid. Our model sheds light on why traders
sometimes drew distinctions among different types of coins.

In a world where the problem of small change has been solved,
the type of coin in which a monetary obligation was paid, pennies or dollars, was irrelevant. But it could become relevant under
medieval monetary arrangements. When exchange rates remained
constant, coins of different types could be treated as though they
were equivalent. Then they could be used indifferently to meet the
cash-in-advance constraints because they carried the same rate of
return. But during times of exchange rate instability, coins ceased to
be equivalent, particularly in economic transactions where rates of
return mattered, like debt contracts. Thus, when e_t changed over
time, a creditor who was owed one coin of type 2 should care if he
were repaid 1 coin of type 2 or e_t coins of type 1.

---

[2] Einaudi (1936), Cipolla (1956, 38–39). Weber (1996) analyzes the unit of
account in medieval Basle using econometrics.

Monetary authorities at times tried to influence units of account and restore the lost equivalence between various coins. They would do so essentially by specifying that an existing debt, denominated in coin 2, could be extinguished by tendering e_L coins 1 for every coin 2 owed. This ultimately was the meaning of the legal tender values[3] assigned by governments in the Middle Ages, ultimately developping into a full list of official relative prices for all denominations. For example, when Venice set the rate of the gold ducat in 1285, it did so in the following words: "that the gold ducat must be current in Venice and its district for 40 soldi a grossi, and that everyone, Venetian or foreigner, must accept the same gold ducat for 40 soldi a grossi in payment, under such penalty as shall be set by the lord Doge" (Cessi 1937, 51).

Monetary authorities sometimes tried to influence units of account.

But if e_L diverged significantly from the market rate e_t, private agents preferred to ignore or evade the law. In Venice and Florence, they did this by the Humpty-Dumpty[4] method: an amount denominated in "coin 2" would be taken to represent, not coins of type 2, but e_L coins of type 1, as the law required. To denote an amount *really* in coin 2, they might use a phrase such as "coin 2 in coin 2" or "coin 2 of coin 2," to which the law did not apply. Sometimes, the authorities intervened again and insisted that the newly emerged "coin 2 of coin 2" be equivalent to e_L coins 1. The private agents would kindly oblige, but then denote real coins 2 as "coin 2 of coin 2 in coin 2." Understandably, this terminology can be confusing for modern historians, who have dubbed these apparitions "ghost monies," because they are not what they seem.

Ghost monies were units of account created by markets.

Such Humpty-Dumpty units of account also emerged when there was no law to evade, but a practical problem needed resolution. When the market exchange rate between coin 1 and coin 2 did remain constant for long periods of time, sometimes a generation, habits formed, contracts were simplified, and one took less care to distinguish among the different types of coins. When the exchange

---

[3] The term "face value" is anachronistic, since the face of coins bore no value.

[4] "'When I use a word,' Humpty Dumpty said scornfully, 'it means just what I choose it to mean—neither more nor less.'" 'Through the Looking Glass,' ch. 6.

rate suddenly changed, there was a need to interpret existing obligations and to have words mean exactly what the parties, or at least the party with more bargaining power, intended. Our model affirms that there can be periods of constant exchange rates alternating with upward movements in e large and permanent enough to require such adjustments. The ghost monies are thus another impression left in the historical record by a phenomenon that our model captures.

Free minting

Free minting was a policy of many late medieval mints.

Free minting meant "unlimited," not "free of charge."[5] Free minting was a common feature of late-medieval mints (Spufford 1988b). By the mid-fourteenth century, it was common place in Italy and elsewhere. Florence instituted free minting for its silver grosso on October 3, 1296 (Bernocchi 1976, 160), Siena did so on March 13, 1350 (Promis 1868, 79), as did Venice for its silver soldino on March 29, 1353 (Lane and Mueller 1985, 162, 346, 447). Genoa also had free minting in the fourteenth century. The merchant's manual of Pegolotti (1936), written around 1340, lists the mint prices in various mints of the Mediterranean, preceded by the same formula: "and to him who brings silver to the mint, the mint returns."

Free minting is not well documented in earlier periods. Of course, neither are other mint policies, so the absence of surviving provisions does not mean that free minting did not exist. But other documents suggest that coins were sometimes minted on government account. For example, surviving documents in Siena show that, in the 1280s, the Consiglio generale decided every year in mid-December whether or not to mint large or small coins, and sometimes left the decision to the discretion of the officials. In 1296, to remedy a perceived shortage of coin, the city lent to the mint 1,000 florins to buy silver and have it coined; the money stayed at the mint to serve as a bullion fund

[5] See chapter 2 for how coining on government account and free minting affect the lower bound on the price level provided by a commodity money.

and was repaid only in 1306 (Paolozzi Strozzi et al. 1992, 425–28).

In the absence of an explicit free minting policy, the authorities could nevertheless have been pursuing a policy that closely approximated it. For example, if the authorities ran the mint by trying to maximize profits, this would lead them to purchase unlimited quantities of silver at a mint price that covered production costs and afforded a monopoly profit. There is evidence of such behavior. In Venice, although free minting of silver was not explicit until 1353, regulations of 1278 enjoined mintmasters to cover their expenses and achieve a prescribed rate of net seigniorage for the commune whenever they could (Lane and Mueller 1985, 166). In practice, this meant that mintmasters would offer to coin silver as soon as the market price of silver reached a certain level; in other words, mint freely at a set price. In Florence, one deliberation of the Consiglio throws a similar light on its motivations. In September 1285, it debated whether to mint grossi. The argument prevailed that no such decision should be taken because of the high price of silver, and that the matter should be considered when it again became possible to mint profitably (Gherardi 1896, 1:290).

The evidence

From a variety of sources across Europe, the rest of part III assembles evidence about the workings of the medieval monetary mechanism. We shall cite evidence of: (1) recurrent shortages of small coins; (2) depreciations of small coins relative to large ones; and (3) debasements of small coins that were justified as attempts to cure shortages of them. We interpret the evidence in terms of our model. We also indicate how monetary authorities gradually became aware of the defects of the supply system that they administered and occasionally experimented, as in Venice and France, with ways to repair it. Those early repair efforts, which implemented parts but not all of the standard formula, were judged to have failed. Thus, the following five chapters of part III mostly paint a picture of the difficult task confronting medieval monetary authorities, given the flawed system that they administered and the imperfect tools at their disposal (including the current state of monetary theory that we described in part II). Part IV will then describe later experiments that ultimately transformed the medieval system for supplying coins into the modern one governed by the standard formula.

❧

CHAPTER 8
Medieval Coin Shortages

Complaints of coin shortages abound in the record since the Middle Ages.[1] The complaints were sometimes general and vague. When they were specific enough, they often mentioned a lack of coins of small denomination. Other concurrent phenomena were sometimes cited, such as exports of metal and invasions of foreign coins, always of lower quality than the domestic coins that they replaced. Our model tells us to expect such things to occur when the penny-in-advance constraint binds. To the witnesses, it often seemed that these symptoms were causes, and they sought palliatives to suppress them.

Shortages occurred throughout Europe.

This chapter reviews some of the evidence, mostly from medieval England and France. In the three subsequent chapters, we will examine in greater detail both the shortages and the policy responses they induced in Venice, Florence, and early modern France.

England

England's problems with small change are well documented qualitatively if not quantitatively. The Reverend Rogers Ruding's *Annals of coinage*, first published in 1817, chronologically present the surviving documentation relating to coins. From the long series of petitions submitted to the king and proclamations and statutes issued by him, one can track the syndrome of currency shortage that we described in the previous chapter.

It should be kept in mind that compared to its continental cousins, the English penny remained singularly weighty. In 1280, it contained 1.33g of silver, compared with 0.34g in France, 0.09g in Florence, and 0.06g in Venice. The Venetian grosso of 1202 was

---

[1] See Spengler (1966, 213), Spufford (1970, 361–62), Carothers (1930, ch. 2), and Cipolla (1956, ch. 3).

only 50% heavier than an English sterling penny, and when Florence issued its quattrino in 1335, it was worth 4d. in Florence but contained ⅙ the silver of an English penny. Thus, when additional denominations were introduced in England during a general recoinage in 1279, they included a multiple of the penny, the groat (4d.), but also subdivisions, the halfpenny (½d.) and farthing (¼d.).

Invasions of foreign coins   Foreign coins were first mentioned in Ruding's documents in 1284 and 1292 when certain foreign coins and counterfeits from Germany were prohibited. Next, in 1299, England banned importation of Flemish small coins and searched incoming ships for them. They were nevertheless allowed to pass current at the rate of 2 for 1d. for a few months. The importation of "false" money was prohibited again in 1310. In 1326, there appeared laws against the export of gold and silver in bullion or coin, repeated in 1331, 1335, 1338, and 1343. In 1335, the statute of York also prohibited melting English coins and import of light and counterfeit money from abroad. This time, the invader denounced was the French penny ("turney"), which had become "commonly current"; incoming ships were again to be searched. The same year, the king ordered "light" halfpennies and farthings to be made. The turneys were also prohibited in Ireland in 1339, but because "great inconvenience had arisen from this prohibition, on account of the scarcity of sterling money," they were tolerated until enough substitutes could be provided for.

Ways to prevent invasions   In 1341, the measures escalated: clearly feeling that the disappearance of money in England was tied to a balance of trade problem, a statute of 1341 required merchants to import silver for all wool exported, and in 1342 it was ordered that all large-scale purchases of corn and victuals be settled with gold. Finally, in 1343 Parliament deliberated on the best way to remedy the great want of money, to prevent the import of false money and the export of good money, and to remedy the high price of gold florins in Flanders, which made imports into England very expensive. It was decided that the English should mint their own gold coin, to be current in both England and Flanders. The new coin, the noble, was 1% lighter than a Florentine florin, and was not legal tender. Simultaneously, the silver money was debased by 10%. Complaints about invasions continued, however. This time, "lushbournes" from Luxemburg were denounced in petitions of 1346 and 1347, until they were prohibited in 1348. Another petition of the time complained of the "great scarcity of coins in the realm" and asked that more money be coined. Finally, silver was debased again by 10% in 1351.

There followed a pause in complaints about invasions, although prohibitions on export of gold and silver appeared in 1353 and 1364, and the Commons asked in 1363 that gold be made required payment for large transactions. In 1367, a new invasion was reported, this time from Scotland. In 1378, and again in 1380, the Commons complained of a great want of halfpennies and farthings, and also of the export of gold and silver, and of clipping. But, during a parliamentary inquiry in 1381, mint officials advised against a debasement, and proposed an array of measures, including making more small coins, having gold circulate by weight, and enforcing balance in trade of goods by requiring importers to match their imports with equivalent exports. When summoning Parliament in 1385, the king recommended a debasement to prevent the export of English currency. In 1393, the commons complained again of scarcity of halfpennies and farthings, and their melting was prohibited once more.

In 1399, there came a new invasion, this time from Venice, in the form of silver halfpennies called "galley halfpennies," three or four of which were "scarcely equal" to a penny, according to the proclamation that banned them. These were soldini, whose fineness was slightly higher than sterling, and whose content was in fact 40% of a penny (see chapter 10). In 1402 and in 1406, the Commons petitioned the king on the want of halfpennies and farthings, and the use of Scottish and Venetian coins in their stead. Because of the "great scarcity of money," a 17% debasement took place in 1411. In 1414, Venetian galleys were searched for coins; Flemish and Dutch coins were prohibited in 1415. Then, in 1423, French coinage that the victorious Henry V had issued came into England: a statute of that year banned the use of "blanks," which were worth 6d. in

France but were 13% light with respect to English pennies. Amidst the litany of bans on foreign coins and renewed penalties for export of money, one notes two unusual measures. The first came in 1421, when the use of gold in payment of taxes was encouraged by having the tax collectors take underweight coins by tale but overweight coins by weight. The other came in 1423, when a "great scarcity of white money" was blamed on the market price of bullion, which stood at 32s. per lb troy, higher than the mint price of 31s. A statute made it illegal to trade bullion at more than 30s. outside the mint.

The record of complaints and measures becomes sparse after that date. One remarkable exception was the detailed petition addressed by the Commons to the king in 1446. The problems created by the lack of halfpennies and farthings was described at length (Ruding 1840, 1:275):

> Men travelling over countries, for part of their expenses of necessity must depart our sovereign lord's coin, that is to wit, a penny in two pieces, or else forego all the same penny, for the payment of a half penny; and also the poor common retailers of victuals, and of other needful things, for default of such coin of half pennies and farthings, oftentimes may not sell their said victuals and things, and many of our said sovereign lord's poor liege people, which would buy such victuals and other small things necessary, may not buy them, for default of half pennies and farthings not had on the part of the buyer nor on the part of the seller; which scarcity of half pennies and farthings, has fallen, and daily yet does, because that for their great weight, and their fineness of allay, they be daily tried and molten, and put into other use, unto the increase of winning of them that do so.

The remedy proposed was to ban the melting of coins, to debase the halfpennies and farthings from 30s. per lb Tower to 33s., to raise the mint price from 29s. to 31s. for those coins only, and to limit their use in payments to a maximum 5% of the sum tendered.

Finally, in 1464, Edward IV debased the coinage by 20%, "by consideration of the great scarcity of money within this his realm of

England, among other things caused of lack of bringing of bullion into his mints, which, as is conceived, is because they that should bring bullion may have more for their bullion in other princes' mints than in his." (Ruding 1840, 1:282).

France

For France, Saulcy (1879–92) made a collection of the documents he found in surviving archives that dealt with money. We do not read the petitions and complaints, but find their echoes in the reasons that kings gave for their orders.

A concern to avoid shortages of petty coinage is apparent in 1322 and 1323. In 1333, the king ordered that a third of all privately owned silverware be minted, at no cost, to provide deniers and *mailles* (halfpennies); it was forbidden to use any but the royal pennies, and to melt them. Also, they were not to be used in payments larger than 10s. In 1337, a debasement of 33% was justified by "the people's suffering and lack of coins," and the same phrase used on the occasion of another debasement in April 1340. Arguably, these debasements had more to do with the start of the Hundred Years War, but the concern for small coinage was apparent in orders of 1339 and 1348 that mints devote one day per month to the production of pennies (Saulcy 1879–92, 1:218–19, 228, 259). In 1347, the king granted a request by the city officials in Narbonne that, "since, by lack of small change, the poorer classes suffer greatly, for the small purchases that they make, and for the alms that cannot easily be made," permission be given to cut coins worth 2d. into halves (Blanchet 1897).

From 1360 to 1417 the French currency was relatively stable. During the same period, shortages manifested themselves repeatedly. In 1365, following a 12.5% debasement, the king ordered his mints to make the new pennies, but only one day every fortnight "for the needs of the people, so that the gold coin may not rise above 16s. by the excessive quantity of small coinage" (Saulcy 1879–92, 1:490). In the southeastern province of Dauphiné, the circulation of

Evidence of shortages in France

"false, clipped, and foreign coins" prompted a debasement in 1370. There were many signs of such invasions: in 1374, the king wrote to the prince of Orange and asked him to stop imitating the French coins. In 1376, the count of Saint-Pol, although a vassal of the king, set up a mint in one of his territories outside the borders and imitated French coins. An order of 1373 for minting halfpennies in the border city of Tournai simultaneously invoked "lack and great need of the people for small coinage" and the need to prevent the circulation of "certain false small coins that are taken and offered in said city." Similar orders were later issued for Rouen (1374) and Paris (1375), citing shortages and invasions at the same time. Export of gold and silver bullion was prohibited in 1374, and goldsmiths were forbidden to buy silver at a price higher than the mint's in 1384. Finally, a 4% debasement allowed the king to raise his mint price, and to issue orders throughout the kingdom for minting coins of ½d., 1d. and 2d., again citing false monies and shortages. It appears that it was still necessary to send orders to various mints specifying quantities of small coins to be minted: one finds such orders every year until 1397, with occasional references to shortages. The record then falls silent, except for a document of 1405 giving a long list of foreign coins of gold and silver whose circulation hindered the French coinage (Saulcy 1879–92, 1:490, 510, 526, 523, 540, 534; 2:10, 20, 23, 31, 130).

The renewal of hostilities with England prompted another long wave of debasements from 1417 until 1429. Shortages are not mentioned again in Saulcy's documents until the 1450s, when the local mint officials in Tournai informed the king that it was necessary to raise the mint price by 10s. in order to find silver for petty coins. In response, the king ordered that the increase be paid for out of the seigniorage levied on large silver and gold coins. The same measure was adopted in Paris in 1461. This was a rare instance of a medieval government subsidizing the production of small coins, but only out of the profits made on other coins (Saulcy 1879–92, 3:225, 234).

The currency was by and large stable in the late fifteenth century. In December 1467, the mailles (½d.) were made 20% lighter than the large silver coins. Within six months, complaints arose of "great quantities of counterfeit *mailles*" around Paris, and it was decided that the new mailles would be blanched to make them harder to imitate. Eventually, in 1474, the rest of the coinage was debased and brought in line with the maille. In 1488, several cities in the west of France asked for more coins of 1d. and 3d. A debasement of 8% soon followed, and orders were sent to various mints for substantial quantities of small coins in the following years (1488 to 1493, 1498 to 1501, 1508 to 1513, 1520 to 1522, etc.). It is apparent, however, that the government remained leery of producing too many coins: the orders always specified the quantity to be produced and "no more, for a great quantity could be detrimental to the king and the public good" (Saulcy 1879–92, 3:346). A final period of shortage started in 1544, with local representatives in Provence complaining of lack of small coins, orders being sent to various mints for minting pennies.[2]

Shortages elsewhere

France and England were not the only countries to suffer bouts of shortages. In the fifteenth century in the Burgundian Netherlands, there was "continual demand for small change, the lack of which was frequent topic of popular complaint. . . . There was a considerable lack of official small change from time to time, accentuated perhaps by hoarding of even the smallest denominations. The government, perhaps on the insistence of the estates, attempted to remedy this deficiency by writing into the monetary ordinances stipulated proportions of bullion to be used in the minting of different denominations. Comparison between the stipulated proportions and the actual quantities of bullion used indicates that such stipulations were completely disregarded by the mintmasters" (Spufford 1970, 51, 44). Munro (1988) has found that the mints of the Netherlands produced very little petty money.

---

[2] In Dauphiné in 1546, the reason given was to "stop the circulation of foreign coins".

In Spain, which consisted of separate kingdoms until the late fifteenth century, there were often shortages of small coins. In Aragon, complaints were voiced from the 1370s. In 1497, to remedy "the great dearth of fractional money in the kingdom," a commission was formed and as a result new billon pennies were minted that were 21% lighter than silver coins (Hamilton 1936, 87–90). The quantity minted was limited to 20% of the total silver coinage, and a legal tender limit of 5d. was imposed. In Navarre, a "great scarcity" of fractional money was noted in 1380 and prompted an issue of billon pennies 18% light. Similar complaints arose in 1430 and in 1481. In 1487, the kingdom was said to "suffer great injury on account of the complete lack of fractional money" (Hamilton 1936, 126–34).[3] In the 1530s, during a scarcity of vellón coinage in Castile, *tarjas* (coins from nearby Navarre) circulated at ⅓ above their intrinsic content. The Cortes of Castile asked the king for issues of vellón in 1518, 1528, 1542, 1551, 1558, 1559, and 1583–85 (Hamilton 1934), and there was a small premium on vellón with respect to silver in the late sixteenth century (Domínguez Ortiz 1960, 238).

Concluding remarks

This chapter has recited scattered complaints about shortages of small coins. The following chapters provide detailed studies of particular episodes in which we know more about the shortages, some of their causes, and policy makers' responses to them.

ↄ

---

[3] Valencia and Barcelona seemed by and large to be free of such problems.

CHAPTER 9

Medieval Florence

This chapter describes the circumstances surrounding the early coins of pre-Renaissance Florence and other Tuscan towns. After they issued multiple denominations, Tuscan towns encountered flaws in the theoretically self-regulating commodity money system, with its set melting points and minting points for coins of various denominations. Shortages and debasements of smaller denomination coins soon occurred. We discuss several episodes in Florence, including one that Carlo Cipolla called the "Quattrini affair." By the time of that episode, the monetary authorities had struggled with limited success to repair the supply mechanism.

Turbulent debut of large coins in Tuscany

Our story begins before Florence had become leader among Tuscan cities. A single silver denomination, the Tuscan penny or *denaro*, descended from Charlemagne's penny, was used by all Tuscan cities. Until about 1150, it was minted only by Lucca. Then prosperous Pisa issued copies of Lucca's penny. That started a period of currency competition between the two cities, while other Tuscan cities chose to use either Lucca's or Pisa's penny. For example, Florence adopted Pisa's currency in return for a rebate of seigniorage. During this period, Pisa and Lucca debased their pennies by half.[1] The currency competition ended in 1181 with a monetary agreement whereby Pisa and Lucca minted intrinsically identical but visually distinct coins, and shared seigniorage revenues. Pisa's penny quickly displaced its rival in transactions throughout Tuscany.

Currency competition in 12th c. Tuscany

---

[1] In chapter 5, we described how this debasement led to Pillius's question and the first discussion of the standard of debt repayment by jurists, setting off a long train of thought over the following centuries.

The next decades saw no changes in the currency system of Tuscany until the late 1220s, when Siena and Pisa introduced a larger silver coin, the grosso worth 12d., with about the same silver content as the grosso of Venice. Within a few years, Florence, Arezzo, and Lucca also issued the grosso. All Tuscan grossi were regarded as equivalent at the time. In 1252, Florence introduced a gold coin, which became known as the *fiorino d'oro*, or (gold) florin.

Tuscan cities debased their pennies.

The introduction of large denominations coincided with several debasements of the Tuscan pennies. In 1251, Siena's authorities learned that their mint had been producing pennies at the same standard as those of Lucca, which were lighter than the standard that then prevailed throughout Tuscany. Siena's authorities ratified that debasement after the fact. In 1255, the Tuscan cities agreed to a new standard and implemented it by 1257. That same year, Florence finally introduced its own penny. Siena cast a suspicious eye on its neighbors, periodically sending officials to assay their coins. Concerned by the variations among coins, Siena left the monetary union in 1266 and stopped coining pennies. When Siena resumed coining pennies in 1279, it did so on a standard of its own choosing. The following year, Florence broke away from Pisa and Lucca after discovering that they had debased their pennies, and adopted the standard of Siena. This ended the instability, and left Tuscan pennies in 1280 at 50% of their content in 1250.

This period also witnessed sharp increases in the exchange rates of pennies for the gold florin and the grosso. We have few quotations of the gold florin before 1275, but the evidence suggests that after being quoted initially at 20s., the florin appreciated to 36s. by 1276. The debasement and resumption of coinage by Siena and Florence temporarily stabilized the florin. At the same time, the grosso's successor, issued at 20d. in 1260, began to appreciate relative to the penny. Premia of 5% occurred in 1264 and rose above 20% by 1277.

Units of account adapted to reflect exchange rates.

In a pattern that recurred again and again, the varying exchange rate between the grosso and the penny brought about new units of account: the *lira a fiorini* (by which was meant silver fiorini, or grossi) represented a particular quantity of grossi, while the *lira di*

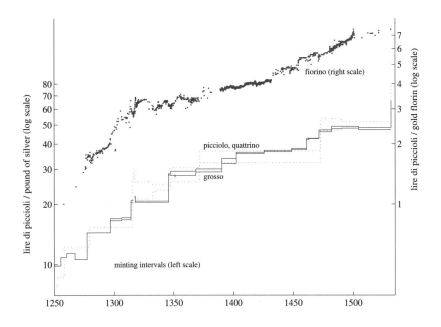

Figure 9.1 Evolution of the mint equivalents and mint prices of the small coins: picciolo (1d.) until 1332, quattrino (4d.) after, and large silver coins: grosso until 1504, barile after, Florence, 1252–1531. Against the right scale, price of the gold florin. *Sources*: Bernocchi 1976, Spufford 1986.

piccioli consisted of 240 pence. The authorities (in this case, the major guilds) tried to fix the exchange rate between grossi and the gold florin, an effort whose consequence was that the *lira a fiorini* became a unit of account tied to the gold florin.[2]

Figure 9.1 summarizes some of Florence's subsequent monetary history. It plots the price of the gold florin in terms of the small coin, the *lira di piccioli*, and also shows the mint equivalent (e_i/b_i in our model) and mint price ($e(1-\sigma)/b_i$ in our model) of a small silver coin, the quattrino, and a large one, the grosso in its various incarnations.[3] The series share an upward trend, while the gold

---

[2] See the passage in chapter 7 on ghost monies.

[3] The name *grosso* designates any of a number of large silver coins, worth from 12d. to 80d. depending on the time period. The *guelfo* is the name of one particular variety of grosso. Tables 9.2 and 9.3 list the various types of silver coins

content of the florin remained almost unchanged throughout the period.[4]

The Quattrini affair

Time series of minting, melting intervals for Florentine silver coins

For much of the fourteenth century, figure 9.1 traces the boundaries of the melting and minting intervals for two silver coins, the quattrino and the grosso. The year-by-year observations on mint prices and mint equivalents underlying the plot are recorded in table 9.2 in appendix A of this chapter. Until 1332, the small coin in Florence was the picciolo (1d.). Thereafter it was mainly the quattrino (4d.). Though piccioli continued to circulate and were minted occasionally, in practice, the quattrino played the role of small change against the grosso (worth 60d.) and the gold florin (worth around 65s. or 780d.). A reform in 1347 had reset the intervals of the quattrino and grosso as shown in the top portion of figure 9.2. Figure 9.2 also shows, in the form of square marks, those semesters during which mint accounts indicate production of a particular coin. These marks incorporate two types of information: numerical records of quantities minted for particular years, and reports from numismatists that a particular coins was minted in a given year. The year-by-year data for both types of evidence are displayed in table 9.4 in appendix A. In our model, a coin is minted when the price level reaches the lower bound of a coin's interval. The middle panel of figure 9.2 shows our estimate of the price level (see appendix B of this chapter), while the bottom panel shows the market quotations of the exchange rate. We shall refer to figure 9.2 to explain some things about the Quattrini affair, and a timing puzzle that we have not yet resolved.

Although the Quattrini affair occurred at the end of the period

---

issued in Florence.

[4] Strictly speaking, our model assumes that the technological rate of transformation between the metals used in large and small coins is constant, which is true when silver is used in both. In the case of the florin, the gold/silver ratio fluctuated over time. Over the long term, however, the ratio was stable, as the roughly constant gap between the series in figure 9.1 shows.

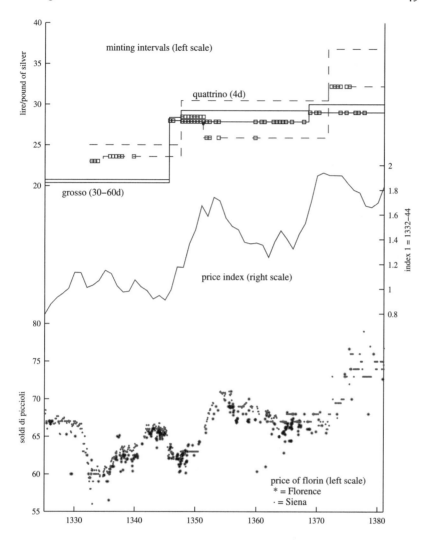

Figure 9.2 (1) Upper and lower bounds on the picciolo, quattrino, and grosso. Minting activity is represented by a square coinciding with the minting bound of a coin for a given semester (appendix A). (2) Consumer price index constructed with a Kalman filter (see appendix B). (3) Price of gold florin in Florence and Siena (Spufford, 1986). Florence, 1325–81.

covered by figure 9.2, we note that the minting intervals for the quattrino were set above those of the grosso when the former was introduced as a new coin in 1332. Only with the reform of 1347 were the two aligned. As the model predicts, no minting of grossi was recorded before 1347, and there are contemporary reports of grossi disappearing after 1332. The motive for issuing the quattrino was "a great scarcity of silver, the fact that payments of small pennies by merchants are greatly delayed, and the fact that it is expedient to have presently a new coin of small denomination in order to supply the needs of merchants and craftsmen of the city and district of Florence" (Bernocchi 1974, 49). Ultimately, however, the scarcity and exporting of grossi prompted the reforms of 1345 and 1347 (Bernocchi 1976, 178–85).

The mint records indicate that after the 1347 reform, both silver grossi and smaller coins (quattrini and piccioli) were minted in large quantities. Eventually, the flows of coinage dried up, and by 1366 foreign pennies, mainly Pisan, were invading Florence, prompting a 36% devaluation of the Florentine picciolo. Despite that, more foreign quattrini and grossi invaded Florence in 1367 and 1368, prompting further responses of the Florentine authorities. A limited debasement of the grosso in 1368, registered in a shift in the interval in figure 9.2, generated only little minting, as indicated in table 9.4. By 1370, the invasion of Pisan quattrini was large enough for the authorities to justify a substantial debasement of the quattrino. As figure 9.2 shows, that debasement put the interval for the quattrino entirely above that for the grosso.

Misaligned intervals provoked coin shortages.   From 1371 to 1403, the interval for the quattrino lay significantly above that for the grosso. Our model predicts that this would spell trouble. Cipolla's account of "the Quattrini affair" confirms it.[5]

Our theory implies the following consequences of putting the interval for the quattrini above that for the grossi: (a) quattrini would be coined, (b) the price level would move upward into the interval for the quattrini, and (c) grossi would disappear. Quattrini

---

[5] See Cipolla's detailed account (1982, 63–85), from which we borrow another beautiful chapter title, and La Roncière (1983, 429–520) on this period.

were indeed minted in large quantities: in the following three years, the mint records (which survive for four out of six semesters) show that £387,000 of quattrini were minted, which is 50% more than the total minting of grossi in the whole decade 1360–69. (See table 9.4 in appendix A for the numbers.) While there was substantial minting of quattrini, as our model would predict, table 9.4 suggests that only small amounts of grossi were minted. Even that small amount puzzles us because when the interval for quattrini is entirely above that for grossi, as in this case, our model predicts *zero* minting of grossi, at least if the minting is done on private and not government account.

Price level movements are shown in the middle portion of figure 9.2, which plots a commodity price index for the period (see appendix B for the method of computation). The bottom panel plots observations of the price of the gold florin over the same period. Both the florin and commodities rose, although the latter seemed to peak before the debasement. Our model predicts that the price level and the exchange rate would move together. The main puzzle for us is the failure of the exchange rate to rise with the price level in the years immediately before 1370. The invasions of foreign small coins that occurred immediately before 1370, representing the 'endogenous debasement' described above, should have increased the price level, as indeed occurred. But our model tells us that to set off that invasion, the exchange rate (the price of grossi in terms of quattrini) should first have risen, which seems not to have occurred. Thus, though it captures many features of this episode, our model misses the detailed timing. We leave the solution of this puzzle to future research.[6]

---

[6] La Roncière studied prices closely and had difficulty tracing the impact of debasements on prices: "whichever coin dominates (picciolo, quattrino, grosso), the alterations it undergoes never have any significant impact on prices" (ibid., 494); "it sometimes happens that the increase in prices anticipates the weakening of the strong currency. The official alteration comes as endorsement of an earlier evolution which has taken place through the abandonment of the strong currency in favor of the clipped version of itself and, thereafter, mainly for illegally imported foreign coins" (ibid., 499).

The rise in prices around 1370 had important political ramifications. The Ciompi revolt of 1378 established a popular government committed to reversing the inflation. It pursued an anti-inflation policy in the form of an effort to reduce the money stock. The government bought back quattrini from October 1380 to February 1382. Within our model, that policy makes sense, though not too much could have been expected of it: a "quantity theory" policy could move the price level downward within the band determined by b_i, σ_i, but could not drive it outside that band.

Ghost monies as legal tender and unit of account

Our model links the problem of small change to the structure of the cash-in-advance constraints: small coins can be used for large purchases but large coins cannot be used for small purchases. We take those cash-in-advance constraints as given, but view them as emerging from the exchange technologies prevailing in the market. However, the government of Florence seems to have tried to alter those exchange relations by declaring exchange rates at which coins constituted legal tender. In this section, we describe how such interventions failed to achieve their goals, but had the unintended effect of creating ghost monies, units of account not corresponding to physical objects.

Traces of those efforts to define legal tenders appear in figure 9.3, which plots prices of the gold florin from 1390 to 1535. Physically, the gold florin was virtually immutable over time.[7] The ambiguity conveyed by figure 9.3 reflects the sometimes simultaneous existence of incorporeal florins, the ghosts of florins past.

In the graph, dots represent "market" prices, either direct observations of the currency market,[8] or exchange rates used in private

---

[7] The florin's weight was higher by 0.4% from 1422 to 1433, a difference that hardly matters, since the standard deviation of the monthly market price series in Spufford (1986, 19–23) is between 0.5 and 1%. A florin 5% below the standard was very briefly minted in 1402, without causing much notice.

[8] Bernocchi (1978) has published the quotations officially recorded by the city

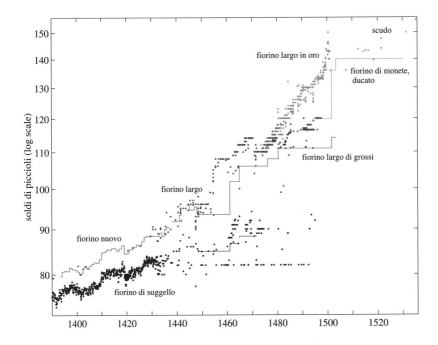

Figure 9.3 Price of various *fiorini d'oro* (*dots*) and some official legal tender values (*lines*) in terms of the silver-based *lira di piccioli*, 1390–1535. *Sources*: Spufford (1986, 11–32), Goldthwaite and Mandich (1994, 97–106), Bernocchi (1976, 274–300).

transactions and recorded in account books. Notice the same upward trend in the market prices, a trend already displayed in figure 9.1. The graph also displays horizontal lines that illustrate a sequence of decisions by Florentine authorities to set legal tender values for gold and silver coins. Figure 9.3 shows that those actions did not prevent the rise in the price of gold coins. However, they did generate several ghost monies. Each time the authorities set a legal tender value for a gold florin, a ghost florin of the same name emerged as a silver-based unit of account, based on the legislated rate. A new name was coined to designate the real coin, and the entire process was later repeated. The names of these ghost monies (*fiorino di suggello, fiorino largo,*

---

for the florin on a daily basis from 1389 to 1432.

fiorino largo in oro) are on the graph.

That market prices usually stood above legal tender values suggests how ineffective these actions were, at least in fixing the exchange rate e_t. One can interpret these actions as mitigating the distributional effects of movements in e_t. The political consequences of the rise in the florin in 1378 seems to have preoccupied Florentine officials more than Venetian officials who, as we will see in chapter 10, were content to let the ducat drift. We are tempted to interpret the distinct actions of the Florentine officials as reflecting an emerging understanding that the rising market premium on florins was somehow linked to the structure of demand for various denominations.[9]

Florentine ghost monies: details

Units of account evolved despite governments' attempts to restrict them.
We now consider the precise nature of these ghost monies and the restrictions that legal tender laws placed on them.[10] We begin with the *fiorino di suggello,* or "sealed florin." In 1294, the city created an office for the certification of gold florins. A set of florins meeting a certain standard of minimum weight was placed in a bag and the bag then sealed by a city officer. The sealed florins were exchanged without being taken out of the bag, and did not need to be weighed or assayed when priced.[11] By the late fourteenth century, the use of sealed florins was common enough that they were the implicit reference for many entries in account books that simply referred to "gold florins." The daily quotations for 1389 to 1432 published by Bernocchi (1978) are plotted in figure 9.3 with the label "fiorino di suggello." The intrinsic content of these sealed florins is not exactly known, but was probably somewhat less than a freshly minted florin (*fiorino nuovo*), because the latter commanded a premium over a sealed florin.

From 1386 to 1464, in a sequence of remarkable operations, the

---

[9] As our model of "within the intervals shortages" says it is. See part V.

[10] The history of these units of account is in Bernocchi (1976, 275–300) and Goldthwaite and Mandich (1994).

[11] In seventeenth- and eighteenth-century Japan, gold and silver coins were wrapped in paper and sealed by the mint and by money-changers; the resulting gold and silver wraps circulated unopened.

city authorities assigned a value to this premium, increasing it over time from 5 to 20%. These legal premia are plotted in figure 9.3 with the label "fiorino nuovo" by augmenting the average market value of the sealed florin. The likely explanation is that, by the 1430s, the government had ceased to seal florins and they no longer denoted physical objects, but were instead gold-based units of account whose value the government set as a fraction of the real gold coin; or, equivalently, the government was assigning a legal tender value to the gold coin when tendered in payment of the unit of account. Since the real gold coin's content was unchanged, the increasing premia represented an effort on the part of the government to lower the gold content of the sealed florin as unit of account. These decreases were presumably intended to offset the increase in the florin's price in terms of silver, that is, to stabilize the value of the sealed florin in terms of silver.

In 1448, the government changed directions and began directly to fix the gold-based unit of account in terms of silver, making fixed quantities of silver coins legal tender for debts denominated in the unit of account. The result of these actions was to turn the sealed florin into a silver-based unit of account, whose price was adjusted a few times before it was abolished in 1471. Corresponding to this, a cluster of prices can be seen in the lower part of figure 9.3, trailing off at a roughly constant level in silver soldi, and disappearing in the late fifteenth century. Meanwhile, the *fiorino largo* or "wide florin" (a slightly wider florin minted from 1422 to match the size of the Venetian ducat) became synonymous with the real gold coin.

In 1464, the government turned to the wide florin and set its legal tender value in silver. Eventually, the "wide florin" became another silver-based unit of account (ultimately called *fiorino largo di grossi* or "wide florin in silver grossi"), while another expression was coined to refer to the actual gold object: *fiorino largo d'oro in oro* or "wide gold florin in gold" (it was also called *ducato* because it was interchangeable with the Venetian ducat). The result in figure 9.3 is a bifurcation of florin prices around 1480, with the gold-based unit continuing its ascent, and the silver-based unit stabilizing.

This process repeated itself yet another time, when, in 1501, the government also tried to make silver legal tender for debts in "wide florins in gold": it, too, became a silver-based unit of account, called *ducato* or *fiorino di monete*, and individuals referred to the real gold coin as a *scudo*. The various legal tender provisions enacted in the fifteenth century are listed in table 9.1, mention being made of the transactions to which each provision applied.

These legal tender laws were passed in response to the rising price of the gold coin. The silver grosso was debased by 7.3% in 1402, 2.2% in 1425, 2.2% in 1448, 12.4% in 1461, by 10.2% in 1471 and by 4.3% in 1481 (see table 9.3). Comparing this with table 9.1 shows that debasements were always accompanied by a change in legal tender laws. The debasements were prompted by scarcity of silver, as the official announcements make clear. In 1448, they cite a scarcity of good grossi, displaced "for the most part" by grossi of Siena of lower fineness and weight. In 1470, a "great lack" of grossi was blamed on the fact that "grossi newly made are just as soon melted and exported" and brought back in the form of foreign coins, from Rome and Naples. Complaints of invasions of foreign black money in 1490 led to a debasement of the quattrino; in 1494, the scarcity of grossi was cited to justify making gold legal tender for silver-denominated debts (Goldthwaite and Mandich 1994, 175, 187, 191–92).

It is particularly interesting to note the attempts made to break the substitutability of silver and gold coins in payments. In 1462, when the soldino (a small coin worth four quattrini) was created, the law defined "important payments" to be those arising out of letters of exchange, government debt, dowries, or sales of real estate or jewelry, for which only gold and large silver coins could be used. The soldini were legal tender for 12d. each only in other payments. In 1464, the city went further and restricted silver grossi to small payments. The experiment quickly failed, and six months later the city made silver legal tender for all payments, large and small.

Table 9.1 Legal tender laws in Florence, fifteenth century. The table shows the rate at which certain coins (gold or silver) could be tendered for a debt denominated in a certain unit (*lira, fiorino di suggello, fiorino largo*), and in which type of payment. A rate of x% means that the (gold) florin could be tendered for $1 + x/100$ account florins. An asterisk denotes a measure that was announced as temporary.

Date	Units owed	Tender	Rate	Payment
1393 (24 Apr)	f di suggello	f nuovo (g)	+5%	
1402 (10 Jun)	f di suggello	f nuovo (g)	+6¼%	
1405	lira di piccioli	f di suggello (g)	73s. 4d.	n.a.
1415 (13 Nov)	lira di piccioli	f di suggello (g)	77s. 4d.	to govt.
1422 (6 May)	f di suggello	f nuovo, f largo (g)	+6⅔%	
1432	f di suggello	f largo (g)	+8¾%	
1442 (23 Dec)	{ f di suggello	f nuovo (g)	+8%	
	f di suggello	f largo (g)	+10%	
1448 (20 Oct)	f di suggello	grossi (s)	85s.	to govt.
1453 (1 Feb)	f di suggello	grossi (s)	85s.	all
1461 (14 Feb)	{ f di suggello	grossi (s)	86s. 8d.	all
	f di suggello	f largo (g)	+17½%	all
1462 (10 Apr)	f di suggello	soldini (s)	87s.	all small
1464 (30 May)	{ f di suggello	grossi (s)	*market*	all small
	f di suggello	f largo (g)	+20%	all large
1464 (9 Sep)	f di suggello	grossi (s)	86s. 8d.	all
1464 (24 Nov)	f di suggello	grossoni (s)	88s.	by govt
1464 (12 Dec)	{ f di suggello	grossi (s)	88s. 4d.	all small
	f largo	grossi (s)	106s.	all large
1470 (15 Feb)	lira di piccioli	f largo (g)	106s.	to govt.
1471 (21 Jun)	f di suggello	grossi (s)	*market*	all large
1471 (22 Oct)	f di suggello	f largo (g)	+20%	all
1471 (22 Oct)	f largo	all silver	*market*	all small
1476 (21 Mar)	f largo	grossi (s)	108s.	by govt.
1476 (21 Mar)	f largo	quattrini (s)	109s.	by govt.
1480 (21 Jun)*	f largo	grossoni (s)	111s.	to govt.
1491 (6 Aug)	f di grossi	grossoni (s)	111s.	all large
1494 (17 Mar)*	f di grossi	f d'oro in oro (g)	+8%	all
1501 (14 Oct)	{ f di grossi	f d'oro in oro (g)	+19%	all large
	f di grossi	all silver	114s. 2d.	all small

Sources: Targioni Tozzetti 1775, 337 n237, Vettori 1738, 299–318, Bernocchi 1974, 314, 324, 342–43, 355–56; Bernocchi 1976, 296.

Concluding remarks

The Quattrini affair has supplied us with a virtual laboratory for illustrating the mechanics of our model of the medieval monetary system. Depreciations and debasements of small coins were woven together as the authorities struggled to realign coins' minting and melting points that had been disrupted by depreciations of the small coins. By the mid-fourteenth century the authorities knew enough about their money supply mechanism to understand that debasements offered at least temporary relief for shortages. By the time of the Ciompi revolt in 1378, the authorities also understood the possible eventual inflationary consequences of those debasements. Committed to a commodity money throughout the denomination structure, policy makers used their flawed remedies for shortages of small change as best they could. We have also seen how policy makers' efforts to manipulate exchange rates kept actual exchange rates unaltered but left a trail of ghost monies, bookkeeping entries that testified to traders' ingenuity in undoing the effects intended by the policy makers.

Appendix A: mint equivalents and mint prices

We follow the figures in Bernocchi (1976) for coin specifications and mint prices (tables 9.2 and 9.3), with some modifications described here.

The early history of Florentine coinage is poorly documented. We do not have actual minting orders until the early fourteenth century. The fineness of the coins can be documented from money-changers' lists of coins of the early fourteenth century (e.g., La Roncière 1973, 254; Bernocchi 1976, 128). The weight of the coins is a matter of conjecture. [12]

---

[12] Bernocchi's method for guessing the weights relies on combining prices of the florin with gold/silver ratios to infer weights of silver coins from the known

Table 9.2 Mint equivalents and mint prices of small silver coins in Florence, in soldi per pound (339.54g) of *popolino* silver (95.8% or 958‰ fine). The *resa* is the number of coins paid by the mint per pound of metal of the requisite fineness. Fineness is expressed in thousandths (‰).

Date	Name	value (d)	fine (‰)	coins per lb	*resa* per lb	ME (s/lb)	MP (s/lb)
1182	d. pisano	1	250	480		7.67	n.a.
1252	d. senese	1	222	480		8.63	n.a.
1258	pic. vecchio	1	156	480		12.27	n.a.
1279	pic. nuovo	1	125	480		15.33	n.a.
1315 (15 May)	picciolo	1	83	540	444	25.88	21.28
1366 (22 Jun)		1	83	840	660	40.25	31.63
1371 (30 Sep)		1	82	864	708	42.28	34.65
1417 (1 Nov)		1	83	996		47.73	n.a.
1472 (6 Nov)		1	21	864	252	165.60	48.30
1491 (30 Jun)		1	21	864		165.60	n.a.
1332 (1 May)	quattrino	4	167	261	240	25.01	23.00
1334 (15 Aug)		4	167	261	246	25.01	23.58
1347 (28 Jul)		4	167	318	297	30.48	28.46
1351 (13 Mar)		4	167	318	270	30.48	25.88
1371 (30 Sep)		4	167	384	336	36.80	32.20
1472 (6 Nov)		4	125	420	366	53.67	46.77
1490 (23 Apr)	quattr. bianco	5	167	432		51.75	n.a.
1491 (30 Jun)	quattr. nero	4	125	420		53.67	n.a.
1509 (25 Oct)		4	83	420		80.50	n.a.
1533 (7 Nov)		4	83	420		80.50	n.a.
1462 (13 Apr)	soldino	12	500	460	446	44.08	42.74
1471 (21 Jun)		12	500	505	483	48.40	46.29
1490 (23 Apr)		12	500	505		48.40	n.a.

There is substantial evidence that Tuscan pennies were minted at the same number of coins per pound (480) from the twelfth to the

weight of the florin. Our model cautions against this method, particularly in the absence of free minting. Furthermore, the gold/silver ratios that Bernocchi uses are in effect themselves derived from prices of the florin (see Castellani 1952, 830, 873), and the method runs the risk of circularity. Indeed, in one instance where Bernocchi uses a florin price of 28s. where Castellani used a price of 29s. to derive the gold/silver ratio, the former concludes that a debasement occurred (Bernocchi 1976, 158).

Table 9.3 Mint equivalents and mint prices of large silver coins, Florence, in soldi per pound of *popolino* silver.

Date	Name	value (d)	fine (‰)	coins per lb	*resa* per lb	ME (s/lb)	MP (s/lb)
1237	fiorino vecchio	12	934	192		9.85	n.a.
1255	fior. di stella	12	906	206		10.89	n.a.
1260	ghibellino	20	885	126		11.36	n.a.
1267	fior. nuovo	12	868	192		10.60	n.a.
1277	guelfo	24	972	146		14.39	n.a.
1296 (3 Oct)	popolino	24	969	171	167	16.92	16.52
1306	popolino	24	958	171	167	17.10	16.70
1314 (1 May)	guelfo del fiore	30	958	167	163	20.88	20.38
1316 (15 May)	bargellino	6	250	313⅛		30.01	n.a.
1317 (30 Jun)	grosso	20	667	183	180	21.92	21.56
1318 (15 Jan)		30	958	166	163	20.75	20.38
1345 (19 Aug)	guelfo	48	958	142	140	28.40	28.00
1347 (19 Jul)		60	958	117	111.6	29.25	27.90
1351 (25 Jan)		60	958	117	110	29.25	27.50
1351 (25 Apr)		60	958	117	111.5	29.25	27.88
1368 (15 Jul)	grosso	24	958	300	290	30.00	29.00
1369 (13 Jun)	guelfo	60	958	120	116	30.00	29.00
1390 (20 May)	grosso	66	958	123	116	33.83	31.90
1402 (30 May)		66	958	132	130	36.30	35.75
1425 (1 Nov)		66	958	135	133	37.13	36.58
1448 (20 Oct)		66	958	138	136	37.95	37.40
1461 (14 Feb)		80	958	128	125⅔	42.67	41.89
1462 (24 Dec)		80	958	128	127.5	42.67	42.50
1471 (21 Jun)		80	958	141	138	47.00	46.00
1481 (21 Nov)		80	958	147	143	49.00	47.67
1490 (23 May)		80	958	147	144	49.00	48.00
1503 (22 Jun)	grossone	84	958	170⅔	166⅔	59.73	58.33
1504 (2 Aug)	carlino	150	958	96⅔	94⅓	60.42	58.96
1506 (3 Jan)	grossone	84	958	173	169	60.55	59.15
1509 (25 Oct)	grossetto	60	958	243⅔	237⅔	60.92	59.42
1510 (15 Feb)	grosso	84	958	173.5	169.5	60.73	59.33
1531 (4 Aug)	barile	160	958	98¾		65.83	

late thirteenth century, and that debasements were carried out by reducing the fineness. The fineness of Tuscan pennies (minted in Pisa, Siena, Lucca) appeared to have remained constant from 1182 to 1250, and a Sienese document of 1250 (Promis 1868, 77) gives us both weight and fineness of pennies of Siena. We simply assume that the specifications given in that document applied earlier, as Herlihy (1974, 185) has surmised. Documents in Paolozzi Strozzi et al. (1992) suggest that Tuscan cities rallied to the standard of Siena in 1257–58, and the money-changers' coin lists cite an "old penny of Siena" at an intermediate fineness: we guess that the Florentine penny of 1258 was minted at that fineness. In 1280, Florence debased again (Gherardi 1896, 1:24, 28) and we identify the new pennies produced at that time with the "denari nuovi" in the coin lists.

For the fiorino vecchio, the fiorino di stella, and the ghibellino, the weight is guessed to match the top of the range of surviving coins, 1.77g, 1.65g, and 2.70g, respectively (Bernocchi 1975); the fiorino nuovo is set at the same weight. The fiorino of 1277 is assumed to be of the same weight as the grosso coined in Siena that year, for which we know the specifications (Promis 1868, 78). The bargellino's weight is set so as to make its value ⅔ of that of the grosso guelfo, to match the contemporary comment by Villani (see Bernocchi 1976, 170). The rest follows Bernocchi (1976), except for the debasement of the grosso in 1448, which is explained in Goldthwaite and Mandich (1994, 176).

Minting

Table 9.4 summarizes existing information on minting activity. The Florentine mint operated on a semester basis (the first semester running from April to October), with different mintmasters in each semester. For some semesters, surviving mint accounts tell us how many coins of each type were minted. But minting records are incomplete in two ways: for some years we only have mention of which denominations were minted but without quantities, and for other years we have no surviving information. In the first case, we denote the unknown but positive quantity by X in the table, and presume that denominations not mentioned were not minted.

Separately, numismatists have been able to date coins by the mintmasters' marks, and have cataloged how many different dies

Table 9.4 Minting activity by semester, 1332–77: quantity minted (in lire) and number of known coin types. X denotes an unknown but positive quantity.

Semester	Grosso minting	Grosso types	Quattrino minting	Quattrino types	Picciolo minting	Picciolo types
1332:I–II	0		X		0	
1333:I	0		X		0	
1334:II–38:I	0		X		0	
1339:II	0		X		0	
1340:II–41:I	0		X		0	
1341:II–44:II	0		0		0	
1345:I	23,228	6	0		0	
1345:II	X	3				
1346:II	0		0		0	
1347:I	66,342	5	11,915	2	0	
1347:II	90,565	9	59,415	6	0	
1348:I	14,069	5	14,241	14	0	
1348:II	61,827	9	7,675	2	0	
1349:I	136,656		22,056		0	
1349:II	140,773	6	16,551	4	0	
1350:I	242,921		10,107		0	
1350:II	301,626	13	1,871	1	0	
1351:I	190,401		6,268		0	
1351:II	8,695		520		0	
1352:II	25,101	8	0		0	
1353:I	13,599	4	0	9	0	
1353:II–58:II	0		0		0	
1359:I	X	3	X	1	0	
1359:II	0		0		0	
1360:I	X	2	0		0	
1360:II	6,423	5	0		0	
1361:II	0		0		0	
1362:I	6,640	1	0		0	
1362:II	38,581	5	0		0	
1363:I	X	7	0		0	
1363:II	41,050	4	0		0	
1364:I	68,504	6	0		0	
1365:I	35,079	5	0		0	
1366:I	0		0		2,415	
1367:I	4,714	3	0		1,995	
1368:I	49,876	14	0		0	
1369:I	X	12	0		0	

Table 9.4 (continued)

Semester	Grosso minting	types	Quattrino minting	types	Picciolo minting	types
1369:II	3,550	10	0		4,855	
1370:I	0		0		1,187	
1371:I	0		0		4,914	
1371:II	0		61,340	7	5,764	
1372:I	0		123,034	11	5,263	1
1372:II				25		
1373:I	6,840	3	161,473		0	
1374:I	0	1	41,564	15	0	7
1374:II			X	13	X	8
1375:II		1				
1376:I	X	4	0		0	
1376:II	0		0		0	
1377:I	X	2	0		0	
1377:II	X		0		0	
1380:II–85:II	0		0		0	

can be identified for each semester (Bernocchi 1975). The number of dies in a semester is an imperfect measure of minting volume. Semesters for which no information of either sort is available are omitted from the table.[13]

Appendix B: a price index for fourteenth-century Florence

The price index used in this chapter was constructed by applying Kalman filtering techniques to a set of price data. The data come from La Roncière (1983). Table 9.5 shows the summary statistics for the series used.

Constructing a price index on the basis of these series presents a number of difficulties. The first one is due to missing data: the

[13] See Cipolla (1982, 75 n22). Known quantities are listed in Bernocchi (1976, 252–58). Unknown but positive quantities are inferred from the original documents (Bernocchi 1974, 48, 56–57, 61–68, 72–77, 91–92, 129–38, 141, 159, 187–96).

Table 9.5 Statistics on available commodity price series, Florence, 1325–81. All series are on a base 1 for 1325–44. *Source*: La Roncière (1983, 821–37).

Commodity	Observations	Mean	Variance
wheat	30	1.26	0.19
barley	42	1.15	0.10
panic	43	1.19	0.21
wine	52	1.58	0.48
kids	31	1.29	0.20
mutton	30	1.57	0.12
chicken	54	1.38	0.18
eggs	50	1.33	0.11
olive oil	53	1.32	0.18
lime	40	1.24	0.07

number of years in the interval is 57, but no series is complete, and some like wheat have substantial gaps. Yet wheat cannot be excluded from the data, since it represented from 26 to 42% of a working family's expenditures (La Roncière 1982, 395).

Another problem stems from the high variance of the series. Wine, which is one of the most complete, is also the most variable series. Wine represented 20 to 30% of an unmarried worker's expenditures (La Roncière 1982, 394). If a consumer price index were attempted, such volatile series would be given a high weight, and their movements would dominate general price level movements. Furthermore, annual series are not available for clothing, housing, and several other important components of a household's typical basket.

One approach is to construct an unweighted average of the available series. An alternative method consists in applying Kalman filtering, which is particularly well suited to handle missing data, and also to recovering common movements in diverse series without taking a stand on the relative weights to apply.

The model is:

$$p_{i,t} = \gamma_i + \beta_i p_t + u_{i,t}$$

$$p_t = \phi p_{t-1} + \epsilon_t$$

$$u_{i,t} = \theta_i u_{t-1} + \eta_{i,t}$$

where $p_{i,t}$ for $i = 1, \ldots, 10$ are the individual price series and p_t is a

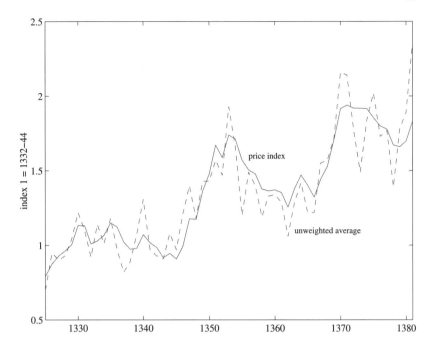

Figure 9.4 Unweighted average of prices (*broken line*) and Kalman-filtered price index (*solid line*).

common factor interpreted as the general price level. The error terms ϵ_t and $\eta_{i,t}$ are assumed normally and independently distributed over time, with no cross-correlations. The parameters γ_i, β_i, ϕ, θ_i, and the variances of ϵ_t and $\eta_{i,t}$ are estimated using maximum likelihood. The series p_t is constructed using the Kalman smoother.

The two approaches are compared in figure 9.4. The Kalman filter index is determined up to a linear transformation of the form $ax + b$. We choose a and b so that the average of the index for 1332–44 and 1372–81 equals that of the unweighted average. The unweighted average is shown by the broken line and displays considerably more variation. The Kalman filter index isolates more clearly the changes in trends.

ℰℐℴ

CHAPTER 10
Medieval Venice

Four episodes

Venice originally used one coin, the penny of Verona. Then starting around 1182, it minted its own penny or *denaro*, a silver coin about 25% fine.[1] In 1201, so the story goes, Venice had exacted ten tons of silver from the leaders of the Fourth Crusade to ferry them to the Holy Land. Turning that mass of metal into pennies at the current standard would have produced 100 million coins. So Venice decided to mint a new silver coin, both heavier and of higher fineness, called the *(denaro) grosso* or "large penny." The penny became known as the *piccolo* or small penny.[2] In 1284, Venice began minting a gold coin known as the ducat, identical in size to the Florentine florin.

Small denomination coins in Venice depreciated in terms of large coins. Figures 10.1 and 10.2 summarize the history of the Venetian monies up to the mid-1450s. For silver coins, figure 10.1 charts the evolution of mint prices $e_i(1 - \sigma_i)/b_i$ and mint equivalents e_i/b_i for the piccolo and the grosso and its successor, the soldino. The graph shows the usual pattern of secular upward movement, reflecting recurrent debasements of the silver coins.

Figure 10.2 shows the market price of the gold ducat in terms of piccoli or equivalents. It displays the same general upward trend we saw in Florence, composed here of sharp accelerations punctuated by periods of stability. The gold content of the ducat, b_2 in our model, remained constant throughout the period. The silver content of silver coins declined, as shown by the mint equivalent of the silver grosso/soldino.

When the standard formula is not or cannot be implemented, our model identifies either a debasement of small coins or a reinforcement

---

[1] This section is mostly based on the account of Lane and Mueller (1985), with some complements from Papadopoli (1893–1909) and Cessi (1937).

[2] Unfortunately, this account of the grosso's origin is doubtful.

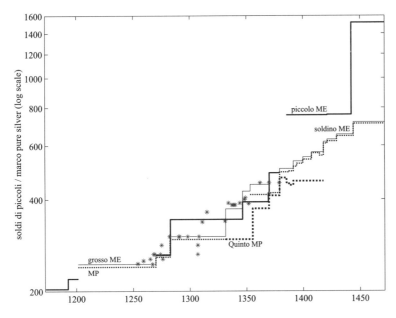

Figure 10.1 Evolution of the mint equivalent (e_i/b_i) and mint price $(e_i(1-\sigma_i)/b_i)$ on small coins (piccolo) and large silver coins (grosso until 1331, soldino and mezzanino after 1331), Venice, 1172–1471 (see the appendix of this chapter). Mint equivalents (ME) are solid, mint prices (MP) are dashed (see page 167 for the *quinto*). The thick solid line corresponds to the piccolo. The thick dashed line plots the price paid for requisitioned silver from 1331 to 1417. The asterisks represent the market price of the grosso in terms of piccoli (Spufford 1986, 85; Lane and Mueller 1985, 1:556, 1:565).

of large coins as a workable policy for keeping both large and small coins in existence. Shortages of small coins occurred in Venice over this period. We shall document how they inspired the frequent exchange rate depreciations and debasements of small coins reflected in figure 10.2.

We shall refer to these figures to discuss four episodes. (1) From 1250 to 1320, the grosso appreciated with respect to the piccolo and there were recurrent shortages of piccoli. (2) From 1285 to 1353, there were fluctuations in the price of gold relative to silver. (3) From 1360 to 1440, the (gold) ducat appreciated with respect to the soldino, a new coin issued around 1331 of size between the grosso

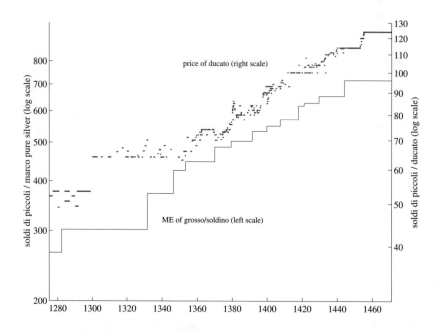

Figure 10.2 Mint equivalent of the silver grosso/soldino (from fig. 10.1, *left scale*), and price of the gold florin (1275–84) and the gold ducat (1285–1471) in silver money (*right scale*), Venice (Lane and Mueller 1985, app. D).

and piccolo. (4) From 1442 to 1457, the government of Venice issued small light coins on its own account that eventually caused inflation. In each episode, Venetian authorities realigned the minting and melting intervals for different coins and also experimented with modifications of the medieval minting institutions. In addition, we discuss an intriguing prelude to episode (4), namely, the Venetian government's issues of overvalued coins intended to circulate in its Greek possessions. Then, as in episode (4), the government of Venice temporarily put in place some but not all elements of the standard formula. Ultimately, in each case those missing elements led the government's emissions of token small coins to cause inflation.

Piccolo and grosso, 1250 to 1320

In this section, we let e denote the exchange rate of the grosso for the piccolo. From 1250 to 1360, e drifted upward in response to recurrent shortages of coins. Sometimes the government tried to remedy the shortage while maintaining the basic coin supply mechanism by debasing the small coin. At other times it tried to change the mechanism, by requisitioning silver for coinage at below market prices. The rises in e were typically "spontaneous," i.e., market determined. However, occasionally the government announced an official e. We regard most of those announcements as belated official confirmations of exchange rates that the market had set.

Soon after the grosso was first issued, authorities set its value at 26d., although it may have been intended initially at 24d. Minting of the piccolo ceased at the same time. The asterisks in figure 10.1 represent the few available observations of the market price of the grosso in that period (or more precisely, the implied mint equivalent of a marc of silver in grossi when computed at a given market price).[3] The exchange rate between grosso and piccolo appears to have been stable for at least two generations at 26 ⅑. However, in the 1250s, an appreciation of the grosso occurred and by 1268 the grosso traded at 28d. An indication that the appreciation of the grosso originated in the short supply of piccoli is a law of May 1268 that made it illegal to export more than £25 in piccoli at a time.

Starting in 1269, important reforms affected the piccolo.[4] In December 1269, the market valuation of 28d. for a grosso was

Depreciations of small denomination coins accompanied recurrent shortages.

---

[3] Lane and Mueller (1985, 556, 565). The "market prices" on page 556 cannot be in soldi a grossi as stated. Instead we interpret them as the value in soldi di piccoli of the mint price of 233 soldi a grossi; we infer a market valuation of the grosso.

[4] The content of the grosso remained unchanged. For the debasements of the piccolo, we follow Cessi (1937, xxix, xxxix) who relies on surviving texts, rather than Lane and Mueller (1985, 497–99) who follow Papadopoli and rely on weights of surviving coins.

officially confirmed; simultaneously, the piccolo's weight was reduced so that its content of silver was ⅟₂₈ that of a grosso. Minting resumed. A law was passed requiring transactions below £50 to be made in piccoli. In the mid-1270s, the minting of piccoli declined again. The export of metal was prohibited in 1274. The grosso's rise resumed, and the city itself used a rate of 32d. in its calculations as early as 1275. Foreign coins minted in Austria were allowed to circulate in 1277, albeit subject to a 5% import tax.[5] In 1282, the grosso's official exchange rate was lowered again to 32d. Simultaneously, the piccolo was debased. This time, however, on the recommendation of mint officials, the piccolo was made lighter than the grosso to cover the piccolo's higher manufacturing costs.

Policies to arrest shortages   In the following years, further measures were adopted to increase minting of piccoli. The government ordered coins from the mint on its own account.[6] For example, the mint was ordered in 1287 to have a reserve fund of £3,000, of which 60% was to be in piccoli, and to pay out piccoli for grossi on request up to £50 per day. Further instructions in 1289 and 1291 ordered the mint to produce piccoli at specific rates (£250, then £500 per month), and a bonus was given to mintmasters for quantities produced in excess of those rates. In 1292, the city raised the mint price for piccoli to the point that seigniorage net of production costs was zero.

Such policies appear to have been successful in arresting the depreciation of piccoli for a long time. The rate of the grosso was maintained at 32d. for about 30 years after 1280. It resumed its rise in the 1310s, and reached 38½d. by 1315. In 1317, the authorities took more measures to increase the production of piccoli, with an order to the mint to produce £1,000 in piccoli every month, with funds appropriated for that purpose. The legal rate of 32d. per grosso was reaffirmed in 1321.

---

[5] In chapter 2 we described these "invasions" of foreign coins as endogenous debasements.

[6] See chapter 2 for a comparison of the consequences of coining on government account versus a regime of unlimited or free minting.

Evolving units of account

As in Florence, a consequence of these exchange rate movements was to create multiple units of account. During the period of the grosso's stable value in terms of piccoli, large payments, although denominated in pence (*lira di denari*), were made indifferently in small coins, with *lira di denari a piccoli*, or in large coins, with *lira di denari a grossi*. These expressions indicated only the type of coin used to make payment for a given sum of piccoli. After the grosso began its sustained appreciation, the form of payment mattered. If the coin composition of the original loan was known, the standard repayment doctrine readily applied: debts should be repaid in coins of the denomination and weight specified in the contract (see chapter 5). But if the original coin was not known, or if wage contracts had not specified a coin of payment, another way to interpret the obligation was required. Two units of account emerged to solve the problem: the *lira di denari a piccoli* continued to contain 240 piccoli (now debased). The *lira di denari a grossi*, which had consisted of $240/26\frac{1}{9}$ grossi for so long, continued to contain $240/26\frac{1}{9}$ grossi (not debased). Debts or contracts denominated in "lire" were then reinterpreted to mean a constant number of piccoli or a constant number of grossi, according to the context, and, presumably, the bargaining power of the parties. Workmen's wages, for example, were indexed to the piccolo. But the wages of city officials, as well as debt payments, were indexed to the grosso. More generally, "the same development probably occurred also in most other accounts of a kind in which payments had been made in grossi" (Lane and Mueller 1985, 130).

Units of account adapted to exchange rates.

Silver and gold, 1285 to 1353

The introduction of a gold coin in 1284 exposed Venice's system of coinage to pressures from swings in the relative price of gold and silver. By shifting the positions of the intervals between the minting and melting points for gold and silver coins, changes in the relative price of gold and silver generated pressures for one coin or the other to be melted or minted. Chapter 11 describes these pressures at work again in France during the sixteenth century.[7]

The coexistence of gold and silver coins added another dimension to exchange rate instability.

In 1285, Venice belatedly followed the example of Florence and issued a gold coin, the ducat. Its weight and fineness matched the florin, although its design was distinct. For the initial run, the mint was authorized to borrow to buy gold; but the mint soon adopted the practice of coining any amount of gold offered at the mint price. A law of 1285 made the ducat legal tender for any debt in grossi, at a rate of 40 soldi a grossi (equivalent to 49 soldi di piccoli in fig. 10.2). The market price of the ducat soon exceeded that official rate.

The relative price of gold to silver changed in the following decades (Spufford 1986, lxii), rising from 11 or 11.5 in 1285 to 15 in the 1320s, at its peak. As a result, the ducat appreciated in terms of both the piccolo and the grosso, reaching 64 soldi di piccoli, or 24 grossi, by 1305. It remained at that level for about 25 years. In 1328, the ducat's legal tender value was officially raised to 24 grossi (or 64 soldi di piccoli), recognizing a now long-standing market value.

Soon after, however, the relative price of gold reversed course, and in the mid-1330s fell from 14 to 11. This sharp depreciation of the ducat's content is not reflected in figure 10.2 because of actions taken by the Venetian authorities. They replaced the grosso with a new coin having a higher mint equivalent, and at the same time requisitioned silver at below-market prices.

Specifically, around 1331, new silver coins called the *mezzanino* and the *soldino* were introduced. Only the soldino became a fixture of the monetary system. Valued at 12d., the soldino stood between the piccolo and the grosso (then around 35 or 36d.). Minting of the grosso slowed considerably, and ended in the 1350s. Ample minting of the soldino and the mezzanino occurred. An indication that shortages of small coins had ended is that the import tax on

---

[7] See chapter 11 for a graphical presentation of intervals for three coins in a bimetallic monetary system.

Austrian coins, which had been repealed in 1332 due to "a need for money," was reinstated in 1338 because "our territory presently has an abundance of coins" (Cessi 1937, 80, 120).[8]

In another departure from the traditional supply mechanisms for coins, the metal supplies for the soldino were secured by imposing a tax on all silver imported into Venice. The tax, called the *quinto*, forced importers to sell 20% of their silver to the mint at a below-market mint price. In figure 10.1, the thick dotted line plots the mint price imposed for silver requisitioned under the quinto. Rather than raising the mint price concurrently with the debasement, authorities maintained it at its previous level by compulsion.

A tax was earmarked to forestall shortages of small change.

The combined effect of the debasement and the quinto was to raise the mint equivalent of silver money, as shown in figure 10.1, and also to widen the interval between the mint equivalent and the effective (cum quinto) mint price. It was soon found, however, that the tax did not provide satisfactory quantities of silver. In 1353, the mint was instructed to coin into soldini all silver offered at a set mint price. That mint price, markedly higher than the price paid on requisitioned silver, is plotted as a normal dotted line in figure 10.1 after 1353. After 1369, the mint price paid on requisitioned silver was brought closer to the market price, and, after the 1390s, it does not appear to have been updated. By then, it was recognized that the quinto was too easily evaded, and the tax was formally abolished in 1417.

The soldino was briefly replaced by a debased mezzanino in 1346, and returned after another devaluation in 1353, minted at the same fineness as the now obsolete grosso. With these operations, the price of the ducat remained stable between 64s. and 70s. The fall of the relative price of gold by a third was matched by a devaluation of

---

[8] Whether the introduction of the soldino was motivated by the impending appreciation of silver, as Lane and Mueller (1985, 392) suggest, or by other difficulties, is not clear. By some accounts, the ducat was rising, not falling, in the years 1329 to 1331 (Cessi 1937, lx). Furthermore, in the account books of the Peruzzi bankers the gold/silver ratio still stood at 14.2 in March 1332, which is the par value for the ducat rated at 24 grossi. By November 1335, in the same source, the ratio had fallen by 20% (Sapori 1934, 108–9).

the silver coinage of the same size (a cumulative 32% from 1331 to 1353).

Adaptation of units of account

An adaptation of the unit of account accompanied the replacement of the grosso as principal silver coin. The lira a grossi, indexed on the grosso, progressively fell out of use and was officially abolished in 1404. Another unit of account tied to the grosso, the *lira di grossi*, contained 240 grossi (in the same way that a *lira di piccoli* contained 240d.). That unit underwent the following transformation. Since the price of the grosso in piccoli had been stable at 32d. from 1282 to the 1310s, a lira di grossi was equivalent to $240 \times 32 = 7680$ piccoli. When the grosso resumed its rise in the 1320s, a unit called the *lira di grossi a monete* (lira di grossi in small coins) made its appearance, containing 7680 piccoli. When the soldino came into circulation at 12d., the lira di grossi a monete became $7680/12 = 640$ soldini. Similarly, in the 1340s, the lira di piccoli became $240/12 = 20$ soldini. The lira di grossi was thus converted from an index of the grosso to an index of the soldino.

Soldino and ducat, 1360 to 1440

More debasements As figure 10.1 shows, the soldino was debased often, in 1369, 1379, 1391, 1399, 1407, 1417, 1421, 1429, and 1444. The cumulative debasement from 1354 to 1444 was 38%. The loss in value of the soldino relative to the gold ducat over the same period was somewhere between 38% and 43%.[9] Our model directs us to look for clues of denomination shortages. These are apparent for the soldino, which largely replaced the now secondary piccolo.

---

[9] Lane and Mueller (1985) give two possible explanations for the depreciation of the soldino. One is the desire to generate seigniorage revenues, but the low net seigniorage rates make this unlikely to be a prime factor. The other is a response to "the rising price of silver" (p. 380), which they attribute to wear and tear of the silver coinage in circulation, although they concede that wear and tear is not sufficient to account for the full extent of the soldino's debasement.

We glean these clues from the laconic preambles to the debasement resolutions taken by the legislative bodies.[10] In 1359 and 1360, complaints about the prevalence of clipped soldini and mezzanini were linked with the observation that gold coins were being exported in large quantities. In 1369, the lack of gold and silver coins was deplored, the good and full-weight coins being exported as soon as they were minted, and only the "vile and bad" coins remaining. In 1368, the melting of soldini was reported: "our soldini are taken out of Venice by some who destroy them for profit, because they can be sold whenever the price of silver reaches £15 7s. per marc, and for this reason these same soldini are lacking, which results in great inconvenience for the whole land and community" (Cessi 1937, 140). The soldino was debased in 1369 to deter melting and "so that there be an abundance of coins, which our territory greatly wants" (Cessi 1937, 144). The order of 1379 made clear the desire to have more coinage, as well as the reluctance to subsidize the mint: "It is useful and good to insure, insofar as can be done without loss for the Commune, that more coins be made" (Cessi 1937, 157).

Monetary difficulties persisted in the following years. Some complaints relate to the shortage or poor quality of the circulating coins. Thus, in 1385, "it is necessary to give attention to the shortage (*strictura*) of coins that is at present in the land, shortage that is extreme as is well known, and particularly for gold coins." In 1387, "it is to the advantage of our land, that as many grossi be made in our mint as possible, also for the good and subsistence of those poor people who work in making coins." Other documents refer to foreign and clipped coins. Measures were taken in 1385 against "extremely poor denari and bad foreign coins." In 1389, it was said that "our silver money and particularly our soldini, as is well known, are clipped and shaved" (Cessi 1937, 160, 181).

England was one destination for exports of soldini. Starting in 1399, English documents mention silver halfpennies brought

Complaints of shortages

Soldini invaded England.

---

[10] Documents up to 1399 are printed in Cessi (1937); later documents are in Bonfiglio Dosio (1984).

from Venice by ship (hence their name of "galley halfpennies"). The Venetian soldino's silver content was about 41% of the English penny's, and soldini circulated in England at ½d. Complaints that 3 or 4 galley pennies "were scarcely equal to one sterling in value" led to prohibitions on their circulation in 1399, 1400, 1409, 1414, 1415, 1423, and as late as 1519 (Ruding 1840, 249, 254, 256, 270, 302).

Other complaints in Venetian documents relate to the drying up of the silver trade. In 1362, it is said that there is only one silver trader left on the Rialto where there used to be eighteen. The 1407 debasement order cites the loss of the silver trade to other venues and the inactivity of the mint. That silver ceased to come to Venice was no doubt linked to the implicit tax that the quinto imposed on silver imports, but the flow of silver was still unsatisfactory after the repeal of the quinto in 1417. The debasement of 1421 was based on the need to "provide for our Mint to coin as much money as possible, for the honor of the city as much as for the support of the poor people, and also to give merchants every possible motive to bring silver to Venice."

The debasement of 1417 was explicitly a response to the fact that silver could not be minted at prevailing prices. The preamble to the debasement decision states that "the orders given to coin money at the rate of £27 4s. per marc, set when the ducat was worth 93s., have not been obeyed for a long time and cannot be obeyed, because making the coins accordingly, no one could bring silver to the mint when the ducat is worth 100s., since they would incur a great loss, and thus silver is never brought to Venice" (Bonfiglio Dosio 1984, 95). This statement explicitly links the unprofitability of coining metal to the high exchange rate between the ducat and the silver coinage, and presents debasement as a response to misaligned intervals.

Difficulties extended beyond the soldino to include the piccolo. The policy concerning that coin is not well documented before 1369. At that date, we learn that the mint was then coining piccoli at a loss, and the Venetian Senate thought it "not good that money be coined by the Commune at its expense" (Cessi 1937, 147). The piccolo was debased, and its mint equivalent aligned with that of the soldino. Few, if any, coins appear to have been coined at the time, however.[11] In 1379, the piccolo's weight and content were reduced again, to make them light relative to the soldino. An order was to be issued by the Signoria calling for the demonetization of all existing small coins, including old Venetian piccoli. A period of one month was allowed during which old piccoli could be exchanged for new light ones, one for one, at the mint. The order was not issued in 1379, however, but a version of it was issued in 1385. Once the delay for exchanging the coins expired, officials were under orders to search and confiscate the demonetized coins, with the right to keep the demonetized coins they found and to receive a new coin for each old coin they found, as a reward (Cessi 1937, 163, 176). To insure that minting of piccoli took place, the mint was required to pay for requisitioned silver partly in new piccoli. Table 10.2 lists the proportions in which the mint was required to make those payments. The mix was more heavily weighted toward smaller coins in periods of debasements.

The rise of the ducat's price led to a new generation of units of account, one indexed to the ducat, the other to silver money. So long as the ducat's price remained relatively stable at 64s. or above in the 1340s, its daily fluctuations had been recorded in account books with the use of a variable premium. When the ducat's price began to rise permanently in the 1350s, another unit of account emerged to represent a constant quantity of gold. The *lira di grossi*, which, as we saw earlier, contained 240 grossi, begat the *lira di grossi a monete*, based on the stable exchange rate of the grosso to the *monete* of the early fourteenth century. Similarly, the ducat's value in grossi had long been stable at 24 grossi; thus, the *lira di grossi* had also come to mean 10 ducats. When the ducat's valuation rose, the *lira di grossi a oro* continued to represent 10 ducats, independently of the silver coins.

New units of account emerged.

---

[11] Papadopoli does not know of any piccolo minted under Andrea Contarini (1368–82) but Majer (1933) describes one, probably minted after 1379.

Figure 10.3 Exogenous increase in Venice's stock of m, prosaically known as Juno bestowing her gifts on Venice, by Valentin Lefebvre after Paolo Veronese. (Author's collection).

Rehearsing fiat money

The following two sections describe two episodes in which the monetary authorities tampered with the supply mechanism to let them issue coins whose exchange value substantially exceeded their intrinsic value. In these episodes, "fiat money" and the "quantity theory of money" appeared.

Light coins were made on government account.

Between 1453 and 1455, the price of the ducat in terms of silver coins rose sharply. This rise was associated with the government's recently having issued large numbers of overvalued small denomination coins for Venice's newly acquired mainland territories.[12] Those coins eventually came to circulate inside Venice. Having been coined on government account to circumvent the normal supply mechanism and the costly discipline imposed by the minting and melting points, excessive issues of those coins caused inflation via a pure quantity theory effect. Soon thereafter, the monetary authorities of Venice, disliking inflation, terminated coining these light coins for the territories on government account. They reinstated the normal supply mechanism, and resisted further proposals to issue light coins on government account.

We compare and contrast that episode with an earlier one in Venice's possessions in Greece. There the Venetian government also issued light small coins on government account. In those isolated Greek possessions, the Venetian monetary authorities held a virtual monopoly on supplying small change, so that market values of light coins above their intrinsic value could be sustained if the government limited their supply. The government managed to do this for some time, but eventually additional issues caused the coins to depreciate toward their intrinsic value. The inflationary effects of this depreciation were reflected in the price of the Venetian ducat in terms of the small currency in Greece. But the effects were confined to Greece because those small coins did not circulate outside Greece.

---

[12] This episode is studied in Mueller (1980). See also Papadopoli (1893–1909, 1:235–36, 259–68, 276, 283–86; 2:573).

However, during the later experiment with light coins in territories adjacent to Venice, quantity-of-coins-induced inflation in the adjacent territories was transmitted quickly to Venice because coins from the territories came to Venice.

The torneselli in Greece

Venice minted overvalued coins for its Greek possessions. After the fall of Constantinople in 1204, the Byzantine empire was divided among the victors, leading to the creation of a number of Latin states in Greece. Venice also acquired territories in Greece, mainly islands including Crete. In the following decades, the currency in Greece consisted of coins imported from western Europe or minted by the Latin states in imitation of the "tournois" penny of their native France. By the mid-fourteenth century, local mints in Greece had become inactive. In 1353, Venice started minting a new billon coin, the *tornesello* ("tournois" in Italian), intended only for the Venetian territories in Greece. Too light to be minted through the usual mechanism,[13] it was minted on government account and soon became the only small coin in the region.[14] Worth 3d., its mint equivalent was about 900s. to the marc, twice overvalued compared to the soldino.

At first, the government restrained the supply of torneselli enough to keep their value high. From 1383 to 1400, under the reign of

[13] Since it was overvalued, its mint price was too low.

[14] The tornesello was extensively studied by Stahl (1985), whom we follow here, with the following exception. The minting order of 1353 appears to specify a fineness of 1⁄9 and weight of 320 coins per marc. However, the surviving torneselli studied by Stahl match the fineness but fall far short of the weight, something that cannot be explained by error or deceit persisting over decades. The mean weights in hoards documented by Stahl (1985, 31, 72–76) might suggest a decline in the weight from 380 per marc to 460 per marc, but there are no documented weight reductions and the standard deviations are large enough to be consistent with a constant weight of 400 to the marc. Furthermore, the tornesello was intended to replace a local Greek coin, the tornesello of Morea, which is known to have been coined at 400 to the marc and 5⁄24 fine (Pegolotti 1936, 116). It is plausible that the Venetians would have issued a coin of same weight, but half as fine. We thus assume throughout that the weight of the tornesello was 400 to the marc.

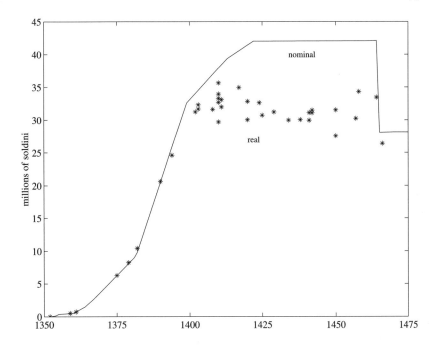

Figure 10.4 Real and nominal stock of torneselli, 1353–1475. *Source*: see text.

Doge Antonio Venier (who, incidentally, had served as governor of Crete just before his election as doge), the annual output of torneselli increased significantly. Production fell back to negligible amounts by the 1420s. The solid line in figure 10.4 plots the cumulative output of torneselli, and the increase in production under Doge Venier is visible as a steep increase in the nominal stock of torneselli.[15]

Officially, the tornesello's value in Venetian money was constant at 3d., or 4 torneselli to the soldino. But starting at the end of the fourteenth century, the quotation of the ducat in Greece, expressed in torneselli, deviated from that of the ducat quoted in soldini in

[15] Stahl (1985, 46, 51) provides an index of annual tornesello output for each doge's reign from 1353 to 1471, and an estimate of the annual output around 1400, allowing us to scale the former by the latter. We then cumulate annual production into an annual series of the outstanding stock, in torneselli, which are converted to "nominal" soldini at the official rate of 4 torneselli per soldino until 1464, and 6 thereafter.

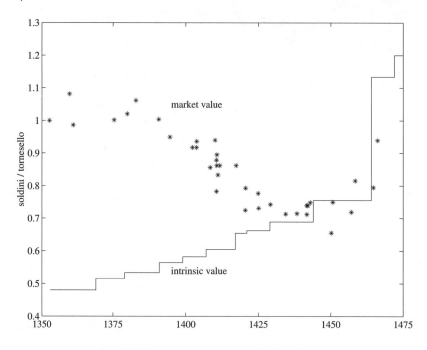

Figure 10.5 Market value and intrinsic value of the tornesello in soldini, 1353–1475. The market value is represented by the ratio of the ducat's price in Venice (in soldini) to the ducat's price in Greece (in torneselli). The intrinsic value is represented by the ratio of the soldino's mint equivalent to the tornesello's mint equivalent. *Source*: Stahl (1985, 87–90).

Venice, signaling a fall in the market value of the tornesello relative to the soldino. We used these quotations to infer a "market value" of the tornesello relative to the soldino, shown in figure 10.5, and to compute the real value of the stock of torneselli in figure 10.4.[16] Figure 10.5 also presents the "intrinsic value" of the tornesello, that is, the soldino value of its silver content. The upward movement in the intrinsic value reflects the progressive debasements of the soldino; the tornesello, to our knowledge, was not altered, until the Venetian authorities changed its official valuation to 6 per soldino in 1464.

---

[16] The stock in torneselli is converted into "real" soldini by dividing by Stahl's (1985, 87–90) prices for the ducat in Greece, in torneselli per ducat, and multiplying by Lane and Mueller's (1985, app. D) prices for the ducat in Venice, in soldini per ducat.

Figures 10.4 and 10.5 show that for a long time the tornesello circulated above its intrinsic value. Figure 10.4 shows that for a long time increases in the cumulative (nominal) stock of torneselli issued were matched by increases in their real value. But after 1410, further issues of torneselli became inflationary, with the real stock of torneselli remaining roughly constant or drifting down. The evaporation of the fiat component of its value was accompanied by an appreciation of the ducat in terms of torneselli. That pattern would be repeated years later in Spain and France, as we shall see when later we discuss figures 14.4 on page 241 and 14.7 on page 247. Figure 10.5 shows that, by 1425, the profit on minting torneselli had disappeared; not surprisingly, the government then stopped producing torneselli.

The inflationary effects of the torneselli were confined to Greece. The ducat did not rise in terms of the soldino because the torneselli did not circulate in Venice. Thus, these disturbances to small change in its Greek territories did not transmit themselves back to Venice. We turn next to an episode in which policy-induced disturbances in the small change designed for possessions adjoining Venice did raise the price of the ducat in Venice.

For years, the tornesello maintained a value exceeding its intrinsic content, without inflation. Then inflation emerged.

Expansion near Venice

Eventually Venice's "monetary imperialism" extended to new landward possessions "da terra" much as it had earlier on the seaward possessions "da mar" in Greece (Mueller 1980). This section describes fluctuations in the price of the ducat emanating from disturbances to the small change of nearby territories that Venice had acquired. At first Venice supplied these territories with new coins whose mint prices and mint equivalents did not threaten to displace the small coins in Venice; that is, the intervals for these new coins were set not to trigger an "invasion" of small change from the adjacent territories.[17] However, later the government of Venice made light coins

The tornesello episode rehearsed a later experiment near the Venetian heartland.

---

[17] Again, see our interpretation of "invasions" of foreign small change in terms

for the territories on government account.[18]   Those coins invaded Venice, eventually leading to an appreciation of the ducat in Venice itself.

In 1405, Venice acquired Vicenza and Verona. Those cities had a different monetary system, the local lira being worth a third more than the Venetian lira. Venice initially extended its own monetary system to the territories. The existing Venetian coins were given legal tender values in local units to conform with the 4:3 exchange rate between Venetian and Veronese lira. New coins were also created, intended for circulation outside of Venice: a full-weight *soldo*, minted to circulate at 12d. of the Veronese lira, and a lightweight penny or *bagatino*, with slightly less than the intrinsic content of ⅓ of a Venetian *piccolo* of the time. The result was merely to adapt Venetian coinage to the local units, along with a one-time modest profit of a recoinage.

In 1442, at the onset of a long armed conflict with Milan that was to last until the peace of Lodi in 1454, the bagatino was debased by cutting its fineness in half. The Venetian piccolo, which circulated in nearby mainland towns like Treviso and Padua, was also debased, as shown on figure 10.1. The motivation for the debasement is noteworthy: "Whereas it is in our Signoria's interest, in this time of penury of money, to regain money by all honest ways and means; and bagatini were formerly coined in our mint for use in Brescia, Bergamo, Verona and Vicenza, with ⅑ silver, stamped with various designs according to the destination; and because these coins are now wanting, some coins from the duchy of Milan called *sesini*, which are silvered but otherwise pure copper, have become current in our territory beyond the Mincio. And if said bagatini were made with 1/18 silver, it would bring great advantage and profit to our Commune" (Papadopoli 1893–1909, 1:259).[19]   The Venetian officials in the

---

of "spontaneous debasements" in chapter 2.

[18] As we explained in chapter 2, coining light coins on government account so widens the intervals that protection against inflation must be provided not by the price guarantee afforded by the intervals but by a limitation on the quantity of the coins supplied.

[19] Note Cipolla's sardonic comment on the "honest means," cited by Mueller

said cities were ordered to use the new coins to replace old bagatini and ship them back to Venice. They were also instructed to make about 5% of their payments in the new coins.

Issues of these coins were thus clearly tied to fiscal needs: they came and went with wars. After peace was made in 1443, further issues of bagatini were forbidden. In 1447, 3,000 marcs (about 1,800 ducats) of bagatini were ordered for Brescia. In 1451, minting was suspended, but resumed two months later, "contrary orders notwithstanding," when the mint was asked to come up with £42,000 (7,000 ducats) in piccoli of Brescia. In August 1453, the Senate ordered 3,000 ducats of Venetian piccoli.

Venice made light coins during periods of fiscal stringency occasioned by wars.

Unlike issues of the tornesello, these issues seemed to raise the price of the ducat in Venice itself.[20] The ducat, which had been stable at 114s. for ten years, rose to 120s. by the end of 1453, and reached 124s. in 1455.

Prices rose in Venice.

In September 1453, the same Senate noted that "due to the great number of piccoli coined in our mint up to now, they have multiplied in our territories and they have already started to be used in payments in rolls,[21] as is done in Padua, which is against all good customs of our city and an affront to our reputation." Mint officials were forbidden to mint Venetian piccoli. By December, however, an order was given to mint 20,000 ducats in quattrini. A final peace was reached in 1454, but in 1456 the Great Council noted that minting of the piccoli had continued and edicted severe penalties for mint personnel. Still, in 1457, another £1,500 worth were ordered minted.

This episode had lasting consequences. In the immediate aftermath, measures were taken to correct these emissions. In 1458, it was decided that all piccoli in Brescia were to be brought to a central office, and only 4,000 ducats' worth to be kept: all those in excess were to be converted into newly made quattrini. In 1463, it was

Venice returned to full bodied coins.

(1980).

[20] The existing quotations of the ducat in mainland cities show no deviation from those in Venice (Lane and Mueller 1985, 606–17).

[21] This refers to the practice of wrapping small coins in rolls and tendering the unopened rolls in payment (see page 254 for a similar practice). Small coins were thus used as substitutes for large coins.

made illegal to circulate small coins in sealed bags, and their legal tender was limited to 5s.

The large issues of the 1440s and 1450s had made piccoli and bagatini common in transactions. Their silver content (5% of weight) was worth about 0.4d. and easily omitted; counterfeiting predictably developed into a serious problem. The Venetian authorities resorted to various measures to deal with it. In 1463, it was ordered that all existing small coins be brought in for examination by officials, and that counterfeits be melted and the metal returned to the owners. Soon after, it was decided to issue a new type of piccolo to replace the old one. All old piccoli were demonetized and made exchangeable for new ones after examination: one for one if genuine, or at the value of their copper content for counterfeits. The exchange program was relatively successful, because the limit on the new issue had to be raised in order to meet the quantities of old piccoli brought in (about 4,000 ducats).

The new piccoli, however, contained the same amount of silver. At the same time, authorities studied the feasibility of issuing pure copper coins. The mint was asked to provide proofs. A proposal to make pure copper piccoli at 64 coins per marc was rejected twice in 1463 and 1464. Given that copper was worth about 40d. to 50d. per marc (Lane and Mueller 1985, 559), the coins would have been fairly heavy (3.7g) but roughly full-bodied. Eventually, a similar proposal was adopted in 1472, and the mint ordered to make piccoli for Verona and Vicenza, "of such manner and size that twelve be worth one mezzanino [12d. in local units], including the costs of production; and let 2,000 ducats be made and sent to said cities, to be exchanged with whomever wants them."

These coins, along with copper coins issued in Naples the same year, were the first pure copper coins issued in Europe since imperial Rome (Grierson 1971). The Venetians had been made cautious by their experiences of the 1440s and 1450s. As the mint's orders make clear, the coins were full-bodied. Not content with this precaution against counterfeiting, the Venetian government tightly controlled the quantities issued. In July 1473, the Council of Ten instructed the mint not to coin copper without its express permission, usually given in response to a petition by local officials about lack of small coins. Often, the amount authorized was not to be issued immediately, but only as ordered from time to time by the Signoria. The Venetian government authorized the issue of 11,500 ducats over the following 35 years, only half of the issues of the year 1453 alone.[22]

Concluding remarks

After experiencing shortages of small coins and the depreciations and debasements that they caused under the medieval mechanism, the government of Venice tentatively experimented with pieces of the standard formula by issuing overvalued coins, first the tornesello for its Greek possessions and then some coins for its mainland possessions. In these experiments, the government tried the "token" part of the standard formula without putting in place the "convertibility" part.[23] But inflation led the government to abandon its attempts to initiate token small denomination coins. We shall see parts but not all of the standard formula being tried again and again before ultimately all parts would be simultaneously implemented.

Appendix: mint equivalents and mint prices

For figure 10.1 we mostly follow Lane and Mueller (1985, appendix A), but with some differences that are explained here. The numbers we use for the mint prices and mint equivalents are in tables 10.1 and 10.3.

Concerning the piccolo's content from 1269 to 1282, we follow the interpretation of Cessi (1937, xxix, xxxix) rather than Lane and

---

[22] The minting authorizations from 1472 to 1506 can be found in Bonfiglio Dosio (1984, 187–277).

[23] See the discussion of the inflation in seventeenth-century Castile in chapter 14.

Table 10.1 Mint price for free and requisitioned (*quinto*) silver, in soldi di piccoli per marc of pure silver, Venice, 1209–1472.

Date	free	quinto
1201	240.35	n.a.
1269	258.84	n.a.
1282	295.82	n.a.
1331	n.a.	295.82
1353 (8 Apr)	414.39	295.82
1355	414.39	372.95
1369 (19 Dec)	420.05	411.65
1379 (4 May)	491.46	470.46
1385 (4 Jun)	491.46	453.66
1387 (1 Aug)	494.61	445.26
1391 (9 Jun)	512.47	459.26
1394 (4 Jun)	524.02	459.26
1399 (7 Oct)	540.82	459.26
1401 (8 Aug)	540.47	459.26
1407 (4 May)	567.07	459.26
1414 (22 Apr)	556.57	459.26
1417 (11 Nov)	610.13	n.a.
1421 (6 Feb)	620.31	n.a.
1429 (9 Jul)	645.63	n.a.
1444 (23 Jan)	620.00	n.a.

Sources: Lane and Mueller (1985), Papadopoli (1893–1909), Cessi (1937); see text.

Mueller. Cessi only sees two debasements of the piccolo, each contemporaneous with the change in legal tender value of the grosso. The debasement order for 1282 is in Papadopoli (1893–1909, 1:121) and, contrary to what Lane and Mueller state (1985, 499 n18), in Cessi as well (1937, xxxix). The debasement order for 1269 does not survive. Cessi interprets his document 30, also in Papadopoli (1893–1909, 1:326), as describing the weight of the piccolo at all times between 1269 and 1282, and assumes that the fineness was unchanged, as numismatic evidence suggests. He also cites a deliberation of 1268 to resume minting of the piccolo on a 1:28 ratio to the grosso, which is consistent with the mint equivalent implied by Cessi's assumptions. This is a simpler hypothesis than Lane and Mueller's, who appear to postulate debasements in 1278 and 1282.

Table 10.2 Mix of denominations in payments on requisitioned silver (*quinto*) and on mandatory refining (*quarto*), 1331–1444.

	Date	*piccoli*	*soldini* *soldini*	mezzogrossi, grossi, grossoni
quinto	1331		100%	
	1353 (15 Jul)		100%	
	1379 (3 May)	*	50%	50%
	1385 (4 Jun)	7.4%	92.6%	
	1390 (29 Apr)	6%	94%	
	1394 (11 Jun)		50%	50%
	1395 (11 Aug)		100%	
quarto	1407 (10 May)	at owner's option		
	1417 (11 Nov)		50%	50%
	1421 (2 Feb)		25%	75%
	1429 (9 Jul)		33%	67%
	1444 (23 Jan)		100%	
	1444 (24 Jan)		50%	33%

*: minting of piccoli at mint officials' discretion, "in the quantity they shall think is necessary for the use and the convenience of the land."

Sources: Cessi (1937, 104, 157, 175, 181, 186, 188), Bonfiglio Dosio (1984, 81, 96, 104, 110, 125, 126).

The piccolo's content between 1343 and 1379 is also a source of difficulty. Lane and Mueller follow Papadopoli's estimate of the piccolo's weight during the reign of Andrea Dandolo (1343–54), but this results in an implausibly heavy standard for the piccolo. In particular, after 1353, it would have made the piccolo minted at a mint equivalent below the contemporaneous mint price, which makes no sense. Papadopoli does not say the size of the sample of coins on which he based his weight estimates. It seems simpler to assume that the piccolo continued to be minted as before under Andrea Dandolo, and that the weight described in Cessi (1937, doc. 158) had been used since Giovanni Gradenigo's reign (1355).

Lane and Mueller (1985, 510) state that the mint price paid on requisitioned silver did not change until 1369. But Cessi (1937, 157) documents that the mint price was 11s. 3d. di grossi a monete before the change of 1369. We assume that this price had been in

Table 10.3 Weight, fine, and mint equivalent (ME) of Venetian coins, 1172–1472. The mint equivalent is in soldi di piccoli per marc (238.5g) of pure silver.

	Date	Coins/marc	fine (‰)	ME
Piccolo (1d.)	1172	658.84	270	203.35
	1193	658.84	250	219.61
	1269 (6 Dec)	788.00	250	262.67
	1282 (6 Oct)	788.00	191	343.72
	1346	900.00	191	392.58
	1369 (13 Apr)	960.00	191	418.75
	1369 (19 Dec)	960.00	188	424.48
	1370 (14 Feb)	1104.00	188	488.15
	1379 (4 May)	1200.00	132	756.10
	1385 (4 Jun)	1200.00	132	756.10
	1390 (8 Jun)	960.00	106	756.10
	1421 (6 Feb)	960.00	105	759.56
	1442 (24 May)	960.00	53	1519.12
Soldino (12d.)	1331–46	249.22	670	371.96
	1353 (8 Apr)	432.00	965	447.54
	1369 (19 Dec)	464.00	952	487.26
	1379 (4 May)	480.00	952	504.07
	1391 (9 Jun)	508.00	952	533.47
	1399 (7 Oct)	524.00	952	550.27
	1407 (4 May)	544.00	952	571.27
	1417 (11 Nov)	589.00	952	618.53
	1421 (6 Feb)	596.00	948	628.75
	1429 (9 Jul)	620.00	948	654.07
	1444 (23 Jan)	680.00	948	717.36
	1472 (20 May)	720.00	948	759.56
Mezzanino (16d.)	1331	192.03	780	328.25
	1346–53	308.10	965	425.58
Grosso (26d. to 48d.)	1201	109.40	965	245.56
	1269 (6 Dec)	109.40	965	264.45
	1282 (30 May)	109.40	965	302.23
	1379 (4 May)	120.00	952	504.07
	1394 (4 Jun)	127.00	952	533.47
	1397	131.00	952	550.27
	1397–1472: grosso's weight = 4 × soldino's weight			

Sources: Lane and Mueller (1985), Papadopoli (1893–1909), Cessi (1937); see text.

use since the reforms of 1355 and the cessation of coinage of the grosso.

A final difference with Lane and Mueller is that we have computed fineness as percentage pure silver, rather than percentage of *argento da bolla*. The reason is that this standard varied over time; furthermore, the fineness of early coins, based on numismatic examination, is stated by Papadopoli in terms of pure silver as well. The difference is very small.

∾

CHAPTER 11

The Price Revolution in France

The "Price Revolution" was a European-wide inflation during the sixteenth and early seventeenth centuries. A century of shortages and depreciations of small coins led the French authorities in 1577 to entertain issuing token small coins as a possible cure for shortages.

In France, a famous dispute about the causes of this inflation arose between a monetary official named Jean Cherruyer de Malestroit and the jurist Jean Bodin. In 1566, Malestroit published the results of his research into this "strange dearness of all things." He claimed that the price of silver relative to commodities displayed no long term trend, and attributed the increase in prices purely to the debasement of the currency. Two years later, Jean Bodin published a reply in which he proposed other causes, chiefly an abundance of gold and silver metals in France, coming in part from "the new lands full of gold and silver" that had been conquered by Spain.[1]

This chapter uses our model to analyze the price revolution in France. From 1510 to 1580, nominal prices increased by a factor of 3.6 (see fig. 11.3), while the metal content of the unit of account declined by a factor of 1.7 (see figs. 11.6 and 11.7), which implies that the value of precious metals declined by a factor of 2.

These numbers make room for contributions from the explanations of both Bodin and Malestroit. Bodin could point to the factor of 2 and attribute it to the American treasure.[2] That leaves a factor

---

[1] The insight that exogenous increases in the supply of precious metals raise the price level was not new. Andrea d'Isernia made the same observations in the thirteenth century (d'Isernia, to 2.F.56, s.v. "moneta"; 1541, 98). In such cases, Isernia thought that a compensating change in the currency was allowable, and that debts should then be repaid in new coins at the old price, a proposal not unlike Fisher's compensated dollar (1920).

[2] The traditional explanation for the decline in value of gold and silver is the influx of American treasure cited among other factors by Bodin (Hamilton 1934). This explanation has been contested on quantitative and chronological grounds

of 1.7 to be accounted for. Our model tells us to look for shortages of small coins as a force pushing prices up and coin contents down. We find such shortages and accompanying subsidiary monetary disturbances, intertwined with depreciation of the two precious metals at uneven rates. This mix of causes perplexed Malestroit and Bodin, as well as the policy makers who urgently tried to make sense of the inflation. Their responses included a remarkable reform in 1577. Although it did not endure, that reform contributed to the long process of learning to master small change.

Relative price change as inflation

Along with Bodin, we need no sophisticated monetary theory, or little monetary theory at all, to explain the upward trend in prices that resulted from the cheapening of metals: elementary price theory can do the job.[3] The money systems in place at the time were designed to link the price level to the relative price of precious metals in terms of consumption goods, and that they did.

Inflation from a lower relative price for gold and silver

A simplified one-coin version of our model illustrates the basic mechanism through which the relative price of silver determines the price level, while the demand function for money determines the nominal supply of silver coins. Temporarily suppose that the only coin is the silver penny. Then our model reduces to:

$$p \in \left[(1 - \sigma_1) \frac{\phi_s}{b_1}, \frac{\phi_s}{b_1} \right], \qquad (11.1a)$$

$$\frac{m_1}{p} = k \qquad (11.1b)$$

where $1/\phi_s$ is the world price of silver in terms of consumption goods, and b_1 is the silver content of the penny, measured in ounces of silver per penny. Equation $(11.1a)$ determines the price level,

---

(see Munro [forthcoming] and references cited there). We will use the traditional label for this decline, but our model only requires *some* exogenous decline.

[3] As Schumpeter (1954, 312), Bodin's explanation of the French inflation relies on nothing more than a downward-sloping demand curve for precious metals.

to within an interval whose width is determined by the seigniorage rate σ_1. A sufficiently big fall in the relative price of silver (i.e., a rise in ϕ_s that is big enough relative to the interval width σ_1) causes the price level to rise. When $\sigma_1 = 0$, (11.1a) determines the price level.[4] The demand function for real balances, equation (11.1b), then determines the supply of nominal balances m_1. The simple "quantity theory" equation (11.1b) carries the implication that the real stock of coins m_1/p measured in terms of consumption goods is a constant k.[5] Therefore, the nominal coin stock must increase proportionately when the price level rises. The money supply increases automatically in response to a rise in ϕ_s because the supply mechanism gives people incentives to bring silver to the mint to purchase coins whenever the price level threatens to fall below $(1 - \sigma_1)\frac{\phi_s}{b_1}$, the "minting point" for pennies.

Disturbances to coin denominations

The one-coin model captures much about how world metal prices impinged on prices in France, but cannot help us understand the interesting disturbances to the denomination structure that were superimposed on the general inflation. This chapter describes these disturbances as well as features of the general inflation, and accounts for them in terms of a three-coin version of our model. The model keeps track of three main categories of coins: silver pennies, larger denomination silver coins, and large denomination gold coins.

Our theory in a nutshell   Briefly, our theory accounts for the observations as follows. A decrease in the relative prices of gold and silver in terms of consumption goods pushed the intervals between the minting points and melting points for all coins to the right. But the price of gold relative to silver itself fluctuated, meaning that the intervals for gold and silver coins moved unevenly. Those uneven movements caused shortages

---

[4] As noted by Sargent and Smith (1997), equation (11.1b) can act as a quantity theory of the price level only within the interval of size σ_1.

[5] This feature leads to Friedman's (1951) calculation that the opportunity cost in terms of consumption goods of the precious metals tied up in a commodity money is independent of the metal used as the commodity money.

Table 11.1 List of symbols for the three-coin version of the model.

Variable	Meaning	Units
m_1	silver pennies	denier
m_2	larger silver coins	teston
m_3	gold coins	écu
ϕ_s^{-1}	world price of silver	cons good / oz silver
ϕ_g^{-1}	world price of gold	cons good / oz gold
b_1	metal in penny	ounces of silver / penny
b_2	metal in teston	ounces of silver / teston
b_3	metal in écu	ounces of gold / écu
e_2	exchange rate of teston	pence / teston
e_3	exchange rate of écu	pence / écu

sometimes of gold coins and other times of silver coins as temporary leftward shifts in one of the intervals induced melting. In addition to shortages caused by uneven movements in intervals for gold and silver coins, we shall describe evidence of the kind of "within the intervals" shortages that indicate a binding "penny-in-advance constraint" in our model. These shortages manifest themselves in rising rates of exchange of large denomination coins (both gold and silver) for small denomination coins. We document how the prices (in pence) of both gold and silver large denomination coins often appreciated during the century.

A three-coin model

Table 11.1 summarizes key notation in a three-coin version of our model. We let m_1 denote the stock of pennies, m_2 the stock of large denomination silver coins, and m_3 the stock of gold coins. Only pennies satisfy the penny-in-advance constraint. We let ϕ_g^{-1}, ϕ_s^{-1} denote the world prices of gold and silver, respectively, denominated in units of the consumption good. We use pence as the unit of account, and let e_2, e_3 be the exchange rates of large denomination silver and gold coins, respectively, for pennies.

Our theory emphasizes irregular shifts in minting and melting intervals caused by fluctuating but secularly declining relative prices of gold and silver.

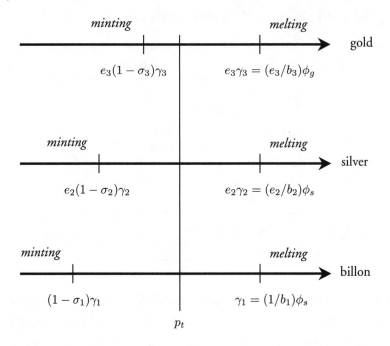

Figure 11.1 Intervals in the three-coin case.

We posit exogenous world-market-determined movements in ϕ_g, ϕ_s that provoke domestic monetary responses in the form of changes in the money supply, in the price level, and the b_i's set by policy makers and the e_i's set by the market. Both ϕ_{st} and ϕ_{gt} moved upward over the century, and both had year-to-year fluctuations.

Figure 11.1 shows intervals for the three types of coins, gold, silver, and small silver or billon. The gold and silver coins are denominated in terms of the smallest coin, the billon coin.

Upward trends in ϕ_{st} and ϕ_{gt} move the intervals for all three types of coins to the right, thus increasing their "minting points." That causes increases in the price level and also in the supplies of all types of coin. However, that the ϕ's did not increase monotonically allowed coin shortages to arise in the following two ways.

Supply: movements in the relative prices of metals

Ignore for now the bottom interval in figure 11.1, and consider the consequences of uneven increases in ϕ_s and ϕ_g. A relative increase in ϕ_g (a lowering of the consumption price of gold) shifts the top interval to the right relative to the middle interval, causing minting of gold coins when p_t hits the minting point for gold. Eventually, the price level rises and reaches the melting point for silver coins, which are now melted. If all silver coins are not to be melted, the silver interval must somehow be shifted to the right (or the gold interval to the *left*), either by decreasing b_2 (or increasing b_3), or by increasing e_2 (or decreasing e_3). The converse holds if ϕ_s increases: silver becomes cheaper, is minted, and eventually gold is melted, until the intervals are realigned. Thus, uneven upward movements in ϕ_g and ϕ_s can explain increases in either e_2 or e_3, but only ones that are not synchronized in time.

Demand: within the intervals shortages

Our model shows how there can be shortages of small coins, even though the price level has not encountered the melting point for any coin. These shortages occur when the penny-in-advance constraint is binding and cause the exchange rates e_{2t}, e_{3t} of the large coins for pennies to *rise*. That shifts the intervals for the larger coins *and*, through the ordinary quantity theory equation, moves the price level (denominated in pence) to the *right*, thereby hastening the day when the penny is to be *melted*. Within the mechanism, the cure for this situation is to debase the penny, thereby shifting its interval also to the right.[6] We keep both sides of the model in mind when we interpret the evidence summarized next.

---

[6] Glassman and Redish (1988) noted that debasements occurred as responses to increases in e_t, which they call undervaluation of the large coins. In their interpretation, these increases are due to movements in the gold/silver ratio, counterfeiting, and wear and tear on the small coins. They see shortages of small coins as a consequence of these increases.

Anatomy of money and inflation

Gold and silver both became cheaper in terms of other goods.

This section describes a variety of facts about monetary arrangements in the sixteenth century, the main ones of which we can summarize as follows. For most of the century, prices were stated in terms of the penny, a small silver coin. There was a general upward trend in the price level but little or no trend in the relative price of gold and silver. There were many depreciations of the metal content of the penny and increases in the rates of exchange of larger coins for pennies. Some increases in the exchange rates of large coins for pennies were decreed by the government, but many others were spontaneous market-determined increases called *surhaussements*. There were few depreciations of the metal content of larger silver and gold coins. There were intermittent shortages of coins of all denominations, especially smaller ones. The exchange rate fluctuations eventually provoked controversies and policy shifts about the appropriate units of account for contracts.

Types of coins and units of account

Our model groups coins into three main types: gold coins, large denomination silver coins, and small denomination billon coins. In practice, these corresponded to, respectively, a gold coin called the *écu soleil*, and its half; a large silver coin called the *teston*, and its half (replaced in 1577 by a similar coin, the *franc*); and several billon coins. The face value of the billon coins remained fixed throughout the period: the *douzain* (from the French *douze*, twelve) at 12d., the *liard* at 3d., the *double* at 2d., and the *denier tournois* or penny, by definition 1d. As had been the case in the Middle Ages, the units of account were multiples of the penny, the *sou* (12d.), and the *livre tournois* (240d.). Prices and debts were quoted in these units of account.[7] Royal edicts also gave the large coins a price in terms of the penny: at the beginning of the century, the gold écu was rated

---

[7] For the period 1483–1575 in Paris, Schnapper (1957, 185) finds 25 long-term debt contracts out of 475 denominated in gold écus, the rest in livres.

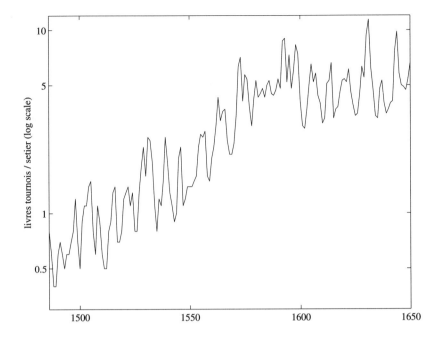

Figure 11.2 Price of wheat in Toulouse, annual average, in livres tournois per setier (93 liters), 1486–1650 *Source*: Frêche and Frêche (1967, 85–88).

at 36s. 3d. The teston, introduced in 1514, was rated at 10s.[8]

The price level

Starting in the 1510s, there was a general upward trend in the price level. Figures 11.2 (prices of wheat) and 11.3 (a regional commodity price index) show the typical profile.[9] Prices are here expressed in the unit of account (livres tournois), which was based on the penny (denier tournois).

Supply: the relative price of gold and silver

Our data indicate that during the sixteenth century, ϕ_s and ϕ_g increased at about the same rate. The stars in figure 11.4 plot the

---

[8] See Wailly (1857) and Lafaurie (1956) for the specifications of French coins.

[9] Note the pronounced cyclical behavior of wheat prices.

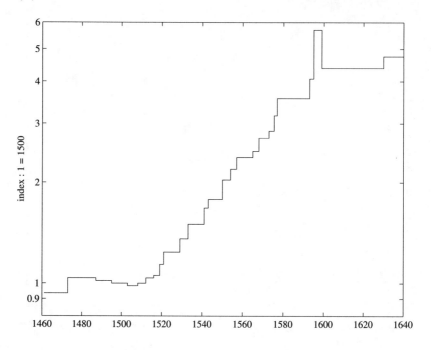

Figure 11.3 Commodity price index, Poitou, 1460–1640. *Source*: Raveau (1929, 2–3).

average legal ratio of silver to gold in Europe, by decade. Until the 1580s, it remained between 10.5 and 11.5, the same range that had prevailed during the late Middle Ages. The solid lines give the upper bounds and lower bounds on the ratio in France. Where ME denotes the mint equivalent and MP the mint price, the upper bound is

$$\frac{ME_g}{MP_s} = \frac{e_3 b_3^{-1} \phi_g}{(1 - \sigma_2) e_2 b_2^{-1} \phi_s}$$

and the lower bound is

$$\frac{MP_g}{ME_s} = \frac{(1 - \sigma_3) e_3 b_3^{-1} \phi_g}{e_2 b_2^{-1} \phi_s}.$$

There were very few changes in b_i for the larger coins. The metal content of the gold écu, minted from 1475 to 1641, was changed only in 1519 and 1561, for a total debasement of 4%. The content of the teston was changed only once in 1521, soon after its first issue,

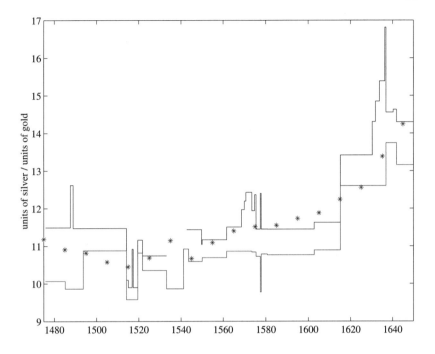

Figure 11.4 Upper and lower bounds on the gold/silver ratio in France, and European average gold/silver ratio (*stars*), 1475–1650. *Sources*: Wailly (1857), Spooner (1972).

by 4%. Its successor the franc was never altered during its life from 1577 to 1641. The frequent movements in figure 11.4 are mainly due to changes in the legal values e_2 and e_3 assigned by royal edicts. These changes track the movement of the gold/silver ratio ϕ_s/ϕ_g over time.[10]

Note that not until after 1600 was there any systematic trend in the bands in figure 11.4. If the market ratio ever rose above the upper bound, it became profitable to melt gold coins and mint silver coins; and *vice versa* whenever the market ratio fell below the lower bound.

Figure 11.5 summarizes quantities that were minted of the three

[10] In fact, Spooner's series is an average of the ratios of mint equivalents for gold and silver across Europe, as there are no series on market prices. The presumption is that those ratios, as in France, tracked the market ratio.

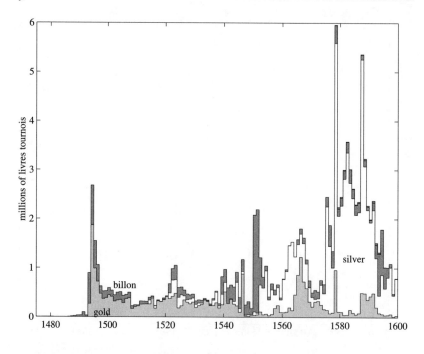

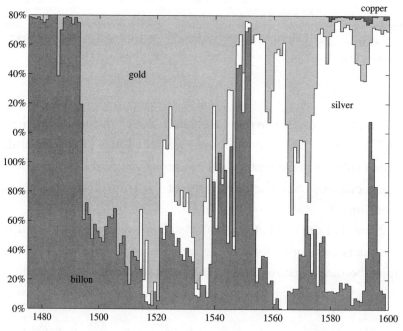

Figure 11.5 Total minting in France, broken down into gold, silver and billon minting: nominal amounts (*top panel*) and shares of total (*bottom panel*), France 1493–1600. *Source*: Spooner (1956, 522–30).

types of coins. Early in the century, until 1530, when figure 11.4 shows that silver was becoming more expensive relative to gold, there was much minting of gold but little of silver, as figure 11.5 shows. By 1550, the trend reversed itself: silver became cheaper relative to gold, and substantially more minting of silver than of gold occurred. This pattern is consistent with the model, which highlights how shifts in the relative values of ϕ_s and ϕ_g influence whether the price level is at the minting point for silver or gold coins.

So far, the model's predictions are not surprising, and our observations are not new. When we turn to smaller denominations, however, the situation becomes more complicated and we contribute something new, including an explanation of the spontaneous debasements known as *surhaussements*.

Debasement of billon coins

Billon coins were debased repeatedly during the century: the penny in 1515, 1541, 1566, and 1572; the douzain in 1519, 1540, 1550, 1572, and 1575. The cumulative debasements from the beginning of the century to 1577 were 52% and 44% for the penny and douzain, respectively. In figure 11.6, the solid lines represent the interval $[(1 - \sigma_1)b_1^{-1}, b_1^{-1}]$, the mint price and mint equivalent, for the douzain. Every movement in the upper solid line corresponds to a reduction in b_1, which denotes the metal content of the douzain.

In this respect, monetary policy for small coins differed markedly from that for large coins. In figure 11.6, the upper dotted line traces the legal value, in terms of pennies, of a constant fine weight of testons. In our notation, this represents $e_2 b_2^{-1}$. The lower dotted line traces $(1 - \sigma_2)e_2 b_2^{-1}$, the mint price. The movements in the dotted lines of figure 11.6 almost always represent changes in the official exchange rate between large silver coins and billon coins e_2, while b_2 remained almost unchanged. By 1577, the rate of the teston had been raised, or "cried up," eight times, from 10s. to 16s.[11]

---

[11] The value of coins was announced by the king's criers at crossroads and markets. Crying up meant increasing the value, crying down or decrying meant decreasing, demonetizing, or more generally prohibiting (as when King James II of Scotland

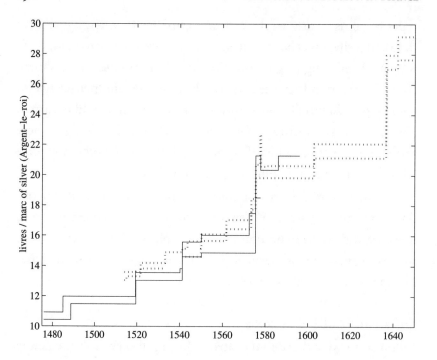

Figure 11.6 Intervals for small silver coins (*solid lines*) and large silver coins (*dashed lines*), France, 1514–1650. The units are livres of account per marc (244.75g) of silver argent-le-roi (^{23}⁄$_{24}$ fine).

This difference was not confined to silver. In figure 11.7, the upper line traces the changing value of $e_3 b_3^{-1}$ for the gold écu. By 1577, its official rate e_3 had been raised ten times, from 36s. 3d. to 65s. Again, as noted earlier, b_3 was almost unchanged throughout the period.

The French authorities did not attempt to make small denomination coins fiduciary to any degree. In figure 11.6, the upper solid line, which is the inverse of the intrinsic content of the penny, is never above, and is often below the dotted line, which corresponds to the larger coin. The solid line ends in the 1590s, however, when the small denominations were replaced with pure copper coins.

---

ordered in 1457, with little success it seems, "That the fute-bal and golfe be utterly cryed downe, and not to be used").

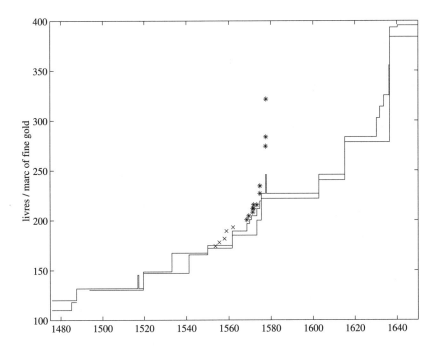

Figure 11.7 Intervals for gold coins, France, 1475–1650. The crosses and stars indicate the market value of the écu-soleil, 1553–62 (see text). The units are livres of account per marc (244.75g) fine gold.

Mysterious movements in exchange rates

Why were billon coins debased so often? There is ample evidence that the rates e_i were determined by the market, and later occasionally ratified by government pronouncements (Glassman and Redish 1988). One form of evidence comes from those pronouncements, which often reflect a frustration on the part of the authorities at their inability to control market rates. Thus, in 1519, the king said that "the prices of gold and silver bullion haven't stopped increasing, and continue to increase from day to day, so much so that our mints remain inactive to the great detriment of our affairs and the public good" (cited in Levasseur (1902, CXL). Malestroit, in his 1566 publication, said that "the opinion of the mob has always ruled, for

kings, whatever resistance they ever oppose, are in the end defeated
and forced to follow the disorderly will of the people, and to raise the
value of the écu day by day." The Cour des Monnaies, in charge of
supervising mint policy, admitted as much in 1577: "Your Majesty
has been forced to increase the rate of the coins, to accommodate
the price that your people gave to them of its own authority" (cited
in Stampe 1932, 35).

We have direct evidence on the free rate at which large French
coins circulated, such as the diary of the sieur de Gouberville, a
squire in Normandy, who routinely recorded those rates when he
made payments, and the correspondence of the Ruiz family, Spanish
merchants established in France. In figure 11.7, crosses indicate
the value $e_3 b_3^{-1}$ implied by the prices noted by Gouberville for the
French écu; the stars indicate similar quotations from other private
accounts of the time. Also, large Spanish coins like the silver *real* and
the gold *escudo* or *écu pistole* were legal tender in France throughout
the period. Figure 11.8 plots the market values of these Spanish coins
from the diary of Gouberville (crosses), and from the correspondence
of the Ruiz (stars and circles). [12]

The crosses and stars of figures 11.7 and 11.8, when compared to
the solid lines that embody the official rates, make clear why the authorities felt powerless, even as they tried to catch up with the market.

The figures also suggest that the period from 1575 to 1577 was
one of accelerating appreciation of the large coins, both gold and
silver. Indeed, contemporaries described the summer of 1577 as one
of crisis. Not only did rates grow faster on average, but geographic
dispersion widened. The gold écu pistole (lower panel of fig. 11.8)
reached 100 sols in September in Nantes, but only 75 to 78 sols in
Paris and 66 sols in Lyon. The silver *real* reached 12 sols in Nantes,
but only 7 or 8 sols in nearby Laval, 8 to 10 sols in Paris. [13] These
extraordinary variations, in both gold and silver coins at the same

---

[12] See Leddet (1928, 191, 201, 208) for the Gouberville prices, Spooner (1956,
163–65) for the other écu price, Lapeyre (1955, 462-3) for the Ruiz prices, and
Stampe (1932, 14–15, 18–19) for legal tender values.

[13] Those rates are literally off the charts of figure 11.8.

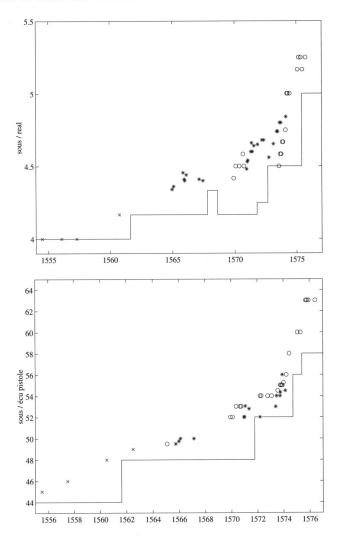

Figure 11.8 Legal tender value (*solid line*) and market price in Normandy (*crosses*), Lyon (*stars*), and Nantes (*circles*) of the silver *real* (*top panel*) and the gold *écu pistole* (*bottom panel*), 1554–77. *Source*: see text.

time, were seen as signs of chaos.

Our model asserts that uneven upward movements in ϕ_g and ϕ_s cannot explain *simultaneous* increases in e_2 and e_3. Further, the movements in the exchange rates induced by shifts in the ϕ values are achieved by deliberate government policies to alter e, but the evi-

We interpret surhaussement as reflecting a binding p.i.a. constraint.

dence shows that the surhaussement was a market phenomenon, and that, as mentioned in our discussion of figure 11.8, increases in the legal face values of coins merely recognized in law what already was fact. Our model of currency shortages emanating from the demand side (i.e., a binding p.i.a. or penny-in-advance constraint) can account for such endogenous increases in the market rates of large coins.

Evidence of small coins shortages

Ordinances and diaries reported shortages of coins.
As in earlier periods,[14] there were reports of shortages of small coins in the sixteenth century, particularly in the late 1530s and early 1540s, and again in the 1570s. The shortages were particularly acute in 1577. Evidence comes from two types of source. In texts of laws and edicts on monetary matters, the king typically described the current situation in order to justify his actions. In addition, diaries were left by contemporaries.[15]

An ordinance of 1538 described in detail the mechanics at play. Many people, French and foreigners, and not only merchants, were driven by profit to gather silver bullion and melt French silver coins, take the metal to the nearby mints of Béarn and Lausanne, convert it into small denomination coins, then import these coins back into France, where they circulated at a mint equivalent higher than that of French coins. As a result, "at present there are few or none of our coins that our poor people might use and aid themselves in their trade of goods, which is the cause of the daily increases in the price of gold and silver bullion and the idleness of our mints" (Fontanon 1585, 2:95; cited in Levasseur 1902, CXLIX).

In 1544, shortages were still reported in parts of France, particularly in the South, and authorizations were given to mint small coins. But the next year, complaints of excessive issues led to a ban on any further minting (Saulcy 1879–92, 4:437; Levasseur 1902,

---

[14] See the examples cited in chapter 8.

[15] See also Levasseur (1902), Liautey (1921), and Spooner (1956) for overviews of the period.

xLVII; Spooner 1956, 133). In 1572, mint officials asked for more douzains to be authorized, on account of their scarcity in most provinces (blamed on taxpayers' use of small coins to pay their liabilities while large coins were hoarded) and the impossibility of getting change of 1s. or 2s. on an écu (Spooner, 1956, 165 n3).

There were many contemporary accounts of acute shortages in 1576 and 1577. The memoirs of Claude Haton, a resident of the town of Provins, note that in February 1576 the price of gold and silver coins started rising again, and "from then on, all small coins such as karolus [10d.], unzains [11d.], douzains [12d.], coins of 3 and 6 blancs [15d. and 30d.], as well as doubles [2d.] and liards [3d.], were so scarce, that one handled as few of them as if there had been none in France. . . . He who owed but 5s. to a man would tender an écu [60s.], a pistole [58s.], a thaler [40s.] or such large coin, at the rate [the creditor] wanted, to receive some change" (Haton 1857, 2:870).[16] In 1577, Pierre de L'Estoile noted in his diary that, in Paris, "there was no small change that the people could use. For this reason the king deposited with city officials quantities of douzains, to relieve the little people and exchange their coins at the rate set in the ordinance, to avoid greater agitation" (L'Estoile 1992, 2:147–48). The diary of Louvet, in the town of Angers, also emphasizes the scarcity of change, and the use of scrip: "In the year 1577, there was such scarcity of money and such great turmoil because of the increase (*rehaussement*) that breadmakers, brewers, and other craftsmen of the town of Angers paid each other with parchment notes, marked with the mark they used on their own silverware, which they received and cashed from one another for 6d. and 12d." (cited in Levasseur 1902, cLxxvII).

Reports of shortages

Policy responses

The difficulties of the system of multiple denominations engendered much debate, and led to a major reform of the coinage in 1577. The

---

[16] This is like buying bubble gum with a $20 bill to make change.

reform embodied several features of the standard formula, including switching the unit of account from the penny to the large gold coin (the écu) and issuing overvalued small coins with limited legal tender.

Perception of the problem by the authorities

We have mentioned the exchange that took place from 1566 to 1568 between Malestroit and Bodin on the sources of inflation. As the problems sharpened into a crisis after 1575, the debates grew more urgent. Many participants in the debate were hampered by their tendencies to confuse cause and effect and were tempted to search for malevolent parties and denounce their failings—for example, foreign merchants (wile and greed), the populace (ignorance and fickleness), or local officials (neglect and incompetence).

Better analyses emanated from the professionals in monetary policy who staffed the Cour des Monnaies.[17] Some of those experts recognized a link between the surhaussement and shortages of small coins. In a memorandum of December 1576, the Cour des Monnaies linked the increase in the valuation of large coins to shortages of small coins and to their export, noting that French importers of foreign goods preferred to pay their foreign bills with small coins (cited in Stampe 1932, 35):[18]

> Merchants have sent thither all our douzains and other billon coins, to avoid the large and excessive loss they would have incurred had they paid in écus or other foreign gold and silver coins, on which, at the rate at which they circulate by the people's will, one would lose 15, 12, 20 and 25% when tendering them abroad, which loss doesn't occur on douzains

---

[17] This body, created in 1358, had executive and judicial roles. As an executive agency, it advised the king on monetary matters and implemented his decisions regarding legal rates, coin designs, and mint prices; it also leased the mints to entrepreneurs. As a judicial court, it had appellate (and, since 1552, final) civil and criminal jurisdiction over cases involving coins, precious metals, and mint employees, regulated jewelers and goldsmiths, and monitored mintmasters. Stampe (1932) reproduces several memoranda originating in the Cour des Monnaies.

[18] This mechanism, and the ensuing necessity to debase small coins, was noted by Lafaurie (1956, x).

and other billon coins which have not been raised in price by
your people as with said gold and silver coins. The scarcity
of those billon coins means that your subjects often cannot
obtain the provisions and other things they need, by lack of
said good coinage, which is less dispensable than high-grade
gold and coins.

This last sentence concisely summarizes the binding "penny-in-
advance constraint" of our model. Recall also that, in our model,
binding penny-in-advance constraints and shortages of small coins
lead to depreciations of their exchange rates. These depreciations
can be large enough to shift the relative positions of the intervals for
large and small coins so much that there will be melting down, or
exporting, of the small coins, further exacerbating the shortage.

The officials of the Cour des Monnaies understood the spontaneous surhaussement as a result of the actions of self-interested
individuals, and sought to identify the incentive driving people to
raise the price of large coins. Removing the incentive, they thought,
would end the disorder. But they saw the shortage as consequence
rather than cause. So they turned elsewhere for the incentive and
found it in the desire of debtors to lighten the burden of their nominal debts. They thus came to see a link between surhaussement and
the choice of units in which to denominate prices and debts, namely
the penny-based sols and livres.

The monetary authorities focussed on the unit of account.

Consequently, the government at first attempted to prevent movements in the exchange rate between coins, and later decided to anchor
the monetary system on the gold coin. At the same time, it decided
to make the small coins out of pure copper and to restrict their legal
tender. Thus, some elements of the standard formula were making
their appearance, albeit in scattered order.

Unit of account and legal tender

French law after 1360 had allowed freedom to denominate contracts
as the parties wished. In the sixteenth century, the king tried to
enforce the face values he assigned to coins. Merchants evaded these
efforts in various ways: by posting multiple prices depending on

Regulations of units of account were evaded.

the denomination of the payment, or by posting a single price but requiring a specific denomination. A law of 1541 explained in its preamble: "Some merchants in their business are wont to ask before closing a deal in what coins they will be paid and at what rate, and accordingly increase or decrease the price of their wares, taking coins at a rate higher than that set by our laws. And everyone immediately follows this, not realizing that this results in *billonements*[19] and export of coins, and a great loss for us and for the public good of the kingdom."

The king outlawed these practices, to no avail. "Billonement" continued unabated, taking the following form according to the government: merchants demanded payment in écus in order to collect them and ship them abroad, to be turned into foreign coins; these coins then came back, circulating above their legal rates. Another attempt was made in 1551 to prevent the first step of this process, that is, the specifying of particular coins for payment, by requiring that prices be posted and contracts denominated only in units of account (sols and livres). However, the Parlement refused to register the law, and it was restricted in 1558 to wholesale and retail merchants only. Finally, it was completely rescinded in 1571, and the freedom to denominate in écus was restored.

The preamble of the law of 1571 reflects a new understanding of the problem: "the surhaussement of coins comes in part from the common accounting in sols and livres in all transactions and contracts; since these sols and livres have depreciated from year to year by the effect of this surhaussement, the creditor receives much less than he should, contrary to the fairness that should prevail in contracts, and loses part of what is owed him, being paid in coins at a higher rate" (cited in Stampe, 1932, 29–32). Officials thought that they had identified a motive for the increases in e_t: debtors tried to pass off large coins for more than they were worth in order to reduce the value of the livre-denominated debts. This was a way to come to grips with the higher rate of return on large coins.

---

[19] The term designates trading in bullion, or billon, the word meaning both low-grade silver alloy and uncoined metal of any kind; see Munro (1974).

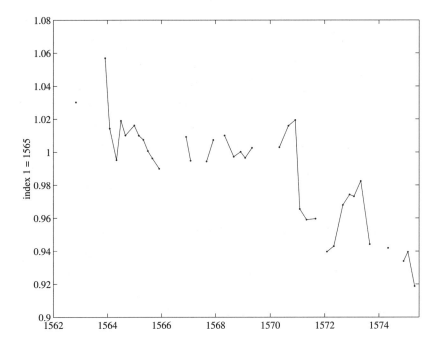

Figure 11.9 Unweighted average of exchange rate indices of the French livre against various currencies in Italy, Spain, Antwerp, and London, 1562–76. Each currency index is 1 in 1565. *Source*: Lapeyre 1955, 464–67.

Units of account and international trade: the fairs of Lyon

The opinion that livre-based units of account were to blame for the increases in e_t became the received theory at the Cour des Monnaies, and the proposed solution was to denominate debts in terms of large denomination coins. The theory received the support of the international bankers of the fairs of Lyon. Descended from the medieval trade fairs, these quarterly events served mainly to clear debts generated in trade rather than to trade the goods themselves. For two weeks, bankers would meet to net clear debts. The balances that had to be settled served as the "excess demands" on whose basis

The fairs of Lyon adopted the gold écu as unit of account.

the exchange rates were set by consensus among bankers.[20]

The exchange rates set at the fairs of Lyon were expressed in foreign currency per French livre. A Seville banker holding a debt payable in Florence only cared about the ratio of the Seville rate to the Florence rate. But holders of claims denominated in French livres cared very much about the value of the livre. That value had been falling since 1570, as shown in figure 11.9, by an amount that reflects the increases in e_t over the same period shown in figures 11.7 and 11.8.

In 1575, the organizers of the Lyon fairs decided to denominate their transactions in the gold écu rather than the livre and also to require that at least ⅔ of any settlement be made in gold. In July 1577, they required the exclusive use of gold (Lapeyre 1955, 449–51). The reform stabilized the quotations of exchange rates in Lyon. It also seemed designed to remedy the ease with which claims on French goods were bought up by foreigners, which monetary officials associated with the reigning disorder.

The reform of 1577

The reform of 1577 made the unit of account the gold écu and minted overvalued small denomination coins with limited legal tender.

While the monetary crisis unfolded, the country was in political turmoil. The Estates General debated various reforms.[21] The Cour des Monnaies took the occasion to press for a comprehensive monetary reform based on a change in the unit of account; so did the Lyon bankers, who sent a delegation to the Estates to plea for reform. Their efforts were successful, and a reform was drafted in September and passed in November 1577. The gold écu was chosen as the basis of the new accounting system. All sums of money greater than the value of one écu were to be denominated in écus only. Existing debts denominated in sols and livres were converted into écus at the rate of 60s. per écu.[22]

---

[20] See Lapeyre (1955) for the fairs of Lyon, and da Silva (1969) for their seventeenth-century counterparts in Italy.

[21] In the second half of the sixteenth century, the Estates General met frequently. After 1614, they met only once, in 1789.

[22] This adjustment foreshadowed Leijonhufvud's (1984, 21) "blueback scheme,"

The gold écu was not made sole legal tender, however. Various combinations of gold and silver coins, down to billon coins of 15d., were made unlimited legal tender for écu-denominated payments, and the creditor could not demand repayment in gold écus. In particular, a new silver coin, the franc, was made equivalent to ⅓ of a gold écu.

For coins smaller than 15d., two measures were taken. One was to provide for minting of pure copper deniers and doubles (1d. and 2d.) in the Mill Mint of Paris, for the first time in France,[23] and for minting of liards (3d.) in fourteen mints throughout France, strictly on government account. The other was to limit the legal tender of the smallest coins (1 to 3d.) to 100s., and that of coins from 6d. to 12d to ⅓ of the payment (art. 21 of the edict).

Finally, several additional measures were taken, all with the intention of removing causes of the price increases. Foreign coins, which were usually allowed to circulate and given a face value for circulation in France, were all demonetized, with the exception of the Spanish escudo and real. Importers were allowed to receive payment in foreign coin, but were directed to bring the coins to the mint. Also, the edict placed restrictions on nonmonetary uses of gold and silver by limiting the size of goldware and silverware and prohibiting the use of gilding, and threatening to impose price controls on goldsmiths' products.

Foreign coins and nonmonetary uses of gold and silver were restricted.

The system created by the reforms of 1577 remained intact until 1602. There are indications that the smallest denominations were produced in adequate quantities, but minting data show that the quantities were small (see fig. 11.5). The rise in prices also seems to have slowed or halted at about that time (fig. 11.3). The price of the gold écu, which had risen 30% from 1560 to 1577, fell back and remained stable. Contemporary evidence points to an

The reforms seemed to work well.

---

a version of which was implemented during the Argentine stabilization of 1986.

[23] The issue of these coins had already been planned in 1575, and they were initially to be made only in the Paris mint, using the new screw press. But, as part of the 1577 reform, their production was extended to all other mints (Lafaurie 1956, 117).

easy adoption of the reform throughout the country, contrary to expectations (Levasseur 1902, CLXXIX–CLXXXI; Lapeyre 1955, 451).

A significant exception to the price stability occurred in the early 1590s, when France was in the grips of a civil war and parts of the country were not under control of the central government. The copper coins issued from 1578 were overvalued.[24] There were some complaints that the coins were not accepted in trade, and the issue officially ended in 1585, but in practice it continued until 1595. From 1589 to 1595, when civil war raged, there were illegal issues of copper coinage in various regions. In Provence, in particular, the inflation seemed to have been substantial: a decree of 1609 deflated debts contracted between 1591 and 1593 by 25 to 50% (Schnapper 1957, 198; see also Spooner 1956, 171, 176, 180–81). Only in 1596 were issues brought under control, and it was decided to restrict production of these copper coins to the screw press in Paris.

Collapse of the reform

The reform of 1577 implemented elements of the standard formula. It removed the provision of the smallest denominations from the classic supply mechanism by making them tokens, minted on government account in limited quantities. It also limited their legal tender. It shifted the basis of accounting from the bottom of the denomination structure, the penny, to the very top, the gold écu, whose size and fineness was to remain constant.

The reform reflected growing understanding of the problems of supplying small change with the medieval money supply mechanism. The authorities understood that the rise in p_t was associated with the rise in e_t: as the edict of 1577 stated (art. 5), "the valuation of all things is made on the basis of the écu's price." Most aspects of the reform were directed, however naively, at suppressing the symptoms of rising e_t. Large foreign coins, whose circulation was seen as giving

---

[24] The copper denier contained 1.57g of copper. If copper is valued at 8.6g of silver per kg of copper (e.g., Parenti 1939, 57*), the intrinsic value of the coin was 27% of its face value.

occasion for speculative bidding, were prohibited. The restrictions
on nonmonetary uses of gold and silver attempted to protect the
large denominations from melting, another symptom of the interval
having shifted because of a rising e_t.

But the reform did not fully implement the standard formula. *Shifting intervals*
Although it prefigured the gold standard of the nineteenth century *made the écu a*
by basing the monetary system on the gold coin and setting a fixed *ghost money.*
exchange rate of smaller silver coins, it kept free minting of silver.[25]
Furthermore, as luck would have it, the gold/silver ratio of 11.0
chosen in 1577 soon compared unfavorably to the rest of Europe
(fig. 11.4). As a result, minting of gold coins stopped almost completely (fig. 11.5) and the gold écu, on which the monetary system
was based, disappeared. In its place, large quantities of the silver
franc were issued. The écu continued as a unit of account, becoming like an Italian ghost money: the écu came to mean three silver
francs rather than one gold coin. Moreover, since gold clauses had
been made illegal, and payment in gold could not be required, gold
coins disappeared from contracts as well.

Finally, the small denominations had been made token, but without convertibility. The disturbances of the 1590s revealed the danger
inherent in unbacked token coinage, as parts of France encountered
copper inflation.

Over the strong protests of monetary officials and businessmen, *The reform was*
the new system was scrapped in 1602. Accounting in livres replaced *abandoned.*
accounting in écus. Limited legal tender for small coins was apparently dropped.[26] The écu, which had been maintained at 60s., was
increased to 66s. Sully, who was prime minister at the time, wrote
in his memoirs (1822, 3:243–48):

I found a remedy that was more effective and less violent than
punishments and confiscations to prevent the exportation of

[25] As we will see in chapter 17, Britain's initial design for the gold standard in
1816 contained the same flaw.
[26] Szlechter (1952, 108) cites a court order of 1607 enforcing repayment of a
debt in gold coins with billon; the edict of 1602, in its article 7, only seems to
maintain the ⅓ limit on billon payment for pre-existing debts.

gold and silver out of the realm; namely, to increase their value. Since there could be no other cause of this abuse than the excessive disproportion between the value of our gold and silver coins, and that of our neighbors, at the same time I established in the realm accounting by livres, where it was previously done by écus. Some may find this notion too subtle, since either method of reckoning ought to come to the same. I do not find so on the experience I have made, that the usage of the écu, by lack of a denomination more suitable for small purchases, imperceptibly raises all items of trade in sale and purchase beyond their true value.

Concluding remarks

Our model prompts us to dismantle and reassemble ingredients that previous commentators and researchers have adduced to explain disturbances to the French currency in the sixteenth century: inflows of gold and silver and debasements of small coins. Relative to past explanations, our model converts the debasement of small coins from cause to effect. We have described how uneven downward movements in the relative price of gold and silver for consumption goods could cause some upward adjustments in the exchange rates of large silver and gold coins for small coins, and how disturbances from the demand side could cause others. In response to such exchange rate changes, the only way to bolster the supply of small coins was to debase them. The debasements were infrequent and followed rather than preceded the increase in the exchange rate of large versus small coins, as shown in figure 11.7.

In 1577, rather than continuing to debase and allowing the coins that formed their unit of account to depreciate, the French attempted a radical reform that embodied elements of the standard formula. In particular, the French chose a single large denomination coin to serve as the unit of account and to anchor the price level. They suspended the medieval supply mechanism for the lowest denomination coins and instead produced coins of pure copper using the new minting technology.

The reform incompletely implemented the standard formula and reflected a partial grasp of the problem. The reform did not make all small denomination coins tokens, nor did it make them convertible. The silver coinage remained within the medieval supply mechanism, at a fixed ratio to the new gold-based unit that soon fell victim to unlucky timing. Gold and silver coins could only be kept in concurrent circulation with more debasements, an action that defeated the purpose of the reform. Instead, only silver remained, and the gold écu's transformation into a ghost money was seen as a failure, as was perhaps the outburst of inflation during the civil wars of 1592–93. More experimenting and more theorizing would be necessary before the standard formula would eventually triumph.

Appendix: mint equivalents and mint prices

Mint equivalents and prices for silver and gold during this period in France are shown in tables 11.2 and 11.3, based on the following sources. Coin specifications can be found in Wailly (1857) and Lafaurie (1956). Edicts concerning legal values are listed in Stampe (1930, 1932); see Richet (1961) for the legal values of foreign coins.

Table 11.2 Mint equivalents and mint prices of the gold écu. The unit of weight is the marc (244.75g) of fine gold.

Date		value (s)	ME (s/marc)	MP
écu: 23⅛ carats, 70 per marc				
1475	(2 Nov)	33	119.9	110.0
1485	(16 Feb)	33	119.9	118.0
1487	(30 Jul)	36¼	131.7	
1493	(31 Aug)	36¼	131.7	130.2
1507	(19 Nov)	36¼	131.7	
1511	(5 Dec)	36¼	131.7	
1516	(22 Nov)	40	145.3	
1517	(25 May)	36¼	131.7	
écu: 23 carats, 71⅙ per marc				
1519	(21 Jul)	40	148.5	147.0
1533	(5 Mar)	45	167.1	
1541	(19 Mar)	45	167.1	165.4
1550	(23 Jan)	46	170.8	172.0
écu: 23 carats, 72½ per marc				
1561	(30 Aug)	50	189.1	185.0
1568	(11 Aug)	52	196.7	
1569	(23 Nov)	53	200.5	
1570	(30 Aug)	54	204.3	
1571	(21 Apr)	54	204.3	
1573	(20 Apr)	56	211.8	200.0
1574	(22 Sep)	58	219.4	
1575	(31 May)	60	227.0	222.0
1577	(15 Jun)	65	245.9	
1577	(20 Nov)	60	227.0	
1602	(30 Sep)	65	245.9	240.5
1615	(16 Feb)	75	283.7	278.3
1630	(28 Feb)	80	302.6	
1631	(31 Aug)	83	314.0	
1633	(31 Jul)	86	325.3	
1636	(5 Mar)	94	355.6	
1636	(28 Jun)	104	393.4	384.0

Table 11.3 Mint equivalents and mint prices of the silver teston and franc. The unit of weight is the marc (244.75g) of silver $^{23}/_{24}$ fine.

Date	value (s)	ME (s/marc)	MP
teston: 938‰ fine, 25.5 per marc			
1515 (6 Apr)	10	13.02	12.50
1515 (17 Feb)	10	13.02	12.75
teston: 898‰ fine, 25.5 per marc			
1521 (20 Sep)	10	13.60	13.25
1533 (5 Mar)	10½	14.28	none
1541 (19 Mar)	10⅔	14.51	none
1542 (20 Sep)	10⅔	14.51	14.00
1543 (27 Jul)	11	14.96	14
1549 (25 Oct)	11	14.96	14.5
1550 (23 Jan)	11⅓	15.41	15.00
1561 (30 Aug)	12	16.32	15.75
1573 (9 Jun)	13	17.68	17
1575 (17 Jun)	14½	19.72	19
1577 (15 Jun)	16	21.76	19
1577 (20 Nov)	14½	19.72	19
1580 (17 Oct)	14½	19.76	19.00
1602 (30 Sep)	15½	21.08	20.27
franc: 833‰ fine, 17¼ per marc			
1575 (17 Jun)	20	19.84	19.00
1577 (20 Nov)	20	19.84	19.00
1602 (30 Sep)	21⅓	21.16	20.27
1636 (28 Jun)	27	26.78	23.50
1636 (22 Sep)	27	26.78	25.90

☙

CHAPTER 12
Token and Siege Monies

For brass I will bring gold, and for iron I will bring silver.
— Isaiah 60 : 17

Precursors of the standard formula

Medieval jurists' preference for full-bodied coinage discouraged but did not entirely stop various forms of tokens or redeemable promises from circulating as currency. Occasionally, siege and other token coins were temporarily issued to relieve extraordinary shortages of small change and other coins. These early siege monies contained lessons about how the medieval monetary mechanism would eventually be reformed with the standard formula. Near the close of the Middle Ages, in Catalonia and Castile, these lessons were brought together to inspire early attempts to implement Cipolla's standard formula, with governments promising to convert token coins. Those attempts were ultimately defeated by the activities of counterfeiters and the governments' lack of a technology to deter them.

Medieval tokens

The numismatic literature treats medieval tokens as part of the large variety of coin-like objects.[1] The reason for segregating them from coins is mainly their content (base metals such as pewter, then lead, and later still brass and copper), but also their functions and the intent of their makers.

---

[1] See Rouyer (1858), Mitchiner and Skinner (1984), Mitchiner (1988–98).

Counters were coin-like objects used by accountants on a checkered counting board, the medieval equivalent of the abacus. Large-scale production of "counting pennies" (*Rechenpfennige*) became a specialty of the German town of Nuremberg. Tokens, on the other hand, were given to furnish proof that some action had been performed, such as payment of a toll or entrance fee. In cases where the action was rewarded after its performance, for example attendance at mass by members of an ecclesiastical chapter, the token was a redeemable claim to future payment. Church bodies and lay confraternities found it useful to issue such redeemable tokens to the needy in order to organize their charitable distributions. The token was usually redeemed by the issuer in kind, such as food in the case of charity; but sometimes redemption was made in cash, and sometimes not by the issuer directly, but by an intermediary who provided the food and then returned the token to the issuer for cash.[2]

Medieval tokens are documented primarily in Flanders and northern France, but also in northern Italy and Catalonia. Their use as substitute for small change is documented early on: in England, a complaint on shortages in 1402 cites the recourse to lead tokens as substitutes. Erasmus, who visited England around 1510, remarked on their use (Ruding 1840, 1:250, 301). By the mid-sixteenth century tokens were used throughout the Low Countries and in neighboring Westphalia (Schrötter 1902). They were subject to counterfeiting: the city of Béthune, in northern France, had to stop its issues in 1531 because of widespread counterfeiting. It redeemed 100,000 outstanding tokens (Rouyer 1862).

The attitude of central authorities varied. In England, where the mint produced very few small denominations, tokens were tolerated and at times officially authorized. In 1582, Elizabeth I allowed Bristol to issue lead tokens to be current within 10 miles of the city. Scarcity of small change led to private issues of substitutes in

---

[2] See Courtenay (1972a, 1972b) for references, and for the role played by these partially convertible tokens as a metaphor in theological discussions of sacraments in the thirteenth century.

lead, brass, copper, or paper, against which no action was taken. In London alone it was estimated that 3,000 tradespeople issued tokens in the amount of £5 each (Craig 1953, 128).

By contrast, in France and the Low Countries, private tokens became victims of government action in the sixteenth century. In 1557, officials of the Cour des Monnaies passing through the town of Mâcon shut down the local cathedral's production of lead tokens. The chapter of the cathedral protested, alleging they had enjoyed the right to make these tokens for several centuries. But the monetary officials were adamant, because the tokens, originally used to pay choristers, had gained circulation throughout the town for 1d., 2d. and 6d. In their eyes, this was money, and they threatened prosecution on grounds of counterfeiting. In a similar case in Autun in 1577, the officials seized the chapter's piles and trussells, but the chapter recovered them after an appeal before the courts (Rouyer 1849, 362, 367).

In the Low Countries, Charles V prohibited the tokens issued by hospitals in Delft because they were circulating in retail trade; it is notable that, after the rebellion against Spain, William of Orange authorized them (Van Loon 1732–37, 1:178). In 1541, Charles V prohibited the circulation of lead pennies in the province of Hainaut; the reason given was that those made by the city of Maubeuge, although legal, had become too widely counterfeited (*Recueil des Anciennes Ordonnances des Pays Bas* 1907, 331).

Siege money

Cities under siege issued token coins. A siege interrupted a city's exchanges with the outside world. The purpose of siege money, also called obsidional currency, was to pay troops lest they stop fighting. A besieged commander, unable to secure funds from outside the city, had to find ways to remunerate his garrison. In some cases, siege money was made of gold or silver, for example when a local ruler or garrison commander had his silver plate cut into pieces and distributed to the soldiers. Numismatists do not class such objects as money because they do not bear the official stamp of a mint. In other cases, the siege money was made with whatever cheap material was at hand, and merely represented a (state-contingent, obviously) promise of payment after the assailants would lift the siege.

The fourteenth-century Florentine chronicler Giovanni Villani (cited in Jesse 1924, 84) told how the German emperor Frederic II ran out of funds while besieging Faenza in 1240. He reportedly paid his troops with leather coins imprinted with the design of his gold *augustales* coins and a promise of redemption that he kept. Similar issues of leather money have been ascribed to King Jean II of France in the mid-fourteenth century and Doge Michiele of Venice at the siege of Tyre in 1124, but these have been shown to be apocryphal.[3] Villani wrote a century after the events. The lack of contemporary evidence suggests that the story of Frederic II may well be an invention too; it was nevertheless believed and frequently cited in sixteenth-century texts on money (Hotman [1573] 1610, 122 [qu. 15]; Grimaudet 1576, 19; Budel 1591, lib. 1, cap. 1 n. 31; Godefroy, to Dig. 18.1.1; [1590] 1688, col. 494).

Aside from this dubious example, siege monies appeared at the end of the fifteenth century.[4] By then, as we have seen, canonists had sanctioned the issue of overvalued currency in cases of emergency. One of the earliest examples, uncovered by Hermand (1846), occurred when the town of Saint-Omer in Flanders was besieged by the French in 1477, and its mayor issued lead tokens of 9d. and 12d. that were ultimately redeemed.

Another early example is cited in several places in the early seventeenth-century literature on money.[5] It took place between

---

[3] See Grierson (1954) for Michiele's coins. The story of the leather money of Jean II does not appear until a century after the facts and was rejected as apocryphal by Dumoulin, along with a similar story for Louis IX of France (1584, §799; 1681, 2:322).

[4] See Mailliet (1868–73) for a catalog of obsidional currencies.

[5] For example Grégoire (*Republica* lib. 3, cap. 6, n. 26; 1609, 43), Carranza (1629, 260 [lib. 4, cap. 1, §7, p. 3]), and González Téllez (to X 2.24.18; 1715, 554).

1483 and 1485, in the town of Alhama de Granada in southern
Spain, not far from Granada itself. Granada was still Arab, and
Alhama had just been conquered by the Christians in 1482. From
1483 to 1485 its commander was Íñigo López de Mendoza, the second count of Tendilla, who later became the first Spanish governor
of Granada in 1492. During that period the Arabs of Granada made
several unsuccessful attempts to retake Alhama. The story is told by
a well-informed contemporary, Fernando del Pulgar, secretary of the
king of Aragon (Pulgar 1943, 2:97–98):

> It happened that there was a shortage of money in that city
> to pay the wages of the soldiers, and for that reason all trade
> necessary for subsistence had ceased between them. The count
> saw this, and ordered that a paper money be made, of various
> denominations high and low, of the quantity he deemed nec-
> essary for carrying out trades between people. On each piece
> of paper he wrote in his own hand the price it was worth;
> and with this money he paid the wages he owed to soldiers
> and workers, and ordered it to be valued among the residents
> of the city, and that no one refuse it. He pledged that when
> anyone left the city, presenting each piece of money to him,
> he would give the value inscribed on it in gold or silver coins.
> And all the people, knowing the trustworthiness of the count,
> trusted him and his word, and accepted their wages in this
> paper money, which circulated between them in the purchase
> of sustenance and other things, and no one refused it, and it
> was a great remedy to the extreme straits in which they were.
> And later, at the time that the count relinquished his post in
> the city, before leaving, he paid to anyone who presented it the
> paper money that they had received, in gold and silver money
> equal in value to that inscribed in his hand on the paper.

The idea of siege money may have come from elsewhere in Spain.
Botet i Sisó (1911, 2:281) cited issues of pennies by the commander
of the besieged town of Gerona in Catalonia in 1462, some of which
may have been of pure copper. In the following decades, there were
only isolated examples of siege monies that were clearly issued for

more than their intrinsic content.[6]

The war fought by the Spaniards to keep the Low Countries prompted a flurry of siege monies.[7] Between 1567 and 1586, token siege money was issued on twenty occasions, in various materials (tin, lead, copper, even paper) and in a range of denominations (up to eight different denominations). The insurgents in Valenciennes issued the first such siege money in 1567. When the war moved to Holland in 1572, siege money was issued by the municipal authorities in Haarlem, Middelburg, and Alkmaar. In Leyden, where a tradition of token money issued by hospitals was well established, the Calvinist municipality issued paper coins made from recycled Roman Catholic prayer books (see fig. 12.1). The siege lasted four months and was lifted on March 21; six days later, the coins were redeemed. The town was besieged again a few months later and another issue of paper coins took place. After these successful precedents, the States of Holland recommended in 1575 that all towns under siege by Spanish armies use siege money, implicitly guaranteeing redemption even if the siege ended with capitulation, as happened at Zierikzee. Sometimes the garrison itself demanded the issue of siege money, as in Deventer in 1578 when the mutinous troops forced the city elders to issue 800 coins of 30s. each to pay their wages.

Van Loon (1732–37, 1:161–62) described an interesting variant of the siege money procedure. In 1573, the existing silver coinage of Holland and Zeeland was subjected to a restamping operation, whereby a small mark was added to coins by government officials. The restamped coins were ordered to circulate temporarily for ⅛ more than their original value, and they were to be ultimately redeemed.[8] We will soon see how the Spaniards used the idea of restamping coins a few decades later.

---

[6] Mailliet documents examples in the Low Countries (L'Écluse in 1492, Tournai in 1521), northern Italy (Novara in 1495, Verona in 1516). The lead coins issued in Vienna besieged by the Turks in 1529 are cited by Budel (1591, 4).

[7] Mailliet (1868–73) catalogs the coinage. Van Loon (1732–37) provides historical details on the sieges.

[8] Van Loon was unable to find any orders of the States-General to confirm this restamping and to determine the actual procedures.

Figure 12.1 Paper money of Leyden, 1574. The stamp in the upper left of the obverse was imprinted at the time of redemption, according to Van Loon. (Copyright Bibliothèque Royale Albert Ier, Bruxelles, Monnaies et Médailles).

The link between the siege monies of the Netherlands and the earlier tokens issued by ecclesiastical and municipal bodies has already been noted. That tokens had developed in the Low Countries, northern Italy, and Catalonia is perhaps not a surprise, since those areas were the most financially developed at the time.[9]

Convertible token currency: an early experiment

Catalonia, in the late fifteenth century, had experience both with tokens, such as those issued by the chapter of Saint-Jean of Perpignan (Mitchiner and Skinner 1984, 33), and with siege money, as with the case of Gerona cited above.

Gerona issued convertible tokens and struggled with counterfeiters.

The coins issued by Gerona's commander Dom Pere de Rocaberti in 1462 were issued and circulated for some time after the siege. Still suffering from a scarcity of small change, the city asked and received permission from the king to issue small change. In 1481, he allowed Gerona to issue coins of any metal, but no more than 200 llivres, and on condition that "the city be known to pledge, and effectively

---

[9]   See de Roover (1948), Lane and Mueller (1985), and Usher (1943), respectively.

pledge to receive said small money from those who might hold it, and to convert it and return for it good money of gold or silver, whenever and however much they be asked." The king required the city to appoint an individual to make the exchange (Botet i Sisó 1908–11, 2:326–37, 3:11–40, 3:480, cited in Usher 1943, 232).

Initially, Gerona withdrew the remaining siege money and restamped it. The collection fell short of the 200 llivres, and it was decided to mint new coins of copper alloyed with 6.25% silver. The resulting coinage contained 25% of the silver in an equal face value of croats, the main silver coin. A total of 1,300 llivres of such coins was minted between 1482 and 1484. The coins depreciated, in part because of counterfeits, and in 1489 the town was authorized to announce a recall for 15 days, after which it was not obliged to convert them anymore. The coins found to be genuine were countermarked and issued again; the next year, another series was issued, of pure copper. In 1494, an interesting episode occurred: as part of a kingdom-wide monetary reform, the king had placed a legal tender limit of 6d. for small change. As a result, people wanted fewer coins of Gerona. They turned in many coins, at great cost to the city. Gerona applied for relief from the king and was authorized to maintain the currency at its original legal tender value for three months, presumably without convertibility. A restamping operation was also carried out. More restampings followed by new issues were carried out in 1510 and in 1515: the latter occasioned difficulties because the city found more than half of the coins to be counterfeits. The new issues were convertible; that of 1515 contained 4% silver. In 1535, the large number of counterfeits gave rise to a rumor that the city would suspend convertibility, and another restamping operation was carried out to remove counterfeits.

Gerona's innovation was quickly imitated by several other Catalonian cities: about a dozen are known to have issued convertible coinage in pure copper or billon. Sometimes the city was required to commit in writing to convert into royal coins of gold or silver current throughout Catalonia. The profits were presumably retained by the city, but sometimes it was specified that they be used to maintain its military installations. The coins were often given legal tender value in a limited range around the city. Indeed, Barcelona, the capital and seat of the official mint, disapproved of these local currencies, maintaining that only it was privileged to mint royal coins. Barcelona prohibited the local issues on its own territory. The problem of counterfeiting was widespread, and the usual response was to restamp coins as in Gerona.[10] Catalonian cities nonetheless continued to issue convertible coins. The last known issue took place in 1576 in Puigcerdà, and it was legal tender throughout the regions of Rosselló and Cerdanya (in spite of the protests from the city of Perpinyà).

First attempt at standard formula

The Catalonian experiments prefigured the standard formula.

These experiments in the Catalonian cities were early attempts to issue a convertible token coinage.[11] The initial experiments were successful enough to be pursued by several cities for decades. But the medieval hammering technology proved too accessible to counterfeiters. The cities' coinages were plagued by depreciation and recurrent crises, which they met by occasionally weeding out counterfeits from the money stock and issuing new types of coins. Before the standard formula was to be explicitly proposed and implemented, many more experiments would occur on larger scales, conducted both by states and private parties.

ぐ

---

[10] In 1532, the city of Vic tried to forestall depreciation by agreeing to buy back counterfeits, but this only increased counterfeiting, and it soon had to resort to restamping.

[11] Another example can be cited: in 1621, the bishop of Verden in Germany issued copper pennies, ordering that, "for these copper coins to remain a subsidiary coin (*Scheidepfennig*) and so that no one be burdened to excess, let no one be obligated to accept more than 9 thaler of these coins in any transaction, and we volunteer to establish an exchange bank in Verden as well as in Rotenburg, where the copper money can be exchanged for imperial coins" (Schrötter 1902, 210).

Part IV

Cures and Side-effects

CHAPTER 13

The Age of Copper

To this next came in course the brazen age,
A warlike offspring, prompt to bloody rage,
Not impious yet.
— *Ovid, Metamorphoses I:125-27, translated by Dryden*

Chapter 4 described a substantial technological change that occurred around 1550, making coins more immune to counterfeiting. As the innovation diffused across Europe, governments sought to dissociate the metallic currency from its intrinsic content, a possibility already contemplated in theory. Governments issued copper coinage, initially as a substitute for small change. For a time it circulated at much more than its intrinsic content. Variations of these experiments occurred across Europe. Some of these experiments sought to improve the efficiency of the money supply mechanism by implementing a version of Adam Smith's thought experiment (see page 101). Theorists soon drew lessons about both the viability and the dangers of fiat currency.

The coinage of pure copper

The sixteenth century saw the emergence of a technology for producing coins with high fixed costs and a large and standardized output. Aside from residual variations due to the imperfection of hand-produced dies, coins were round, sharply imprinted, and nearly identical. These characteristics presented high barriers to counterfeiting. It became possible for governments to produce pure copper coins whose intrinsic content was considerably lower than their face value.

Several countries experimented with the new technology by using

The advent of the new technologies allowed governments to produce token coinage.

it for small change.[1]   Spain[2] began issuing token copper coinage
in 1596, for reasons of efficiency, but soon embarked on a large-
scale fiat money experiment that lasted several decades. England
issued its first copper coinage in 1613 (Spufford 1988a, 372), but
remained leery of token coinage and kept its coins nearly full-bodied.
France, which first experimented with mechanized minting of small
change in 1577, vacillated, and started down the road of large-scale
token issues without following through.   Several other countries
experienced episodes of replacement or displacement of large coins
by token coinage. In Russia, this resulted from an outright policy
decision to replace silver with overvalued copper coins, whereas the
German experience resulted from a lack of adequate small coinage,
ultimately met by states vying for seigniorage revenues.[3] Some of
these experiments created large inflations. We examine them in turn.

Skepticism about a   Use of copper was a response, not to shortages of silver, but
"bullion shortage"   to possibilities opened by new coin making technologies and new
monetary theories.   Others have noted the prominence of copper
in seventeenth century monetary history, but explained it differently. Spooner (1972, 41) wrote that "it was not possible, actually,
for silver alone to meet the total monetary demand. As a result,
copper achieved exceptional success, promoted almost to the status
of a precious metal. . . . There was a temptation, and perhaps an
obligation, to use [coins of pure copper] when bullion was relatively
scarce." Our interpretation of the seventeenth century "Age of Cop-

---

[1] There had been occasional issues of pure copper coinage before. We noted
the example of Venice on page 180. The Spanish Low Countries minted pure
copper coins in 1543. The value of the copper represented around 20% of the
face value (*Recueil des Anciennes Ordonnances des Pays Bas* 1907, 448, for the
coin specifications, Parenti 1939, 57* for copper prices). Curiously, the reason
given for this innovation was the widespread counterfeiting of existing billon
denominations.

[2] Or more precisely, Castile. The kingdom of Aragon, while part of Spain, had
its own monetary system, and it was not affected by the events in neighboring
Castile.

[3] Although the new minting technology was not clearly a factor in the German
and Russian cases, both showed governments to be grappling with the consequences of circulating fiat coinage.

per" differs. Policy makers were free to choose whether or not to use copper, and different policy makers made different choices. At least in Castile, for a number of years, they managed to substitute inconvertible tokens for silver coins without causing inflation. But ultimately inflation caused the Castilian authorities to restore more full-bodied coins.

Experiments in many countries

The next five chapters describe a sequence of experiments with token copper coins. The earlier experiments were ultimately judged to have failed, because they replaced the problem of shortages of small coins with a greater evil of a surplus of coins that caused inflation. The failures were associated either with an inadequate appreciation of the importance of making token coins convertible, or a lack of resources to make them convertible. In response to those failures, governments abandoned token coins for many decades. Nevertheless, as chapters 16 and 17 will describe, the British government came to allow private citizens to issue tokens, some of which were convertible. These chapters describe the interaction of private and government measures to supply small coins in Britain, and how in important respects the private market taught the government the standard formula. Chapters 17 and 18 will tell how the standard formula ultimately prevailed, and how its triumph was connected with the rise of the gold standard and the demise of bimetallism.

ℰℐ

CHAPTER 14

Inflation in Spain

Elements of the standard formula

Tokens, seigniorage, and convertibility   The standard formula recommends that the government make over-valued tokens that it redeems for full-bodied coins. To create tokens, the government should terminate free minting of small denominations and thereby end the associated automatic mechanism governed by the minting and melting points, with the purpose of divorcing the value of small coins from that of the metals they contain. To determine the exchange value of the small coins, the standard formula instructs the government to offer to convert token coins into full-bodied coins. The possibility of pushing overvalued small coins into circulation was discovered before the importance of convertibility was appreciated.

Government revenues from issuing tokens.   The standard formula ties up smaller stocks of valuable metals in a country's coins than did the comprehensive medieval commodity money system. A government hungry for revenues might be expected to recognize that. By moving from a full-bodied to a token system, a government could, at no cost in inflation, collect one-time revenues equal to the value of the precious metal in its subsidiary coinage. This chapter describes how the government of seventeenth-century Castile tried to do just that, thereby implementing part, but only part, of the standard formula.[1] The government did not promise to convert the subsidiary coins into silver. However, it eventually realized that market fundamentals alone could not determine

---

[1] The story of vellón inflation in Castile is told in Schrötter (1906), Hamilton (1934), Domínguez Ortiz (1960), Motomura (1994), Lozanne (1997), García de Paso (2000b). The exact chronology of monetary operations between 1597 and 1664, as well as the data and calculations used in this section, are described in Velde and Weber (2000), and summarized in the appendix of this chapter. This chapter benefited from the comments of José García de Paso.

the exchange rate for these token coins[2] and used announcements
to manipulate the rate of exchange of token coins for full-bodied
coins.

It is not surprising that the role of convertibility was not immediately appreciated, because theoretically a token system can work
without convertibility. Without convertibility, a token coin system
is incomplete but it is not incoherent. With wide bands for the
subsidiary coinage and without convertibility, our model asserts that
there are many exchange rates that are consistent with equilibrium.
Technically, the exchange rate is *indeterminate*.[3] The theoretical indeterminacy of the exchange rate means that government attempts to
pin it down by directive or persuasion make sense. In the episodes to
be described in this chapter, watch how the government manipulated
the exchange rate.

The Castilian experiment

In chapter 4, we described the arrival of the new cylinder press
technology in Spain, and the construction of a new machine called
the *Ingenio*. King Philip II recognized that this new technology
offered possibilities beyond those of simply making better versions
of the old coins. In a royal decree of 1596, he announced that pure
copper coins produced in the cylinder presses of the Segovia mint
would replace the billon coinage previously produced for the smaller
denominations. The text explained his decision to substitute copper
for silver (Del Rivero 1918–19, document 14):

*Philip II's advisors
recommended that
token coins replace
silver coins.*

> We have been advised by men of great experience that the
> silver put in those billon coins is lost forever and that no profit
> can be drawn from it, except in their use as money, and that

---

[2] Without a promise to redeem, the "fundamentals" of a token coin are necessarily weak.

[3] Kareken and Wallace (1981) write about the indeterminacy of international
exchange rates in environments where there is no special source of demand for
domestic over foreign currencies.

the quantity of silver that is put to that use for the necessities of ordinary trade and commerce in this kingdom is large. We have also been advised that, since we have established a new Ingenio in the city of Segovia to mint coins, if we could mint the billon coinage in it, we would have the assurance that it could not be counterfeited, because only a small quantity could be imitated and not without great cost if not by the use of a similar engine, of which there are none other in this kingdom or the neighboring ones. And it would thus be possible to avoid adding the silver.

Until then, copper, silver, and minting costs each formed a third of the face value of billon[4] coinage. With Philip II's decree, the silver was withheld and the copper content reduced.[5]

Philip II sought to raise government revenues without generating inflation. The same decree of 1596 ordered that a limited quantity of the new coins be minted each year, and that an equal quantity of existing small denomination coins be retired, until the outstanding billon coins were eliminated. Gold and silver coins were not changed. In terms of our model, the aim was to replace m_1 (small denomination coins) with token coinage, but to maintain a narrow interval between the melting and minting points for the large denomination silver coins composing m_2. The price level would stay within the interval between the melting and minting points for silver coins so long as they continued to circulate.

Philip II died in 1598. His successors Philip III (1598–1621) and Philip IV (1621–65) used the Ingenio to produce copper coins far in excess of the quantity of m_1 of 1596, so much that the silver coins composing m_2 disappeared. That released the price level from the constraints imposed by the melting and minting points for silver coins, and set loose the quantity theory cast in terms of copper coins as the determinant of the price level.

---

[4] The Spanish word for billon is *vellón*, which later came to designate the pure copper coins.

[5] In response to parliamentary opposition, 0.3% of silver was actually put in the new coins until 1602.

The Castilians struggled with exchange rate indeterminacy. They discovered that the face value of token coins, the number inscribed on them, could be made irrelevant. They learned to manipulate that number either to collect more seigniorage or to fight inflation. At first sight, some of these manipulations may seem absurd, but on closer study they were not. For example, on occasion the government "cried down" coins by saying that the numbers on copper coins represented not what the Roman numerals usually meant, but something else decreed by the government. We see these measures as serious attempts to respond to the government's growing awareness of the exchange rate indeterminacy implicit in the system of token coinage it had set up.

The Castilian monetary authorities managed exchange rates.

Monetary manipulations

The complexity of the Castilian episode requires additional notation to keep track of units of account, exchange rates, and government operations designed to alter them.

The unit of account was the maravedi (mr), originally representing 1/34 of a silver real, or 0.094g of fine silver. After copper coins had been issued, people distinguished between silver mr, the original unit, and copper mr. Copper mr were the units in which the government assigned numbers to copper coins. The actual copper coins were not called maravedis, but for example, *cuartillos, cuartos, ochavos,* and *blancas,* to which the government initially assigned the numbers 8, 4, 2, and ½, respectively. We shall take the cuarto as our representative token coin.

Starting in 1602, the copper coins were stamped with numbers (see fig. 14.1), originally denoting the number of copper mr assigned to those coins. We say "originally" because the government recurrently tampered with the numbering system in two ways, restamping or "crying down" particular coins.

Figure 14.1 Two 8-maravedis coins ("cuartillos") minted at the Segovia mint (1622, *left*, and 1604, *right*). The original face value VIII (8 mr) is marked to the right of the central coat of arms. Both coins were reduced to 4 maravedis in 1628. The coin on the right was stamped "XII" (12 mr) in 1642 in Burgos. (Author's collection.) Photograph: Robert Lifson.

Restamping

The government manipulated exchange rates by restamping coins.

In this operation, the government took a coin that was initially stamped x and restamped it jx, where j might equal 2, 3, or 4. Figures 14.1, 14.2, and 14.3 show various restamped coins. Figure 14.1 shows two coins that testify to both restamping and crying down. Both coins, called cuartillos, were originally stamped VIII mr. Figure 14.2 shows one coin that was restamped three times and another coin that had originally been issued over 100 years earlier and that was restamped in 1603. Figure 14.3 shows a coin originally issued in the time of the Roman emperor Domitian that was restamped fifteen centuries later to circulate at 12 mr; evidently, only the most recent marking mattered.

Restamping operations were administered as follows. The government offered a citizen the opportunity to bring to the mint j coins originally worth x maravedis, have all be stamped with jx, allow the government to keep $j - 1$, and to retain the last coin.[6]

---

[6] We say "originally worth" rather than "originally stamped" because the coin

Figure 14.2 Two 2-maravedis coins ("ochavos"), restamped in the seventeenth century. The coin on the right was restamped three times: "IIII S" in Seville in 1603, "VI G" in Granada in 1636, and "IIII" in 1654 (the date is visible at the bottom, the numeral is on the other side of the coin). The coin on the left still bears the recognizable legend of Ferdinand and Isabel (1480–1504): it was thus over a hundred years old when it was restamped in 1603. (Author's collection.) Photograph: Robert Lifson.

Figure 14.3 Bronze coin of Emperor Domitian, 1st c. A.D. This coin was stamped 12 mr in Granada in 1636. (Photograph: Bibliothèque nationale de France, Cabinet des Médailles, Paris.)

---

that was brought in might have been cried down earlier, for example, as the coins in figure 14.1 both were.

Such an operation left the coin owner indifferent. To break indifference, the mints of Castile offered a small premium, in the form of an allowance for the costs of travel to the mint.

Crying down coins

The government also reset exchange rates by "crying down" coins.

When the government cried down a coin, it told people to disregard the number stamped on the coin when using it, and instead to refer to another number from a government edict. Let x denote the prevailing number of copper mr per cuarto, either written on the coin or in the pertinent government edict, depending on the momentarily prevailing convention. The government cried down the cuarto by saying that a coin originally stamped x_1 mr was now to be regarded as x_1/j mr, where j might be 2, 3, or 4, regardless of the stamp. This cry-down operation reset x from $x = x_1$ to $x = x_1/j$. Thus, sometimes the number on the coin mattered and sometimes it did not. The actual number of mr represented by a given coin could be set by the edict that had cried down the coin.

The two coins in figure 14.1 were marked 8 at issue. In August 1628, both were cried down to 4. Later, in 1642, the one on the right was restamped XII as part of the factor-of-3 restamping. So for this cuartillo, 8 became 4 (by being cried down in 1628) and 4 became 12 (by being restamped in 1642).

Theory of the Castilian tokens

We modify our model to accomodate restampings and cry-downs.

Additional notation

Table 14.1 summarizes notation. We let m_2 denote the stock of silver coins, measured in silver mr, and m_1 the *number* of copper coins called cuartos. We use the parameter x to denote the number of copper mr per cuarto, as determined by the cumulative effects of successive stampings and government edicts crying down the cuarto. Changes over time in x induced by restamping and crying down

Table 14.1 Notation for the Castilian episode.

Variable	Meaning	Units
m_1	cuartos, vellón coins	number of disks
m_2	silver coins	silver mr
x	number assigned to a cuarto	copper mr / cuarto
e	exchange rate	copper mr/silver mr
$e^* = e/x$	exchange rate	cuarto / silver mr
p	price of cons goods	cuarto/cons good
$p^* = p/e^*$	silver price of cons goods	silver mr / cons good
ϕ^{-1}	world price of copper	cons goods / oz copper
b_1	content of a cuarto	ounces of copper / cuarto
$\frac{b_1 p^*}{\phi}$	silver price of a cuarto	silver mr /cuarto
$e^{*-1}m_1$	stock of cuartos	silver mr
b_2	content of silver coins	ounces of silver / silver mr
ϕ_2^{-1}	world price of silver	cons goods / oz silver

will be a big part of our story. We let e be the exchange rate of copper maravedis per silver maravedi, and $e^* = e/x$ the cuarto-silver maravedi exchange rate; p is the price of consumption goods in cuartos and $p^* = p/e^*$ is the price of consumption goods in silver maravedis. We let ϕ^{-1} be the world price of copper and ϕ_2^{-1} the world price of silver, each denominated in consumption goods per ounce of the metal. As we shall see, Castile was ultimately to use enough copper in making coins to move the price of copper in European markets.[7]

Multiple regimes

The list in table 14.1 contains exogenous variables that the government took as given, policy variables directly under the government's control, and endogenous variables. We take ϕ and ϕ_2 as exogenous, and we note that b_2 remained fixed throughout the period.[8] The government, manipulated the policy variables m_1, b_1, x, in order

---

[7] See chapter 18 for an account of a worldwide model of bimetallism in which the monetary authority's choice of commodity affects its equilibrium price.

[8] With one shortlived exception from December 1642 to March 1643, when the silver real was cried up by 25%.

to achieve particular outcomes in terms of the endogenous variables m_2, p, and e. We see the Spanish king's advisors as seeking to diminish m_2, and thereby reap the resulting silver as government revenues. We also see them as concerned with keeping the price level subject to the discipline of the silver standard. They discovered that several regimes were possible, depending on whether m_2 was positive or not.

To see this, consider these bounds imposed by the supply mechanism. The upper bound was the melting point for silver, $\gamma_2 = \phi_2/b_2$, expressed in silver maravedi per consumption good. In other words, γ_2 is the price level in terms of silver mr above which it is profitable for people to melt silver mr. The lower bound is $(1-\sigma_2)\gamma_2$, the price level associated with the minting point for silver mr. For simplicity, we will assume that $\sigma_2 = 0$, so that the two bounds coincide and the price level in silver mr, px/e, must be γ_2 so long as silver mr have not all been melted:

$$p^* = p\left(\frac{x}{e}\right) = \gamma_2 \text{ if } m_2 > 0 \qquad (14.1)$$

$$m_2 = 0 \text{ if } p\left(\frac{x}{e}\right) > \gamma_2, \qquad (14.2)$$

where p^* is the price level measured in silver mr per unit of consumption good.

The quantity theory of money $(2.7a)$ in terms of prices denominated in cuartos is

$$\frac{m_1 + \left(\frac{e}{x}\right)m_2}{p} = k, \qquad (14.3)$$

while in terms of prices denominated in silver maravedis the quantity theory is

$$\frac{\left(\frac{x}{e}\right)m_1 + m_2}{\left(\frac{x}{e}\right)p} = k. \qquad (14.4)$$

Two regimes are possible, depending on whether or not $m_2 > 0$. In each regime, the quantity theory equation plays a different role.

The noninflationary regime   When equation (14.1) prevails, the price level is determined by (14.1). Then the role of the quantity theory equation (14.4) is to determine the mix of the currency stock between m_1 and m_2. That is, it determines m_2 as a function of $(\frac{x}{e})m_1$:

$$m_2 = k\gamma_2 - \left(\frac{x}{e}\right) m_1. \qquad (14.5)$$

The government set x, by what it stamped on the coins or proclaimed in government documents, and it affected m_1 through its minting policies. The market set e. The government's purpose was to stay in this first $m_2 > 0$ regime but to lower m_2.

In another regime, $m_2 = 0$. The restriction on the price level p^* imposed by the melting point of silver (14.1) vanishes. This makes the quantity theory equation (14.4) collapse to a quantity theory cast purely in terms of cuartos:

The quantity theory regime

$$\frac{m_1}{p} = k. \qquad (14.6)$$

We can measure both m_1 and p in silver mr by making a pure units change, and multiplying both the numerator and the denominator by $\left(\frac{x}{e}\right)$.

Depending on the regime in which it found itself, the government experimented with different policies. Within the $m_2 > 0$ regime, it used several methods to increase $\left(\frac{x}{e}\right) m_1$ and to reduce m_2 to its benefit. One was simply to mint new coins and increase m_1 to purchase silver coins. Another was to reduce the b_1 parameter, and then use a restamping to exchange new, lighter coins for the outstanding heavier ones. Finally, a direct restamping, or j-fold increase in x, allowed the government to collect a fraction $(j-1)/j$ of the existing money stock.

Within the $m_2 = 0$ regime, the government tried to *decrease* p^* enough to bring back some silver mr, that is, to make $m_2 > 0$ again by equation (14.1), and thereby discipline the price level with the silver standard. Since $p^* = p\left(\frac{x}{e}\right)$, it could do so by acting on p through equation (14.6), that is, by decreasing the actual quantity of cuartos in circulation (by "consuming vellón," to use the phrase of the time). Or it could try to change x/e by a cry-down, that is, a reduction in x.

Cry-downs as anti-inflation policy

We see the government of Castile learning about properties of our model, such as the existence of the two regimes we have just described. The price data from the beginning of the seventeenth century are symptomatic of the $m_2 > 0$ regime. However, chapter 6 told how Juan de Mariana had warned earlier of a possible $m_2 = 0$ regime. Either the king's advisors learned the hard way, or they deliberately ran the risks that Mariana foretold because they saw no better way to meet their goals.

More learning: aspects of indeterminacy

Various equilibria are possible. Our model has another property with which the government appeared to wrestle, namely indeterminacy. What matters in the quantity theory formulas (14.3) and (14.4) is x/e. While the government acted upon x through restampings and cry-downs, the market set e. It is theoretically possible, though not necessary, that the market could always have reset e proportionally with x, thereby removing the effects of restampings or cry-downs on m_2 or the price level denominated in silver mr. However, the time series evidence about e and x in figure 14.6 (later in this chapter) shows that movements in e did not always cancel movements in x, so that the restampings and cry-downs mattered. We want now to mention some of the theoretical possibilities for the co-movement of x and e.

The form of equation (14.4) indicates that multiple equilibria are possible, because in response to a change in x, either m_1, e, or p can adjust. We mention two types of equilibria:

1. *Equilibria with x/e a constant.* In such equilibria, fluctuations in x are irrelevant changes in units. Notice that if equation (14.4) holds for one $x > 0$ with $m_1 > 0$, it also holds for any other positive value of x with x/e held constant. Here the market immediately cancels the effects of any government adjustments of x.

2. *Equilibria in which e stays fixed while x is altered.* In these equilibria, movements in x affect either the stock of silver coins m_2 (if $m_2 > 0$) or the price level denominated in silver mr (if $m_2 = 0$). We consider each possibility in turn.

a. Suppose that $m_2 > 0$, so that some silver coins circulate. Then an increase in x is consistent with fixed e and fixed $p^* = (\frac{x}{e})p$, provided that m_2 shrinks in response to the increase in x. Notice that the price level p denominated in cuartos varies inversely with x in this case. Philip II's advisors wanted that. The melting point for silver prevents the price level from rising in response to an increase in xm_1/e while $m_2 > 0$.

b. If $(x/e)m_1 \geq k\gamma_2$, where γ_2 is the upper bound on the price level implied by the melting point for silver, then further rises in x cause either the price level measured in silver mr or the exchange rate e to rise. Which form inflation takes is irrelevant because both lead to the same value of the price level p denominated in cuartos.

The evidence presented in the next section shows that x/e fluctuated over time, ruling out a pure type 1 equilibrium. But aspects of a type 1 equilibrium were reflected in particular episodes.

The evidence

Figures 14.4, 14.5, and 14.6 summarize the Spanish monarchs' experiments with token coinage (see the appendix of this chapter for sources).[9] Figure 14.4 plots the nominal ($m_1 x$, in copper maravedis) and real ($\frac{m_1 x}{e}$, in silver maravedis) values of the vellón stock.

For a single vellón coin called the cuarto, figure 14.5 shows the intrinsic value and the value in exchange or the market value, each measured in silver maravedis per cuarto.[10] The intrinsic value measures $b_1 p^*/\phi$ in our model; b_1 is the ounces of copper per

---

[9] Compare figure 14.4 with figure 10.4 on page 175.

[10] The intrinsic value is constructed as the market value, in silver mr, of the copper content of the coin, copper prices taken from Motomura (1994) until 1626, and from Amsterdam prices for Swedish copper (Posthumus 1946, 271–72) with a 30% markup for transport costs. The market value is constructed as the face value of the coin at each point in time, deflated by the premium on silver as for figure 14.4.

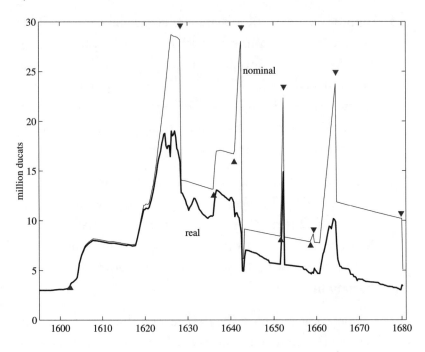

Figure 14.4 Nominal value $m_1 x$ (in copper mr) and real value $\frac{m_1 x}{e}$ (in silver mr) of the vellón stock, 1595–1680. 1 ducat (D) = 375 maravedis (mr). The dates of restampings and cry-downs are marked by $\triangle$ and ∇, respectively.

cuarto, ϕ is the ounces of copper per unit consumption good, and p^* is silver maravedis per unit consumption good. The market value measures e^{*-1}, in units of silver maravedis per cuarto. Note that $b_1 p^*/\phi < e^{*-1}$ implies $p^* < \frac{e^{*-1}}{b_1}\phi = e^{*-1}\gamma_1$. Thus, a larger gap between $\frac{b_1 p^*}{\phi}$ and e^{*-1} implies a larger "fiat component" to the value of cuartos. The figure implies that, most of the time, the exchange value of cuartos exceeded their melting point, often substantially.

Figure 14.6 plots the movements in x and e. We observe fluctuations in both series. Movements in x are dictated by the government's sequences of restampings and cry-downs. The series e represents observations on the market-determined exchange rate between copper mr and silver mr.

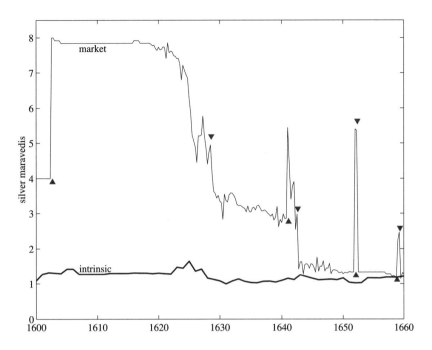

Figure 14.5 Market value ($e^{*-1} = x/e$) and intrinsic value ($b_1 p^*/\phi$) (in silver mr) of a vellón *cuarto* coin, 1600–1660. The dates of restampings and cry-downs are marked by $\triangle$ and ∇, respectively.

The chronology of operations was roughly as follows (see table 14.4 for details). Implementation of Philip II's edict of 1596 led to a gradual replacement of older, partly silver small coinage with the new copper coins minted in Segovia. In 1602, the government decided to produce new copper coins with half as much copper as the previous ones. In figure 14.5, the cuarto's intrinsic value became only ⅛ of its market value. The government observed that e remained constant. It then recalled the coins minted before 1602 and restamped them (increased x) by a factor of 2. In figure 14.6, x doubled. The operation was successful, in that large quantities of coins were voluntarily brought to the mint for restamping, and the government collected 50% of the amounts brought. No inflation ensued, encouraging the government of Castile to mint large quantities

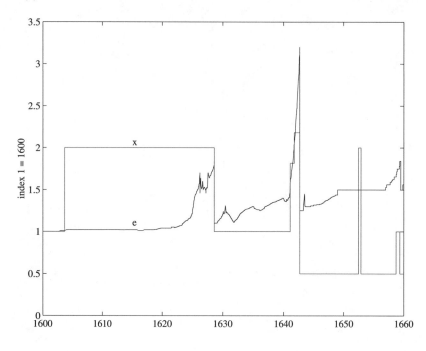

Figure 14.6 Index numbers of x (copper mr/cuarto) and e (copper mr/silver mr) for a vellón *cuarto* coin, 1600–1660.

of the new coins, not just in Segovia but in the other mints as well, even though these other mints continued to rely on the medieval technology, producing poor quality coins known as "thick billon" (*vellón grueso*). Figure 14.4 shows two periods of substantial minting: from 1602 to 1608, when a concerned parliament extracted from the king a promise to halt minting, and again from 1618.

In 1626, Mariana's 1609 prediction came true.

These expansions of m_1x continued until 1626, when the vellón coinage had completely replaced silver as medium of exchange. Comparing the nominal and real balances of the vellón coinage in figure 14.4 indicates that by 1626 an upper bound on real balances had been reached, corresponding to k, the demand for all real balances.[11] Inflation set in, as e began to increase rapidly (fig. 14.6).

---

[11] Velde and Weber (2000) estimate the pre-existing silver stock at 15 to 25 million ducats, based on the population of Castile and estimates of per capita money holdings in other countries at the time. Hamilton (1934, 91) states

Alarmed policy makers abruptly halted the minting of copper coins, a measure that stabilized e for a while. They spent two years deliberating over the best way to stem the inflation and the incipient fall in real balances shown in figure 14.4. They started an open-market operation to exchange copper coins for bonds but soon cancelled it. That they contemplated this operation shows that they understood how the price level was under sway of a quantity theory cast in terms of the vellón coins of the form (14.6). That is, they believed that p^* varied directly with $m_1 e^{*-1}$. Eventually, in 1628, they devalued (lowered $e^{*-1} \equiv x/e$), by crying down x, halving the face value of the copper coinage overnight. This brought the market exchange rate between copper and silver coins part of the way back to its pre-1602 value: the premium on silver fell overnight from 84% to 10%.

Castile issued no more copper coinage until 1660, and therefore ceased to act on m_1 directly. But it carried out four restamping operations (increases of x) to multiply the face value of the copper coins by 2, 3, or 4. These restampings are detailed in table 14.4 of the appendix; they are also marked by upward-pointing arrows in figure 14.4, and recognizable as sharp increases in x in figure 14.6.[12] Each of these restamping operations was soon followed by a cancelling cry-down or reduction in x. The devaluations are marked by downward-pointing arrows, and their effects appear in the downward movements in nominal values in figure 14.4 and figure 14.5, and in x in figure 14.6. Each restamping operation generated revenues, as individuals brought in coins to exchange them unit per unit, affording seigniorage rates of ½, ⅔, or ¾. But the government found that the revenues it could raise were diminishing. As shown in figure 14.4, the real balances of vellón fell over time.

Figure 14.6 shows abrupt adjustments in x that were not accompanied by abrupt movements in e (for example, in 1602 and in

---

that 95% of transactions used vellón. Castilian vellón even began circulating in bordering areas of France in 1626 (Spooner 1972, 178).

[12] Since figure 14.6 charts the story of a pure copper coin, only three restampings appear; compare with table 14.4, right columns.

Table 14.2 Extent of restampings. The first column gives the number of existing coins called for restamping, the second gives the number of coins that were presented.

	Existing Stock (m D)	Amount Stamped (m D)	Ratio (%)
1603	3.6	2.3	64
1636	2.4	2.1	87
1641 (Feb)	9.1	9.0	99
1641 (Nov)	1.7	1.4	82
1651	4.8	3.7	77
1658	4.4	0.9	20

Table 14.3 Responses of e to changes in x.

Date	Change in: x	e
Aug 7, 1628	-50%	-40%
Sep 15, 1642	-75 to -83%	-61%
Jun 21, 1652	-75%	0%
Jun 30, 1659	-50%	-18%

1651) so that the data are not consistent with the straight type 1 equilibrium mentioned earlier. The restamping of 1651 is particularly noteworthy, for it had no effect on the silver premium, either in Hamilton's monthly series or in Micón's daily notations. Yet government accounts show that the restamping was very successful, as appears in table 14.2. On the other hand, movements in e during cry-downs at times came close to matching the movements in x, as shown in table 14.3 which compares the overnight changes in x with the corresponding overnight changes in e.

The end of the token coin experiment

From 1660 to 1680, Castile issued small coins made of a mixture of copper and 7% silver, this time using the cylinder press technology

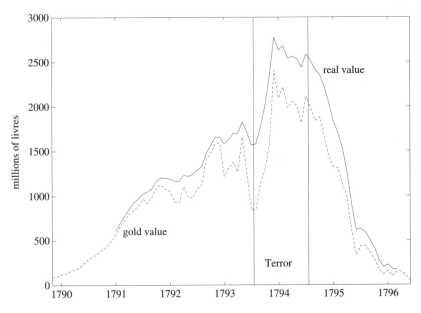

Figure 14.7 Real balances of assignats during phases of the French hyperinflation, 1789–96. *Source*: Sargent and Velde (1995).

in all mints. Initially, the government tried to give the coins a face value above intrinsic content, but depreciation forced it to abandon that project, and the coins were issued at close to intrinsic value, like medieval billon. Extensive counterfeiting (in spite of the use of the new technology) ultimately forced the government to abandon billon altogether: the government's technological advantage had been lost. After 1680, the small coinage in Castile was, like elsewhere in Europe, full-bodied copper, with a return to the hammering method. Not until after the advent of the Borbón dynasty were the hammers and the cylinder press replaced with imported screw presses in 1728. The Castilian experiment with token coins was over. [13]

---

[13] See García de Paso (2000a) for the reform of 1680–86.

Comparison with inflation during the French Revolution

The shape of the time series for real balances in figure 14.4 resembles a graph for real balances of the French paper assignats issued during the French Revolution, figure 14.7 (taken from Sargent and Velde 1995). The assignat was first issued in 1789 as a claim redeemable at auctions of church land nationalized in 1789. The government nationalized the land so that it could get revenues by then selling it. The government intended to use proceeds from the land sales to service and retire the national debt. The state issued assignats to pay for goods and services and to service its debt. To absorb or "back" assignats, the government auctioned church lands in exchange for assignats. It promised to burn the assignats redeemed at these auctions, and for a while actually did so. Vertical lines in figure 14.7 divide the period into three broad regimes of monetary policy. The line in 1793 indicates the beginning of the Terror, when price and wage controls and prohibitions on holding stores of value other than the assignat were enforced with instruments of Terror. The line in mid-1794 indicates the end of the Terror.

Before mid-1792, nominal issues of assignats saw mild inflation and large and steady increases in the real value of the total stock. During this period, assignats displaced metal as a means of exchange. The metal left France for other countries.[14] During this first period, the French government was mostly faithful to the auction scheme. But war raised the government's need for revenue and induced it to suspend the auctions and to print assignats. Inflation accelerated and real balances started to fall. The policy response to this situation was the set of economic measures enforced by the Terror. Thus, our second regime was the Terror, whose economic components included a set of harshly enforced legal restrictions designed to stimulate the demand for assignats and thereby increase the base of the inflation tax. The Terror arrested the inflation and the fall in real

---

[14] See Hawtrey (1919) and Sargent and Velde (1995).

balances. Vast quantities of assignats were printed without causing inflation. In July 1794, with France winning the war and the coalition that supported the Terror eroding in France, the Terror ended. This began the third regime, with deficits again being financed by printing assignats. This policy produced the classic symptoms of hyperinflation: accelerating inflation and falling real balances.

Apart from their time scales, figures 14.4 and 14.7 have similar patterns and witness similar monetary experiments. The different time scales show a much more rapid pace of events during the French Revolution. In both cases, a token currency was issued. In Spain it was made of copper, in France of paper. In both cases there initially occurred a buildup of real balances of the token currency, accompanied by only modest depreciation of the token money. In both cases, real balances of the token currency eventually constituted virtually the entire stock of real balances, driving out other monies and threatening to activate the quantity theory. In both cases, there eventually emerge periods of persistent inflation accompanied by declining real balances of the tokens. Thus, in the Castilian example, in the period from 1602 to the early 1620s, the token currency replaced other currencies, with little observed inflation, as occurred at first when the French revolutionaries introduced a paper currency.[15]   In the French case, the subsequent period of declining real balances of the token money exhibited all of the features of the twentieth-century hyperinflations described by Cagan (1956). It is likely that related forces account for the long decline in real balances in figure 14.4, because the repeated restampings and subsequent devaluations must eventually have been expected, prompting people to economize on m_1.

Unintended consequence for Sweden

An unintended consequence of Spain's monetary reform was to bring a full-bodied copper money and also inflation to Sweden.[16]   An

---

[15]   A notable difference is that, in the Castilian case, there was no explicit backing for the token coinage.

[16]   See Friedman and Schwartz (1963, 699–700) and Brandt and Sargent (1989)

important element in the story is reflected in figure 14.5, where the intrinsic value $\frac{b_1 p^*}{\phi}$ shows interesting movements in the 1620s. Its rise in the early 1620s was partly caused by the rise in the price of copper in terms of silver that accompanied Spain's massive coining of vellón coins. Its fall after 1626 reflects Spain's suspension of new coining.

Partly in response to developments in Spain, Sweden adopted a copper standard.

Mechanization came to Sweden in 1625. The following year, Spain stopped minting copper. When Spain withdrew from copper, it caused the demand for copper from Sweden (the biggest producer in Europe) to fall, because Spain had been consuming an amount equal to half of Sweden's copper output (Wolontis 1936, 221).[17] The Swedish king, Gustavus Adolfus, repeatedly pressed his French ally to buy Swedish copper and to mint it. In 1636, he nearly succeeded, but the project was blocked at the last minute by the French Cour des Monnaies (Spooner 1972, 189–90). To promote demand for Swedish copper, Sweden then moved to a copper standard, which it retained until the mid-eighteenth century, when it went to a paper currency. The Swedish experience differed from the Spanish because the coins were full-bodied rather than fiduciary. The Swedish government's aim was to enhance the demand for copper; a full-bodied coinage achieved this aim more aptly than a token one. The inflation that occurred in Sweden came from a declining copper content of the unit of account (Heckscher 1954, 88–91).

Concluding remarks

The governments in seventeenth-century Castile experimented with token coins. They understood and implemented parts but not all of the standard formula. Informed by advisors who recognized that the state could reap revenues by instituting a token subsidiary

---

for differing analyses of the Roosevelt administration's silver purchase program on the world price of silver and thereby on monetary affairs in China.

[17] In figure 14.5, note the fall in the world price of copper after the mid 1620s, roughly coinciding with the termination of Spain's producing new copper coins.

coinage, kings of Spain issued inconvertible token coins, at first in moderate amounts that let them gather revenues without causing inflation. But the kings eventually issued enough token coins to cause the first big fiat money inflation in Europe. For decades after inflation had emerged, the kings struggled sometimes to repair the system but other times to raise more revenues from it. In doing so they used a variety of measures that led contemporary observers to formulate early versions of the quantity theory of money. Following their footsteps, we have interpreted these Castilian experiments in terms of key parameters of our model. For us as well as for the early quantity theorists, purposefully or not, the kings of Castile performed wonderful and informative experiments. They were to be copied.

Appendix: money stocks and prices

Table 14.4 presents a chronology of monetary operations on copper coinage in Castile between 1597 and 1680, pieced together from various sources.[18] We distinguish between *calderilla*, that is, coins made any time before 1602 and containing some silver, like the coin on the right in figure 14.2, and the pure copper coinage that followed. Monetary ordinances and reforms treated those two types of coins differently.[19]

Our estimates of the copper stock of money are constructed by keeping track of the stock of calderilla and pure copper separately. The starting point for both series is in 1596: the initial stocks are

---

[18] The account in Hamilton (1936) is useful but incomplete and in places erroneous. It needs to be complemented with Domínguez Ortiz (1960). A good study of the Valladolid mint (Pérez García 1990) is very helpful as well. See also Carrera i Pujal (1943–47). Numismatists provide precious information: in particular, Fontecha y Sánchez (1968) catalogs the stamps used in the various restamping operations.

[19] In 1641, a difference was even made between the *segovianos*, coins minted in the *Ingenio* of Segovia like those of figure 14.1, and the other coins, variously called *vellón grueso*, *pechelingues*, or *moneda de Cuenca*.

Table 14.4 Chronology of billon and pure copper coinage (vellón grueso, segovianos) in Castile, sixteenth and seventeenth centuries. The mint equivalent is expressed in mr per marc (230g).

Date	Billon (calderilla, vellón rico)			Copper	
	Fine	ME	Change in x	ME	Change in x
1566–97	1.4%	110			
Jul 19 1597	0.4%	140	*calderilla* minted		
Jun 3 1602				280	*vellón* minted
Sep 18 1603		280	restamped ×2		
Nov 2 1608					minting halted
Sep 30 1617					resumed
May 8 1626					halted
Aug 7 1628		140	cried down ÷2	140	cried down ÷2
Mar 11 1636		420	restamped ×3		
Oct 22 1641				420	restamped* ×3
Sep 15 1642		70	cried down ÷6	70	cried down ÷6
Mar 12 1643		280	cried up ×4		
Nov 11 1651				280	restamped ×4
Jun 21 1652				70	cried down ÷4
Nov 14 1652		0	demonetized		
Oct 21 1654		280	remonetized		
Oct 29 1658				140	restamped ×2
May 6 1659				70	cried down ÷2
Sep 11 1660				204	minted
Oct 29 1660	6.9%	816	*vellón rico*	0	demonetized
Oct 14 1664	6.9%	408	cried down ÷2		
Feb 10 1680		204	cried down ÷2		
May 22 1680		0	demonetized	76	new *vellón*

∗: non-Segovia coinage was ordered restamped by 2 on Feb 11, 1641.

3 million ducats (1 ducat = 375mr) for calderilla (Domínguez Ortiz 1960, 252) and 0 for pure copper.

Quarterly time series for the nominal stocks are then constructed by accounting for increases due to minting of new coins, crying up and restamping, and decreases due to by crying down and depreciation. Like Motomura (1997), we set depreciation at 1% per annum, which is consistent with what is known about wear and tear of coinage and allows us to match contemporary estimates of the money stock. Output, whether due to minting or restamping, is computed from Motomura's figures until 1642 and Domínguez Ortiz (1960, 273) for later restampings. See García de Paso (2000a, 2000b) for more precise estimates. For the restampings of February and November 1641, we keep track of Segovia coinage and non-Segovia coinage separately (the former representing 15% of the total copper coinage).

The silver premium series, which is quarterly before 1650 and monthly after 1650, is in Hamilton (1934, 93, 96; 1947, 28). For the period 1618 to 1667, we have a daily premium series collected by a Genoese banker based in Madrid named Cosme Micón (see García de Paso, whom we thank for alerting us to these data).

☙

Chapter 15

Copycat Inflations in Seventeenth-Century Europe

This chapter describes how several European countries were tempted to replicate the Castilian experiment with token coins. Some resisted but others accepted the temptation and took the inflationary consequences.

France: flirting with inflation

France twice began to issue large quantities of token coinage, but retreated from the brink of inflation.

France was tempted to copy the Spanish experiment, but ultimately refused. In France, the realization that mechanized minting allowed a fiduciary coinage dawned at the same time as in Spain. Before 1575, France's small denomination coins had been made of billon. The French had set up the Mill Mint, a mechanized mint, in 1552 (see chapter 4). In 1575, it produced the first pure copper coins, with an intrinsic content worth about 45% of the face value. To quote Blanchet and Dieudonné (1916, 172): "The date of this reform is important: in distinction with medieval currency which, however alloyed, had never had value but for its content of fine metal, we see the birth of subsidiary fiduciary coinage, thanks to the progress in public credit, as well as to a sharper understanding of the relative roles of metals in circulation."

Limited minting of pure copper coins continued for a time. In 1596, it was decided that all pure copper coinage would be made exclusively at the Mill Mint, and little was produced. From 1602 to 1636, however, the French king began granting private individuals licenses to produce copper coins using presses. The coins were legal tender. The licenses limited the total coinage, and the Cour des Monnaies tried to restrict these issues. Throughout this period, imitations of French copper coins were minted in foreign enclaves and territories adjacent to the French kingdom (see fig. 4.8), and typically circulated in rolls.[1]

However, when mechanized minting was extended to all mints in 1640, new emissions of pure copper soon followed, small amounts in 1642 and 1643, and much larger ones between 1653 and 1656, at a time of extreme political crisis.[2] The minting was subcontracted to private entrepreneurs who established presses in small towns with water mills. The amounts remained small, however, at least in comparison with the Spanish experience. The output of 1653–56 was equivalent to 1.6 million Spanish ducats and amounted to 2 or 3% of the French money stock. France had thus considered following Spain's policies but had refrained from excessive issues of token coins after numerous warnings from monetary officials.[3]

Catalonia

In 1640, the Catalonians rebelled against the king of Spain and signed a treaty with France that made the king of France the count of Barcelona and prince of Catalonia. It took the Spanish troops until 1652 to retake Barcelona and most of Catalonia, but the Roussillon region around Perpinyà (Perpignan) remained in French hands. Fighting continued inconclusively until 1659, when Spain ceded the part of Catalonia north of the Pyrenees to France.

During that period, a number of Catalonian towns (Mailliet 1868–73 lists over twenty) issued copper coins; some, like Vic, Perpinyà, Gerona, Puigcerdà, and Villafranca del Panadès, had issued convertible small change in earlier years. It appears, however, that this time the convertibility of the copper coin was not guaranteed, and large emissions followed.

Usher (1943, 459–63) and Colson (1855) provide information on copper issues in Barcelona and Perpignan respectively. In Perpignan,

---

[1] Spooner (1972, 174–78, 185–92, 336–39).

[2] The output was 300,000 livres in 1642–43 and 7.3 million livres in 1654–56.

[3] Spooner (1956) documents the opposition of the Cour des Monnaies.

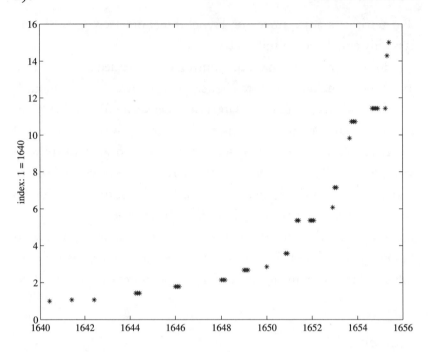

Figure 15.1 Index of the price of the gold doubloon in sous, Perpignan, 1640–56. *Source*: Colson (1855, 141–42).

the city council asked the French viceroy in 1643 to authorize issues of coins of 6d., 12d., and 24d. with the usual content. A few months later, however, citing difficulties in securing the silver content, they asked permission to put less silver in the 12d. and 24d. coins, and none at all in the 6d. coins; the viceroy, initially reluctant, finally agreed. In 1646, a further issue was authorized. Counterfeiting immediately became a problem. Inspectors were appointed to stamp the authentic coins and destroy the fakes. Surrounding towns refused to accept the copper coins, but Perpignan took them to court and won a ruling by the supreme court of Catalonia.

Significant inflation resulted, as shown in figure 15.1 which plots the price of the gold coin in Perpignan.[4] The scale of the inflation,

---

[4] The price series for Barcelona (Usher 1943, 466) tracks figure 15.1 closely, but stops in 1653 when the town came under Castilian control again.

a factor of 15, indicates that the market value of the copper coinage, initially overvalued by a factor of 13 to 14, had been driven to its intrinsic value. After the inflation ended, the French government tackled the problem of debts contracted during the inflation. To index repayments, it established a price series for the gold coin, which forms the basis of figure 15.1.

Germany

In Germany, efforts by successive Emperors since the fifteenth century to coordinate the coinage policies of the many constituent states of the Empire culminated in an imperial mint ordinance (*Reichsmünzordnung*) of 1559. This left the responsibility for minting coins to selected group of princes, but fixed the intrinsic content of coins throughout the whole denomination structure, and made small coins full-bodied. This arrangement led the official mints to produce only large denomination coins (silver thalers thaler and guldiner) and caused a shortage of small change that was increasingly met by unauthorized mints that produced light-bodied coins. Over time, these coins became lighter, so that by 1610 they were already 20 to 25% lighter than prescribed in the mint ordinance.

Widespread inflation developed in Germany between 1619 and 1623 (the Kipper- und Wipperzeit).

When the Thirty Years War began in 1618, the stage had been set for what became known as the *Kipper- und Wipperzeit*, "the clipping and culling times."[5] Throughout Germany and the Habsburg lands, local princes as well as private mints competed with each other and produced progressively more debased petty silver coinage (*groschen, kreutzer, pfennig*), driving the intrinsic content to ⅛ of the amounts prescribed in 1559. Some states even issued pure copper coinage. People queued at the mints to turn their copper pots and pans into

---

[5] Gaettens (1955, ch. 4), Rittmann (1975, ch. 9–12), and Sprenger (1991, ch. 7) for general surveys and references to the numerous regional studies. See also Schmoller (1900) in the context of the evolution of monetary policy with respect to small coins. A brief treatment in English is Kindleberger (1991). This episode has attracted little interest in the English language literature, even though German writers called it "the Great Inflation"—until 1923, that is.

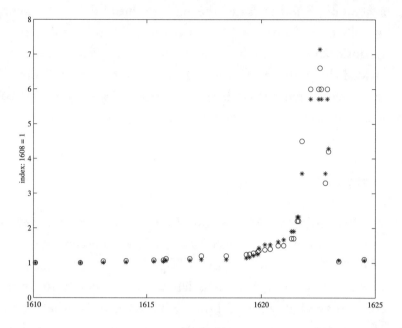

Figure 15.2 Price of the Gold florin (*circles*) and the silver thaler (*stars*) in terms of Kreutzer coins, Bavaria. *Source*: Altmann (1976, 272–73).

coins. The metal content of the large coins remained unchanged. The prices of such large coins (the gold florin and the silver thaler) in terms of the small coins are tracked in figure 15.2. Commodity prices also increased greatly, although not quite as much. The inflationary episode ended abruptly in 1623, when the princes' deteriorating tax revenues from issuing coins induced them to return to a better standard. However, another episode of inflation, less spectacular and more drawn out, was to take place in the late seventeenth century (the so-called second *Kipper- und Wipperzeit*).[6]

The scale of inflation evident in figure 15.2 even surpasses Castile's experience, with the price of silver coins tripling from March 1621 to March 1622.[7] Minted quantities for all of Germany cannot

---

[6] See also Schönberg (1890, 1:336) on the large-scale recourse to copper coinage in Prussia between 1764 and 1806.

[7] Redlich (1972, 12) notes the similarity with the Castilian inflation.

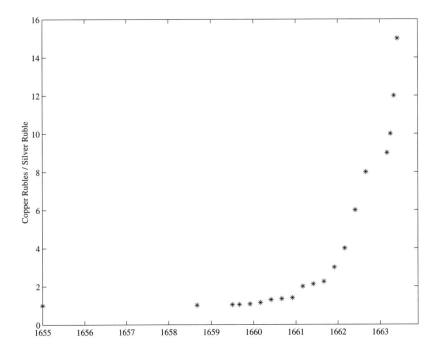

Figure 15.3 Exchange rate of copper rubles to silver rubles, Russia, 1655–63. *Source*: Chaudoir (1836, 1329–30).

be known, but there is information for Saxony, a major state and important silver-producing area. In the twenty years preceding the inflation, Saxony minted 0.4 million fl. per year, almost all in large silver coins. During the four years of the Kipperzeit, at least 12.5 million fl. in small coins were minted, 5.5 million fl. in Dresden alone. During the following 28 years, 0.1 million in large silver coins were minted per year (Wuttke 1894, 142).

As Richard Gaettens wrote (1955, 95): "From the point of view of monetary history the Kipperzeit had undoubtedly also a positive side. Indeed it became apparent that alongside the main currency a fiduciary money was needed for small change. . . . The development of subsidiary coinage received in the Kipperzeit its decisive impulse."

Russia

Poland and Russia experienced inflation due to copper coinage in the 1650s and 1660s.

In the second half of the seventeenth century, large issues of small coins and a consequent appreciation of the large currency recurred in eastern Germany and in Poland. While engaged in a war against Poland, the Russian czar began to mint pure copper imitations of silver rubles in 1655, and decreed that they should exchange at par with the latter. Initially successful, this currency collapsed after a few years. The pattern shown in figure 15.3 (stable exchange rate for several years, followed by a rapid collapse) resembles the Castilian experience. In 1663, the mint repurchased the copper rubles at 1% of their face value.[8]

The Ottoman empire

A final example comes from the Ottoman Empire. In the 1680s, the Ottoman rulers hired a Venetian convert to construct screw presses and replace the old hammering method. The first use of the new machines was to produce massive amounts of copper coinage from 1687 to 1690, when the *mankur*, whose copper content was worth about 0.14 silver *âkçe*, was ordered to pass for 1 *âkçe* (Sahillioğlu 1983, 289; Pamuk 1997).

෴

---

[8] See Chaudoir (1836, 128–30) and Bruckner (1867) on Russia, Bogucka (1975) on Poland.

Chapter 16

England Stumbles toward the Solution

This chapter and the next describe the mixture of experience and theorizing that eventually led England to adopt the standard formula. Experience held the upper hand. During the seventeenth and eighteenth centuries, England used privately issued tokens and counterfeits for much of its small denomination coins. In 1661, Sir Henry Slingsby propounded the standard formula. The government did not implement it, even after 1787, when Boulton's steam press made Slingsby's proposal practical. But private firms quickly exploited Boulton's technology to make redeemable tokens that were difficult to counterfeit. For a generation after 1787, these private tokens supplied small change for England. The government effectively nationalized the issuing of tokens after 1817. Later in the nineteenth century, the British government explicitly stated the operating rules needed to affirm the standard formula.

Impelled by experience and private innovations, Britain evolved toward the standard formula.

Thus, England's path from the medieval cycle of shortages and debasements to implementing the standard formula and the gold standard was circuitous. The period that extends from 1560 to the nineteenth century contains several interesting episodes that exemplify the slow process of learning about the standard formula.

Britain's Great Debasement and the abhorent reaction to it set the stage. Unlike England's medieval debasements,[1] the Great Debasement of Henry VIII and Edward VI from 1550 to 1560 reduced fineness rather than weight. Intended to raise revenues, it was the kind of debasement that jurists and philosophers had condemned. In 1560, Elizabeth I repaired the Great Debasement by restoring

---

[1] We interpret many of these debasements as having been designed to cure shortages of small change, not primarily to gather seigniorage. Angela Redish (2000, 9) remarks that the motive for most debasements was to maintain adequate supplies of coins, not to raise government revenues.

a strong standard for the silver coins: 60d. per troy ounce of sterling silver. The standard was slightly modified in 1601, to 62d.,
and thereafter it remained unchanged until 1816. The Great Debasement cast a long shadow. It inspired the British government's
subsequent reluctance to issue anything but sterling coinage, effectively precluding government issues of small denomination silver
coins. It also gave the English an enduring aversion to debasements
that played a decisive role in policy debates.

Regimes with   To supply the smaller denominations that the royal mint would
private tokens not produce, England experimented with various methods of issuing copper coinage: private monopoly, government monopoly, and
laissez-faire. We examine these regimes in the first part of this chapter and see them as implementing tentative and partial versions of
the standard formula. In chapter 14, we saw how Castilians tried
the "token" part of the standard formula without the "convertibility"
part. In their experiments, the English actually implemented convertibility, more or less completely, as part of the private monopoly
and laissez-faire regimes, although not with the government monopoly regime. But their attempts at making the coins overvalued ran
into predictable problems, in spite of intense efforts to improve the
existing technology and defeat counterfeiters. In the midst of one of
these experiences, Sir Henry Slingsby proposed the standard formula
in 1661.

The debate   In the late seventeenth century, the problem of small change
preceding the Great emerged higher in the denomination structure, among the silver
Recoinage ended coins. By 1695, a preponderance of markedly underweight silver
with a set back to coins caused the gold coin, the guinea, to appreciate abruptly in
prospects for the terms of the silver coins, which were still the unit of account. The
standard formula appreciation of the guinea precipitated two important events: the
in Britain.   Great Recoinage of 1696, which was preceded by a fascinating debate over the proper remedy; and the eventual emergence of gold
coins as the unit of account and a de facto gold standard in the
eighteenth century.[2] The second part of this chapter uses our model

---

[2] Adopting the gold coin as the unit of account would set the stage for Britain's
eventual adoption of the standard formula, with subsidiary silver coins becoming

to illuminate these events and debates, which engaged some of the brightest men in England including John Locke, William Lowndes, and Isaac Newton.

The government's decision to resolve the Locke-Lowndes debate largely in Locke's favor retarded progress toward the standard formula. Britain's monetary experiments before 1690 had inched toward the standard formula with privately issued tokens that were sometimes convertible. Despite theoretical insights from the Renaissance that had made price level stability, not the weight of coins in silver, the criterion of good monetary policy, Locke reverted to the medieval "communis opinio" when he insisted that a government's coin represented a claim on a set amount of silver. Locke's authority as forbearer of the gold standard rests mostly on that.[3]

Locke's writings about the recoinage belie his reputation as an empiricist philosopher. Against Lowndes's carefully documented account of historical facts about British coinage and his rich model designed to account for them, Locke stubbornly held to a simplified model despite its inconsistency with some salient facts. But politically Locke triumphed over Lowndes the empiricist. Sir Henry Slingsby's standard formula would have to wait.

Free-token and other regimes

Monetary theory is silent about the physical object on which a promise to pay is recorded, so that, except maybe for their denominations, theory treats token coins and banknotes in the same way. In 1776, Adam Smith proposed that banks be allowed to issue paper notes if they would promise to convert them into specie on demand (see page 101). We believe that Smith did not create that idea out of thin air. Smith lived in a country that for nearly two centuries had allowed private firms to issue redeemable subsidiary token coins. If

---

convertible tokens for gold coins.

[3] See Bernstein (2000, 180–88) for another account of the debate between Locke and Lowndes.

the costs of manufacturing tokens were sufficiently low, firms could profit from issuing convertible tokens because people who held them in effect supplied interest-free loans. It is a small leap of the imagination from such a "free token" regime to the "free banking" regime advocated in Smith's "real bills doctrine." [4]

Laissez-faire or monopoly: England's hesitations

From the mid-sixteenth century to 1816, England's policy to supply small change alternated between private monopoly, government monopoly, and laissez-faire. Slingsby stated the standard formula for token coinage. Technological difficulties made the government adhere to full-bodied copper coinage until the late eighteenth century, but to tolerate private issues.

From 1560 to 1817, England alternated between three regimes for supplying small change: private monopoly of partially convertible token coinage, government monopoly of full-bodied coinage, and free private competition in supplying convertible token coinage.

English coins had always been made of sterling silver, except during the Great Debasement of 1540–60. The smaller denomination coins, from the farthing to the penny, had become too small to be made of silver and by the mid-sixteenth century, royal coinage of these smaller sorts had ceased altogether. In the following century and a half, small change in England took the form of unalloyed base metals issued by various private parties. There were two periods of laissez-faire. Both were terminated by the government after it had adopted a new minting technology: mechanization in the 1670s and the steam engine in the 1820s. The latter episode ended when the government implemented the standard formula after the private sector had profited for a generation from using a technology for producing high-quality coins that were difficult to counterfeit.

Private monopoly (1613–44)

A private monopoly prevailed from 1613 to 1644. By a proclamation of May 19, 1613, the king reclaimed his prerogative to issue currency and outlawed private moneys. He also granted to an individual the exclusive right to manufacture copper farthings. The coins were to be made "artificially by engines and instruments." The patent set a minimum weight for the coins, but that minimum was low: 1 pound of copper, costing 1s., was turned into 25s. in tokens (Ruding 1849, 1:381, and Beveridge et al. 1965, 677, for the price of copper).

---

[4] See Sargent and Wallace (1982) for an analysis of Smith's real bills regime.

The coins were thus issued at a high rate of profit, to be shared with the king.[5] The coins were not made legal tender: the king's proclamation of 1613 said that the coins were "to pass for the value of farthings . . . with the liking and consent of his loving subjects." The patent further required the manufacturer to sell the tokens at a rate of 21s. in tokens for 20s. in silver; it also imposed the obligation to repurchase them at the same rate, but only for one year "until the said tokens should have grown into more general use and were well dispersed." The arrangement therefore consisted of a highly overvalued but only partially convertible token. Both aspects of the arrangement ran into trouble and had to be refined.

Some difficulties came from the overvaluation. Complaints had arisen that the tokens were inconvertible and that their selling price was below par. Their circulation remained limited, and unlicensed private issues continued in spite of their prohibition. So "that everie person may be left without all excuse, if againe they should presume to infringe Our Royall commandment," the king in 1617 changed the selling price to 20s. in tokens per £ silver (it was changed back to 21s. in 1625). The buying price remained at 21s. in tokens per £ silver, but the king ordered that a "continuall rechange for them" be established in London only, to buy and sell tokens.

Another problem was counterfeiting. Counterfeiting either the tokens or the engines was prohibited again in 1615 and 1618. In 1625, the importation of counterfeits was also prohibited. By 1631 the counterfeiters were so busy that they were underselling the king's monopolists by offering tokens at 24 to 26s. for 20s. silver.

The first problem fed on the second, as counterfeiting hindered convertibility. Complaints grew that the monopolists were not maintaining convertibility, to which the monopolists responded that they were refusing only counterfeits. An indication that excessive quantities could not be redeemed came in a prohibition against tendering more than 2d. in tokens in 1634, and a renewed statement that they

---

[5] A disappointed competitor attempted to discredit the patent holder by spreading the rumor that the profits would be higher than initially disclosed, prompting the king to renegotiate with the incumbent a higher share for himself.

were not legal tender in 1636.

To combat counterfeiting, the tokens were redesigned in 1636 and a brass insert added. Impressing a plug of a different metal required a sufficiently powerful mechanical press, which made counterfeiting a more costly and more detectable activity. The patentees were instructed to exchange both old and new tokens for sterling, but only "from time to time," and the old ones were in effect repudiated, creating much resentment against the tokens.

After the Civil War began, the monopoly soon ended. Parliament investigated it in 1642, confiscated its assets in 1643, and seized £5000 from the estates of the patentees to redeem outstanding tokens.[6]

Laissez-faire

A laissez-faire regime prevailed intermittently, from the mid-sixteenth century to 1613, from 1644 to 1672, and from the 1740s to 1817. During each episode, the government desisted from making its own coins and encouraged, or at least did not discourage, private suppliers of coins.

We have seen that private tokens were widespread in the early sixteenth century (see page 217). After restoring the English coinage, Elizabeth I considered issuing copper coinage. Citing complaints "against the tokens of lead and tin, generally coined and uttered . . . by grocers, vintners, chandlers and alehouse-keepers," a proposed proclamation of 1576 was to announce the issue of royal copper farthings and halfpennies, providing that "such cost and charge should be employed thereon as that any, so evil-disposed, should hardly attain to counterfeit the same"; the coins were to have limited legal tender, and privately issued tokens were to be forbidden. But the proclamation was never issued, nor did the government issue any coinage of its own.[7] Instead, the government tolerated private

---

[6] Ruding (1840, 1:369, 371–72, 378, 381, 386, 388, 389, 399–402); see also Peck (1960, 19–49); Larkin and Hughes (1973–83, 1:287–90, 308–10, 350–51, 363–65, 2:39–41, 500–503).

[7] Peck (1960, 9–10, 581–82).

coinage, and in the case of the city of Bristol granted official permission to issue square lead tokens in 1577. The proclamation of May 19, 1613 that established the private monopoly (see page 264) describes in detail the situation prevailing at the time (Ruding 1840, 1:369): farthing tokens, made of lead, passed between vintners, tapsters, chandlers, bakers, and other tradesmen and their customers.

Over 12,700 different types of tokens have been cataloged for the period from 1644 to 1672, issued in 1,700 different English towns. An estimated 3,000 were issued in London alone. Suppliers were city councils, owners of firms, and local retailers. Tokens usually bore the name and location of the issuer. The circulation of each token was limited geographically to a few streets, but there existed in London at least one "changer of farthings" in Drury Lane, who issued his own farthings (Berry 1988, 5).

One of the better documented issuers was the city of Bristol, which had issued tokens in the sixteenth century. Then the second or third largest city in England, Bristol obtained permission to issue copper farthings in 1652, and made further issues in 1660 and 1669 (Thompson 1988, vii–xxxiii). As to convertibility, we know of a city ordinance of June 1652 by which the mayor and magistrates "to the end also that no person or persons shall or may suffer any loss or prejudice by them, have published and declared that they will from time to time receive and take them in and allow them after the rate of penny for 4 of them."

The Bristol farthings are the most common of surviving tokens, and almost no other tokens are known from the city of Bristol. They circulated regionally, examples having been found in various places around Bristol; they were successful enough that they were counterfeited. Furthermore, they set a standard, since Gloucester in 1669 decided to issue farthings of the "full weight of a Bristol farthing" (Thompson 1975). We do not know that weight, but surviving tokens suggest that they were made at 32d. to 40d. per pound of copper. This compares with the standard of 22d. to the pound adopted for the royal coinage in 1672, which was as close to intrinsic value as possible, based on a price of copper of 14d.

per pound. Thus, the Bristol farthings were somewhat overvalued, but probably not excessively, considering the likely returns to scale enjoyed by the royal mint.

The Slingsby doctrine

Sir Henry Slingsby proposed the standard formula in 1661.

During the Commonwealth, from 1649 to 1660, proposals were put forward to replace these private tokens with government issues. Shortly afterwards, Sir Henry Slingsby (1621–90) stated the standard formula. Slingsby (fig. 16.1) was master of the London Mint from 1662 to 1680 and supervised the mechanization of coin production by Blondeau (Challis 1992b, 343). In a memorandum to King Charles II, dated June 5, 1661, Slingsby proposed to mint farthings of ¼d, the smallest existing silver coin being 1d. He made what may be the earliest statement of Cipolla's standard formula, when he wrote (Peck 1960, 601):

> Copper is the fittest metal; a contract should be made with Sweden for the supply thereof, and it should be coined at so little increase of price as to make counterfeiting disadvantageous. To avoid a danger of glut, the Mint should be always ready to exchange farthings for silver money, if requested, and should forbear to make more than demanded.

Slingsby's proposal was not implemented until more than one hundred years later. Perhaps, in spite of the new minting process, the government's cost advantage over its competitors remained insufficient. Or perhaps the lesson Slingsby taught was not widely learned.

Government monopoly

Slingsby's proposal was ignored.

Instead, soon after implementing mechanization in 1660, the royal government decided to mint its own copper farthings and halfpennies for the first time. The proclamation of August 1672 asserted that "our subjects would not easily be wrought upon to accept the farthings and half-pence of these private stampers, if there were not some kind of necessity for such small coins to be made for public use, which cannot well be done in silver, nor safely in any other metal, unless the intrinsic value of the coin be equal, or near to that

Figure 16.1 Portrait of Sir Henry Slingsby (Hailstone 1869). Courtesy of the Yale University Library.

value for which it is made current." The mint was ordered to make halfpennies and farthings "to contain as much copper in weight as shall be of the true intrinsic value and worth of a half-penny and a farthing respectively, the charges of coining and uttering being only deducted." The new coins were made legal tender for payments up to 6d. Privately issued tokens were outlawed. Slingsby was put in charge of the copper coinage, and contracted with a Swedish merchant to purchase copper. The face value of a pound of copper was 22d., the cost of the copper was 14½d. and expenses were 4d. (Craig 1953, 175); net seigniorage was thus 16%. The coins were widely counterfeited. Minting stopped in 1676, after about £40,000 had been minted.

The English government sought ways to deter counterfeiting by adding milled edges to coins or by using plugs of a different metal inside the coin, or by looking for better alloys. Tin was tried between 1684 and 1694, although more as a means of subsidizing Cornish producers at a time of a low price of tin. The net seigniorage rate was high, at 40%. To defeat counterfeiters, the coins not only had a copper plug as the tokens of 1636 did, but their edge was inscribed with Castaing's machine (Peck 1960, 107–8, 151–52). In spite of those measures, the House of Commons found those coins wanting in value and too easily counterfeited, and ended their production in 1694, over the protests of the Cornish mine owners.

While Philip II of Spain could be led to believe that the technological superiority of his mechanical press was secure, a century later English officials could not be put under such an illusion. Small-scale screw presses had been used during the "free token" era of the Commonwealth; one such press used by an apothecary in Derbyshire was described in an eighteenth-century magazine (Peck 1960, 579–80). The government admitted defeat in the Plate Act of 1696 by offering to buy any press capable of making coinage from individuals (Challis 1992b, 391).

The failure of measures against counterfeiting moved English monetary officials to endorse a full-bodied copper coinage. The copper coinage of 1694–96 was issued at 21d. per pound, even closer to intrinsic value than in 1672. When the government decided to resume copper coinage in 1718, Sir Isaac Newton, the mintmaster, insisted that it be minted at intrinsic value plus costs,[8] and small quantities of copper coins were issued in the eighteenth century (1717–24, 1729–55, 1770–75).

Another "free token" era then followed. "By the 1740s competition had driven the copper in private coins of mixed metal down

---

[8] "Halfpence and farthings (like other money) should be made of a metal whose price among Merchants is known, and should be coined as near as can be to that price, including the charge of coinage. . . . All which reasons incline us to prefer a coinage of good copper according to the intrinsic value of the metal" (in Shaw [1896] 1967, 164–65).

to one-eighth of that in legal coin" (Craig 1953, 253). In 1754, official coinage was stopped on a petition from London retailers complaining that copper had overtaken gold and silver in retail coinage. Counterfeits, which had appeared after 1725, became numerous after 1740. In 1751, the first "evasions" appeared: coins that imitated the general appearance of the official coinage, but were clearly differentiated in the details, such as the legend "Britannia" altered to read "British girl," or the king's name replaced by Shakespeare's. The government and the courts construed the laws on counterfeiting not to apply to these imitations. Counterfeiters sold them at half-price to wholesalers, who resold them at 28s. to 30s. for a gold guinea of 21s. By 1753, 40 to 50% of the stock of copper in circulation was counterfeit, and by 1787, the mint estimated that only 8% of copper coins in circulation "had some tolerable resemblance to the king's coin." To remedy the situation, the mint recommended issuing royal copper coins twice as heavy as before.[9]

After James Watt first harnessed the steam engine to a minting press in 1787, trade tokens issued by firms and employers became extremely common: convertible tokens once again emerged as the predominant form of small change in England. Most of the trade tokens were made by Birmingham firms. They were of the same weight as the official coinage and carried the issuer's name in promise of redemption. This system of reliable convertible token coins was the market's way of supplying small change. The market thus prepared the way for the government to implement the standard formula. The government had only to nationalize and administer this system, which it began to do in 1816.

The Great Recoinage of 1696

By 1690, Slingsby's theorizing and numerous experiments with convertible private tokens and government tokens had taken Britain

---

[9] Peck (1960, 205–15).

far toward the standard formula. However, in 1695 Parliament resolved a public debate about the shortage of small coins in a way
that arrested progress toward the standard formula. By accepting
John Locke's view that a government coin represented a set amount
of silver, Parliament reverted to the "communis opinio" of medieval
monetary theory, and did so at great public expense.

The theme of this book is that implementing the standard formula required several things: a good technology to make coins, an
understanding of the relevant monetary theory, and a government
wanting to convert token coins into full-bodied coins on demand.[10]
The Great Recoinage of 1696 showed some of these prerequisites

*The standard
formula required
technology,
monetary theory,
and a trustworthy
government.*
to be present but others still lacking.[11] Thus, after 1661, a well-
informed monetary theorist should have known about the standard
formula from Sir Henry Slingsby, not an obscure scholarly writer
but an important British public official from a recent time. Not
only was the relevant monetary theory available, but a new technology for producing milled coins had been introduced in 1662 that
might have allowed the government to solve the problem of small
change. But two problems remained. One was that the minting
technology still might not have offered enough of a cost advantage,
as recurring problems with counterfeiters were to show. The other
was that the reigning Stuart dynasty could not be trusted to honor its
financial commitments.[12] So under the Stuarts, England continued
to mint full-bodied silver coins and full-bodied copper coins without
convertibility. The silver coinage was of poor quality. The newly
minted coins were often melted down immediately, and the state of
the coinage seemed to be slowly deteriorating.

The underweight state of the silver coinage attracted more attention after the Glorious Revolution of 1688. The revolution brought

---

[10] Here "wanting" is taken to mean "credibly committed." See French finance
minister Jacques Necker's remarks on credibility cited by Sargent and Velde (1995).

[11] We have substantial documentation about the Great Recoinage: Feavearyear
(1963, ch. 6–7), Craig (1953, ch. 11), Horsefield (1960), Li (1963), and Challis
(1992a).

[12] See North and Weingast (1989) for a modern "Whig view" of the opportunistic
behavior of the Stuarts, including defaults on a variety of commitments.

a regime that demonstrated its attachment to making and keeping commitments by engineering a costly recoinage at government expense in the midst of an expensive war. Though it completely followed the recommendations of no single advisor, Parliament heard sophisticated analysts, including Lowndes and Locke. The advice of each of these opposing figures can be interpreted as reflecting alternative versions of our model. We think that Lowndes's analysis was more consistent with the evidence. But Locke's argument that the state's coins committed it to deliver a particular amount of silver, not a particular value in exchange for goods, nevertheless carried the day. [13]

The monetary system under the Restoration (1660–88)

England used both gold and silver coins. It did not issue coins at a standard less than sterling (92.5%). The silver coinage in circulation ranged mostly from the sixpence (6d.) to the half-crown (30d.). The gold coinage consisted mainly of guineas.

Chapter 4 described how England used the screw press to produce new silver coins in 1662. The technology let the government produce coins that were distinctly sharp and regular, with milled edges. After 1662, these milled coins coexisted with the hammered coins that had been minted with the older technology. [14] The new milled money inhibited clipping and so gave the government a technological advantage over counterfeiters. The government began in a limited way to address the problem of low denominations (1d. and below).

The large denomination silver and gold coinage then moved center stage. In 1666, gross seigniorage was set to 0 by the Free Coinage Act (18 Car. II. c. 5), and a specific tax was levied on alcohol to finance minting expenses (Feavearyear 1963, 95). The recommendation of the Romanists was finally implemented. [15]

---

[13] The personal motto of William Camden (see page 17) still carried much force in British public policy.

[14] Since the coins were produced by a mill, coins with engraved edges came to be known as "milled money."

[15] The policy was briefly imitated in France in 1679.

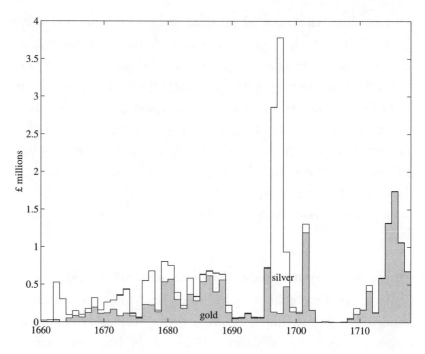

Figure 16.2 Minting volumes in England, 1660–1718. *Source*: Challis 1992a.

Figure 16.2 shows the minting volumes in the years that followed. For a while, there was substantial minting. The market price of silver remained at or slightly above the mint price (now equal to the mint equivalent) of 62s. per pound troy. But by 1690, gold minting had displaced silver minting, which practically ceased.

Milled and hammered money coexisted. The cumulative output of milled money after 1662 was £4.3 million. Most of it was hoarded, melted, or exported (Feavearyear 1963, 122–23; Craig 1953, 167: "the new machine-struck coins were reserved for illegal export or the melting-pot"). In 1694, the silver circulation was estimated to consist of £13.5 million: £2.5 million in milled money (minted since 1662), £10 million in hammered money (minted before 1662), and £1 million in counterfeits (Horsefield 1960, 258). Thus, most of the silver currency consisted of hammered money, by nature more susceptible to clipping.

The silver currency, however, seemed not to have deteriorated much before 1672. Deterioration was widely noted only after 1686. Government treasurers, who accepted all silver coins by tale regardless of their condition,[16] found them to be increasingly underweight, from 11.4% in 1686 to almost 50% in 1695 (Challis 1992b, 380–82). By the mid-1690s, complaints about the underweight state of the coins and the export of bullion had increased.

Of this period of deteriorating silver coins, Macaulay ([1855] 1967, 4:187) tells us:

The coinage deteriorated under the Stuart kings.

> Meanwhile the shears of the clippers were constantly at work. The coiners too multiplied and prospered: for the worse the current money became the more easily it was imitated. . . . It was to no purpose that the rigorous laws against coining and clipping were rigorously executed. At every session that was held at the Old Bailey, terrible examples were made. Hurdles, with four, five, six wretches convicted of counterfeiting or mutilating the money of the realm, were dragged month after month up Holborn Hill. One morning seven men were hanged and a woman burned for clipping. But all was vain. The gains were such as to lawless spirits seemed more than proportional to the risks. Some clippers were said to have made great fortunes. One in particular offered six thousand pounds for a pardon. His bribe was indeed rejected: but the fame of his riches did much to counteract the effect which the spectacle of his death was designed to produce.

Of the consequences of the underweight currency, Macaulay ([1855] 1967, 4:188–90) says:

Macaulay described the evils of an underweight and not uniform subsidiary coinage.

> The evil proceeded with constantly accelerating velocity. At length, in the autumn of 1695 it could hardly be said that the country possessed, for practical purposes, any measure of the value of commodities. It was mere chance whether

---

[16] Gold coins could be refused if more than 2% underweight, by a proclamation of Elizabeth I of 1587 renewed by James I in 1611 (Ruding 1840, 1:351, 366); silver coins could be refused if clipped, by an act of 1503 (Horsefield 1960, 59).

what was called a shilling was really a tenpence, sixpence, or a groat. . . . The evils produced by this state of the currency were not such as have generally been thought worthy to occupy a prominent place in history. Yet it may well be doubted whether all the misery which had been inflicted on the English nation in a quarter of a century by bad Kings, bad Ministers, bad Parliaments, and bad Judges, was equal to the misery caused in a single year by bad crowns and bad shillings. . . . When the great instrument of exchange became thoroughly deranged, all trade, all industry were smitten as with a palsy. The evil was felt daily and hourly in almost every place and by almost every class, in the dairy and on the threshing floor, by the anvil and by the loom, on the billows of the ocean and in the depths of the mine. Nothing could be purchased without a dispute. Over every counter there was wrangling from morning to night. . . . The ignorant and helpless peasant was cruelly ground between one class which would give money only by tale and another which would take it only by weight.

The deteriorated state of the silver coinage attracted the attention of Parliament. In 1690, 1691, and 1692, bills were introduced in Parliament to devalue the currency from 62s. an ounce to 64s. or 65s., then the market price of bullion. Before 1695, every such measure was defeated. Pamphlets were published, debating the issue. Although Locke's first intervention occurred in 1691, until late 1694 there was still a limited sense of urgency and Parliament did not act. In 1695, a rise in the price of the guinea ignited a crisis.

The crisis

The high price of guineas provoked the government to act.

Figure 16.3 shows the price of the gold guinea in terms of the silver coins in the late seventeenth century. When the guinea was first issued in 1663, it was intended to circulate at 20s.,[17] but over the

---

[17] The proclamation of December 24, 1663 indicates that this rate is a target rather than a mandate: "That our Twenty shilling piece of Crown [i.e., 22 carat] gold to be coyned by the Mill and Presse may be even Twenty shillings in

following twenty years its value varied between 21s. 2d. and 21s. 8d. (Feavearyear 1963, 120–21, Li 1963, 51). Suddenly, in late November 1694, the guinea's price moved above 22s. and climbing to 30s. by June 1695.

Horsefield (1960, 26–28) noted that the guinea rose relative to silver because "it was in demand as a substitute for silver coins." We read Horsefield's phrase as alluding to a "within the interval" penny shortage in our model, when a binding penny-in-advance constraint makes large coins appreciate in terms of small ones. However, Horsefield did not isolate a cause for the depreciation of small coins, although he too cited fears of devaluation of the silver coinage. He noted that the nominal value of the money supply $m_1 + em_2$ had increased, largely because e increased, and said that "which was cause and which effect in all this remains obscure."

But the period from 1694 to 1696 also witnessed broader inflation. Figure 16.4 shows the movements in the prices of bullion, expressed in units of account per unit of weight of metal. To render the series for gold and silver comparable, we show them as percentage deviations from "par," where par is defined on the basis of the face value assigned to the gold and silver coinage as a result of the recoinage in 1696. Silver bullion appreciated, but less than gold. Gold's price relative to silver, which had been between 15 and 15.5, remained at 17 in late 1695. Horsefield (1960, 252) reported an index of non-agricultural commodities that rose by 18% from March 1695 to a peak in March 1696.

Feavearyear attributed the rise in prices to the expansion of credit that the Bank of England began in August 1694 with the its first loans to the government (Feavearyear 1963, 128–30).[18] He noted that the prevalence of underweight silver coins raised the melting point of silver coinage and therefore the upper bound on the price

---

value . . . or as neere as conveniently may bee" (Li 1963, 38). No law made the guinea legal tender at any particular rate.

[18] Feavearyear (1963, 131) ascribed the sudden rise in the guinea to fears of an impending debasement of silver (also cited by Craig 1953, 184), increased demand for gold as reserve currency, and speculation.

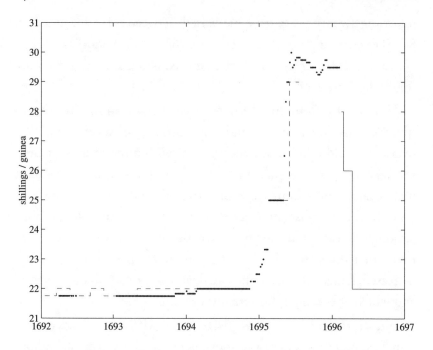

Figure 16.3 Market price and legal limits on the guinea, 1692–96. *Dashed line:* rate at which the Treasury accepted guineas (see text). *Solid line:* maximum rate set by Parliament (Horsefield 1960, 81). Prices: weekly series from Houghton (1692–1702).

level given by the commodity money. The widened band made room for an expansion of circulating paper IOUs to raise the price level by expanding m_2. Had the silver coinage been full-weight, the notes would have displaced coins and the price level would have remained constant (Feaveryear 1963, 135).[19]

A model with underweight coins

We now describe and analyze the debate about how to reform the coinage. To understand the debates and evidence, we have modified

---

[19] Thus, we read Feaveryear too as using elements of our model. Note that the Bank's notes became inconvertible in May 1696 and went at a discount, as low as 22% in February 1697; they became convertible again in December 1697 (Feaveryear 1963, 143; Rogers 1887, 170 for the time series on the discount).

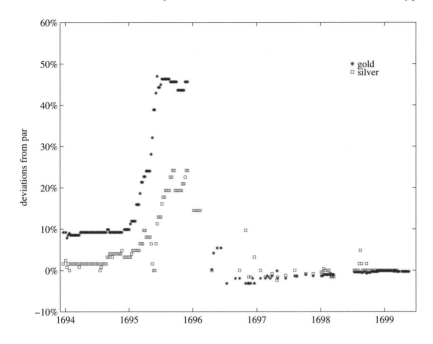

Figure 16.4 Market price of gold and silver bars in London, 1693–99, shown as deviation from par. Par is 5s. 2d. per troy oz of sterling (92.5%) silver (see text for gold par). *Sources*: Houghton (1692–1702), Proctor (1696–98), Whiston (1696–98), Castaing (1698–99).

our basic model to include underweight coins in the way of Sargent and Smith (1997). We will describe the modifications carefully later (in a passage in chapter 22 that begins on page 361); here we briefly summarize that modified version and some of its implications. To interpret events in Britain in the 1690s, we think of silver as playing the role of the small denomination coins and gold as playing the role of the large coins in the model.

At time $t = 0$, we assume that part of the stock of small coins is underweight. In the model, the mint does not make underweight coins. They just spontaneously emerge, for example, through exogenous depreciation. The price level that inspires melting of underweight coins exceeds that which would prompt melting of full-weight coins. For example, let an underweight coin weigh a fraction δ of a full-

When extended to include underweight coins, the model captures an essential aspect of the Lowndes-Locke debate.

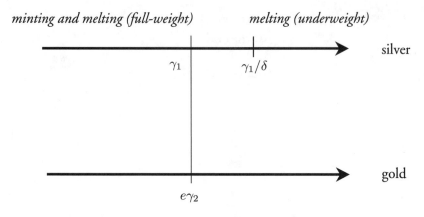

Figure 16.5 Intervals with full-weight and underweight silver coins.

weight coin. Assume zero seigniorage, which was true in England at that time. Then the melting point for underweight small coins will be γ_1/δ, while the minting and melting points for full-weight coins will both be γ_1 (see fig. 16.5). This situation implies that full-weight coins will be melted or exported before underweight ones. We let both full and underweight small coins satisfy the cash-in-advance and the penny-in-advance constraints. Start from a steady state with the intervals (now points) aligned for large and small full weight coins. Suppose that a shortage of small coins develops, say because income has grown. Then the model in chapter 22 yields the outcomes that the large coin appreciates, the price level rises proportionately, full-weight small coins are melted, and the value of additional large coins that are newly minted exceeds the value of small coins that are melted. What allows the price level to rise is that the melting point for underweight small coins is higher than the "official" melting point. Then not only does the exchange rate rise, but m_2 rises while m_1 falls, so that in the model of chapter 22, the ray $e(m_2)/m_1$ has risen.

Thus, the modified model seems to fit many of the facts, including the appreciation of the guinea, the rise in the price level, and the melting of full-weight silver coins. We will use features of this model again in chapter 17 to explain the apparent widening over the eighteenth century of the ranges within which prices of gold and silver fluctuated even while the exchange rate between gold and silver coins had stabilized.

The Locke-Lowndes debate

The recoinage episode sheds special light on the social learning process. In addition to Parliament's involvement, hundreds of pamphlets were published in the space of a few years by many writers. We also have reports from within the government, as well as opinions that the government solicited from outside experts (see Horsefield 1960 for a survey).

In 1695, it was recognized that the deteriorated state of the silver coinage was the source of the rising price level and price of gold guineas shown in figures 16.3 and 16.4. By rendering much of the silver currency underweight, wear, tear, and clipping had effectively widened the intervals, which were supposed to have been reduced to points by the Free Coinage Act of 1666. That allowed movements in exchange rates between large and small coins, increases in prices, and shortages of denominations. Instead of a uniform coinage with a distribution of coin weights for a particular type of coin massed at one point, there prevailed a nondegenerate distribution, with individual coins widely ranging in weights. To repair the coinage, policy makers sought to reduce the distributions of coin weights to point masses. To do so, they would replace the old hammered coins with coins from the new milling technology.

What should be the weight and fineness of the new coins? Debate crystallized around two positions. One was presented by the Secretary of the Treasury Lowndes in a report of September 1695 written at the request of the Keeper of the Seals Sir John Somers and the Chancellor of the Exchequer Charles Montagu. Another position was advocated by John Locke in his comment published within weeks of Lowndes's report.

Lowndes's solution was to debase the silver coinage by exactly the amount needed to make the 1695 price level become the new minting point for silver. He calculated that a 20% debasement was

Lowndes proposed a noninflationary debasement.

required. He justified his proposal with the observation that the market price of bullion was about 77d., while the current standard (represented as $1/b$ in our model) was 62d. He predicted that the debasement would not increase prices, and so would minimize redistributive consequences. It would trigger minting activity and thereby implement the desired recoinage and end the inflows of gold. By relieving the shortage of coins, it would "thereby hinder the increase of hazardous Paper-credit, and the inconveniency of Bartering." [20]

Lowndes carefully assembled historical evidence. Lowndes also justified his proposal by an appeal to historical practice. He drew a table of the content of the pound sterling since 1300. These are the data plotted in figure 2.1 on page 16. Although he could not prove that the past debasements were indeed responses to the same problem of shortages of small change that now prevailed in 1695 (as both Lowndes and we suspect they were), he could at least make the case that debasements to cure those shortages formed a time-honored practice.

Lowndes's report apparently did not satisfy Montagu and Somers, who solicited opinions from other experts, including Charles Davenant, a high official in the customs and a writer on economics; Sir Josiah Child, governor of the East India Company and also a writer; John Houblon, governor of the newly created Bank of England; the architect Sir Christopher Wren; the physicist Isaac Newton; and a medical doctor John Locke. Their reports survive. [21] Locke's comments especially influenced the public debate.

John Locke had published his views earlier, when debasement was proposed in Parliament in 1691. The bad state of the silver currency had been known then, but prices had not yet risen (see fig. 16.3 and 16.4). Although the events in 1695 could be seen as falsifying Locke's views, he did not modify them, and maintained his opposition to debasement. We first examine his 1691 views.

---

[20] See Sargent and Smith (1997) for a theoretical analysis of a noninflationary debasement or "raising" along the lines that Lowndes proposed.

[21] Those of Wren, Davenant, Newton, and Locke are in Li (1963).

In important parts of his reasoning, although not in all of it, Locke argued as though the intervals were always reduced to points, that variations in the exchange rate e between large (gold) and small (silver) coins were due to uncontrollable variations in the relative price ϕ_g/ϕ_s, and that minting and melting flows resulted solely from the need to settle an exogenously determined trade balance.

Locke posited empty intervals with $p_t = \gamma$.

To Locke, "it is evident, that an equal quantity of Silver is always of equal value to an equal quantity of Silver" (1695). Therefore, "Silver, i.e., the quantity of pure Silver separable from the Alloy, makes the real value of Money. If it does not, Coin Copper with the same Stamp and denomination, and see whether it will be of the same value." (1691, 145). Expressed in terms of our model, Locke said that because the intervals are points, the inverse of the price level coincides at all times with the legally defined intrinsic content γ. It followed that a devaluation has only nominal effects—it increases prices by the extent of the debasement—and redistributive effects— it hurts creditors. Locke said that the melting and exporting of full-weight coins that were observed in 1691 could only be due to the balance of trade, which is determined by real factors. Hence, devaluation can have no effect on this: as long as gratuitous coinage is in place, such melting will take place when silver needs to be exported (1691, 154). As for multiple metals, his view was that silver is the standard, and gold coins should be produced for convenience but left to be priced like a commodity. He said that legal tender laws could not be continuously adjusted to match the exogenous relative prices of silver and gold, and would either be ignored or be damaging (1691, 169).

The coexistence of underweight and full-weight coins creates an anomaly within Locke's $p_t = \gamma_1$ model. Locke tried to deal with this problem by acknowledging that in 1691 clipped money passed by tale as equal in value to full-weight money. He said that this did not reject his view that prices were always set in terms of the full-weight coins: as long as the two coins traded one for one, no one cared if they were paid in light coins, since they were able to exchange them for heavy coins. And he predicted that if the full-weight coins

By making the interval nonempty, underweight coins created difficulties for Locke.

disappeared, then prices would have to rise and "here you see you have your Money without this new trick of Coinage, raised 5 per Cent" (1691, 161).

This last passage shows that Locke seemed to admit equilibria only at either end of the interval: at the lower end, where full-weight and underweight coins coexist and the price level is determined by the full-weight of coins ($p_t = \gamma_1$), and at the upper end, where only underweight coins remain, and $p_t = \gamma_1/\delta$. The latter equilibrium would be inconsistent with his assertion that only the *legal* value of γ mattered. That is, after full-weight coins disappear, the price level jumps from γ_1 to γ_1/δ, where δ is the ratio of an underweight to a full-weight coin.[22]

By 1695, the full-weight coins had evidently disappeared, and prices had indeed risen. Yet, when the equilibrium materialized, Locke did not acknowledge the incoherence, and saw instead the correctness of his "out-of-model" prediction as a validation of his model.

Indeed, his opposition to debasement strengthened. Whereas in 1691 he saw the mooted 5% debasement as mostly pointless, Lowndes's 20% debasement was more dangerous. "Men in their bargains contract not for denominations or sounds, but for the intrinsick value; which is the quantity of Silver by publick Authority warranted to be in pieces of such denominations," namely 62d. per ounce. A debasement would thus subvert contracts.

Lowndes had started from the observation that the price of silver was 77d. per ounce. Such a price made no sense if it were based on full-weight pennies, as Locke tiresomely demonstrated. Did it not follow that men, in their bargains, contracted for something else than the legal content of coins, contradicting Locke's basic tenet? To this, Locke merely replied: "If the Author means here, that an Ounce of Standard Silver is risen to 6s. 5d. of our clip'd Money, I grant it him, and higher too. But then that has nothing to do with the raising our Lawful Coin, which remains unclip'd; unless he will

---

[22] Note that his analysis did not allow for $p_t < \gamma_1/\delta$ when only underweight coins circulated. See our analysis of the modified model below.

say too, that Standard Bullion is so risen, as to be worth, and actually to sell for 6s. 5d. the Ounce of our weighty mill'd Money. This I not only deny, but farther add, that it is impossible to be so" (1695).

Locke dismissed the historical precedents of repeated debasements that Lowndes had cited because "we are not from matter of Fact informed, what were the true Motives that caused those several changes in the Coin" (1695). As for solving the shortage of money, he said that a debasement would not help any more than changing the definition of the yard could provide more cloth for the army (cited in Li 1963, 233).[23] That purely deductive argument ignored historical evidence, some of which Lowndes had cataloged, more of which is contained in previous chapters, that time and again monetary authorities had used debasements to cure shortages of small change.[24]

Locke argued mostly from a priori grounds.

Clipping was the problem: to remove the consequences of clipping, and also limit the incentive for clipping, Locke recommended that the government order that underweight coins circulate by weight. He particularly criticized the government's accepting coins by tale.[25] But he did not favor demonetizing clipped money, and he advised against a general recoinage on practical grounds. Instead, he recommended waiting for clipped money to be recoined over the course of time.

The Great Recoinage

Lowndes had recommended a recoinage at a debased standard, while Locke had recommended no recoinage and no debasement. Parliament enacted a recoinage with no debasement and undertook measures to induce people to bring coins to the mint.

Locke prevailed.

---

[23] But Locke proposed to alleviate the absence of denominations smaller than 6d. by making coins of 4d., 4½d., and 5d., which, combined with the 6d. coin, could produce any multiple of ½d. For the literature on optimal denomination structure, see Van Hove (2001) and the references there.

[24] Also see Redish (2000, 9).

[25] That underweight coins circulated by tale and not weight should have pushed Locke towards Lowndes's richer model of a widened interval $[\gamma, \gamma/\delta]$ for the price level. See the modified model below.

When the new Parliament met on November 23, the king's speech drew attention to the monetary situation. On December 10, the Commons resolved to recoin clipped money at the old standard at public expense. Montagu introduced a bill a few days later, which was blocked by the Lords; another bill introduced on January 13 received royal assent on January 21.

First, no matter what their condition, the government accepted coins at tale in payment of taxes and dues until May 24, 1696 and in purchases of bonds until June 24, 1696. The silver thus collected was sent to the mint for recoinage. During that time £4.7 million was received at face value, at a cost to the government of £2.2 million. For those coins, the loss was wholly on the government.

This was far short of the estimated outstanding stock of hammered money (about £10 million, excluding counterfeits), so further measures were taken in July 1696: for another year, hammered money was accepted by weight (62d. per ounce) plus a slight premium at the mint (2d. premium) or in payment of taxes (6d. premium). Between July 1696 and July 1697 £4.9 million, was received by weight. The silver content was recoined into £3.3 million, resulting in a gross loss of £1.6 million. But the government conceded a small premium to coin-holders, taking on about £0.25 million of that loss.

Hammered money was fully demonetized in December 1697. After that date, the remaining hammered money, some £0.5 million, found its way to the mint as bullion. This brought the total collection to £10 million.

Government expenses for recoinage were large. The total silver output of the recoinage (including £0.4 million in silver purchased as plate at prices slightly above market) was £6.8 million, at a cost of £2.7 million to the government (Craig 1953, 193–94; Challis 1992b, 388). For comparison, we may note that, in 1696–97, tax revenue was £3.4 million and government spending was £8 million, of which £6 million was for war. The cost of the recoinage was thus very large.

The recoinage was chaotic. The mint did not have the capacity to process the mass of silver, and a long delay followed the removal of currency from the public's hands before new coins could be brought out. The year 1696 saw an intensification of the public debate, with increasing sentiment in favor of a debasement.[26]   But Parliament resolved in October 1696 to keep its course, and the debate died down.

Locke: genius or idiot?

Locke stands tall in political theory and political history.   His *Essays on Government* made him "interpreter of the Revolution," the theorist of the events of 1688.   Politicians long regarded him as defender of sound money and forbearer of the gold standard.   In the nineteenth century, Lord Liverpool, whose Act founded the gold standard, cited Locke for authority.   Macaulay, who was not aware that Newton's 1695 report had survived,[27] believed that Newton agreed with Locke and wrote ([1855] 1967, 4:192–93):

Macaulay saw Locke and Newton as a team.

> Never had there been an occasion which more urgently required both practical and speculative abilities united in an alliance so close, so harmonious, and so honorable as that which bound Somers and Montague to Locke and Newton. It is much to be lamented that we have not a minute history of the conferences of the men to whom England owed the restoration of her currency and the long series of prosperous years which dates from that restoration. It would be interesting to see how the pure gold of scientific truth found by the two philosophers was mingled by the two statesmen with just that quantity of alloy which was necessary for the working. It would be curious to study the many plans which were propounded, discussed, and rejected, some as inefficacious, some as unjust, some as too costly, some as too hazardous, till at length a plan was devised of which the wisdom was proved by the best evidence, complete success.

---

[26] Macaulay ([1855] 1967, ch. 21) reported considerable commercial distress in 1696 and associated it with temporary shortage of coins accompanying the recoinage. He alluded to the service done by temporary expedients such as bank note and circulating credit issued by opulent men to relieve the shortage of coins.

[27] Neither was Feavearyear (1963).

Newton sided with
Lowndes.

But Macaulay had mistakenly assigned Newton to Locke's side of the debate. In fact, Newton agreed with Lowndes and directly disputed Locke's main arguments. Newton (Li 1963, 217) said that "it seems more reasonable to Alter the extrinsick than the Intrinsick Value of Milled Money, that is, to raise a Crown Piece to the Value of an Ounce of Bullion, wch. at present is at least 6s. 3d. than to Depress Bullion to the present Value of Mill'd Money." About the redistributional consequences of "raising," Newton said (Li 1963, 218):

> If it be said that by raising the Extrinsick Value of Milled Money, the King in receiving Excise, Custom and Taxes, and all Persons in receiving Annuitys Rents and other debts must be content with a Crown-Piece instead of 6s. 3d. & so lose 1s. 3d. wch. is $1/5$ of his Money: I answer, that if the Loss be computed in the Extrinsick value of Money, it will be none at all, because a Crown-Piece after it is raised, will be of the same Extrinsick Value with 6s. 3d. at present, and go as far in a Market or in buying Land. But if it be Computed in the Intrinsick Value, it will be no New Loss, because Taxes, Rents, Annuitys & all other Debts are Payable by Law in Unmill'd Money which has already lost at least $2/5$ parts of it's Intrinsick Value by Clipping and Adulteration.

Although Locke's writings on the recoinage were praised by Macaulay and Whig politicians, to monetary historians, Locke's venture into economics has been an embarrassment. On Locke's assertion that "an equal quantity of silver is always of equal value to an equal quantity of silver," the nineteenth-century historian Ruding remarked: "this is undeniably true in every instance except that to which the author applied it, namely, to the coinage" (Ruding 1840, 2:42). William Shaw was no kinder when he commented: "The interference of the philosopher Locke in the monetary debates which centred round the great recoinage of 1696, affords one of the most conspicuous instances of the weakness of even piercing intellects before a purely practical and technical question, and of the danger at such junctures of preferring broad generalisations before expert sense" (Shaw [1896] 1967, 103).

We see Locke as doggedly defending a simple version of our model that set seigniorage to zero and usually abstracted from the existence of underweight coins.[28]   Lowndes was using a modified version (see chapter 22, page 361) that allows for coexistence of full-weight and lightweight coins. Both models are coherent, Locke's model being simpler and easier to present. Lowndes's version fits the facts better.[29]   In particular, it permits the coexistence of full-weight and lightweight coins at a price level consistent with the old standard ($p_t = \gamma$), but leaves room for preference or income shocks to induce a spontaneous debasement, sudden increases in the value of the guinea and in the price level, minting of gold, melting of silver, and a coincident shortage of small currency. Locke could only ignore these facts or treat them as exogenous. But accounting for these facts was central to the problem at hand.[30]

Each man's policy prescription made sense within the context of his model. Lowndes also relied on the medieval experience of debasements as a response to shortages. Locke saw the same history, and noted that it stopped with the Great Debasement of Henry VIII. That led him to think that the motive of all earlier debasements might have been to raise seigniorage revenue rather than to repair a shortage of small change, as is possible both in our model and Lowndes's.

Locke and Lowndes both seem to have used versions of our model.

---

[28] Locke conveyed important insights. For example, he crisply expressed the idea that clipping was a spontaneous debasement: "Clipping of Money is raising it without publick Authority; the same denomination remaining to the piece, that hath now less Silver in it, than it had before." (1695).

[29] We don't know how much Lowndes actually understood, but his views were at least consistent with the observations.

[30] Macaulay ([1855] 1967, 4:194–95) was a strong proponent of Locke and an unjust critic of Lowndes. He wrote: "[William Lowndes] was not in the least aware that a piece of metal with the King's head on it was a commodity of which the price was governed by the same laws which govern the price of a piece of metal fashioned into a spoon or a buckle, and that it was no more in the power of Parliament to make the kingdom richer by calling a crown a pound than to make the kingdom larger by calling a furlong a mile. . . . Had [Lowndes's] arguments prevailed, the evils of a vast confiscation would have been added to all the other evils which afflicted the nation: public credit, still in its tender and sickly infancy, would have been destroyed; and there would have been much risk of a general mutiny of the fleet and army." Macaulay had not learned Slingsby's lesson.

Locke's recommendation in 1695 reflected his concern about the redistributional consequences of a debasement and for what he saw as its adverse effects on the government's credibility as administrator of the unit of account. He deplored debasements because they subverted private contracts, whose protection was the government's duty. Locke was the interpreter of the Revolution.[31] A debasement seemed to be the wrong way to build trust at the beginning of a new regime with a Parliament that was supposed to monitor the king for abuses of his prerogative. As Locke wrote: "It will weaken, if not totally destroy the public faith, when all that have trusted the public, and assisted our present necessities, upon acts of parliament in the million lottery, bank act, and other loans, shall be defrauded of twenty per cent of what these acts of parliament were security for" (cited in Li 1963, 90).

Moved by the politicians Montagu and Somers, Parliament rejected debasement, but recoined despite Locke's advice. For insisting that the state should preserve the sanctity of contracts, Locke would long be remembered among the fathers of the gold standard.

෴

---

[31] The financial aspects have been studied by North and Weingast (1989).

CHAPTER 17

Britain, the Gold Standard, and the Standard Formula

Take care of the pence, and the pounds will take care of themselves.
— *William Lowndes*

With the Great Recoinage of 1696, Britain withdrew from its earlier experiments with token subsidiary coins and reaffirmed the medieval idea of a full-bodied commodity money throughout the denomination structure. It thereby arrested its earlier substantial progress toward the standard formula. Nevertheless, in the eighteenth century, market pressures and a government policy neglecting subsidiary coinage propelled Britain again toward the standard formula. These developments contributed to the gradual process by which Britain approached the gold standard in the early nineteenth century, when it explicitly made its subsidiary coins into tokens that it promised freely to exchange for gold coins.[1]

Time and neglect undid the Great Recoinage

When the eighteenth century began, the unit of account for Britain was still in silver. In terms of the silver unit of account, the gold guinea issued by the government fluctuated in price. Because they affected tax collections, those fluctuations attracted the government's attention in the mid-1690s. The government tried in vain to regulate the price of the guinea from the 1690s to the early eighteenth century. A leading monetary authority, Sir Isaac Newton, asserted the futility of those attempts. However, gold eventually emerged as unit of account.[2]

Gold emerged as the unit of account.

---

[1] The importance for the gold standard of using token subsidiary coins is one of the important themes of Angela Redish (2000).

[2] The temporary French reform of 1577 had made a large gold coin the unit of account as part of a set of policy measures to cope with depreciating silver coins (see chapter 11).

In addition, the price of silver coins expressed in terms of gold stabilized after 1717. Persistent depreciation of small denomination coins, the telltale sign of shortages of small change found in figure 2.1 on page 16, is absent in eighteenth-century Britain. Thus, besides transforming the unit of account, eighteenth-century Britain effectively solved the problem of small change. Counterfeiters and other suppliers of tokens somehow produced enough small change to have allowed the exchange rate between large (now gold) coins and smaller silver coins to stabilize after 1720.

Coins deteriorated again. Meanwhile, the government's neglectful policy toward the coinage allowed the stocks of both gold and silver coins to deteriorate until many coins became substantially underweight. The prevalence of underweight coins widened the effective intervals between minting and melting points for both gold and silver coins. Wider intervals facilitated a fixed exchange rate between gold and silver coins because they allowed larger fluctuations in the relative price of uncoined gold and silver before they would trigger melting of underweight coins or minting of full-weight coins.

Thus, by the end of the eighteenth century, wear and tear of the coinage and a government policy of benign neglect had eradicated many intended effects of the Great Recoinage. By 1770, Britain again used underweight and token coins, many of them privately issued. After 1787, Boulton's steam press could be applied to make high-quality tokens. The government was slow to use this technology, but private firms were not. They soon issued substantial numbers of high-quality convertible token coins. They created a system of convertible token coins that the government eventually nationalized. That is how the standard formula was implemented in Britain.

The accidental standard

The standard formula takes for granted that a large denomination coin is the unit of account, and that the values of subsidiary coins are stated in terms of the larger coin. Before the standard formula was implemented in Britain, a large gold coin, the guinea, had already become the unit of account. But the eighteenth century began in England with a smaller silver coin being the unit of account and most everyone taking for granted that the guinea was a commodity whose price would fluctuate.

How did the guinea convert from commodity to unit of account? We do not know for sure. In this section, we describe some evidence of the government's attitude toward the guinea that hints at how fluctuations in the price of the guinea raised concerns about their re-distributional consequences. By the end of the seventeenth century, the government was trying to influence or regulate the price of the guinea, without much success. However, these regulations showed a concern with units of account that eventually led private contracts to be denominated in guineas. This section describes some of the government's policies that aimed to influence or regulate the price of the guinea. It also describes some of Isaac Newton's views on the market for gold and guineas.

The evolution of the gold standard

Laws and ceilings

After the Great Recoinage, the government set a legal ceiling on the value of the guinea, and lowered it several times, until 1717. After that the ceiling value remained 21s. per guinea. That value became the definition of the unit of account in Britain.[3] Accepting that unit of account put Britain on a de facto gold standard. By making a large denomination coin the unit of account, guinea-denominated debts made people think of small denominations as fractional coins, and prepared the way for the standard formula.

The guinea and legal tender laws

The government's main purpose in setting a legal ceiling on the guinea was to protect the revenues it received when it accepted gold in payment of taxes at a high rate. Until 1696, the government had never tried directly to regulate the price of the guinea; indeed,

Tax collections motivated the government's concern about units of account.

---

[3] It replaced the 5s. 2d. per ounce of silver that had preceded it.

during the crisis of 1695 it found that it had little power to do so.[4]
When the guinea was first issued, 20s. was treated as a reference or
"par"; until the early 1690s, the price of the guinea was quoted as
a premium over 20s.[5] Government officials accepted the guinea at a
discretionary rate that tracked market variations. The dashed line in
figure 16.3 shows the rate at which Treasury tellers were instructed to
accept guineas in payment for taxes or loans.[6] During the height of
the crisis, the Treasury was reluctant to accept the guinea at its rapidly
rising market value, inspiring the government to try to deprive the
gold coin of its legal tender status for payment of taxes. But on
June 1, 1695 the cashiers of the Exchequer stated that their refusal
to accept guineas for more than 25s. "would not at all keep down
the price in the town" and that it also interfered with marketing
government loans. Thus, they were forced to take guineas at 29s. In
July 1695, the cashier of the Excise was instructed to "discountenance
taking guineas, but if there be a necessity he must not refuse them, as
this might cause the King's subjects not to bring in the tax; he must
make the collectors think that guineas will not be taken for the next
installment of the tax." This last instruction reveals an attempt to
discourage demand for the guinea. Tax collectors in Bristol found in
October that "by reason of the badness and scarcity of silver it was
impossible to make good their collections unless they were permitted
to receive and pay guineas at 30s.," which the government refused
to do. On October 16, the king was informed of the impact on tax
collection but told his officials to "hold it as long as they can." The
question of the rate at which to accept the guinea was set aside when
the recoinage was being planned, and no measures were taken until
the recoinage was under way.[7]

---

[4] Proclamations on coinage did assign rates to other gold coins, which were
declared to be "current" at certain values, but no penalties were edicted.

[5] Examples in Houghton (1692–1702) before 1694, in *Calendar of Treasury
Books* 1904–58, 9:30.

[6] *Calendar of Treasury Books* 1904–58, 9:30, 44, 225, 266, 679, 750, 1038,
1195, 1310, 1554, 1650, 1805, 1899; 10:174, 521, 1383, 1395.

[7] *Calendar of Treasury Books* 1904–58, 10:1383, 1395, 1409; *Calendar of Treasury Papers* 1868–89, 1:464.

In 1696, the House of Commons began to regulate the guinea, by passing resolutions that put a maximum on the coin's market price, first 28s. (February 15), then 26s. (February 26). An Act (7 & 8 Will. III c. 10, s. 18) confirmed this last value, by stipulating that after March 25, 1696 "noe Person shall receive take or pay any of the pieces of Gold Coine of this Kingdom commonly called Guineas att any greater or higher rate than 26 shillings for each Guinea" (Horsefield 1960, 81; Horton 1887, 243). The penalty for violating this law was a fine of £20 plus twice the value of the guineas so exchanged, and the fine was shared with the informant. But it was made clear that "nothing in this Act contained shall extend or be construed to compel any person or persons to receive any Guinea or Guineas at the said Rate of 26 Shillings." The guinea was therefore not made legal tender at 26s. (or any other rate). The ceiling was lowered to 22s. on April 10, and remained there until 1717. These successive values are represented by the solid line in figure 16.3, and also serve as the basis for "par" after 1696 in figure 16.4.[8]

We do not know the effect of these laws on the market price of the guinea.[9] By 1698, however, the price of gold had fallen to a level consistent with the guinea at 22s. or less (fig. 16.4).

In October 1697, the Treasury decided to accept guineas at 21½s. in payments for loans only, but maintained the rate of 22s. for taxes (Horsefield 1960, 82). The following year, a report to Parliament, signed by John Locke among others, recommended lowering the guinea's rate by 6d., because the gold/silver ratio was lower in the rest of Europe (Li 1963, 126–28). No legislation followed, but in February 1699 the Treasury decided to refuse guineas at more

---

[8] The "par" value of a troy pound of standard gold was taken to be 44.5 times the value assigned to a guinea.

[9] The source for figure 16.3 is a weekly newspaper called *Collection for the Improvement of Husbandry and Trade*. The last price for the guinea was for Feb. 4 until the guinea reappeared on April 14 at 22s., and remained unchanged until it ceased to be reported in 1699. But Horsefield (1960, 82) cited contemporary evidence that the legal ceiling was evaded. A buyer, knowing that a seller had a guinea, would bet 3s. with the seller that the seller couldn't find him a guinea at 22s. The seller would promptly produce the guinea and the buyer, losing the bet, would pay 22 + 3 s.

than 21½s. Although the legally enforceable ceiling of 22s. was not modified, the market price of gold immediately adjusted to the Treasury's new buying rate, so no change in the ratio of that market price to "par" is visible in figure 16.4.

Finally, in December 1717 a royal proclamation was issued to "forbid all persons to utter or receive any of the pieces of Gold, called Guineas, at any greater or higher rate than 21 shillings for each guinea . . . upon pain of our highest displeasure and upon pain of the greatest punishment that by law may be inflicted upon them for their default, negligence and contempt in this behalf" (Li 1963, 156).[10]

These are the laws upon which Britain's monetary system was based until Lord Liverpool's Coinage Act of 1816 made gold the basis of the British coinage, with gold coins unlimited tender at a fixed value.

Newton's forecasts

Sir Isaac Newton's writings tell us something about the purposes behind the government's monetary actions in 1717, and whether it foresaw the consequences of its actions. Unlike Locke, Newton was a professional monetary authority. He was master of the mint from December 1699 until his death in 1727. Between 1701 and 1717 he advised the Treasury on monetary matters, including public policy about the price of the guinea (texts in Horton 1887 and Shaw [1896] 1967; see also Craig 1953, 212–29; Feavearyear 1963, 153–58; Li 1963, 143–60).

In 1702, Newton estimated that the guinea was higher in England than it would be in France, Holland, Germany, or Italy, and recommended lowering its rating by 6d., 9d., or 12d.; but he advised against an "alteration of the standard," by which he meant the silver coinage (Shaw [1896] 1967, 137). In 1717, Newton estimated that the gold/silver ratio was 15.57 in Britain with the guinea at 21½s,

---

[10] What penalties this clause actually implied is not clear. The proclamation was issued under the royal prerogative, albeit at the request of Parliament, but was not backed by statutory penalties.

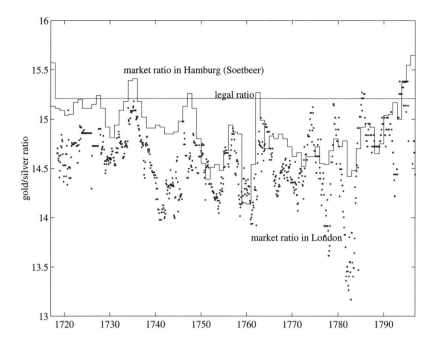

Figure 17.1 Market ratio of gold to silver prices, London (*dots*); legal ratio (ratio of par prices); market ratio in Hamburg (annual averages, *lines*); 1694–1797. *Sources*: figures 16.4, 17.3 for London; Soetbeer 1879, 128–30 for Hamburg.

compared to 14.8 to 15 in the rest of Europe, 12 in East India, and 9 or 10 in China and Japan (Shaw [1896] 1967, 168). He expected arbitrage to reduce these disparities and that the ratio in Britain would fall into line with the rest of the world. John Conduitt, who succeeded Newton as master of the mint, identified further reasons to expect the ratio to fall throughout Europe, including increased supplies of gold from Brazil, and increased demand for silver from the European affluent (Shaw [1896] 1967, 187). Those expectations were broadly confirmed, as figure 17.1 shows.[11]

Newton suggested again that England's ratio be brought closer to that in the rest of Europe, by reducing the value of the guinea by 6d. But he did not think that government action was necessary: "if

---

[11] We lack observations on the gold/silver ratio in London from 1698 to 1717, which is why we use the ratio in Hamburg as a proxy.

things be let alone till silver money be a little scarcer, the Gold will fall of itself. For people are already backward to give Silver for Gold, and will in a little time refuse to make payments in Silver without a premium. . . . And so the question is whether Gold shall be lowered by the government, or let alone till it falls of itself by the want of silver money."

Newton on units of account   Newton still regarded silver as the standard of value. According to Cantillon's testimony, Newton rejected the suggestion to debase silver, saying: "according to the fundamental Laws of the Kingdom silver was the true and only monetary standard and as such it could not be altered" (cited in Li 1963, 159). Newton thought that even if gold coins were not valued properly by the government, they would be correctly priced by the market. Similarly, Locke in 1698 had written that it was "impossible, that more than one Metal should be the true Measure of Commerce," that "Gold as well as other Metals is to be looked upon as a Commodity, which varying in its Price as other Commodities do, its Value will always be changeable" (Li 1963, 127).[12]

Gold becomes the unit of account

Belying Newton's dictum that "silver was the true and only monetary standard," the unit of account in Britain turned from silver to gold during the eighteenth century.

In 1717, Parliament had lowered the guinea by 6d., which brought the "legal ratio" to 15.2 (see fig. 17.1). The gold/silver ratio fell further. But no silver was minted, silver coinage went at a discount, and the guinea stayed at 21s. By the late eighteenth century, England was on a de facto gold standard: the unit of account (in Locke's words, what "men in their bargains contract for") had become an amount of gold, namely, $20/21$ of a guinea.

---

[12] Locke regarded attempts at rigidly setting the value of gold to be "prejudicial to the Country which does it." He explained why in his 1691 tract (Locke 1691, 162–64): setting the guinea above its value forces creditors to accept it, but setting it under its value doesn't. In the latter case, either gold is hoarded or else the law is ignored, but in the former case gold is imported by debtors. See Garber (1986) for more about the option value of currency under bimetallism.

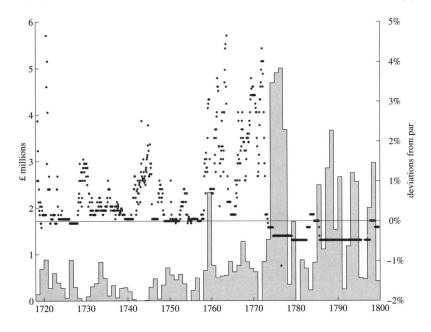

Figure 17.2 Annual minting of gold (*left scale, solid line*) and market price of gold bars as premium over par (*right scale, dots*), London, 1718–1800. Par is based on a guinea at 21½s. before December 1717, 21s. after (£3 19s. 8¾d. per troy oz of standard [22k] gold before December 1717, £3 17s. 10½d. after). *Source:* figure 17.3, Challis 1992a.

Underweight coins

Figure 17.2 presents evidence that the amount of gold in a guinea was not actually stablilized until the last quarter of the eighteenth century because wear and tear left a distribution of underweight coins.

Assuming that melting occasionally took place, the maximum value of the percentage premium of gold bars estimates the size of the interval between the minting and melting points.[13] Figure 17.2 shows that the width of the interval increased significantly after 1760 until 1774, when the government recoined underweight gold coins.

Underweight coins and widths of minting and melting intervals

---

[13] This is δ^{-1} in the model of chapter 22.

The widening interval before 1774 reflects a gradual deterioration of the weight of the outstanding stock of gold coins in Britain. That the market price of bullion could deviate as much as 4% above par indicates that an average guinea, if valued at 21s., could contain as much as 4% less than its official content. Progressive wear and tear widened the distribution of weights among circulating coins, thereby widening the interval between the melting point and the minting point. A wider interval allowed the price of bullion to fluctuate more.

By 1774 it was estimated that the average guinea was 9% under-weight (Li 1963, 163). In that year, Parliament ordered a recoinage of gold at government expense. That had the effect of reducing to a point the distribution of guineas by weight, as the recoinage of 1696 had for silver. It therefore equated the guinea to its official content, and the market price of gold remained slightly below par.[14] Figure 17.2 confirms that the margin of movement for gold narrowed after 1774.

Figure 17.2 shows both the premium on gold bullion over par and minting volumes between 1718 and 1773. Although the coincidence is imperfect, before 1760 it appears that when the market price of bullion was markedly above the mint price, minting slowed. From 1760 to 1771 there was substantial minting of gold despite what was often a significant premium on gold (the price level was higher than the minting point for gold).

Figure 17.3 shows that the interval between the minting and melting points for silver coins widened even more for silver than for gold. By weighing bags of coins at the mint, Conduitt estimated that the wear on silver coinage ranged from 1 to 3.4% in 1728. The government's policy toward silver, however, differed from that toward gold. The recoinage of 1774 only involved gold. Silver was left to depreciate further, so that by 1798, the wear on silver ranged from 3 to 38% (Li 1963, 163, quoting Liverpool). On the contrary, the government progressively deprived silver of its legal

---

[14] The effect of wear and tear on coinage continued in Britain and concerned Jevons (1875). Another recoinage at government expense took place in 1896.

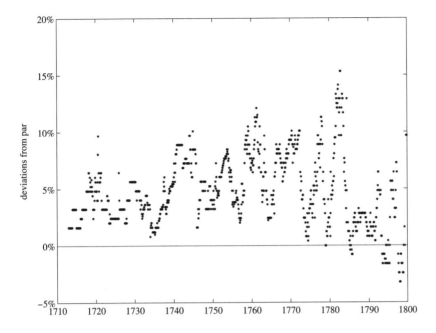

Figure 17.3 Market price of silver bars in London 1713–1800, shown as deviation from par. Par is 5s. 2d. per troy oz of sterling (92.5%) silver. *Sources*: Commons (1811), Castaing (1713–1800), Shaw ([1896] 1967, 195).

tender quality: between 1774 and 1783, and again between 1798 and 1816, it was limited to £25 by tale, and any amounts larger could be paid in silver by weight only. In the late 1790s, when silver bullion fell to a discount for a sustained period of time, the government acted temporarily to suspend the free coinage of silver.

Neglect the pence

We have already described how the British authorities tolerated private supplies of small change in the eighteenth century even in the form of counterfeit copper coins. Benign neglect extended to the silver coinage, which gradually became token, while the pound sterling, taking care of itself, became gold.

We remain ignorant about many details of the process by which Britain adopted the gold standard. However, an important piece of the story was the persistence of a stable exchange rate between the guinea and the subsidiary coins in the eighteenth century. This somehow emerged when the government got out of the business of supplying small change, the policy of benign neglect alluded to earlier. Thus, the path of the exchange rate of large for small coins in eighteenth-century Britain did not display the age-old persistent depreciations depicted in figure 2.1 on page 16. We interpret the absence of depreciations as evidence that somehow the entrepreneurs who produced small change managed to supply enough to avoid the shortages that our model registers as a binding penny-in-advance constraint.

To understand how the exchange rate between coins of different metals could remain constant, we use a modified version of our model. We allow underweight coins of both metals to coexist with full-weight coins, as described in chapters 16 and 22. The modified model allows a constant exchange rate between two coins made of different metals so long as two conditions are met: (1) that the intervals be broad enough to accommodate movements in the relative prices of gold and silver while still overlapping at a constant value of e; (2) that there occur no shortages of small denominations that would trigger a binding penny-in-advance constraint and an increase in e.[15] The wear and tear of the coin stock can account for the first condition. We conjecture that the "benign neglect" policy resulted in sufficient amounts of small change to maintain the second condition.[16]

Implementation of the standard formula

The market led the way. We described on page 271 how Boulton's application of James Watt's steam engine allowed private firms to issue high-quality convertible

---

[15] Above, we have interpreted the rise in e observed in 1695 as reflecting a binding penny-in-advance constraint.

[16] Feavearyear (1963) and others have also argued that Britain, as it grew more prosperous, needed less small coinage.

tokens. After 1787, many firms issued such tokens, and they formed much of the subsidiary coinage of Britain. Thus, by 1800, the market had chosen a gold coin as the unit of account and had also found a technology and set of private institutions to provide token subsidiary coins convertible into gold. Britain had mostly solved the problem of small change in practice. The complete triumph of the standard formula in Britain waited for laws to catch up with practice and for the government to nationalize the business of supplying small change.

With the Coinage Act of 1816, the British government began to implement the standard formula not just for small denomination copper or bronze coins, at the lowest end of the denomination scale, but for all of its silver coinage. In doing so, Britain implemented the first full-fledged gold standard. But it did so in a piecemeal fashion, rather than carrying out a preconceived plan.

Redish (1990) discusses in detail the adoption of the gold standard shortly after the installation of Watt's steam-driven minting presses at the Royal Mint in 1805. The gold standard was officially adopted by the Coinage Act of 1816, also known as Liverpool's Act (56 Geo. III c. 68), based on Lord Liverpool's 1805 proposal. The act proclaimed gold coin to be the sole standard of value, and made silver coins representative; however, it still allowed for free minting of silver, at the existing mint price of 62s. per pound. Seigniorage, which had been abolished in 1666, was levied again on silver by reducing the weight of the coins from 62s. to 66s. per pound troy, and their legal tender was limited to £2. Finally, the Act of Suppression of 1817 (57 Geo. III. c. 46) made private coinage illegal. The Mint resumed copper coinage in 1820.[17]

Formally, the 1816 act did not completely implement the standard formula. A key element, that the small denominations be minted on government account, seemed to be contradicted by a clause of the act specifying that free minting of silver would begin at a date to be announced. But because the market price of silver

---

[17] The coins were issued at 24d. per pound; the price of copper in 1820 was around 10d. per pound. Britain switched to bronze in 1860.

remained below the mint's legally set price of 62s., the mint forever refrained from announcing a date, lest it be flooded with silver. Free minting of silver was not actually removed from the statutes until 1870. In addition, convertibility of the token coinage was not explicitly mentioned. Instead, the Bank of England voluntarily adopted a policy of accepting silver coins at face value in exchange for gold or its notes. Only in 1836 did the Bank come to an arrangement with the Treasury to sell its inventory of silver coins at par value to the Mint, establishing convertibility in fact if not in law (Redish 2000, 152).

According to Redish (2000, 149), Mint officials believed that restricting the quantity of silver coins would be sufficient to maintain a constant exchange rate with gold coins, and it took the Bank some time to convince them otherwise. Four ingredients of the standard formula were thus progressively and quietly put in place from 1816 to 1836: (1) a token coinage; (2) a government monopoly of token coin production; (3) minting on government account; and (4) convertibility.

The gradual process by which Britain slid into practicing the standard formula rendered its monetary arrangements and practices ambiguous to some observers. Thus, in 1829, when the United States Congress debated changes to its monetary system, several influential voices rejected the British model, at least as they understood it. Jefferson's former Secretary of the Treasury, Albert Gallatin, thought that British token money "is in fact, an issue of adulterated money which does not regulate itself" because it is "irredeemable" (cited in Redish 2000, 220). John Stuart Mill's description of the British monetary system (1857, book III, ch. 10, sec. 2) lists the first three ingredients from the previous paragraph, but not convertibility.[18] As late as 1918, Cannan (1935, 39) did not consider convertibility to be part of the English system, but rather a "slight

_____

[18] That convertibility would be sufficient to maintain the value of token small change had nevertheless been made clear by Jean-Baptiste Say in 1803: "If the government were to pay silver on demand for the copper coins presented, it could, almost without inconvenience, give them a very low intrinsic content. . . . There would only be counterfeiters to fear" (Say 1841, 262).

improvement" made by other countries to Britain's system, a system that he nevertheless deemed "perfectly successful." Despite having no formal commitment to convertibility, Britain practiced the standard formula.

☙

CHAPTER 18

The Triumph of the Standard Formula

This chapter describes how the standard formula spread beyond Britain in the course of the nineteenth century. While Britain adopted the standard formula along with the gold standard, in 1838 the German Monetary Union implemented the standard formula but remained on a silver standard. When Germany unified in 1871, it switched to a gold standard. Meanwhile, the United States and a group of countries led by France put in place important features of the standard formula while maintaining bimetallism. All eventually followed Britain onto the gold standard.

By the early nineteenth century, shortages of small change of the type we have studied in medieval Europe were less frequent.[1] However, various problems with small change persisted. They occurred in France and the United States as both countries moved from a "double standard" (bimetallism) toward the gold standard.

In this chapter we shall describe how the final triumph of the standard formula was intimately related to the "battle of the standards" and ultimately coincided with the end of bimetallism. First, however, we describe how Germany formally adopted the standard formula.

Germany's monetary union of 1838

Germany implemented the standard formula. Given the ambiguity that long surrounded aspects of Britain's implementation of the standard formula, Germany should be considered the first country to implement it completely. Germany did so explic-

---

[1] France suffered a severe shortage in the early days of the Revolution, around 1790 (Marion 1919, 270–78). Private coins such as the one shown in figure 4.7 were produced to meet this shortage.

itly in 1838.[2] It was on the silver standard then, had no single monetary authority, but participated in a currency union. The Dresden treaty established a currency union among sovereign states. It represents the first pure implementation of the standard formula. Aside from the unquantified commitment to limit issues, the only restrictions on token coinage were limited legal tender and convertibility.

Germany's earlier long-standing problems with gluts of small change had come from the hundred rival issuers of currency and their inability to commit to a common standard, as we saw in chapter 15. After the Congress of Vienna in 1815, the number of sovereign states in Germany had been reduced to 39. They formed a customs union in 1834. Coalescing into a currency union was helped by the fact that most German states were on one of three silver standards (the convention thaler in Bavaria and Austria, the gulden in southern and western Germany, and the Prussian thaler in northern and eastern Germany).[3] Also, most German mints had adopted the steam-driven presses devised by the engineer Uhlhorn in 1817.

The first step toward monetary union was taken when the states in southern and western Germany formally defined their common standard in August 1837, the silver gulden of 60 kreutzer. The terms of the union concerning denominations below the gulden are remarkable. The union defined the weight and fineness of the 6-kreutzer and 3-kreutzer pieces to be struck by the individual states as 9.3% below full weight, and required that the issuing state redeem its small coins in gulden pieces, when presented in amounts of 100 gulden or more. Mindful of their history, members of the union established a rotating monitoring system whereby member i monitored the quality of member $i + k$'s coins in year k of the union. Coins of 1 kreutzer and smaller were left unregulated.

The currency union was considerably enlarged in July 1838 at Dresden. The gulden and the Prussian thaler were established as concurrent units at a fixed ratio. The terms of the Dresden union

---

[2] See the overview in Sprenger (1993).

[3] Gold coins were minted in some parts of Germany, but they had no fixed legal tender value.

concerning small change were slightly different. Small denomination underweight coins could be minted by individual states subject
to a convertibility requirement, and demonetization could only be
carried out with prior notice and with redemption of outstanding
coinage. The states also committed themselves not to issue more
than necessary for the needs of trade, and small coins could not be
legal tender for more than the denomination of the smallest full-
bodied coin.

The currency union of Dresden covered 85% of the German population. By 1857 it had been extended to 95% of the population,
and it even included the Austro-Hungarian empire until 1866. It remained in force until 1871, when the newly formed German empire
decided to abandon the silver standard for the gold standard. The
monetary law of 1873 established the same system for its subsidiary
coinage (with per-capita limits and redemption). The existing large
silver thalers, however, remained legal tender but were not made
convertible.[4]

Bimetallism versus the gold standard

In countries adhering to the "double" or bimetallic standard, such as
France and the United States, full adoption of the standard formula
did not come until after bimetallism had collapsed. While bimetallism was not incompatible with adopting the main features of the
standard formula for some denominations, the nearly simultaneous
decisions of Germany, France, and the United States to leave silver
in 1873 had important ramifications for how France and the United
States would implement the standard formula.

Bimetallism is a monetary system in which the mint stands ready
to convert either of two metals (gold and silver) into coins, and those
coins are unlimited legal tender at given rates.[5] The original purpose
of bimetallism was to allow silver to be used for small denominations

---

[4] See the discussion of limping standards at the end of this chapter.

[5] See Redish (2000) for an extensive study of bimetallism.

and gold for large ones, and to maintain a constant exchange rate between the two.[6]

Because a given weight of gold is so valuable, small denominations in a gold standard cannot be full-bodied. This fact urgently recommended the standard formula under the gold standard. By comparison, maintaining bimetallism made adopting the standard formula less pressing. Large denominations could consist of full-bodied gold coins, small denominations of full-bodied silver coins, and the exchange between them could under the proper circumstances[7] be fixed by the rules of bimetallism. But in 1873, France and the United States both ended the free coinage of silver. The ensuing fall in the market value of silver promptly made their existing silver coins into overvalued tokens, for which convertibility was ultimately provided.

To understand why this happened, we briefly review two theories of bimetallism, the first of which assumes that relative prices of silver and gold are exogenous (a "small country" assumption), the second of which makes relative prices of gold and silver respond to the choice of monetary regime of a government or a coalition of governments.

The standard formula was more urgently required under the gold standard.

Bimetallism in a small country

The model of chapter 11 can be used to study bimetallism for a small country that takes relative prices of gold and silver to be exogenous. Bimetallism adds to the chapter 11 model a government rule that makes gold and silver coins legal tender at a fixed ratio.

However, if there are frequent and substantial changes in the relative prices of the metals in terms of consumption goods (ϕ_g, ϕ_s), it is difficult to sustain a fixed exchange rate for very long in the model of chapter 11. To maintain concurrent circulation of coins of both metals in the face of such changes, the government has to

---

[6] Its proponents in the late nineteenth century emphasized other properties such as its superior ability to stabilize the price level in the face of separate fluctuations in the price of gold and silver. This argument was made by French officials as early as 1867 (Willis 1901, 76).

[7] See the discussion in the section on page 310 entitled "Worldwide bimetallism."

adjust coin specifications (i.e., debase or reenforce coins of one of the metals) to realign the intervals.

Appreciations in ϕ_s and ϕ_g have very different ramifications for potential shortages of small change. An increase in the price of goods in terms of silver, ϕ_s, (a cheapening of silver) shifts the silver interval to the right and ultimately leads to minting of silver and melting of gold. At worst, all currency becomes silver, which leads to no shortages of the small denomination silver coins. But an increase in the gold price of goods, ϕ_g, makes silver disappear; and in our model, large gold coins cannot take the place of small silver coins.

Thus, even if a bimetallic system could potentially provide several tiers of denominations within the old medieval system of coin production, it remained vulnerable to a cheapening of gold.[8] That would force the monetary authorities to contemplate a debasement of the silver coin or to think of alternate ways of providing smaller denominations.

Monetary authorities confronted just that problem after the gold discoveries in California and Australia in 1849 sparked an increase in ϕ_g. Within a few years, the United States resorted to token coinage for their smallest denominations, albeit without convertibility. Several European countries reacted similarly, until a desire to coordinate their responses led them to create the Latin Monetary Union, centered in France. But both the United States and the Latin Union maintained free coinage of silver and unlimited legal tender for their main silver coins, the 5F and the $1 pieces. They remained committed to bimetallism for parts of their denomination structures. Their attachment to bimetallism has been the subject of much debate. To understand that debate, we use a different model, which we describe next.

Worldwide bimetallism

When a large country or a large coalition of countries adopts bimetallism at the same rate, it is no longer appropriate to take the relative

---

[8] We have seen such an event take place in the 1340s, in chapters 9 and 10.

prices of gold and silver (ϕ_g, ϕ_s) as exogenous because they can be affected by the demands for monetary stocks of gold and silver, which in turn depend on the choice of standard. The endogeneity of relative prices means that for a large country or coalition of countries, bimetallism can be less susceptible to the problems mentioned in the previous section. This point was recognized and formalized by Walras ([1900] 1977), Fisher (1911, ch. 7), and Velde and Weber (2000).

To make gold and silver prices endogenous, Velde and Weber's model focuses on the substitution between monetary and nonmonetary uses of gold and silver. Velde and Weber set our seigniorage parameters σ_i to zero for each type of coin, thereby collapsing the minting and melting intervals to zero. They impose a single cash-in-advance constraint cast in terms of the nominal value of all gold and silver coins. The cash-in-advance constraint applies to consumption of three consumption goods, one a nondurable consumption good, the remaining two being durables, namely, gold and silver jewelry, to capture the nonmonetary uses for these metals. Velde and Weber study a pure endowment economy, so that the supplies of three types of consumption good are taken to be exogenous. The consumers have preferences over the nonmonetary stocks of gold and silver (jewelry) that are represented by a concave utility function. The single cash-in-advance constraint applies to the sum of gold and silver coins, weighted by the exchange rate. This means that at any constant exchange rate between gold and silver coins, the money holder is indifferent between holding gold and silver coins.[9]

Bimetallism was tenable for a large coalition of countries.

There are potentially six endogenous variables: stocks of gold and silver coins, stocks of gold and silver jewelry, the price level, and the exchange rate. Alternatively, the "legal ratio" of gold to silver, rather than the exchange rate, can be taken to be endogenous. While there might be six endogenous variables, there are only five independent restrictions on these six variables: the resource constraints for gold and silver, the first-order conditions for gold and silver jewelry, and

The monetary authority of a large coalition of countries influences the relative price of gold and silver.

---

[9] Velde and Weber's formal model thus abstracts from the differing denominations that gold and silver coins took in practice, and does not include a penny-in-advance constraint. Gold and silver coins are treated symmetrically.

the cash-in-advance constraint. Accordingly, there are multiple equilibria. Within limits, this allows the government to choose the legal price ratio of gold to silver; given that government-set price, competitive forces will then cause the stocks of gold and silver coins and also the stocks of gold and silver jewelry to adjust.[10] Provided that they are not too large, disturbances to supplies and demands of gold and silver are consistent with a fixed government-set relative price of gold for silver because there is room for the monetary and nonmonetary stocks of the metals to adjust to assure equilibrium. Thus, Velde and Weber show that for a large country bimetallism can be much more robust than the analysis of the previous section based on the model of chapter 11 would suggest. Bimetallism is feasible for a range of exchange rates: given a "legal" ratio between gold and silver, quantities of metal can move between monetary and nonmonetary uses so that the relative value of the metals in nonmonetary uses, the market ratio, matches the legal ratio.

Velde and Weber model the world as a single economy, and consider a single legal ratio holding for all countries on a bimetallic standard, a state of affairs that presupposes some form of coordination among countries. Velde and Weber also show that changes in the legal price ratio can be necessary with more or less frequency, depending on the sizes of disturbances and on parameters that are influenced by the size of the bimetallic coalition. Such adjustments in the legal price ratio would require ongoing coordination among countries in a bimetallic coalition.[11] A lack of coordination bedeviled European countries in the sixteenth and seventeenth centuries, when big movements in the gold/silver ratio prompted haphazard responses from a multitude of political units. Isaac Newton's reports to the Treasury are filled with detailed comparisons of the gold/silver ratio in various European countries. But coordination gradually became easier. One of Napoleon's legacies was a gold/silver ratio of

---

[10] See Velde and Weber (2000, 1216–17), in particular the quotation ascribed to Walras.

[11] The need for international coordination was keenly felt by proponents of bimetallism in the nineteenth century.

15.5, on which a number of European countries converged. The
market price of gold in terms of silver remained remarkably stable
in the vicinity of that ratio, even in the face of such large events as
the California gold discovery. Consequently, for a long time in the
nineteenth century, international bimetallism was viable with very
few adjustments in the legal ratio. And it seems that it would have
been viable for many years after that. Nevertheless, for reasons apparently unconnected to the prospects then prevailing for sustaining
a stable legal ratio, bimetallism suddenly collapsed in 1873.[12]

Passage to gold

The United States and France adopted the standard formula when
they reassembled coherent monetary policies after the wreck of
bimetallism. In the United States, political forces striving for a
return to bimetallism long delayed the extension of the standard formula to the outstanding stock of silver coinage. In the Latin Union,
member states had to negotiate an arrangement suitable to all.

The United States
In the United States, the process of adopting the standard formula
was long and arduous.[13] The Mint Act of 1792 (1 *Statutes at Large*
246) established a bimetallic system with gold and silver coins freely
minted on demand and unlimited legal tender. Full-bodied copper
coins were minted on government account. The ratio between gold
and silver was initially set at 15:1, but in the 1820s it came under reconsideration. Congress explicitly decided to maintain bimetallism,
but debased the gold coins and changed the ratio to 16:1.

When the gold discoveries in 1849 pushed the intrinsic value of

---

[12] Friedman (1990), Flandreau (1996), Velde and Weber (2000), and Redish
(2000, 202–6) discuss whether that collapse was inevitable. Velde and Weber
discuss the welfare implications of various choices of the legal ratio, and find that
in general they cannot argue that bimetallism was welfare-improving relative to a
uni-metal standard.

[13] See Carothers (1930) and Redish (2000, 209–39).

the silver coinage above its legal tender value, Congress sought to remedy the situation without forsaking bimetallism. The result was an Act of 1853 (10 Stat. 160). It modified the coinage of 5¢, 10¢, 25¢, and 50¢ silver pieces by ending their free coinage, making them 6.9% below weight with respect to the $1 silver coin, and making them legal tender for private debts for up to $5. The Secretary of the Treasury was to regulate the quantities minted, and the coins were to be sold at par by the mint in exchange for gold coins or silver dollars. At the same time, Congress made explicit its intention to maintain bimetallism, and declined to follow the English model.[14]   The measures were considered temporary, the diminution in weight was minimal, and there was no mechanism for redemption. According to Carothers (1930, 126–27), Congress expressed concerns over the perceived risks in government-issued token coinage: not only the possibility of private duplication, but also over-issue on the part of government and consequent depreciation. The ambiguities of the British model led to serious misunderstandings: "There was an almost universal belief that a coin legally rated at a value above its bullion value was a debased coin of doubtful honesty."

The U.S. restored convertibility.   After the Civil War ended, and as the greenback episode drew to a close, the United States prepared to return to a metallic standard. Instead of returning to the bimetallic standard, it instead adopted a gold standard in 1873. Silver was no longer freely minted. The silver dollar, still legal tender, was henceforth minted on government account only (albeit in quantities set by law from 1878 to 1893). Coins of 1¢, 3¢, and 5¢ in copper and nickel were created, with legal tender limited to 25¢. Finally, by an act of 1879 (21 *Statutes at Large* 7) the legal tender limit was also raised to $10, and, more importantly, it was provided that "the holder of any of the silver coins of the United States of smaller denominations than one dollar, may, on presentation of the same in sums of twenty dollars, or any multiple thereof, at the office of the Treasurer or any assistant Treasurer of the United States, receive therefor lawful money of the

---

[14]   Congress was aware of the English model, described upon request by the U.S. ambassador to Britain (Carothers 1930, 114).

United States."

Thus, for the first time, the standard formula was adopted in the United States for subsidiary coinage smaller than $1. The silver dollar remained inconvertible. Its metallic content started to lose its value as events in Europe triggered a collapse of the price of silver.

The Latin Monetary Union

The Latin Monetary Union bound France, Belgium, Italy, and Switzerland from 1866 to 1926 (Greece joined in 1868).[15] It was formed to coordinate policies regarding subsidiary coinage, and became the framework within which the member countries conducted their passage to the gold standard.

The center of the union was France, its largest member. France's monetary unit, the franc, had been defined as 4.5g of silver by a law of 17 Germinal XI (in the Revolutionary calendar, or April 7, 1803). The same law provided for the coinage of gold francs at a 15.5 ratio to silver francs, and coins of both metals were unlimited legal tender. Full-bodied silver coins ranged from 0.25F to 5F, and a few bronze coins of 0.05F and 0.10F were occasionally minted at cost on government account. As new countries formed nearby, they adopted an identical system, with an identical content of the unit of account: Belgium in 1832, Switzerland in 1850, Italy in 1862.

In the early 1850s, the relative price changes caused by the gold discoveries in California made silver coins disappear from circulation. Several countries reacted as the United States did in 1853, by making the smallest coins token. Switzerland reduced the silver content of its subsidiary coins (2F and lower) by 11% in 1860. Italy made its subsidiary coinage 7% lighter in 1862. France reduced by the same amount the content of its smallest coins only (0.50F and lower) in 1864. Belgium then called for a coordinated approach to subsidiary coinage; a monetary convention in 1865 resulted in the Latin Monetary Union, which went into effect in August 1866 for fifteen years, renewable by tacit consent.

---

[15] We largely follow Willis (1901) on the history of the union.

The union adopted a surfeit of protective measures: a common standard of token coinage was set for all coins smaller than 5F; the subsidiary coins had limited legal tender; their issue was limited on a per capita basis country by country; they were accepted by all governments up to 100F and redeemable on demand into full-bodied silver or gold coins. Switzerland had asked for further precautions, in particular that each country keep the profit made on token issues in a reserve fund, as it had done since 1860. This 100 percent reserve requirement for token coinage was rejected by the other countries.

The union also specified the silver and gold contents of the full-bodied coins. Because it did not *require* that those coins be freely minted, and made them unlimited legal tender only for debts to governments, the arrangement did not embody an explicit bimetallic standard. The other members had wanted the gold standard, but France wished to maintain its existing system intact. The treaty did make the 5F piece legal tender throughout the union, and the members continued to allow silver be freely minted, as in the United States (a 5F piece was very close in size to a $1 piece). France's position that bimetallism was sustainable and that the world gold/silver ratio could be stabilized so long as enough countries adhered to a common ratio makes sense in the model of worldwide bimetallism that we described earlier.

Free riders in monetary unions

Coordination problems bedeviled the Latin Monetary Union. The treaty had fully accepted token coinage but not fiat money. The union was soon tested.[16] On April 30, 1866, Italy declared war on Austria. The next day, Italy suspended convertibility of its banks' notes and required Italian banks to buy government bonds. During the war, Italy acquired Venice and also inflation. Small denomination notes soon appeared, privately issued at first (Fratianni and Spinelli 1997, 76). Italy's token coinage was legal tender everywhere in the union and soon flooded it. When the union came up for renewal in 1878, the sum of Italian small denomination notes and

---

[16] Zarazaga (1995) presents an equilibrium model of the coordination problems inherent in a system with multiple issuers of fiat money.

coins exceeded Italy's legal quota by 100%. The negotiations for renewal of the union centered on depriving Italian subsidiary coins of their legal tender status in the rest of the union and on forcing Italy to reacquire them. Italy grudgingly agreed to redeem its subsidiary coins circulating in other member countries for full-bodied coins, and to use those subsidiary coins to redeem its small notes. Soon Italy was able to restore convertibility of all its notes, and its coins were legal tender again throughout the union. But another crisis in 1893 prompted another suspension, followed by another agreement with other members of the union for Italy to repatriate its subsidiary coinage. Greece's subsidiary coinage was likewise "nationalized" in 1908.

The accident of 1873

The end of bimetallism in Europe, as in the United States, posed the same problem of convertibility for what had previously been a full-bodied silver coinage. In 1871, Germany adopted the gold standard and embarked on a program designed to replace its silver coins with gold coins. To do so, it sold silver and bought gold at the prevailing exchange rate of 15.5. For reasons that remain unclear,[17] the Latin Union proved unwilling to absorb Germany's stocks of silver, and its members suspended free coinage of silver in quick succession in 1873, at the same time as the United States. Bimetallism disappeared abruptly. The market price of gold in terms of silver increased substantially, devaluing the stocks of silver of the formerly bimetallic countries and formerly silver-standard countries like Germany. These silver coins became effectively tokens in terms of the countries' units now based on gold.

Silver coins became tokens when countries abandoned bimetallism for the gold standard.

Members of the Latin Monetary Union were quick to impose on themselves annual caps on silver minting. Then in 1878, they agreed to suspend minting of silver and to resume it only by unanimous decision. France had already suspended free coinage of silver by a law of August 5, 1876. The preamble of the law presented the suspension not as the collapse of a system, but as the final step in an evolution:

---

[17] Flandreau (1996) has speculated on the relevance of the 1870–71 war between France and Germany.

"The theory of the double standard, on which our monetary law of the year XI is based, has been called into question ever since its origin. It is, in our view, less a theory than the result of the primitive inability of the legislators to combine together the two precious metals otherwise than by way of an unlimited concurrence—metals, both of which are destined to enter into the monetary system, but which recent legislators have learned to coordinate by leaving the unlimited function to gold alone and reducing silver to the role of divisional money."

The standard formula limps into place

By 1900, Britain, France, Germany, and the United States all had implemented the standard formula in practice, though curiously enough, the promise of convertibility had not been universally formalized. Thus, Britain remained officially silent about convertibility, but had made convertibility a longstanding practice. To be sure, Cannan (1935, 40) saw this practice as having built a set of expectations: "In this country, there is little doubt that in case of a considerable falling off of demand [for subsidiary coins] the Government would be compelled to take back enough of the coin to keep up its value, and the obligation might just as well be acknowledged at once." Cannan had written this in 1918, and a footnote added in later editions cited withdrawal of silver coin from 1921 to 1924 as proof that the expectations were valid.

A limping standard used large stocks of silver coins.

The formerly bimetallic countries were confronted with the issue of convertibility to a greater degree. Their belated adoption of the gold standard had saddled Germany, France, and the United States with large stocks of previously standard silver coins, creating a situation known as the "limping standard."

Those silver coins (thalers in Germany, 5-franc pieces or "écus" in France and the Latin Monetary Union, dollars in the United States) were legal tender but de facto token, as the value of their silver content had plummeted along with the world price of silver after 1873.

In the United States, as a result of political tussles, considerable quantities of silver dollars were produced after the suspension of silver coinage and until 1893. Only by an act of March 14, 1900 (31 *Statutes at Large* 45) did Congress make it the Treasury's duty to maintain parity to the gold dollar of "all forms of money coined and issued by the United States." This firmly established the gold standard, and set in law a practice to which the Treasury had held fast until then, sometimes at considerable cost (Dewey 1918, 444–55).

Members of the Latin Monetary Union, alert to the free-rider problems inherent in their union, dealt more quickly with the status of their silver coinage. In 1878, they bound themselves to keep the stock of silver coins constant. But the coins remained legal tender for their face value throughout the union, and circulated widely outside their countries of origin. Nothing had been said about the status of the coins should the union dissolve or a country secede, which could happen with a year's notice. In 1884, France made clear that it wanted the issue addressed, and a new treaty was negotiated the following year. The negotiations were difficult: expecting to be a net debtor, Belgium initially opted out and won some last-minute concessions. Ultimately, the members committed themselves to redeeming their net balances of 5F pieces in gold or gold-denominated instruments within five years of the dissolution of the union (Belgium and Italy committed to redeem only half of their balances). Meanwhile, as long as the union remained in force, the Bank of France promised to accept all 5F pieces at par.[18] As in Britain, the commitments were ultimately honored.[19]

∽

---

[18] A similar policy on the part of the German Reichsbank kept the silver thalers at par until they were retired in 1907 (Mises 1953, 55).

[19] When World War I came, all belligerent countries suspended convertibility, and Switzerland became the unwilling recipient of their subsidiary coinage. France and Belgium made good on their obligations when the union came to an end in January 1927.

Chapter 19

Ideas, Policies, and Outcomes

Evolutions of ideas and institutions

James Laurence Laughlin (1931, 87) concluded his textbook exposition of the standard formula as follows:

> It might seem at first blush that, as subsidiary moneys play only a secondary part, the principles governing them are not of first importance. On the contrary, the questions raised in early monetary experience down to the present day of necessarily combining different metals of varying relative values in one monetary system have led to the evolution of general principles of far-reaching influence.

Laughlin cited the role of these principles in managing the silver money stocks in formerly bimetallic countries, and also in maintaining "the value of paper and credit representatives of the established metallic standard" and in supporting "devices for avoiding the actual transfer of the valuable standard metal" such as paper money, banknotes, checks, and bills of exchange.

Contemporaries of Laughlin also sought timely lessons from episodes in the history of small change. The German hyperinflation of 1922–23 prompted German scholars to study how medieval jurists had dealt with units of account during periods of fluctuations in exchange rates. We owe to Germany's 1923 hyperinflation a wealth of scholarship devoted to those concerns (Nussbaum 1950, 171–80, 217; see also Täuber 1933, 20–29).

This chapter summarizes what we have learned from studying the history of the big problem of small change. We recall themes that connect many episodes.

Our history

Our story began after Charlemagne first issued the silver penny, which for hundreds of years was the only coin and unit of account in Europe. In the 1200s, states began to issue at first silver and then gold coins in larger denominations. The unit of account remained the penny. The larger denominations contained more silver than the penny, and were meant to be that much more valuable; coins of different denominations were supposed to exchange for one another like lumps of silver of different sizes. Governments set up a mechanism to supply the coins needed for trade. They chartered mints and instructed them to sell (but not buy) particular coins for specified amounts of silver. The public decided how many coins to mint and how many to export or to melt. This mechanism was designed automatically to supply the amounts of coins that traders wanted.

But almost from the beginning, that supply mechanism produced shortages of the smaller denomination coins. Those shortages were often accompanied by appreciations of the large denomination coins in terms of the penny. The administrators of the mints learned how to cure shortages, at least temporarily, by debasing small denomination coins. Debasements provided incentives for people to bring silver to the mint to purchase new small coins. That cure for shortages produced centuries of appreciating rates of exchange of the large for the small denomination coins. Those debasements also caused price levels to drift upward, because pennies were the unit of account in which prices were stated. A principle cause of many debasements was not governments' thirst for seigniorage revenues, but their wish to provide adequate supplies of small denomination coins.

Recurring appreciations of large denomination coins relative to small denomination coins preoccupied lawyers who confronted conflicts about the units of account used in contracts. Beginning in the twelfth century, secular lawyers created a body of opinion about money, mainly by selecting from among conflicting passages that

they found within the body of Roman law that had been system-
atized under Justinian. Roman law and ancient commentaries on
it had expressed an array of views on money. They ranged from a
commodity view that money acquired value from the metal within
it, to the view that money was worth more than its constituent
material because it facilitated exchange by alleviating the absence of
double coincidence of wants, a view that had been expressed by the
Roman jurist Paulus. The medieval lawyers chose to ignore Paulus
and to adopt the view that money is a commodity whose value is
determined like that of any other commodity. They thought that
people bargained and contracted for the amounts of silver within
coins, not the names on those coins.

Weight versus tale   Fluctuations in exchange rates of different denomination coins
and features of the technology for producing coins bedeviled the
medieval lawyers' theory. Small denomination coins cost proportionately more resources to produce than large ones. Allowing producers of coins to recover their costs and governments to tax the
coin producers put a wedge between the value of the metal inside
and the exchange value of newly minted coins, for otherwise no
one would have the incentive to take silver to the mint to purchase
coins.[1] Because the costs of production were greater, wedges were
typically larger for small coins than for large. Those wedges meant
that coins were actually valued partly by *tale* (i.e., in proportion to
their number rather than their weight) and made room for exchange
rate fluctuations between coins of different denominations, even in
the absence of any change in their metallic contents.

Theorists struggled   For centuries medieval and Renaissance lawyers and monetary
to reconcile facts theorists tried to apply an idealized theory that held that money is
with the principle a commodity to facts indicating that the market often valued coins
of valuation by partly by tale. The theory had to adapt to fit the facts. Theorists
weight. emerged who recognized and even made virtues of the facts. Eventually, they used their new theories to make proposals to amend the
medieval money supply mechanism in ways that would avoid the

---

[1] This made the wedge necessary. What made the wedge *possible* was that coins
fulfilled a particular purpose that could not be served by uncoined metal.

recurrent shortages of small change.

Those theorists did not work in a vacuum. They sought to explain outcomes of accidental and purposeful monetary experiments. Lawyers adjudicating disputes occasioned by exchange rate fluctuations sometimes argued that what had implicitly been contracted for were not particular quantities of silver but values of a more comprehensive bundle of goods. That pushed value in exchange to the foreground, not weight. Towns under siege issued tokens of various forms. Although some of them appear to have been backed by a leader's promise that they would be redeemed for metal coins after the siege was lifted, others seem to have been unbacked. During a siege, token coins were valued, even when they were not backed by an explicit promise of convertibility, supporting Paulus's ancient observations.

Partly inspired by such observations, theorists discussed circumstances under which it would be wise or just to issue token coins. From experiences with siege monies, they knew that counterfeiters threatened to undermine a system of token coins. As late as the seventeenth century, coins continued to be created by the same ancient technology of hammering them by hand from dies. That technology required little capital, so that the costs of entry into the counterfeiting business were low. The technology produced low quality coins that were easy to copy. The medieval way of deterring counterfeiting was simply to abstain from issuing token coins and to let the high cost in terms of metal content of making full-bodied coins deter counterfeiters.

Experiments

Disturbances to supplies of small change in the sixteenth century brought new ideas and experiments to France and Spain. In France, shortages of small change played an important part in generating the persistent rise in the price level of the sixteenth and seventeenth centuries called the Price Revolution. The inflation was partly caused by inflows of Spanish treasure into Europe from the New World, which drove down the relative prices of both gold and silver in terms

The Price Revolution and units of account

of goods in general. But more inflation occurred than could be accounted for by cheaper gold and silver alone. The penny remained the unit of account for most of the sixteenth century in France. Exchange rates for larger silver and gold coins appreciated persistently, to the accompaniment of recurring shortages and debasements of small denomination coins. Those debasements and depreciations of the small coins accounted for perhaps half of the inflation in France during the sixteenth century. The exchange rate fluctuations between large and small denomination coins provoked disputes about the unit of account.

In response, in 1577 the government imposed a reform that made a large coin, the gold écu, the unit of account. The French government also experimented with issuing token small denomination coins in small amounts. These were remarkably progressive reforms, because making the large coin the unit of account and using small coins as tokens were to be crucial elements in what two centuries later would become a standard formula for solving the problem of small change. But for some reason, after 25 years, France abandoned the reforms of 1577 and returned to the medieval mechanism. The unit of account reverted to the penny and token small coins were abandoned.

Castile's experiment with token coins   In 1596, Castile started a longer and more comprehensive experiment that tested elements of the standard formula, including token small change. Fiscal exigencies motivated Castile's monetary experiments. For years before 1596, it had been known that a government could raise resources by replacing small denomination silver coins with token coins. But the prevailing hammering technology had made token coins easy to counterfeit, which meant that a government would lose much of the potential revenue to counterfeiters. In the late sixteenth century an expensive new technology for producing high-quality coins arrived, the cylinder press. Knowing how token coins could be substituted for silver coins without causing inflation, the monetary advisors of King Philip II of Spain proposed that the cylinder press be used to make inconvertible token copper coins. Philip II and his successors performed that experiment.

The experiment succeeded for twenty-five years. Substantial numbers of token coins were issued without deteriorating in value relative to silver coins, raising substantial revenues for the government in the process. However, eventually so many of these small denomination token coins were issued that inflation began. The Spanish monetary authorities then struggled for half a century, sometimes to arrest inflation, and sometimes to extract more revenues from the token coinage. In the process, they performed marvelous experiments and tried to manipulate exchange rates. After the experiment was over in 1660, Spain renounced token coins, and returned to the medieval monetary system.

The Castilians had tried the "token" part of the standard formula, *Convertibility* but had omitted convertibility. In 1661, the British monetary official Sir Henry Slingsby understood how convertibility would automatically have regulated the quantity of token coins issued and thereby prevented the Castilian inflation. The advisors to the king of Spain hadn't recognized the role of convertibility, or had recognized it too late. But the Castilian experiment generated valuable time series data that led empiricists to draw an association between the quantity of such token coins issued and the price level. The wreckage of the Castilian experiment gave token coins a bad name, but created an important database that helped analysts like Sir William Petty induce the quantity theory of money.

Shortages of small change in seventeenth- and eighteenth-century *Trust and tokens* Britain led to further and more successful experiments with elements of the standard formula. During the seventeenth century, under the opportunistic Stuart kings, Britain let private firms and cities supply tokens. Those tokens formed much of Britain's small denomination coinage. Sometimes the firms or cities offered to convert those tokens into silver. Towards the end of the period that those tokens flourished, in the 1660s, there emerged a new technology for making milled coins that were difficult to counterfeit. By deterring counterfeiting, that technology improved the prospects for implementing a convertible token coinage. The government under the Stuart kings used that technology to produce some silver coins, but not to produce tokens. Perhaps that was because to implement a system of convertible token coins, the public had to believe the government's commitment to redeem the tokens into full-bodied money on demand. As North and Weingast (1989) have reminded us, the Stuart kings could not be trusted.

Reaction   Presumably the new regime formed by Parliament and King William III after the Glorious Revolution of 1688 was more trustworthy. Ironically that new regime never contemplated issuing token coins, precisely *because* it cared about credibility in monetary and fiscal affairs. At the time, John Locke made a famous argument that by restoring the weight of the small denomination coins, the government would be upholding the sanctity of contracts. Locke reiterated the medieval view that when people signed contracts for deferred payment of coins, they understood a coin to be a quantity of metal. For asserting that, the statesman Lord Liverpool and the Whig historian Lord Macaulay continued to praise Locke in the mid-nineteenth century.

In 1696, Parliament in Britain went beyond Locke's recommendations, and recoined at the old weights at government expense. It thereby incurred expenses that accounted for a considerable fraction of its budget in the midst of a European war. The new regime thus expended considerable resources to restore a full-bodied coinage and to reinstate the medieval monetary mechanism. It thereby turned its back on the progress that the market had made in moving toward the standard formula and reinstated full-bodied and revalued silver small denomination coins.

The standard   Despite the setback of the Great Recoinage, the progress that *formula prevailed.* Britain had made toward the standard formula under the Stuart kings resumed again during the second quarter of the eighteenth century. Wear and tear on the coins and a neglectful government policy toward subsidiary coinage allowed counterfeits and private issues of subsidiary coinage to proliferate. After 1720, the exchange rates of large for small denomination coins stabilized. By mid-century, the guinea, a gold coin, had replaced silver coins as the unit of account. That transformation in the unit of account came not from government legislation but from the decisions of private contractors. In 1787, the invention of Boulton's steam press made it feasible to issue token coins that were difficult to counterfeit. Private firms soon exploited the new technology to issue convertible token coins. After a generation in which those coins served as the small change in Britain, the government nationalized the business of supplying small change, thereby practically implementing the standard formula. Meanwhile, the standard formula was more deliberately adopted by the German monetary union, which remained on a silver standard. Later in the 19th century, France and the United States embraced the standard formula when they abandoned bimetallism for the gold standard.

Major themes

We conclude part IV by recalling recurring themes.

Beliefs and interests

Much of modern economics and political economy assumes that while people might have diverse interests, they nevertheless share a common and correct model of the economy. That all decision makers know the correct model underlies both the Nash and the rational expectations equilibrium concepts. Different people might prefer different policies, but all know their consequences.

Though the formal model in part V assumes rational expectations, our narrative assumes that policy makers frequently used incorrect or incomplete models. Only after a long process of learning did society and policy makers discover what we think is a correct model. Only then were they able to set up a good mechanism for managing supplies of coins. Much of our story is about how intelligent and well-informed people used and debated different models, contributing to a social process of model adaptation and discovery.

That process of model adaptation and discovery would be difficult to formalize, and we have not tried to do. Most formal theories of learning in economics study easier problems in which people know the model. Models that use Bayes' law assume that people know a correct specification or set of specifications that they never alter. The accumulation of evidence allows them to sharpen estimates and resolve uncertainty, but does not prompt them to uncover new specifications. As Marimon (1997) noted, a Bayesian learner knows the truth from the beginning: he may lack data but believes he has an adequate model specification.

Disputes about models were central to many episodes and propelled a slow social process of learning that eventually led societies to abandon commodity money and to embrace the idea of token money. Progress occurred when someone proposed a new model, or added a new feature to an old one. We have not modeled those leaps of imagination and paradigm shifts, but have observed them in our history.[2]

Thus, we assign an important role to model disagreement and discovery in explaining outcomes,[3] while modern political economy assumes away any such disagreements and explains outcomes as reflecting the polity's mechanism for resolving conflicts of interest. Conflicts of interest play a role in our story too, but they are not the whole story. Numerous episodes of inflation in units of account set debtors against creditors. The debate about the Great Recoinage between Locke, Lowndes, and Newton brought out both their different models and their different preferences about the distributional consequences of proposals to recoin at an historic or a depreciated rate.

Units of account and nominal contracts

How people choose to denominate contracts is an important question in modern macroeconomics. "Price stickiness" and "nominal rigidities," if they exist, emerge from contracting decisions. An enduring question in macroeconomics, often posed as a challenge to

---

[2] See Kreps (1998) for a discussion of the issues. Kreps sketched a learning process that features model respecification and experimentation.

[3] See Sargent (1999) for a similar perspective on the U.S. inflation and deflation of the 1970s and 1980s.

particular models of sticky prices, is why people don't index contracts against inflation.

That question runs through our narrative. By focusing on the content of the coins initially lent and the intent of the parties, medieval law seemed equipped to index contracts and protect parties from fluctuations in exchange rates. Yet when exchange rate stability prevailed, contracts ceased to take note of the form in which money was lent, and parties seemed happy enough to denominate all transactions in the same unit of account. Only when rates fluctuated again was it urgent to reconsider conventional units of account and index the unit to one coin or another.

At times, the monetary authorities tried in vain to defend a hitherto conventional unit of account by legislating the exchange rate. Their efforts invariably failed to affect the exchange rates that traders actually used, and succeeded only in producing a string of ghost monies, units of account that let traders evade government-mandated units of account.

By the sixteenth century, jurists were assigning to the public authorities the power to regulate the unit of account. Those public authorities saw it as their duty to provide a stable unit of account in which all transactions, small or large, could be denominated. That was the intention of the French reform of 1577, with the innovative shift from the small coin to the large coin as unit of account. At the same time, theorists described money, not as a lump of metal, but as "the measure of all things," and struggled with ways to keep it as constant as the yard or the ounce, a concern not shared by their medieval predecessors.[4] But the inflationary experiences of the seventeenth century also made those authorities reluctant to relinquish the tight constraints on the price level that full-bodied coinage provided. Their desire to maintain a constant vector of exchange rates and full-bodied coinage for both gold and

Price level targeting emerged.

---

[4] Medieval philosophers thought of money as a measure (Kaye 1998), as did Oresme. This led them to condemn debasements as an alteration of this measure, not necessarily to advocate policies to maintain its constancy (see the footnote on page 186 for an exception).

silver ultimately gave birth to bimetallism.

John Locke said that although people made contracts in units of account, by a unit of account they meant a fixed quantity of metal. In his view, it was the government's duty to fix that quantity, and thereby to uphold the intentions of all parties in a way that private law could not. Disregarding Locke, who had said that people bargain for weights of metal and not "for sounds" (see page 284), on June 5, 1933 the U.S. Congress declared that contracting for a fixed quantity of metal was "against public policy" (48 Stat. 112) and at one fell swoop substituted sounds for intrinsic value.[5]

Small change and monetary theory

The evolution of monetary doctrines about small change was an important part of the process by which a managed fiat currency system came to be understood and implemented. Apart from the inessential detail of the substance on which a "promise" is printed, a token coin is like a paper bank note. A token coin is an IOU written on a piece of metal whose intrinsic value is less than the amount owed. At first, token coins were issued by local governments and private firms, as well as by some national governments. Eventually, national governments monopolized the issuing of banknotes and token coins. Thinking about the feasibility of a system of token small coins uncovered and refined the quantity theory of money as well as its main rival, Adam Smith's real bills doctrine (page 101).

Currency boards, dollarization, and the standard formula

Currency issued by a currency board resembles token coinage. Many of the theoretical justifications for the standard formula apply when modern policy makers consider the drastic step of abandoning their national currency or the somewhat less drastic step of linking their national currency to a foreign currency via a currency board. A currency board behaves much like the managers of small change under the standard formula: it issues and redeems tokens convertible into foreign currency. Delegating monetary policy to a currency

---

[5] The Duchess paraphrased Lowndes's dictum (see page 291) : "take care of the sense, and the sounds will take care of themselves." Alice in Wonderland, ch. 9.

board is supposed somehow to alter a government's incentives in a way that increases the markets' trust in the future value of its currency. (Recall that an essential prerequisite for the standard formula was having a government that could be trusted to redeem tokens for full-bodied money, and that it took a long time before the idea was accepted that governments could be so trusted.) Like token subsidiary coinage, the notes of a currency board tie up fewer resources in a nation's currency stock than does a fully "dollarized" system. In a dollarized system, a government exits the business of creating token currencies and uses the currency issued by a foreign government. [6] Thus, the choice of a currency board versus dollarization involves the same basic theoretical principles that his advisors taught King Philip II. [7]

Learning by markets and by governments

Both governments and private sectors played important roles in solving problems and pushing forward the learning process. A slogan in economics is that if something is a big problem, the market will adapt to solve it. We have encountered examples that validate that bromide. One set of examples were the repeated "invasions" of foreign coins that were the market's way of implementing a spontaneous debasement to cure shortages of small coins in the absence of timely government action. A second set of examples occurred when the market created ghost monies, units of account that private traders used to circumvent a government-mandated unit of account. Third, firms issued tokens, and eventually convertible tokens, thereby giving the government working examples of the standard formula. Since convertible tokens are interest-free IOUs, firms had incentives to issue them.

Although the standard formula calls for the government to take the lead in administering a system of token coinage, it was actually the market that took substantial steps toward the standard formula in

---

[6] By the act of dollarizing, the government in effect performs the *reverse* of the "small country" experiment of Adam Smith that we described on page 101.

[7] See page 231.

seventeenth– and eighteenth–century Britain. Ultimately the British government implemented the standard formula by nationalizing a smoothly operating system of privately issued tokens.

જી

Part V

A Formal Theory

CHAPTER 20

A Theory of Full-Bodied Small Change

We present a model of supply and demand for large and small metal coins designed to simulate the medieval and early modern monetary system, and to show how its supply mechanism lay vulnerable to alternating shortages and surpluses of small coins.[1] We extend Sargent and Smith's (1997) model to incorporate demands and supplies of two coins differing in denomination and possibly in metal content. We specify cash-in-advance constraints to let small coins make purchases that large coins cannot. As in the Sargent-Smith model, for each type of coin, the supply side of the model determines a range of price levels whose lower and upper boundaries trigger coin minting and melting, respectively. These ranges let coins circulate above their intrinsic values. The ranges must coincide if *both* coins are to continue to circulate. The demand side of the model delivers a sharp characterization of "shortages" of small coins. Shortages make binding our additional cash-in-advance constraint—the "penny-in-advance" constraint that requires that small purchases be made with small coins. This means that small coins must *depreciate* in value relative to large coins during shortages of small coins. Thus in our model, shortages of small coins have two symptoms: (1) the quantity theory of money splits in two, one for large coins, another for small; and (2) small coins must depreciate relative to large ones in order to render binding the "small-change-in-advance constraint" and thereby provide a motive for money holders to economize on small change. In conjunction with the supply mechanism, the second response aggravates the shortage.[2]

---

[1] Part V is a revision and expansion of Sargent and Velde (1999).

[2] The standard formula solves the exchange rate indeterminacy problem inherent in any system with an inconvertible and less than full-bodied fractional currency. Remember that Russell Boyer's (1971) original paper on exchange rate indeterminacy was titled "Nickels and Dimes." See Kareken and Wallace (1981)

We use these features of the model to account for various historical outcomes, including why debasements of small coins were a common policy response to shortages of small change. Then we modify the original arrangement by including one or more of the elements in the formula recounted by Cipolla, and show the consequences. In parts II, III, and IV of this book, we have compared some of these consequences with the predictions and prescriptions of contemporary monetary theorists, and with episodes in monetary history.

The remainder of this part is organized as follows. Chapter 21 describes the model environment, the money supply arrangement, and the equilibrium concept. Chapter 22 uses "back-solving" to indicate possible co-movements of the price level, money supplies, and national income; to illustrate perverse aspects of the medieval supply arrangements; and to interpret various historical outcomes. Chapter 23 uses the model to study how aspects of Cipolla's standard formula remedy the perverse supply responses by making small change into tokens. Chapter 24 concludes.

ৎ৽

---

for an analysis of exchange rate indeterminacy in a model with multiple fiat currencies. A one-sided exchange rate indeterminacy emerges from the cash-in-advance restrictions in our model, and determines salient predictions of the model.

CHAPTER 21
The Model

In a small country there lives an immortal representative household that gets utility from two nonstorable consumption goods. The household faces cash-in-advance constraints.[1] "Cash" consists of a large and a small denomination coin, each produced by a government-regulated mint that stands ready to coin any silver brought to it by household-owned firms. The government specifies the amounts of silver in large and small coins, and also collects a flat-rate seigniorage tax on the volume of newly minted coins; it rebates the revenues in a lump sum. Coins are the only storable good available to the household. The firm can transform either of two consumption goods into the other one-for-one and can trade either consumption good for silver at a fixed international price. After describing these components of the economy in greater detail, we shall define an equilibrium. For any variable, we let $\{x\}$ denote the infinite sequence $\{x_t\}_{t=0}^{\infty}$. Table 21.1 lists the main parameters of the model and their units.

The household

The representative household maximizes

$$\sum_{t=0}^{\infty} \beta^t u\left(c_{1,t}, c_{2,t}\right).　\tag{21.1}$$

We assume that the one-period utility function is of the form $u(c_{1,t}, c_{2,t}) = v[g(c_{1,t})] + v(c_{2,t})$ where $v(\cdot)$ is strictly increasing, twice continuously differentiable, strictly concave, and satisfies the Inada

---

[1] The model modifies Sargent and Smith (1997), which in turn modified Lucas (1982) and Lucas and Stokey (1987). See Barro (1979), Sargent and Wallace (1983), and McCallum (1989) for other models of commodity money.

Table 21.1 Symbols.

Variable	Meaning	Units
ϕ	world price of silver	oz silver / cons good
b_1	intrinsic content of penny	oz silver / penny
b_2	intrinsic content of dollar	oz silver / dollar
γ_1	melting point of penny	pence / cons good
γ_2	melting point of dollar	dollars / cons good
σ_i	seigniorage rate	(none)
b_1^{-1}	mint equivalent of penny	pence / oz silver
b_2^{-1}	mint equivalent of dollar	dollars / oz silver
m_1	stock of pennies	pence
m_2	stock of dollars	dollars
e	exchange rate	pence / dollar
p	price of cons goods	pence / cons good

condition $\lim_{x \to 0} v'(x) = +\infty$. For illustrative purposes we will sometimes use $v(\cdot) = \log(\cdot)$. The function g is monotonic, twice continuously differentiable, and satisfies $g(0) = 0$ and $g(x) = x + \alpha$ with $\alpha > 0$ for x greater than some small number $\underline{c}$.[2] We use consumption of good 1, c_1, to represent "small" purchases, and c_2 to stand for "large" purchases.

There are two kinds of cash: pennies, whose stock is m_1, and dollars, whose stock is m_2. Each stock is measured in number of coins, pennies or dollars. Both coins can be used for large purchases, but only pennies can be used for small purchases.[3] A dollar exchanges

[2] The composition with the function g makes preferences nonhomothetic and assures that Inada conditions hold for both c_1 and c_2. Such restrictions on preferences could also be represented in a variety of alternative ways. The behavior of g in the interval $(0, \underline{c})$ accounts for the curvature of the expansion paths in Figures 22.1 and 22.3. We shall typically assume that equilibrium outcomes occur at consumption allocations for which $g(x) = x + \alpha$, for example, in the the arguments on pages 353, 357, and 362.

[3] The assumption that pennies can be used for the same purchases as dollars is motivated by several episodes in history during which small denominations overtook the monetary functions of large denominations with great ease (see for example chapter 14).

for e_t pennies. Thus, the cash-in-advance constraints are:

$$p_t \left(c_{1,t} + c_{2,t}\right) \le m_{1,t-1} + e_t m_{2,t-1} \qquad (21.2)$$

$$p_t c_{1,t} \le m_{1,t-1}, \qquad (21.3)$$

where p_t is the penny price of good i. We call (21.3) the "penny-in-advance" constraint. The household's budget constraint, expressed in pence, is

$$p_t \left(c_{1,t} + c_{2,t}\right) + m_{1,t} + e_t m_{2,t} \le \Pi_t + m_{1,t-1} + e_t m_{2,t-1} + T_t, \quad (21.4)$$

where Π_t denotes the firm's profits measured in pence, and T_t denotes lump sum transfers from the government, both items that will be described shortly.

The household faces given sequences $\{p\}$, $\{e\}$, $\{\Pi\}$, $\{T\}$, begins life with initial conditions $m_{1,-1}$, $m_{2,-1}$, and chooses sequences $\{c_1\}$, $\{c_2\}$, $\{m_1\}$, $\{m_2\}$ to maximize (21.1) subject to (21.2), (21.3), and (21.4).

Production

A household-owned, profit-maximizing firm carries out two activities: it sells consumption goods to the household, and also makes decisions about minting and melting.

Production of goods

The firm owns an exogenous sequence of an endowment $\{\xi\}$ from which goods can be produced. Furthermore, one unit of either consumption good can be traded in the international market for $\phi > 0$ units of silver,[4] leading to the following restrictions on feasible allocations:

$$c_{1,t} + c_{2,t} \le \xi_t + \phi^{-1} S_t, \qquad t \ge 0 \qquad (21.5)$$

---

[4] Alternatively, there is a reversible linear technology for converting consumption goods into silver.

where $c_{1,t} \geq 0, c_{2t} \geq 0$ and S_t stands for the net exports of silver from the country.[5]

Production of coins
Stocks of coins evolve according to

$$m_{i,t} = m_{i,t-1} + n_{i,t} - \mu_{i,t} \tag{21.6}$$

where $n_{i,t} \geq 0, \mu_{i,t} \geq 0$ are rates of minting and melting of pennies, $i = 1$, and dollars, $i = 2$. These rates are chosen by the firm. The absence of any upper bound on the rate of minting embodies "free" or "unlimited" minting.

Coins are melted or minted to finance net exports of silver in the amount

$$S_t = b_1 \left(\mu_{1,t} - n_{1,t} \right) + b_2 \left(\mu_{2,t} - n_{2,t} \right). \tag{21.7}$$

Net exports of silver S_t correspond to net imports of $\phi^{-1} S_t$ of consumption goods.

Government
The government sets b_i, the number of ounces of silver in a penny, $i = 1$, and in a dollar, $i = 2$. It also levies a seigniorage tax on minting: for every new coin of type i minted, the government charges a flat tax at rate $\sigma_i > 0$.

The quantities $1/b_1$ and e_t/b_2 (measured in number of pence per minted ounce of silver) are called by Redish (1990) "mint equivalents." The quantities $(1 - \sigma_1)/b_1, e_t(1 - \sigma_2)/b_2$ are called "mint prices," and equal the number of pennies paid out by the mint per ounce of silver.

---

[5] Equation (21.5) can be recovered from the budget constraints holding at equilibrium prices, as usual. By substituting $\Pi_t = p_t \xi_t$, (21.8), and (21.6) into (21.4) we obtain

$$p_t \left(c_{1,t} + c_{2,t} \right) \leq p_t \xi_t + \mu_{1,t} + e_t \mu_{2,t} - (1 - \sigma_1) n_{1,t} - e_t (1 - \sigma_2) n_{2,t}.$$

Using the no-arbitrage conditions (21.12) in this expression and rearranging leads to

$$c_{1,t} + c_{2,t} \leq \xi_t + \left[\gamma_1^{-1} \left(\mu_{1,t} - n_{1,t} \right) + \gamma_2^{-1} \left(\mu_{2,t} - n_{2,t} \right) \right],$$

where $\gamma_i = \phi/b_i$. The term in square braces equals net imports of consumption goods.

Depending on citizens' minting decisions, the government collects revenues T_t in the amount

$$T_t = \sigma_1 n_{1,t} + \sigma_2 e_t n_{2,t}, \tag{21.8}$$

which are rebated in lump-sum fashion to the household. Below we shall describe other interpretations of σ_i partly in terms of the mint's costs of production. The only modification that these alternative interpretations require would be to alter (21.8).

Timing

The firm receives the endowment, sells it, mints and melts, pays seigniorage, and pays all earnings to the household at the end of each period.

We adapt the usual shopper-worker decomposition of the household to support the following within-period timing of events at t. We use a small country interpretation of the "technology" for transforming consumption goods from and into silver. First, the household separates into a shopper and a worker. The worker owns the firm, which receives the endowment ξ_t and net imports of goods $\phi^{-1} S_t$. The firm converts $\xi_t + \phi^{-1} S_t$ into $c_{1,t}$ and $c_{2,t}$ subject to equation (21.5), and sells the goods subject to the cash-in-advance constraints to the shopper. The firm then mints and melts coins and uses the net proceeds of metal to settle its import account. The firm pays the seigniorage tax to the government, which immediately transfers the proceeds to the household as T_t. Finally, the firm pays its net nominal proceeds ($m_{1,t}$ and $m_{2,t}$) to the "worker." At the end of the period, the firm has nothing, while the household gets the goods that it consumes and money stocks that it will carry into period $t+1$.

The firm's profit measured in pence is

$$\Pi_t = p_t \xi_t + p_t \left(\frac{b_1}{\phi} \mu_{1,t} + \frac{b_2}{\phi} \mu_{2,t} \right) - \left(\mu_{1,t} + e_t \mu_{2,t} \right) + \left(n_{1,t} + e_t n_{2,t} \right)$$
$$- \left(\sigma_1 n_{1,t} + \sigma_2 e_t n_{2,t} \right) - p_t \left(\frac{b_1}{\phi} n_{1,t} + \frac{b_2}{\phi} n_{2,t} \right). \tag{21.9}$$

The first term measures revenues from the sale of the endowment. The next terms are melting revenues (the value of the silver in the melted coins), followed by melting expenses (the number of coins melted), minting revenues (the number of coins minted), seigniorage payments on new minting, and minting expenses (the value of the silver turned into coins).

In every period t, the firm takes the prices (p_t, e_t) as given and chooses minting and melting $n_{1,t}$, $n_{2,t}$, $\mu_{1,t}$, $\mu_{2,t}$ to maximize (21.9) subject to (21.6).

Equilibrium

A *feasible allocation* is a triple of sequences $\{c_1\}, \{c_2\}, \{S\}$ satisfying (21.5). A *price system* is a pair of sequences $\{p\}, \{e\}$. A *money supply* is a pair of sequences $\{m_1\}, \{m_2\}$ satisfying the initial conditions $(m_{1,-1}, m_{2,-1})$. An *equilibrium* is a price system, a feasible allocation, and a money supply such that given the price system, the allocation and the money supply solve the household's problem and the firm's problem.

Analytical strategy

We proceed sequentially to extract restrictions that our model places on co-movements of the price level and the money supply. The firm's problem puts some restrictions on these co-movements, and the household's problem adds more.

The firm's problem

The firm's problem puts restrictions on the price level in the form of two intervals. Define $\gamma_i = \phi/b_i$ and rearrange (21.9):

$$\Pi_t = p_t \xi_t + \left(1 - \sigma_1 - p_t \gamma_1^{-1}\right) n_{1,t} + e_t \left(1 - \sigma_2 - p_t \left(e_t \gamma_2\right)^{-1}\right) n_{2,t}$$
$$+ \left(p_t \gamma_1^{-1} - 1\right) \mu_{1,t} + e_t \left(p_t \left(e_t \gamma_2\right)^{-1} - 1\right) \mu_{2,t}. \qquad (21.10)$$

Each period, the firm chooses $n_{i,t}$, $\mu_{i,t}$ to maximize Π_t subject to non-negativity constraints $n_{i,t} \geq 0$, $\mu_{i,t} \geq 0$ and to the upper bound on melting: $m_{i,t-1} \geq \mu_{i,t}$, for $i = 1, 2$. The form of (21.10) immediately implies the following no-arbitrage conditions:[6]

$$p_t \geq \gamma_1 (1 - \sigma_1) \qquad (21.11a)$$

$$p_t \geq e_t \gamma_2 (1 - \sigma_2) \qquad (21.11b)$$

and the following first-order conditions:

$$n_{1,t} \geq 0; \quad = \quad \text{if } p_t > \gamma_1 (1 - \sigma_1) \qquad (21.12a)$$

$$n_{2,t} \geq 0; \quad = \quad \text{if } p_t > e_t \gamma_2 (1 - \sigma_2) \qquad (21.12b)$$

$$\mu_{1,t} \geq 0; \quad = \quad \text{if } p_t < \gamma_1 \qquad (21.12c)$$

$$\mu_{2,t} \geq 0; \quad = \quad \text{if } p_t < e_t \gamma_2 \qquad (21.12d)$$

$$\mu_{1,t} \leq m_{1,t-1}; \quad = \quad \text{if } p_t > \gamma_1 \qquad (21.12e)$$

$$\mu_{2,t} \leq m_{2,t-1}; \quad = \quad \text{if } p_t > e_t \gamma_2. \qquad (21.12f)$$

Implications of the arbitrage conditions for monetary policy

The no-arbitrage conditions (21.11) place a lower bound on the price level. Furthermore, the first-order conditions constrain the mint's policy if both coins are to exist.[7] The constraints put p_t within both of two intervals, $[\gamma_1(1 - \sigma_1), \gamma_1]$ (corresponding to pennies) and $[e_t\gamma_2(1 - \sigma_2), e_t\gamma_2]$ (corresponding to dollars), as illustrated in figure 21.1. Only when the price level p_t is at the lower end of either interval might the associated coin be minted. Only when the price is at the upper end might that coin be melted.

Thus, if the lower ends of the intervals do not coincide (i.e., if $\gamma_1(1 - \sigma_1) \neq e_t\gamma_2(1 - \sigma_2)$), then only one type of coin can ever be minted. Equating the lower ends of the intervals (by the government's choice of (b_i, σ_i)) makes the mint stand ready to buy silver for the same price, whether it pays in pennies or dollars. If the upper ends of the intervals don't coincide, then one type of coin will be melted before the other. Equating the upper ends of the intervals makes the ratio of metal contents in the two coins equal the exchange rate: $e = b_2/b_1$. In such a case, pennies are said to be "full-bodied."

---

[6] These restrictions must hold if the right side of (21.10) is to be bounded (which it must be in any equilibrium); their violation would imply that the firm could earn unbounded profits.

[7] See the related discussion in Usher (1943, 197–201).

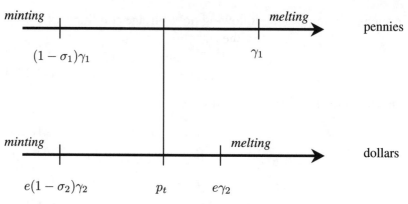

Figure 21.1 Constraints on the price level imposed by the arbitrage conditions.

Household preferences and equations (21.2) and (21.3) imply that $p_t \leq \max\{e_t\gamma_2, \gamma_1\}$ (both monies cannot disappear) and $e_t\gamma_2 \leq \gamma_1$ (pennies cannot disappear). If this last inequality is strict, the intrinsic content of pennies is less than proportionate to their value in dollars, in which case pennies are "light" or "overvalued."

Thus, if pennies are not full-bodied, a sufficient rise in the price level will make large coins disappear. If the mint prices differ, a sufficient fall in prices will prompt minting of only one of the two coins. The perpetual coexistence of both coins in the face of price fluctuations requires that pennies be full-bodied and that equal mint prices prevail for both coins; that is, the intervals must coincide, and therefore the seigniorage rates must be equal. This is not possible if we reinterpret the σ_i's in terms of the production costs for the two types of coins, because per unit of value it is cheaper to produce large than small denomination coins.

Interpretations of σ_i

In using (21.8), we have interpreted σ_i as a flat tax rate on minting of coins of type i. But so far as concerns the firm's problem and the arbitrage pricing restrictions, σ_i can be regarded as measuring *all* costs of production borne by the mint, including the seigniorage it must pay to the government. On this interpretation, in setting σ_i, the government names the sum of the seigniorage tax rate and the mint's costs of production. If a government were unwilling to *subsidize* production of coins, then the costs of production would serve as a lower bound on σ_i.

The government could decide to set gross seigniorage σ_i to 0, by subsidizing the mint. In this circumstance, our two coins could coexist only if pennies were full-weight (their intrinsic content being proportional to their face values), and if the price level never deviated from $\gamma_1 = e\gamma_2$.

We discussed earlier the attitudes of medieval writers as well as the actual policies followed by governments. One tradition of thought advocated setting $\sigma_i = 0$, but it was not followed in practice until the seventeenth century; other jurists thought that σ_i should remain close to production costs, except in cases of clearly established fiscal emergency.

On the other side, restraints were placed on the government's freedom to set σ_i by potential competitors to the mint, such as counterfeiters or foreign mints, and by the government's ability to enforce laws against counterfeiting and the circulation of foreign coins. Let $\bar{\sigma}_i$ be the production costs for counterfeiters, or for arbitrageurs taking metal to foreign mints and bringing back coins (inclusive of transport costs). A wide gap between σ_i and $\bar{\sigma}_i$ was difficult to maintain unless a government's enforcement powers were strong. If they were not, $\bar{\sigma}_i$ placed an upper bound on σ_i.[8]

A government could maintain positive seigniorage if the costs of production of licensed mints were smaller than those of competitors. For example, Montanari ([1683] 1804, 114) argued that the death penalty for counterfeiting, while impossible to enforce strictly, adds a risk premium to counterfeiters' wage bill, thereby increasing $\bar{\sigma}_i$ when the same technology is used by all. Furthermore, if a

---

[8] See Usher (1943, 201): "Seigniorage presented no special problem unless the amount exceeded the average rate of profit attractive to gold and silversmiths, or to mints in neighboring jurisdictions. Beyond this limit, the effective monopoly of coinage might be impaired by illegal coinage of essentially sound coins, or by the more extensive use of foreign coin."

government were able to restrict access to the mint's technology, or if it could secure the exclusive use of a better technology, it could set seigniorage above the mint's production costs, up to the level of competitors' costs.

Per coin production costs differed between small and large denomination coins. The medieval technology made it significantly more expensive to produce smaller denomination coins.[9] In situations that tied the σ_i's to the costs of production, different production costs implied different widths of our no-arbitrage intervals. This meant either that pennies had to be less than full-bodied or that the mint prices differed. In either case, price level fluctuations could arrest production or, by stimulating melting, cause the disappearance of one coin.

Full-weight and underweight coins

So far, our model assumes that all coins of a given denomination are of the same weight. Actual coins deteriorated over time. One cause was wear and tear, that is, physical and chemical alteration inevitably resulting from handling in trade. A coin owner could purposefully make a coin deteriorate through sweating, clipping, or shaving. Sweating is an artificial form of abrasion in which the losses are collected, while clipping and shaving are outright removal of pieces of metal from the edges of the coin.

Wear and tear can, by itself, be consequential. Figure 21.2 plots estimates of wear for coins in nineteenth-century Britain, France, Canada, and the United States. Estimates for medieval abrasion on English silver coinage are from 0.2 to 0.3% per annum (estimates of Grierson and Mayhew cited in Lane and Mueller 1985, 24 n1), a rate comparable to those observed in the nineteenth century. Such rates of abrasion deprive coins of 10 to 20% of their weight after 30 years.

---

[9] This was true of competitors' costs as well: Montanari notes that the risk premium induced by the death penalty is the same across denominations. For arbitrageurs taking metal to foreign mints, transportation costs made the operation worthwhile only for the larger coins; the near-uniformity of medieval seigniorage rates on gold coins, contrasted with much greater variation on smaller coinage, bears this out.

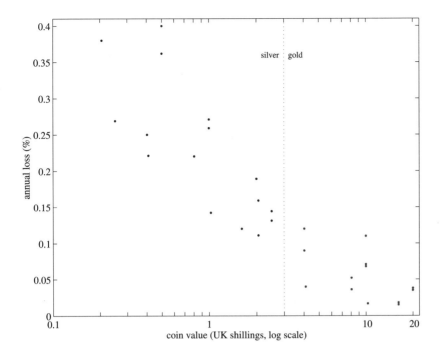

Figure 21.2 Annual rate of loss for various denominations, based on coin surveys in Britain (1833, 1868, 1881), France (1868, 1884), Canada (1914), and the United States (1886). The coin denominations are converted to British shillings. *Sources*: Nanteuil (1928) for France; Grierson (1963) for Britain; U.S. Mint (1886, 119) for the United States; U.K. Mint (1914, 168) for Canada.

We can incorporate the presence of underweight coins in our model, following Sargent and Smith (1997). Assume that, at any time t, the stock of small coins $m_{1,0}$ is composed of coins containing their legal weight in silver b_1, and of coins containing δb_1, with $\delta \in (0, 1)$. The stock of full-weight coins is $m_{1,t}^f$ and that of underweight coins is $m_{1,t}^u$. Only full-weight coins can be minted. Both coins can be melted for their respective silver contents. In the cash-in-advance and penny-in-advance constraints (21.2) and (21.3), only the total stock $m_{1,0} = m_{1,0}^f + m_{1,0}^u$ enters as before, with no distinction made in the purchases of goods between the two types of coins.

The only required modification to the model occurs in the firm's profit function and its first-order conditions. Let $\mu_{1,t}^f$ and $\mu_{1,t}^u$ be the number of full-weight and underweight coins melted, respectively: then (21.12c) is replaced by:

$$\mu_{1,t}^{f} \geq 0; \quad = \quad \text{if } p_t < \gamma_1 \tag{21.13a}$$

$$\mu_{1,t}^{u} \geq 0; \quad = \quad \text{if } p_t < \gamma_1/\delta. \tag{21.13b}$$

The interval for small coins is modified: it now has two melting points, one for full-weight coins at γ_1, the other for underweight coins at γ_1/δ. The price level can now rise above γ_1 without leading to a complete disappearance of small coins: but the heaviest coins are melted down first. The result is a broader interval, as if σ_1 were larger, but with possible changes in the stock of small coins within the broader interval.

Below, we shall typically assume that only full-weight coins exist. We shall make it clear when we do admit underweight coins in order to use our model to shed light on British monetary controversies of about 1695.

The household's problem

We have extracted the preceding restrictions from the requirement that equilibrium prices should not leave the firm arbitrage opportunities. We now turn to additional restrictions that the household's optimum problem imposes on equilibrium prices and quantities.

The household chooses sequences $\{c_1\}$, $\{c_2\}$, $\{m_1\}$, $\{m_2\}$ to maximize (21.1) subject to (21.4), (21.2) and (21.3), as well as the constraints $m_{i,t} \geq 0$ for $i = 1, 2$. Attach Lagrange multipliers λ_t, η_t, θ_t and $\nu_{i,t}$, respectively, to these constraints. Using the notation $u_{i,t} = \partial u(c_{1,t}, c_{2,t})/\partial c_i$, the first-order conditions are:

$$\frac{u_{1,t}}{p_t} = \lambda_t + \eta_t + \theta_t \tag{21.14a}$$

$$\frac{u_{2,t}}{p_t} = \lambda_t + \eta_t \tag{21.14b}$$

$$-\nu_{1,t} = -\lambda_t + \beta \left(\lambda_{t+1} + \eta_{t+1} + \theta_{t+1} \right) \tag{21.14c}$$

$$-\nu_{2,t} = -e_t \lambda_t + \beta e_{t+1} \left(\lambda_{t+1} + \eta_{t+1} \right) \tag{21.14d}$$

with corresponding relaxation conditions. Conditions (21.14a–c) lead to the following:

$$u_{1,t} \geq u_{2,t} ; \quad = \text{ if } m_{1,t-1} > p_t c_{1,t} \quad (21.15a)$$

$$\beta e_{t+1} \frac{u_{2,t+1}}{p_{t+1}} \leq e_t \frac{u_{2,t}}{p_t} ; \quad = \text{ if } m_{2,t} > 0 \text{ and}$$

$$m_{1,t-1} + e_t m_{2,t-1} > p_t \left(c_{1,t} + c_{2,t} \right) \quad (21.15b)$$

Multiplying (21.14c) by e_{t+1}, subtracting it from (21.14d), rearranging, and imposing that $\nu_{1,t} = 0$ (because of the Inada conditions on u), we find:

$$\lambda_t \left(e_{t+1} - e_t \right) = \beta e_{t+1} \theta_{t+1} - \nu_{2,t}. \quad (21.16)$$

Suppose $\theta_{t+1} > 0$ and $\nu_{2,t} = 0$: this implies that $e_{t+1} > e_t$. In words, if the penny-in-advance constraint is binding and positive holdings of dollars are carried over from t to $t + 1$, dollars must *appreciate* in terms of pennies from t to $t + 1$.

The intuition for this paradoxical result is as follows. The household holds money from t to $t + 1$, and also wishes at $t + 1$ that it had held a higher proportion of pennies (i.e., if [21.3] is binding at $t + 1$), yet it chose not to. It must be that pennies were dominated in rate of return by dollars, that is, $e_{t+1} > e_t$. Thus shortages of pennies occur only after dollars dominate pennies in rate of return.

To describe the rate of return on pennies further, write (21.14c) and (21.14d) at t, and (21.14a) and (21.14b) at $t + 1$, and make the necessary substitutions (recalling that $\nu_{1,t} = 0$) to find that, if $m_{2,t} > 0$:

$$\frac{e_{t+1}}{e_t} = \frac{u_{1,t+1}}{u_{2,t+1}} \geq 1. \quad (21.17)$$

In models with only one cash-in-advance constraint but two currencies, this equation holds with equality. Inequality (21.17) embodies a form of one-sided exchange rate indeterminacy and makes possible a class of equilibrium exchange rate paths along which the small change is not appreciating relative to large coins.

Having set out the equilibrium conditions, in the next chapter we use back-solving to create some equilibrium examples.

☙

CHAPTER 22

Shortages: Causes and Symptoms

This chapter computes some sample equilibria and uses them to highlight key operating characteristics of the model. We utilize the back-solving strategy employed by Sargent and Smith (1997) to describe possible equilibrium outcomes. Back-solving takes a symmetrical view of endogenous and exogenous variables.[1] It views the first-order and other market equilibrium conditions as a set of difference inequalities putting restrictions *across* the endowment, allocation, price, and money supply sequences, to which there exist many solutions.

We use back-solving to display aspects of various equilibria. For example, we shall posit an equilibrium in which neither melting nor minting occurs, then solve for an associated money supply, price level, endowment, and allocation. We shall construct two examples of such equilibria, one where the penny-in-advance constraint (21.3) never binds, another where it occasionally does. We choose our sample equilibria to display particular adverse operating characteristics of our money supply mechanism.

Equilibria with neither melting nor minting

When neither melting nor minting occurs, $c_{1,t} + c_{2,t} = \xi_t$, and $m_{i,t} = m_{i,-1} \equiv m_i$, $i = 1, 2$. In this case, the equilibrium conditions of the model consist of one or the other of the two following sets of inequalities, depending on whether the penny-in-advance restriction binds:

---

[1] See Sims (1989, 1990) and Díaz-Giménez et al. (1992).

when (21.3) does not bind:

$$m_1 + e_t m_2 = p_t \xi_t$$

$$m_1 \geq p_t c_{1,t}$$

$$c_{1,t} + c_{2,t} = \xi_t$$

$$\frac{u_{1,t}}{u_{2,t}} = \frac{e_t}{e_{t-1}} = 1$$

$$\frac{e_t u_{2,t}}{p_t} \geq \beta e_{t+1} \frac{u_{2,t+1}}{p_{t+1}}$$

or

when (21.3) binds:

$$e_t m_2 = p_t c_{2,t}$$

$$m_1 = p_t c_{1,t}$$

$$c_{1,t} + c_{2,t} = \xi_t$$

$$\frac{u_{1,t}}{u_{2,t}} = \frac{e_t}{e_{t-1}} \geq 1$$

$$\frac{e_t u_{2,t}}{p_t} \geq \beta e_{t+1} \frac{u_{2,t+1}}{p_{t+1}}$$

Notice that when (21.3) does not bind, there is one quantity theory equation in terms of the total stock of coins, but that when (21.3) does bind, there are two quantity theory equations, one for large purchases cast in terms of dollars, the other for small purchases in terms of the stock of pennies.

Notice also that the exchange rate e_t can only be constant or rising. It rises from $t-1$ to t if there is a shortage at t. Thus, in our model, a plot of the exchange rate over time will look much like the graphs in figure 2.1.

In what follows, we begin by examining equilibria where the first set of conditions applies at all times. We will show how to construct stationary equilibria. Then we will study a variation in the endowment that brings into play the second set of inequalities, when the penny-in-advance constraint binds, all the while maintaining the requirement that neither melting nor minting occurs. Throughout, we take the mint policy (σ_i and γ_i) as fixed.

Stationary equilibria with no minting or melting

We describe a stationary equilibrium with constant monies, endowment, consumption rates, price level, and exchange rate.

Proposition 1. (A stationary, "no-shortage" equilibrium)
Assume a stationary (i.e., constant) endowment sequence ξ, and initial money stocks (m_1, m_2). Let (c_1, c_2) solve

$$u_1 = u_2 \tag{22.1}$$

$$c_1 + c_2 = \xi. \tag{22.2}$$

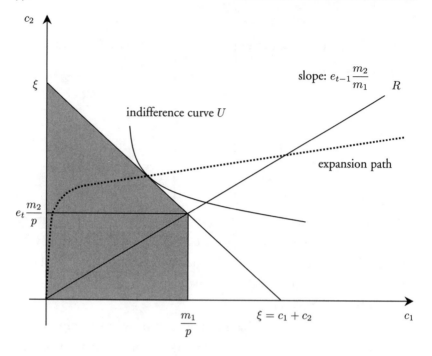

Figure 22.1 Stationary equilibrium, non-binding constraint.

Then there exists a stationary equilibrium without minting or melting if the exchange rate e satisfies the following:

$$I = (\gamma_1 (1 - \sigma_1), \gamma_1) \cap (e\gamma_2 (1 - \sigma_2), e\gamma_2) \neq \emptyset \qquad (22.3)$$

$$\frac{m_1 + em_2}{\xi} \in I \qquad (22.4)$$

$$\frac{\xi m_1}{m_1 + em_2} \geq c_1. \qquad (22.5)$$

Proof: Let $p = (m_1 + em_2)/\xi$. By (22.4), p will satisfy (21.12) in such a way that coins are neither melted nor minted. Condition (21.2) is then satisfied with equality and (21.3) is satisfied with inequality by (22.5). Since (21.3) does not bind, $\theta_t = 0$ and conditions (21.14) are satisfied with a constant e. ∎

Condition (22.3), a consequence of the no-arbitrage conditions, requires that the exchange rate be set so that there exists a price level compatible with neither minting nor melting of either coin, of the type described in proposition 1. Condition (22.4) means that the *total* nominal quantity of money (which depends on e) is sufficient for the cash-in-advance constraint. Condition (22.5) puts an upper bound on e: the share of pennies in the nominal stock must be more than enough for the penny-in-advance constraint not to bind. Conditions (22.4) and (22.5) together imply that $pc_2 \geq em_2$, that is, dollars are insufficient for large purchases.

Figure 22.1 depicts the determination of c_1, c_2, p, and satisfaction of the penny-in-advance constraint (21.3) with room to spare. There is one quantity theory equation cast in terms of the total money supply. That there is room to spare in satisfying (21.3) reveals an exchange rate indeterminacy in this setting: a range of e's can be chosen to leave the qualitative structure of this figure intact. Notice the ray drawn with slope $\frac{e_{t-1}m_2}{m_1}$. So long as the endowment remains in the region where the expansion path associated with a unit relative price lies to the northwest of this ray, the penny-in-advance constraint (21.3) remains satisfied with inequality. But when movements in the endowment or in preferences put the system out of that region, it triggers a penny shortage whose character we now study.

Small coin shortages

Using the back-solving method, we display some possible patterns of endowment shifts that generate small coin shortages.

First, note that another way to interpret (22.4) and (22.5) is to take m_1, m_2, e as fixed and to formulate these conditions as bounds on ξ:

$$\frac{m_1 + em_2}{\gamma_1} < \xi < \frac{m_1 + em_2}{\gamma_1 (1 - \sigma_1)} \tag{22.6}$$

$$\frac{m_1 + em_2}{e\gamma_2} < \xi < \frac{m_1 + em_2}{e\gamma_2 (1 - \sigma_2)} \tag{22.7}$$

$$\xi \leq \alpha \frac{m_1 + em_2}{em_2 - m_1} \tag{22.8}$$

(where [22.8] is written for the logarithmic utility case). These equations reveal a variety of ways of generating small coin shortages with a change in ξ, starting from a given stationary equilibrium. The simplest, which we explore first, is a one-time change in ξ within the strict intervals defined in (22.6) and (22.7) but that violate (22.8): no minting or melting occurs, but a shortage ensues. Another way is as follows: a shortage of small change arises when the stock of pennies is insufficient relative to dollars. Suppose the lower bound in (22.6) is lower than that in (22.7). Then a shift in the endowment can lower the price level to the minting point for dollars without triggering any minting of pennies, resulting in a (relative) decrease in the penny supply; for some values of the parameters, this can violate (22.8) and generate a shortage in the period following the minting of dollars.

Small coin shortage, no minting or melting

We begin by studying the situation that arises when, following an epoch where constant money supplies and endowment were compatible with a stationary equilibrium, there occurs at time t a shift in the endowment. In figure 22.1, for the utility function $v(g(c_{1,t})) + v(c_{2,t})$ we drew the expansion path traced out by points where indifference curves are tangent to feasibility lines associated with different endowment levels. The expansion path is $c_1 = \max(0, c_2 - \alpha)$, and so has slope 1 or infinity, for $c_1 > \underline{c}$. If $\frac{em_2}{m_1} < 1$, i.e., if pennies compose a large enough fraction of the money stock, then the ray c_2/c_1 equaling this ratio never threatens to wander into the southeastern region described above and render (21.3) binding. However, when $\frac{em_2}{m_1} > 1$, growth in the endowment ξ can push the economy into the southeastern region, which makes (21.3) bind and triggers an appreciation of dollars.

Thus, suppose that ξ_t is high enough that the intersection of the expansion path with the feasibility line ($c_1 + c_2 = \xi_t$) is below the ray $e_{t-1} m_2 / m_1$. This means that at t, our second subset of equations determines prices and the allocation. If we assume that ξ_t is such that neither minting nor melting occurs (an assumption that must in the end be verified), then equilibrium values of c_1, c_2, e, p can be

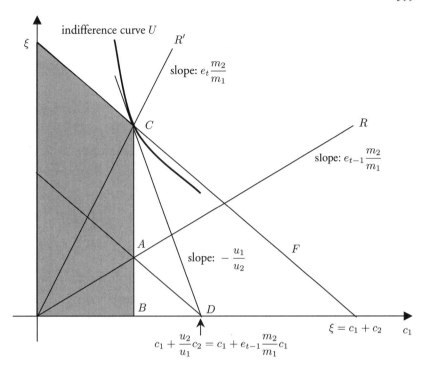

Figure 22.2 Effect of a shift in endowments.

computed recursively as follows.

Given e_{t-1}, the following three equations can be solved for c_1, c_2, e at t:

$$c_{1,t} + c_{2,t} = \xi_t \tag{22.9}$$

$$\frac{u_{1,t}}{u_{2,t}} = \frac{e_t}{e_{t-1}} \tag{22.10}$$

$$\frac{e_t m_2}{m_1} = \frac{c_{2,t}}{c_{1,t}}. \tag{22.11}$$

These can be combined into a single equation in $c_{1,t}$:

$$u_{2,t}\left(c_{1,t}, \xi_t - c_{1,t}\right) - u_{1,t}\left(c_{1,t}, \xi_t - c_{1,t}\right)\frac{e_{t-1}m_2}{m_1}\frac{c_{1,t}}{\xi_t - c_{1,t}} = 0 \tag{22.12}$$

to which there exists a solution.[2] Then c_2 is determined from

─────────────────
[2] Call $f(c_{1,t})$ the left-hand side of (22.12). Since the expansion path intersects

(22.9), and e_t (which satisfies $e_t > e_{t-1}$ by construction) is given by (22.10). It remains to check that $p_t = m_1/c_1 \in I$ and that the Euler inequality (21.15b) holds. There is room to satisfy the inequality if $\frac{\beta p_{t-1}}{p_t}$ is small enough.

Figure 22.2 illustrates the situation. We use the intersections of various lines to represent the conditions (22.9), (22.10), and (22.11), and to determine the position of the consumption allocation (point C) and e_t, given e_{t-1}. First, the feasibility line F, on which C must lie, represents (22.9). Second, condition (22.11) means that the ray passing through point C has slope $e_t m_2/m_1$: this defines e_t.

Finally, condition (22.10) relates the rate of return on large coins (the slope of R compared to the slope of R') with the slope of the indifference curve at C. To represent this geometrically, (22.11) can be used to transform (22.10) into the following:

$$c_1 + \frac{u_{2,t}}{u_{1,t}} c_2 = c_1 + \frac{e_{t-1} m_2}{m_1} c_1. \qquad (22.13)$$

Define point A to be the vertical projection of C onto the ray $e_{t-1} m_2/m_1$. The right-hand side of (22.13) is the point at which a line, parallel to the feasibility line and drawn through point A, intersects the x-axis. The left-hand side is the point where the tangent to the indifference curve at C intersects the x-axis. Condition (22.10) requires that these intersections coincide. When they do, the segments AB and BD have same length (because AD has slope -1), and therefore the ratios CB/BD and CB/AB are equal. The former is the slope of the indifference curve at C, and the latter is the ratio of the slopes of R' and R, in other words the rate of return of large coins relative to small coins.

Permanent and transitory increases in ξ

Having determined the new exchange rate e_t after a shift in the endowment ξ_t, we can determine what happens if the shift is permanent or transitory. If it is *permanent*, then the constraint (21.3)

---

the feasibility line above the ray $e_{t-1} m_2/m_1$, the coordinates of that intersection $(c_1, \xi - c_1)$ satisfy $f(c_1) < 0$. Also, $\lim_{c_1 \to 0} f(c_1) = u_2(0, \xi) > 0$.

will continue to bind. The reason is that, since $e_t > e_{t-1}$, the ray $e_t m_2/m_1$ is in fact even higher than $e_{t-1} m_2/m_1$, which means that the expansion path remains below the ray, and the penny constraint continues to bind. This situation cannot continue indefinitely without minting or melting, however. Thus, a permanent upward shift in the endowment from the situation depicted in figure 22.1 to that in figure 22.2 would impel a sequence of increases in the exchange rate until eventually the price level is pushed outside the interval I.

As for a *temporary* (one-time) increase in ξ_t, it might prompt further increases in the exchange rate even if the endowment immediately subsides to its original level. The reason is that the increase in e induces a permanent upward shift in the $\frac{em_2}{m_1}$ ray that enlarges the southeastern region where (21.3) is binding.

Logarithmic example

We can go further in analyzing the results of shifts of endowments by supposing that $v(\cdot) = \ln(\cdot)$ in equation (21.1). For this specification we can compute solutions by hand.

Consider a steady state with constant $\xi_t = \xi_0$, m_1, m_2, and $e_t = e_0$, such that the constraint (21.3) does not bind. The equilibrium objects are

$$c_{1,t} = \frac{\xi_0 - \alpha}{2}, \quad c_{2,t} = \frac{\xi_0 + \alpha}{2},$$
$$p_t = \frac{m_1 + e_0 m_2}{\xi_0}.$$

The condition that ξ_0, m_1, m_2 and e_0 must satisfy for (21.3) not to bind is:

$$\xi_0 < \alpha \frac{e_0 m_2 + m_1}{e_0 m_2 - m_1} = \bar{\xi}. \tag{22.14}$$

The income level $\bar{\xi}$ corresponds to the intersection of the expansion path and the ray $e_0 m_2/m_1$ in figure 22.1.

Suppose that, at $t = 1$, ξ increases above $\bar{\xi}$ so that (22.14) is violated. Then e_0 cannot be the exchange rate at $t = 1$ and (21.3) binds at $t = 1$. The equilibrium objects at $t = 1$ become:

$$c_{1,1} = \frac{m_1}{e_0 m_2 - m_1} \alpha = \frac{\bar{\xi} - \alpha}{2}, \quad c_{2,1} = \xi_1 - c_{1,1}$$

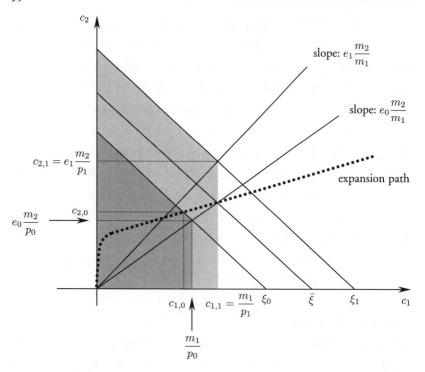

Figure 22.3 Effect of a shift in endowments (logarithmic case).

$$p_1 = \frac{m_1}{c_{1,1}}, \quad e_1 = \frac{m_1}{m_2}\frac{c_{2,1}}{c_{1,1}}.$$

It can be shown that $p_1/p_0 = \xi_0/\bar{\xi}$ so that the price level initially falls at $t = 1$, although to a level independent of ξ_1. (It must be checked that p_1 is not so low as to reach one of the minting points, since we are assuming throughout that m_1 and m_2 do not change.) Consumption c_1 is also unrelated to ξ_1, and is limited to the amount that would be consumed at the income level $\bar{\xi}$, just where the constraint begins to bind.

Figure 22.3 illustrates the effect of a shift in the endowment from ξ_0 to $\xi_1 > \bar{\xi}$. The corner in the new budget set (light shade) is vertically aligned with the intersection of the expansion path and the ray $e_0 m_2/m_1$. The position of that corner also determines the new exchange rate, since the ray going through that corner has slope

$e_1 m_2/m_1$. It is also apparent from the graph that p_1 is lower than p_0 (because m_1/p_1 is greater than m_1/p_0) and that it has the same value for all $\xi_1 \geq \bar{\xi}$. The exchange rate e_1, however, is increasing in ξ_1.

Consider now the case where ξ remains fixed at ξ_1 permanently after $t = 1$. The penny-in-advance constraint continues to bind, implying that the exchange rate continues to increase. In every period, the ray $e_t(m_2/m_1)$ moves up, and $c_{1,t} = m_1/(e_{t-1}m_2 - m_1)$ falls, moving further away from the first-best allocation and indicating that the shortage of small change becomes increasingly severe. Furthermore, the price level $p_t = m_1/c_{1,t}$ now rises, and the rate of inflation is

$$\frac{p_t}{p_{t-1}} = \frac{e_{t-1}m_2 - m_1}{e_{t-2}m_2 - m_1} > \frac{e_{t-1}}{e_{t-2}} > 1,$$

that is, the price level rises faster than the exchange rate did the previous period.

Suppose now that, after jumping from ξ_0 to ξ_1, income falls back to its earlier value ξ_0 and stays there. If ξ_1 was large enough (specifically, if $\xi_1 > (c_{1,1}/c_{1,0})\xi_0$), then the ray $e_1(m_2/m_1)$ has moved high enough that the expansion path is in the southeastern region, as depicted in figure 22.3. In that case, the shortage will continue, and e_t will continue to increase as in the case of a permanent change in ξ.

Money shortages bring inflation

If we return to the supply side as shown in figure 21.1, we see that the price level initially fell. It might fall enough to reach the minting point for dollars, in which case the shortage is worsened, as we will see shortly. Assuming as we did that p_1 did not reach either minting point, the shortage continues, and e_t rises, which shifts the lower interval to the right at a "speed" e_t/e_{t-1}. But the price level now moves to the right as well, and at an even higher speed. This suggests that the price level will reach the melting point for either dollars or pennies before it is caught up by the minting point for dollars. If pennies are melted, the shortage is aggravated further.

The two forms of inflation, in e_t and in p_t, are linked because the quantity theory equation has split into two separate, albeit related components $e_t m_2 = p_t c_{2,t}$ and $m_1 = p_t c_{1,t}$. The link is subtle because the quantities c_1 and c_2 are changing as well.

An enduring shortage of small change without minting or melting leads to the paradoxical situation of sustained inflation in the absence of any change in the stock of money. Stranger still, it is the shortage of (one type of) money that causes the general inflation. Ultimately, the price level is bounded by γ_1, the melting point for pennies. If pennies were initially light, then γ_1 could be substantially above the initial price level, and the shortage-induced inflation could be significant.

Shortages of small coins through minting of large coins

A shortage of small coins can also occur as a consequence of minting, independently of the "income effect" we have described. Assume that all coins are full-bodied, so that the bounds of the intervals coincide to the right ($\gamma_1 = e\gamma_2$), but that production costs require that a higher seigniorage be levied on small coins ($\sigma_1 > \sigma_2$), so that the left boundaries do not coincide ($\gamma_1(1 - \sigma_1) < e\gamma_2(1 - \sigma_2)$).

In the previous section, we considered "small" increases in the endowment ξ; that is, increases that led to movements in the price level p_t *within* the intervals dictated by the arbitrage conditions. We now consider "large" increases that will induce such a fall in the price level that it reaches the minting point for large coins ($p_t = e\gamma_2(1 - \sigma_2)$). The structure of coin specifications and minting charges means that small coins will not be minted. As a result, m_2 increases while m_1 remains unchanged, and the ratio em_2/m_1 rises. The intuition garnered from figure 22.2 suggests that, for large enough increases in m_2, trouble may occur; a shortage of small change results, because the share of pennies in the total money stock falls too far. We verify that this can indeed happen.

We begin again from a stationary equilibrium with no minting or melting. Suppose that, at time t, the endowment increases from ξ_0 to ξ_t, with the latter satisfying $\xi_t > (m_1 + em_2)/e\gamma_2(1 - \sigma_2)$ so as to violate (22.7). Then minting occurs at t, and the price level is known: $p_t = e\gamma_2(1 - \sigma_2)$.

As before, two situations can arise, depending on whether (21.3) is binding or not at t. We will look for equilibria where it is not. Then $u_2 = u_1$, which, combined with the binding cash-in-advance constraint (21.2), allows to solve for $c_{1,t}$ and $c_{2,t}$. Now we know the amount minted, namely, $\xi_t - c_{1,t} - c_{2,t}$ (positive by assumption), and the addition to the money stock is $n_{2,t} = \gamma_2(\xi_t - c_{1,t} - c_{2,t})$.

At $t + 1$, it can be shown that

$$e\gamma_2 (1 - \sigma_2) < \frac{m_1 + e_{t-1}m_{2,t}}{\xi_t} < e\gamma_2$$

or, in other words, that no more minting occurs if (21.3) does not bind. But (21.3) binds if the following holds:

$$\frac{e_{t-1}m_{2,t}}{m_1} > \frac{\xi_t + \alpha}{\xi_t - \alpha}.$$

At equality, this becomes a second-degree polynomial in ξ_t, which, for large enough values of ξ_t, will have a positive root. Thus, if enough dollars are minted, pennies become relatively short of supply.

Shortages through melting of full-weight small coins

In this section, we modify the model to include underweight small denomination coins. The modifications are designed to capture the circumstances that prevailed in England around 1695, described in chapter 16. In this case, an initial shortage of small coins leads to melting of some of the small coins, as well as minting of large coins.

We make two modifications. One is to assume that $\sigma_1 = \sigma_2 = 0$, which was true in England in the 1690s. The other is to introduce underweight coins, as described above. Specifically, we assume that, at $t = 0$, the stock of small coins is divided between $m_{1,0}^f$ full-weight coins and $m_{1,0}^u$ underweight coins, weighing a fraction δ of the full-weight coins. We assume that the stock of underweight coins is inherited from the past, and for simplicity we do not model the creation of underweight coins.[3]   As described on page 346, the existence of underweight coins creates two melting points, one for full-weight coins at γ_1 and another for underweight coins at γ_1/δ.[4]

We consider an experiment in which an initial steady state prevails with the penny-in-advance constraint (21.3) not binding, followed by an increase in income at $t = 1$ that makes the constraint binding. As above, in the logarithmic case, the initial equilibrium values are

$$c_{1,t} = \frac{\xi_0 - \alpha}{2}, \quad c_{2,t} = \frac{\xi_0 + \alpha}{2},$$
$$p_t = \frac{m_1 + e_0 m_2}{\xi_0},$$

with $e_0 = \gamma_1/\gamma_2$ and $p_0 = \gamma_1 = e_0 \gamma_2$.

At $t = 1$, income is $\xi_1 > \bar{\xi}$ and the penny-in-advance constraint binds. It follows that $e_1 > e_0$. Since the no-arbitrage conditions impose $p_1 \geq e_1 \gamma_2$, the price level rises and $p_1 > \gamma_1$. This implies that all full-weight small denomination coins are melted. Assume that $p_1 < \gamma_1/\alpha$ so that no underweight small denomination coins are melted.

Although minting and melting take place at $t = 1$, quantities $c_{1,1}$ and $c_{2,1}$ are determined by the incoming stocks of money $m_{1,0}$ and $m_{2,0}$, along with the new price level p_1, via the two quantity theory equations.

The quantity theory equations $p_1 c_{1,1} = m_{1,0}$ and $p_1 c_{2,1} = e_1 m_{2,0}$ imply

$$c_{2,1} = e_1 \frac{m_{2,0}}{m_{1,0}} c_{1,1}. \qquad (22.15)$$

This, along with (21.17), gives

$$c_{1,1} = \frac{m_1}{e_0 m_2 - m_1} \alpha = \frac{\bar{\xi} - \alpha}{2}, \qquad (22.16)$$

---

[3] See Sargent and Smith (1997) for a simple model of physical depreciation of coins.

[4] Feavearyear (1963, 123) cited evidence that underweight coins were more likely to be counterfeited in England: "Meanwhile its (the Mint's) workmen made copies of the old clipped groats, and issued them, at a good profit, to people who apparently accepted them freely and used them. Nobody troubled to counterfeit milled money, for there was no profit in it."

while feasibility gives

$$c_{2,1} = \xi_1 + \gamma_1^{-1} m_1^f + \gamma_2^{-1} \left(\mu_{2,1} - n_{2,1} \right) - c_{1,1}. \qquad (22.17)$$

Equations (22.17) and (22.15) allow us to solve for the change in the stock of large coins $\mu_{2,1} - n_{2,1}$ as a function of $c_{1,1}$, which is known from (22.16). One finds

$$\mu_{2,1} = 0 \quad \text{and} \quad n_{2,1} = \gamma_2 \left(\xi_1 - \bar{\xi} + \gamma_1^{-1} m_1^f \right),$$

which means that the stock of large coins increases, and by more than the stock of small coin decreases. Finally, one finds $c_{2,1} = (\bar{\xi} + \alpha)/2$.

Our model thus predicts the following symptoms of a small coin shortage: the heavier small coins will be melted or exported, coinage of the large coins will increase substantially, prices will rise and so will the exchange rate between large and small coins. All of these symptoms were present in the second half of 1695, as we saw in chapter 16.

Consider now the new ray $e_1(m_{2,1}/m_{1,1})$ and note that, from $t = 0$ to $t = 1$, e and m_2 have increased while m_1 has fallen. As a result, the ray is now higher than before. The shortage situation is thus likely to persist, whether the change in income ξ is permanent or transitory.

The opposing policies of Lowndes and Locke can readily be formulated in terms of the model. Lowndes advocated a debasement so that γ_1 becomes $\bar{\gamma}_1 = p_1 = e_1 \gamma_2$. He argued for an increase in the supply of small coins (if necessary by subsidizing the mint) and claimed that it would not be inflationary. In our model, Lowndes is correct: if it were of the proper amount, such an increase in m_1 would not be inflationary because it would relax the constraint on consumption of small goods.

In 1695, the government of England decided to remint at its expense, at the old standard: that is, the mint was ordered to melt $\mu_1 = m_{1,0}^u$ into $\alpha b_1 m_{1,0}^u$ ounces of silver, and to make at the old standard b_1 the quantity of coins $n_1 = \mu_1/b_1 = \alpha m_{1,0}^u$. The net result would be to decrease the stock of small coins m_1 by a fraction $1 - \alpha$, the cost borne by the taxpayer.

Perverse effects and their palliatives

We have thus shown two ways that endowment growth can induce small coin shortages, with or without minting. We now discuss how such episodes affect the monetary system over time, in particular the relation between small and large coins.

A shortage of small coins manifests itself in a binding penny-in-advance constraint (21.3), and is associated with two kinds of price adjustments, one "static," the other "dynamic." First, the quantity theory breaks into two separate equations, one for small, another for large coins taking the forms $p_t = m_{1,t}/c_{1,t}$ and $e_t = \frac{m_{2,t}}{p_t c_{2,t}}$. The mitosis of the quantity theory is the time-t consequence of a shortage of small coins. A second response is dynamic, and requires that $e_t > e_{t-1}$, so that dollars appreciate with respect to the pennies. This response equilibrates the demand side but has perverse implications because of its eventual effects on supply. For fixed b_2, an increase in e shifts the interval $[e(1 - \sigma_2)\gamma_2, e\gamma_2]$ to the *right*, leaving the interval $[(1 - \sigma_1)\gamma_1, \gamma_1]$ fixed. This reduces the intersection I and hastens the occasion when either more dollars will be minted or pennies will be melted, depending on which bound the price level hits first. Thus, shortages of small coins ultimately reduce their supply, relatively or even absolutely, a perverse outcome.

This penny-impoverishing implication of a rise in e induced by a shortage isolates a force for the government to adopt a commensurate reduction in b_1. This shifts the penny interval in line with the dollar interval, eventually resupplying the system with a new, lighter penny. Sargent and Smith's (1997) analysis of a noninflationary debasement in a one-coin system can be adapted to simulate such a debasement.[5]

---

[5] This experiment stresses the extent to which a "circulation by tale" axiom is embedded in our framework: for the purposes of the cash-in-advance constraint (21.3), a penny is a penny, whatever its weight. To analyze a debasement as described in the text, one has to keep track of two kinds of pennies, old and new.

An alternative way to realign the two intervals in response to a shortage-induced increase in e would be to *raise b_2*, thereby counteracting the rightward shift of the dollar interval. A shortage-induced debasement of small coins and a "reinforcement" of large coins have different implications for the price level in terms of pence: the former lets it rise with e, the latter stabilizes it. The price level in terms of dollars would remain constant with the former, fall with the latter. In a world with nominal debt contracts, the two policies have different implications for debtors and creditors.

Parts III and IV cited many examples of historical shortages of small change that we interpreted in terms of the theoretical shortages that can emerge in our model. The following chapter describes how some remedies for shortages, such as the standard formula, work in our model.

∽

CHAPTER 23

Arrangements to Eliminate Coin Shortages

This chapter describes two money supply mechanisms that, within the context of our model, prevent shortages of small coins. We scrutinize these mechanisms in terms of how they incorporate some or all of the ingredients in Cipolla's recipe, and study whether some ingredients of the recipe are redundant.

A standard formula regime

We change the supply mechanism to implement a version of Cipolla's standard formula, retaining the demand side of the model. It is as if the government tells the mint to set up a "pennies department" that operates like a currency board for pennies. The rules for supplying dollars are not changed from those described above. But now the mint is required to convert pennies into dollars and dollars into pennies, upon demand and at a fixed exchange rate e, named by the government. Assume that pennies are produced costlessly by the mint, and so are truly tokens ($b_1 = 0$). The government requires the mint to carry a non-negative inventory of dollars R_t from each date t to $t + 1$. The mint increases its inventory of dollars only when it buys dollars, and decreases it only when it buys pennies.

This regime imposes the following laws of motion for stocks of dollars and pennies:

$$m_{1,t} = m_{1,t-1} + e^{-1}\left(R_t - R_{t-1}\right)$$
$$m_{2,t} = m_{2,t-1} + n_{2,t} - \mu_{2,t} - \left(R_t - R_{t-1}\right)$$
$$R_t \geq 0,$$

where R_t is the stock of dollars held by the mint from t to $t + 1$. The law of motion for dollars can be rewritten as

$$\left(m_{2,t} + R_t\right) = \left(m_{2,t-1} + R_{t-1}\right) + n_{2,t} - \mu_{2,t}.$$

For the firm, it does not matter whether it melts dollars or whether pennies are exchanged for dollars that are then melted; only the total stock of dollars $m_{2,t} + R_t$ counts.

Under this money supply mechanism, the firm's profits become:

$$\Pi_t = p_t \xi_t + e\left(n_{2,t} - \sigma_2 n_{2,t}\right) - p_t \frac{b_2}{\phi} n_{2,t} + p_t \frac{b_2}{\phi}\mu_{2,t} - e\mu_{2,t}, \quad (23.1)$$

subject to the constraints

$$n_{2,t} \geq 0 \quad \text{and} \quad m_{2,t-1} + R_{t-1} \geq \mu_{2,t} \geq 0.$$

The absence of R_t from its profits signifies the firm's indifference to the choice of $m_{1,t}$ (as long as $R_t \geq 0$), because the firm always breaks even when it buys or sells pennies.[1] The firm's indifference lets the demand side of the model determine the stock of $m_{1,t}$ appropriately. More precisely, one can find paths for the money stocks that are consistent with the firm's profit maximization and satisfy the household's first-order conditions with (21.3) not binding.

A subset of the no-arbitrage conditions now obtains:

$$n_{2,t} \geq 0; \quad = \quad \text{if } p_t > e\gamma_2 \left(1 - \sigma_2\right) \quad (23.2a)$$

$$\mu_{2,t} \geq 0; \quad = \quad \text{if } p_t < e\gamma_2 \quad (23.2b)$$

$$m_{2,t-1} + R_{t-1} \geq \mu_{2,t}; \quad = \quad \text{if } p_t > e\gamma_2 \quad (23.2c)$$

This regime forces p_t into the interval $[e(1 - \sigma_2)\gamma_2, e\gamma_2]$. In particular, p_t can never rise above $e\gamma_2$ because that would mean melting all dollars, including those backing the pennies, and the economy would have no money stock. This regime also solves the exchange rate indeterminacy problem by administering a peg. The positive stocks of R_t carried by the mint are socially wasteful, as indeed are the stocks of silver being used in large coins.

---

[1] The condition $R_t \geq 0$ can be ensured by choosing initial conditions such that $m_{1,-1} \leq R_0$.

Variants of the standard formula

The preceding version of a standard formula regime omits Cipolla's stipulation to "limit the quantity of the small coins" in circulation. Though our model renders that stipulation redundant, various writers insisted on limiting the legal tender of small coins and strictly limiting the quantity issued, often as supplements—though occasionally apparently as alternatives to pegging the exchange rate e_t by converting either coin into the other at par.[2]

The effect of limited legal tender is evidently to modify the cash-in-advance constraint (21.2), because pennies are no longer accepted in payment of large purchases. Instead, two separate cash-in-advance constraints are imposed:

$$p_t c_{2,t} \leq e_t m_{2,t-1} \tag{23.3}$$

$$p_t c_{1,t} \leq m_{1,t-1}. \tag{23.4}$$

The household's first-order conditions now imply:

$$\beta \frac{u_{1,t+1}}{p_{t+1}} \leq \frac{u_{1,t}}{p_t} , \quad = \text{ if } m_{1,t} > 0 \text{ and}$$

$$m_{1,t-1} > p_t c_{1,t} ; \tag{23.5a}$$

$$\beta e_{t+1} \frac{u_{2,t+1}}{p_{t+1}} \leq e_t \frac{u_{2,t}}{p_t} , \quad = \text{ if } m_{2,t} > 0 \text{ and}$$

$$e_t m_{2,t-1} > p_t c_{2,t} ; \tag{23.5b}$$

$$\frac{e_{t+1}}{e_t} = \frac{u_{1,t+1}}{u_{2,t+1}} \quad \text{if } m_{1,t} > 0 \text{ and } m_{2,t} > 0. \tag{23.5c}$$

---

[2] Thus, Feavearyear (1963, 172) noted: "Adam Smith, writing just after the recoinage of gold in 1774, suggested with some hesitation that the silver money should be deliberately overrated and made legal tender only in payments up to a guinea. The provision of a limited legal tender was necessary because he did not contemplate closing the Mint to the free coinage of silver. No one seems to have entertained for one moment the idea of giving the Mint the right to buy silver as required at the market price, to issue the coins definitely as tokens in just sufficient quantities to meet the demands of the public, and to withdraw at face value any excess. When this is done a limit upon legal tender is of little importance except to prevent creditors from having large quantities of small change dumped upon them." As we saw in chapter 6, Sir Henry Slingsby had indeed entertained instructing the mint as Feavearyear wanted.

Furthermore, Inada conditions require that holdings of both coins be positive. Condition (23.5c) says that whichever coin will be most needed in period $t + 1$ will depreciate relative to the other from t to $t + 1$. The two coins now play a symmetric role, and either one can appreciate. The exchange rate would no longer exhibit the generally monotone increasing pattern in figure 2.1, but would wander up and down depending on which of the two cash-in-advance constraints binds. In this sense, the limited legal tender provision 'cures' the persistent depreciation of small coins.

Consider the case of a constant endowment ξ_0 and initial money holdings m_1, m_2. Let $(c_{1,0}, c_{2,0})$ solve $u_1 = u_2$ and $c_{1,0} + c_{2,0} = \xi_0$. If $p_0 = m_1/c_{1,0}$ lies in the intervals dictated by the firm's first-order conditions, then the constant prices p_0 and $e_0 = (m_1/m_2)(c_{2,0}/c_{1,0})$, constant allocation $(c_{1,0}, c_{2,0})$, and constant money supplies m_1, m_2 form an equilibrium.

Suppose a small shift in endowment at time 1, from ξ_0 to ξ_1, such that no minting or melting occurs. Could the allocation $(c_{1,1}, c_{2,1})$ solve $u_1 = u_2$ and $c_{1,1} + c_{2,1} = \xi_1$? This would imply $u_{1,1} = u_{2,1}$, hence the exchange rate would be constant from 0 to 1: but our non-homothetic preferences imply that the ratio $c_{2,1}/c_{1,1}$ would have to differ from $c_{2,0}/c_{1,0}$, and therefore e could not be unchanged unless money supplies changed. The allocation at time 1 is found instead as the solution of

$$\frac{u_{1,1}}{u_{2,1}} = \frac{m_1}{e_0 m_2} \frac{c_{2,1}}{c_{1,1}},$$

and the new exchange rate is $e_1 = (m_1/m_2)(c_{2,1}/c_{1,1})$.

The standard formula without convertibility: the Castilian experience

One striking feature of the standard formula and its reserve requirement is the apparent wastefulness of R_t (in fact, of $m_{2,t} + R_t$). We now consider a regime in which the convertibility requirement is simply removed. As before, the rules for supplying dollars are identical to the earlier ones. Pennies are token that are costless to produce. The government does not require an inventory of dollars to back the pennies, but sets the seigniorage rate on pennies $\sigma_1 = 1$. The firm's profit is then (23.1), to be maximized subject to $n_{2,t} \geq 0$ and $m_{2,t-1} \geq \mu_{2,t} \geq 0$. Again, the firm is indifferent to the values taken by $\mu_{1,t}$ and $n_{1,t}$. Those values are set exogenously by the government, and $m_{1,t}$ follows the law of motion (21.6). The government's budget constraint (21.8) is

$$T_t = n_{1,t} + \sigma_2 e_t n_{2,t}.$$

From the firm's no-arbitrage conditions (23.2), we can bound p_t below, by the minting point $e\gamma_2(1 - \sigma_2)$. But there is no upper bound on p_t. If $p_t > e\gamma_2$, $\mu_{2,t} = m_{2,t}$ and dollars disappear, but pennies remain in circulation. Then the cash-in-advance constraint (or quantity theory equation) determines the price level:

$$p_t \left(c_{1,t} + c_{2,t} \right) = m_{1,t-1}.$$

We start from given initial stocks $m_{1,-1} + e m_{2,-1}$ and a constant endowment ξ, such that $e\gamma_2(1 - \sigma_2) < (m_{1,-1} + e m_{2,-1})/\xi < e\gamma_2$, and consider alternative policies for the path of the penny stock. Suppose that a shift in endowment occurs as in chapter 22, so that no minting or melting of dollars takes place. In the absence of any change in $m_{1,-1}$ a penny shortage would develop. The shortage can be remedied, or prevented, by an appropriate increase in m_1, one that lowers the ray of slope $e m_2/m_1$ in figure 22.1 so as to put the intersection of the expansion path and the resource constraint in the northwestern region.

Issues of pennies can proceed in the absence of any further shifts in endowments. Suppose ξ remains constant, but the government issues quantities of pennies every period. When constraint (21.3) isn't binding, the price level is determined by the binding constraint (21.2), and the issue of pennies will lead to a (non-proportionately) rising price level, until $p_t = e\gamma_2$. At that point, dollars begin to be melted, and successive increases in the penny stock displace dollars at the constant rate e, maintaining $m_{1,t} + e m_{2,t} = e\gamma_2\xi$. Once all dollars have been melted, the economy becomes a standard cash-in-advance fiat currency economy, whose price level is governed by the quantity theory equation (21.2), namely $m_{1,t-1} = p_t\xi$. Further

increases in the penny stock result only in increases in the price level
(and in seigniorage revenues for the government).

Should a government wish to bring about the return of dollars, it
must lower the price level to $e\gamma_2(1-\sigma_2)$. It can do this acting on
$m_{1,t}$: either by retiring a portion of $m_{1,t}$, a costly option envisaged
by the Castilian government between 1626 and 1628 and ultimately
rejected; or through a re-denomination or cry-down, the policy
followed in 1628.

The re-denomination and the consequent change in e_t have to
occur "overnight," in an unanticipated fashion, or (21.16) would
be violated. We look for an equilibrium in which minting of dollars
occurs, which requires $p_t = e\gamma_2(1-\sigma_2)$. The household enters the
period holding only pennies, so that (21.2) is $e\gamma_2(1-\sigma_2)(c_{1,t}+c_{2,t}) =
m_{1,t-1}$. (Note that, since the household holds only pennies, [21.3]
cannot be binding). The resource constraint becomes $c_{1,t} + c_{2,t} =
\xi - \gamma_2^{-1}n_{2,t}$. The two conditions combine into

$$\gamma_2\xi = n_{2,t} + m_{1,t-1}/e_t(1-\sigma_2), \qquad (23.6)$$

a joint condition on $n_{2,t}$ and e_t. The requirement that $\gamma_2\xi > n_{2,t} >
0$ puts a lower bound on e_t, namely

$$e_t > \frac{p_{t-1}}{\gamma_2(1-\sigma_2)}$$

where p_{t-1} was the price level prior to the monetary operation.

In the following period $t+1$, neither minting nor melting occurs,
because equation (23.6) implies

$$e_t\gamma_2(1-\sigma_2) \leq \frac{m_{1,t-1} + e_t n_{2,t}}{\xi} < e_t\gamma_2.$$

However, to ensure that (21.3) does not bind at $t+1$, the stock of new
dollars $n_{2,t} = m_{2,t+1}$ must not be too large: $e_t m_{2,t+1} \leq p_{t+1}c_{2,t+1}$,
or $(c_{1,t+1}/\xi)n_{2,t} \leq m_{1,t-1}$. This places a further restriction on e_t,
namely:

$$e_t < p_{t-1}\frac{c_1 + (1-\sigma_2)c_2}{c_1(1-\sigma_2)\gamma_2} \qquad (23.7)$$

where c_1 lies on the expansion path and on the feasibility line in
figure 22.1.

Conditions (23.6) and (23.7) require the government to engineer a devaluation of pennies of the "correct" extent. If it is too small, no dollars are minted; if it is too large, too many dollars are minted and another increase in m_1 will be required to relieve the binding penny-in-advance constraint.

We have assumed that the government carries out this operation in an unanticipated manner. After 1628, the Castilian public surely viewed subsequent manipulations of m_1 with some suspicion. Expectations of further reforms altered the demand for pennies, but our simple model is not equipped to pursue the analysis in that direction.

Fiat currency

To attain a version of Lucas's (1982) model of fiat money, we would suspend the original technology for producing both coins, and let them be produced costlessly. Alternatively, we can think of widening the bands—i.e., driving the γ_i's to infinity. Like Lucas, we would simply award the government a monopoly for issuing coins. We get a pure quantity theory. The government fixes paths for $m_{i,t}, i = 1, 2$, being careful to supply enough pennies (i.e., to keep [21.3] from binding). Condition (21.2) at equality determines the price level as a function of the total money supply. Condition (21.3) imposes a lower bound on the quantity of pennies needed to sustain a fixed e equilibrium; equation (21.2) imposes an upper bound on the amount of pennies that can be issued via "open-market operations" for dollars.

☙

CHAPTER 24

Our Model and Our History

We designed our model to help us understand problems with the arrangements for minting more or less full-bodied coins that prevailed for centuries throughout western Europe. Our model ascribes rules for operating the mint that copy historical ones, and focuses on the difficulty those rules create for simultaneously maintaining two commodity currencies. The model extends insights from single-currency commodity money models,[1] where minting and melting points impose bounds within which the price level must stay to arrest arbitrage opportunities. In those one-commodity money models, when the price level falls enough (i.e., when currency becomes scarce), new coins will be minted; and when the price level rises enough, coins will be melted.[2]

With two currencies, there are distinct melting and minting points for each currency, and this causes trouble. We posit a particular model of demand for coins that, in conjunction with the two sets of melting and minting points, makes shortages of the smaller denomination coins arise when national income fluctuates. We analyze the perverse price adjustments fostered by the historical supply arrangement, how they served to aggravate shortages over time, and how they left debasement as the preferred relief.

The vulnerability to recurrent shortages of small coins that characterized the historical supply arrangement eventually prompted its repair in the form of a huge "once-and-for-all debasement" of small coins, making a permanent system of token small change. In that system, the government acts as a monopolist for small coins. It can peg

---

[1] See Sargent and Smith (1997).

[2] Sargent and Smith (1997) analyze two-commodity monies in the form of gold and silver coins, but do not link these metals to *denomination* as we do here. In particular, they have no counterpart to our constraint (21.3).

the exchange rate of small for large coins, either by always choosing a proper quantity of small ones, or by maintaining convertibility.

Establishing a system of token small change was a fateful step on the road to creating a fiat money system for *all* currency. As we have seen, refining the idea of fiat money and actually implementing it took centuries. Historical episodes, such as that in Castile in the seventeenth century, highlight the difficulty of establishing a token system even for small coins in the face of technological limits on making coins and persistent pressures on governments to raise revenues from the money supply mechanism.

℘

Glossary

In some cases, terms are considered only in their relationship to money and coinage. Some definitions are taken from the Oxford English Dictionary, *2d edition (OED).*

billon. An alloy of silver and copper in which the share of silver is less than 50%.

brassage. Fee charged by the mint operator to cover production costs (excluding the price of metal).

brocard. An elementary principle or maxim (OED).

bullion. Uncoined metal.

coin. *a.* A die used to stamp a design on a metal disk; *b.* a metal disk so stamped.

convertible. Currency that can be exchanged or converted into another currency, usually upon demand at a fixed rate.

counterfeit. Imitation of a coin produced by an official mint. See *duplication*.

cours forcé. French, literally "forced circulation." Said of a currency that is both inconvertible and legal tender (Nussbaum 1950, 58). See *legal tender, fiat*.

cry-down. A lowering of the face value of a coin.

cry-up. A raising of the face value of a coin.

debasement. A lowering of the intrinsic content of a coin or currency. See *inflation*.

decry. To withdraw a coin from use as money.

duplication. Making a coin that is not, but is materially identical to, a coin produced by the official mint.

face value. Legal tender value of a particular coin, or its official value in terms of other coins. Values were not inscribed on the faces of coins until the late sixteenth century.

fiat. (Latin phrase meaning "let it be done," with which kings signed orders). Command or decree. Fiat money: money with *cours forcé*. Intrinsically worthless money with positive market value.

fiduciary. Not full-bodied. See also *overvalued*.

fractional. Of lower denominations. In the U.S., coins or notes smaller than $1. Traditionally, coins made of silver were called *subsidiary*, and those made of copper or bronze were called *minor*.

full-bodied. Said of a coin whose metallic content is worth as much as the face value or market value (net of production costs in some definitions).

ghost money. Not a coin but a unit of account representing a fixed number, greater than one, of a particular coin.

glossarist. One who writes glosses; one who compiles a glossary (OED).

glossator. A writer of glosses; particularly, medieval commentators who wrote glosses on the texts of Roman and canon law (OED).

imaginary money. See *unit of account*.

inflation. A fall in the value of money.

intrinsic. Intrinsic content, the metal contained in a coin. Intrinsic value, the value of a coin's intrinsic content.

legal tender. That which cannot be refused by a creditor when tendered by a debtor to fulfill an existing obligation.

mint equivalent. Value (in units of account or number of coins) of a unit of weight of coined metal.

mint price. Price (in units of account or number of coins) paid by the mint for a unit of weight of metal.

nominalism. The doctrine that all coins are legal tender at their face value.

obsidional. Of coins struck in a besieged city to supply the want of current coins (OED).

overvalued. Taken for more than its intrinsic value.

penny.   *a.* a coin (plural "pennies");   *b.* a unit of account (plural "pence").

promissory. Containing or implying a promise of redemption.

reinforcement. A raising of the intrinsic content of a coin or currency. Sometimes called currency reform.

seigniorage. Fee charged on the coining of money to cover production costs and to provide revenue to the king. Also, profit earned by the monetary authority from the issue of currency.

subsidiary. Of lower denominations. In the U.S., fiduciary silver coins below $1.

tale.   *a.* A recounting of events.   *b.* A counting of objects. By tale: by number, as determined by counting rather than by weighing.

token. A stamped piece of metal, often coin, issued as a medium of exchange by a private person or company who promises to exchange it for its nominal value for goods or legal currency (OED).

token money. State coinage of money not having the intrinsic value for which it is current, but bearing a fixed value relative to gold coin, for which it is exchangeable (OED).

underweight. Below its normal or legal weight.

unit of account. A unit in which accounts are kept; a particular coin (or a number of particular coins) in terms of whose value sums of money are expressed.

weight (by). See *tale*.

References

d'Afflitto, Matteo. 1598. *Commentaria in Librum feudorum*. Frankfurt-am-Main: Andreas Wechel.

Altmann, Hans Christian. 1976. *Die Kipper- und Wipperinflation in Bayern*. Munich: Neue Schriftenreihe des Stadtarchivs München.

Arrow, Kenneth J. 1951. An Extension of the Basic Theorems of Classical Welfare Economics. In *Proceedings of the Second Berkeley Symposium on Mathematical Statistics and Probability*, ed. Jerzy Neyman, 507–32. Berkeley: University of California Press.

Barro, Robert J. 1979. Money and the Price Level under the Gold Standard. *Economic Journal* 89 (March): 13–33.

Bartolo da Sassoferrato. 1570–71. *Opera*. Venice: Giunta.

Baulant, Micheline. 1971. Salaire des ouvriers du bâtiment de Paris de 1400 à 1726. *Annales* 26 (Mar–Apr): 463–83.

Bernocchi, Mario. 1974. *Le monete della Repubblica fiorentina I: Il libro della Zecca*. Florence: L. S. Olschki.

—————. 1975. *Le monete della Repubblica fiorentina II: Corpus Nummorum Florentinorum*. Florence: L. S. Olschki.

—————. 1976. *Le monete della Repubblica fiorentina III: Documentazione*. Florence: L. S. Olschki.

—————. 1978. *Le monete della Repubblica fiorentina IV: Valute del fiorino d'oro, 1389–1432*. Florence: L. S. Olschki.

Bernstein, Peter. 2000. *The Power of Gold*. New York: John Wiley & Sons.

Berry, George. 1988. *Seventeenth Century England: Traders and Their Tokens*. London: Seaby.

Beveridge, William H., et al. 1965. *Prices and Wages in England from the 12th to the 19th Century*. London: F. Cass.

Biel, Gabriel. 1930. *Treatise on the Power and Utility of Moneys*. Trans. Robert B. Burke. Philadelphia: University of Pennsylvania Press.

Blanchet, J.-Adrien. 1897. Les monnaies coupées. *Revue numismatique*, 4th ser. 1:1–13.

Blanchet, Adrien, and Adolphe Dieudonné. 1916. *Manuel de numismatique française*. vol. 2. Paris: Auguste Picard.

Bogucka, Maria. 1975. The Monetary Crisis of the XVIIth Century and its Social and Psychological Consequences in Poland. *Journal of European Economic History* 4 (1): 137–52.

Bonfiglio Dosio, Giorgetta, ed. 1984. *Il "Capitolar dalle Brocche" della Zecca di Venezia (1358–1556)*. Padua: Editrice Antenore.

Borden, D. G., and I. D. Brown. 1984. The Milled Coinage of Elizabeth I. *Numismatic Journal* 53:108–12.

Bornitz, Jakob. 1608. *De nummis in republica percutiendis et conservandis.* Hanover: Wechel.

Botet i Sisó, Joaquim. 1908–11. *Les monedes catalanes.* Barcelona: Institut d'estudis catalans.

Boyer, Russell. 1971. Nickels and Dimes. Manuscript. London, Ontario: University of Western Ontario.

Boyer-Xambeu, Marie-Thérèse, Ghislain Deleplace, and Lucien Gillard. 1994. *Private Money and Public Currencies: The 16th Century Challenge.* Armonk, New York: M. E. Sharpe.

Brandt, Loren and Thomas J. Sargent. 1989. Interpreting New Evidence about China and U.S. Silver Purchases. *Journal of Monetary Economics* 23 (1): 31–51.

Bruckner, Alexander. 1867. *Finanzgeschichtliche Studien: Kupfergeldkrisen.* St. Petersburg: Buchdruckerei der kaiserlichen Akademie der Wissenschaften.

Brundage, James. 1995. *Medieval Canon Law.* London and New York: Longman.

Bruno, Alberto. 1609. Tractatus augmenti et diminutionis monetarum. In *De monetarum augmento variatione et diminutione tractatus varii,* 614–738. Turin.

Budel, René. 1591. *De monetis et re numaria.* Cologne: Johann Gymnich.

Buridan, Jean. 1637. *Quaestiones in decem libros Ethicorum Aristotelis ad Nicomachum.* Oxford: H. Cripps.

Burns, Arthur Robert. 1927. *Money and Monetary Policy in Early Times.* London: K. Paul, Trench, Trubner & Co.

Butigella, Girolamo. 1608. Repetitiones in legem cum quid. In *Repetitionum in varias iuris civilis leges,* ed. Pompeius Limpius, 2:83–86. Venice: sub signo aquilae renovantis.

Butrio, Antonio de. [1578] 1967. *In libros Decretalium commentarii.* Venice: Giunta. Reprint, Torino: Bottega d'Erasmo.

Cagan, Phillip. 1956. The Monetary Dynamics of Hyperinflation. In *Studies in the Quantity Theory of Money,* ed. Milton Friedman, 25–117. Chicago: Chicago University Press.

Calendar of Treasury Books 1660–1718. 1904–58. London: His Majesty's Stationery Office.

Calendar of Treasury Papers 1557–1728. 1868–89. London: Longmans, Green, Reader, and Dyer.

Cannan, Edwin. 1935. *Money: Its Connexion with Rising and Falling Prices.* London: P. S. King & Son.

Carothers, Neil. 1930. *Fractional Currency.* New York: John Wiley & Sons.

Carranza, Alonso de. 1629. *El aiustamiento i proporcion de las monedas de oro, plata i cobre.* Madrid: F. Martinez.

Carrera i Pujal, Jaume. 1943–47. *Historia de la economía española.* Barcelona: Bosch.

Castaing, John, ed. 1698–1810. *The Course of the Exchange.* London.

Castellani, Arrigo. 1952. *Nuovi testi fiorentini del Dugento*. Florence: G. C. Sansoni.

Cessi, Roberto. 1937. *Problemi monetari veneziani fino a tutto il secolo XIV*. Documentari finanziari della Repubblica di Venezia, 4th ser., vol. 1. Padua: Casa editrice Dott. Antonio Milani.

Challis, Christopher E. 1992a. Appendix 2. In *A New History of the Royal Mint*, ed. Christopher E. Challis, 699–758. Cambridge: Cambridge University Press.

———. 1992b. Lord Hastings to the Great Silver Recoinage, 1464–1699. In *A New History of the Royal Mint*, ed. Christopher E. Challis, 179–397. Cambridge: Cambridge University Press.

Chaudoir, Stanislaw de. 1836. *Aperçu sur les monnaies russes et sur les monnaies étrangères qui ont eu cours en Russie depuis les temps les plus reculés jusqu'à nos jours*. St. Petersburg: F. Bellizard et Co.

Cipolla, Carlo M. 1948. *Studi di storia della moneta I: I movimenti dei cambi in Italia dal secolo XIII al XV*. Pavia: A. Garzanti.

———. 1956. *Money, Prices, and Civilization in the Mediterranean World, Fifth to Seventeenth Century*. New York: Gordian Press.

———. 1982. *The Monetary Policy of Fourteenth-Century Florence*. Berkeley: University of California Press.

———. 1990. *Il Governo della moneta a Firenze e a Milano nei secoli XIV–XVI*. Bologna: Società editrice il Mulino.

Colson, Achille. 1855. Notice sur des monnaies frappées dans la principauté de Catalogne, le Roussillon et la Cerdagne pendant la révolution de 1640 et l'occupation française jusqu'en 1659. *Revue Numismatique*, 1st ser. 20:117–46.

Cooper, Denis R. 1988. *The Art and Craft of Coinmaking: A History of Mint Technology*. London: Spink.

Corpus juris canonici. 1959. Graz: Akademische Druck- und Verlagsanstalt.

Corpus juris civilis. 1598. Venice: Giunta.

Costa, Giovanni Battista. 1603. *De facti scientia et ignorantia*. Pavia: Roberto Meietto.

Courtenay, William J. 1972a. The King and the Leaden Coin: The Economic Background of "Sine qua non" Causality. *Traditio* 28:185–209.

———. 1972b. Token Coinage and the Administration of Poor Relief During the Middle Ages. *Journal of Interdisciplinary History* 3 (2): 275–95.

Craig, John. 1953. *The Mint: A History of the London Mint from A.D. 287 to 1948*. Cambridge: Cambridge University Press.

Davanzati, Bernardo. [1588] 1807. Lezione delle monete. In *Scisma d'Inghilterra con altre operette*. Milan: Società tipografica de' classici italiani.

Day, John. 1987. *The Medieval Market Economy*. Oxford: Blackwell.

Debreu, Gerard. 1954. Valuation Equilibrium and Pareto Optimum. *Proceedings of the National Academy of Sciences* 40:588–592.

Del Rivero, Casto María. 1918–19. El Ingenio de la Moneda de Segovia, Parts 1–5. *Revista de archivos, bibliotecas y museos* 38:20–31, 191–206; 39:28–36, 288–306; 40:141–155.

Dewey, Davis Rich. 1918. *Financial History of the United States.* New York: Longmans, Green and Co.

Diaz-Giménez, Javier, Edward C. Prescott, Terry Fitzgerald, and Fernando Alvarez. 1992. Banking in Computable General Equilibrium Economies. *Journal of Economic Dynamics and Control* 16 (March): 533–60.

Domínguez Ortiz, Antonio. 1960. *Política y hacienda de Felipe IV.* Madrid: Editorial de derecho financiero.

Doneau, Hugues. 1847. *Opera omnia.* vol. 10. Florence: Clius.

Duaren, François. 1598. *Omnia quae quidem hactenus edita fuerunt opera.* Frankfurt-am-Main: Andreas Wechel.

Dumoulin, Charles. 1681. *Omnia quae extant opera.* Paris: Charles Osmont.

Dupuy, Claude, ed. 1989. *Traité des monnaies de Nicole Oresme et autres écrits monétaires du XIVe siècle (Jean Buridan, Bartole de Sassoferrato).* Paris: La Manufacture.

Durant, Guillaume. [1574] 1975. *Speculum judiciale.* Basel: Frobenius. Reprint, Aalen: Scientia Verlag.

Einaudi, Luigi. 1936. La teoria della moneta immaginaria nel tempo da Carlomagno alla rivoluzione francese. *Rivista di storia economica* 1:1–35.

Feaveryear, Albert. 1963. *The Pound Sterling.* Oxford: Clarendon Press.

Fisher, Irving. 1911. *The Purchasing Power of Money.* New York: The Macmillan Company.

———. 1920. *Stabilizing the Dollar.* New York: The Macmillan Company.

Fisher, Irving, and Hans L. R. Cohrssen. 1934. *Stable Money: A History of the Movement.* New York: Adelphi Company.

Flandreau, Marc. 1996. The French Crime of 1873: An Essay on the Emergence of the International Gold Standard, 1870–80. *Journal of Economic History* 56 (4): 862–97.

Fontanon, Claude. 1585. *Les edicts et ordonnances des roys de France depuis S. Loys jusques à present.* Paris: Jacques Dupuys.

Fontecha y Sánchez, Ramón de. 1968. *La moneda de vellón y cobre de la monarquía española (años 1516–1931).* Madrid: Artes gráficas.

Forcadel, Étienne. 1595. *Opera.* Paris: Guillaume Chaudière.

Fratianni, Michele, and Franco Spinelli. 1997. *A Monetary History of Italy.* New York: Cambridge University Press.

Frêche, Georges, and Dominique Frêche. 1967. *Les prix des grains, des vins et des légumes à Toulouse (1486–1868).* Paris: Presses universitaires de France.

Friedman, Milton. 1951. Commodity-Reserve Currency. *Journal of Political Economy* 59 (3): 203–32.

———. 1959. *A Program for Monetary Stability.* New York: Fordham University Press.

———. 1990. The Crime of 1873. *Journal of Political Economy* 98 (6): 1154–94.

Friedman, Milton, and Anna J. Schwartz. 1963. *A Monetary History of the United States.* Princeton, NJ: Princeton University Press.

Gaettens, Richard. 1955. *Inflationen, das Drama der Geldentwertungen vom Altertum bis Gegenwart.* Munich: R. Pflaum.

Galeotti, Arrigo. [1930] 1971. *Le monete del granducato di Toscana.* Bologna: Forni.

Garber, Peter M. 1986. Nominal Contracts in a Bimetallic Standard. *American Economic Review* 76 (5): 1012–30.

García de Paso, José I. 1999a. La economía monetaria del Padre Juan de Mariana. *Moneda y crédito* 209:13–44.

———. 1999b. The 1628 Castilian Crydown: Origins and Failure. Manuscript. Madrid: Universidad Complutense.

———. 2000a. La estabilización monetaria en Castilla bajo Carlos II. *Revista de historia económica* 18 (1): 49–77.

———. 2000b. La Política monetaria castellana de Trastámaras y Austrias, 1400–1700. Manuscript. Madrid: Universidad Complutense.

Gherardi, Alessandro. 1896–98. *Le consulte della Repubblica fiorentina dall'anno mcclxxx al mccxcviii.* Florence: G. C. Sansoni.

Glassman, Debra, and Angela Redish. 1988. Currency Depreciation in Early Modern England and France. *Explorations in Economic History* 25 (1): 75–97.

Glück, Christian Friedrich. 1841. *Ausfürliche Erläuterung der Pandecten nach Hellfeld: Ein Commentar.* vol. 12. Erlangen: Johann Jacob Palm.

Godefroy, Denis. [1590] 1688. *Corpus iuris civilis.* Frankfurt-am-Main: Balthasar Christoph Wust.

Goldthwaite, Richard A., and Giulio Mandich. 1994. *Studi sulla moneta fiorentina.* Florence: Leo S. Olschki.

González Téllez, Manuel. 1715. *Commentaria perpetua in singulos textus quinque librorum Decretalium Gregorii IX.* Lyon: Anisson & Posuel.

Grégoire, Pierre. 1609. *De republica.* Lyon: J. Pillehotte.

Grice-Hutchinson, Marjorie. 1978. *Early Economic Thought in Spain, 1177–1740.* London: George Allen & Unwin.

———. 1993. *Economic Thought in Spain.* Brookfield, VT: E. Elgar.

Grierson, Philip. 1954. Deux fausses monnaies vénitiennes du Moyen âge. *Schweizer Münzblätter* 5 (3): 86–90.

———. 1963. Coin Wear and the Frequency Table. *Numismatic Chronicle,* 7th ser. 2:iii–xvii.

Grierson, Philip. 1971. The Monetary Pattern of Sixteenth-Century Coinage. *Transactions of the Royal Historical Society,* 5th series 21:45–60.

Grimaudet, François. 1576. *Des monnoyes, augment et diminution du pris d'icelles.* Paris: Martin Le Jeune.

Hahn, Emil. 1915. *Jakob Stampfer, Goldschmied, Medailleur und Stempelschneider von Zürich, 1505–79.* Zürich: Beer & Co.

Hahn, Frank H. 1965. On Some Problems of Proving the Existence of an Equilibrium in a Monetary Economy. In *The Theory of Interest Rates,* ed. Frank H. Hahn and F. P. R. Brechling, 126–35. London: Macmillan.

Hailstone, Edward. 1869. *Portraits of Yorkshire Worthies: Selected from the National Exhibition of Works of Art at Leeds, 1868, with Biographical Notices.* London: Cundall.

Hamilton, Earl J. 1934. *American Treasure and the Price Revolution in Spain, 1501–1650.* Cambridge, MA: Harvard University Press.

————. 1936. *Money, Prices and Wages in Valencia, Aragon and Navarre, 1351–1500.* Cambridge: Harvard University Press.

————. 1947. *War and Prices in Spain, 1651–1800.* Cambridge, MA: Harvard University Press.

Harsin, Paul. 1928. *Les doctrines monétaires et financières en France du XVIe au XVIIIe siècle.* Paris: F. Alcan.

Haton, Claude. 1857. *Mémoires, contenant le récit des événements accomplis de 1553 à 1582, principalement dans la Champagne et la Brie.* Paris: Imprimerie impériale.

Hawtrey, Ralph G. 1919. *Currency and Credit.* London: Longmans, Green.

Heckscher, Eli F. 1954. *An Economic History of Sweden.* Cambridge, MA: Harvard University Press.

Herlihy, David. 1974. Pisan Coinage and the Monetary History of Tuscany, 1150–1250. In *Le zecche minori toscane fino al XIV secolo: Atti del 3º convegno internazionale di studi, Pistoia, 16–19 settembre 1967,* 169–93. Bologna: Rastignano.

Hermand, Alexandre. 1846. Premières monnaies de nécessité. *Revue de la numismatique belge* 2:196–201.

Hocking, William John. 1909. Simon's Dies in the Royal Mint Museum, with Some Notes on the Early History of Coinage by Machinery. *Numismatic Chronicle,* 4th series 9:56–118.

Horsefield, J. Keith. 1960. *British Monetary Experiments, 1650–1710.* Cambridge, MA: Harvard University Press.

Horton, S. Dana. 1887. *The Silver Pound and England's Monetary Policy since the Restoration, Together with the History of the Guinea Illustrated by Contemporary Documents.* London: Macmillan and Co.

Hostiensis (Segusio, Henry of). [1581] 1965. *In quinque Decretalium libros commentaria.* Venice: Giunta. Reprint, Torino: Bottega d'Erasmo.

Hotman, François. [1573] 1610. *Liber quaestionum illustrium.* Hanover: Wilhelm Anton.

Houghton, John. 1692–1702. *A Collection for Improvement of Husbandry and Trade.* London: Randal Taylor.

Hubrecht, Georges. 1933. Compte-rendu. *Revue historique de droit français et étranger* 12:776–83.

———. 1955. Quelques observations sur l'évolution des doctrines concernant les paiements monétaires du XIIe au XVIIIe siècle. In *Aequitas et Bona Fides: Festgabe zum 70. Geburtstag von August Simonius*, ed. juristische Fakultät der Universität Basel, 133–44. Basel: Helbing & Lichtenhaan.

Innocent IV. 1570. *Commentaria super quinque libros Decretalium*. Frankfurt-am-Main: Sigmund Feyerabend.

d'Isernia, Andrea. 1541. *Commentaria in usus Librum feudorum*. Lyon: Iacobus Giunta.

Jesse, Wilhelm. 1924. *Quellenbuch zur Münzgeschichte*. Halle-Saale: A. Riechmann & Co.

Jevons, William Stanley. 1875. *Money and the Mechanism of Exchange*. London: H. S. King.

Johnson, Charles, ed. 1956. *The "De Moneta" of Nicholas Oresme and English Mint Documents*. London: Nelson.

Kareken, John H., and Neil Wallace. 1981. On the Indeterminacy of Equilibrium Exchange Rates. *Quarterly Journal of Economics* 96 (2): 207–22.

———, eds. 1980. *Models of Monetary Economies*. Minneapolis: Federal Reserve Bank of Minneapolis.

Kaye, Joel. 1998. *Economy and Nature in the Fourteenth Century*. Cambridge: Cambridge University Press.

Kindleberger, Charles P. 1991. The Economic Crisis of 1619 to 1623. *Journal of Economic History* 51 (1): 149–75.

Kiyotaki, Nobuhiro, and Randall Wright. 1989. On Money as a Medium of Exchange. *Journal of Political Economy* 97 (4): 927–54.

Kreps, David M. 1998. Anticipated Utility and Dynamic Choice. In *Frontiers of Research in Economic Theory: The Nancy L. Schwartz Memorial Lectures, 1983–97*, ed. Donald P. Jacobs, Ehud Kalai, and Morton I. Kamien, 242–74. Cambridge: Cambridge University Press.

Kohn, Meir. 2001. The Origins of Western Economic Success: Commerce, Finance, and Government in Pre-Industrial Europe. Manuscript. Dartmouth College: Dartmouth, NH.

Lafaurie, Jean. 1956. *Les monnaies des rois de France de François Ier à Henri IV*. Paris: Émile Bourgey.

Lane, Frederic C., and Reinhold C. Mueller. 1985. *Money and Banking in Medieval and Renaissance Venice: Coins and Moneys of Account*. Baltimore: Johns Hopkins University Press.

Lapeyre, Henri. 1955. *Une famille de marchands: Les Ruiz*. Paris: Armand Colin.

Lapidus, André. 1997. Metal, Money, and the Prince: John Buridan and Nicholas Oresme after Thomas Aquinas. *History of Political Economy* 29 (1): 21–53.

Larkin, James F., and Paul L. Hughes. 1973–83. *Stuart Royal Proclamations*. Oxford: Clarendon Press.

La Roncière, Charles-M. de. 1973. *Un changeur florentin du Trecento: Lippo di Fede del Sega (1285 env. - 1363 env.)*. Paris: S.E.V.P.E.N.

———. 1982. *Prix et salaires à Florence au XIVe siècle (1280–1380)*. Rome: École française de Rome.

Laughlin, J. Laurence. 1900. *Report of the Monetary Commission of the Indianapolis Convention of Boards of Trade, Chambers of Commerce, Commercial Clubs, and Other Similar Bodies of the United States*. Indianapolis: The Hollenbeck Press.

———. 1931. *Money, Credit, and Prices*. Chicago: University of Chicago Press.

Laures, John. 1928. *The Political Economy of Juan de Mariana*. New York: Fordham University Press.

Law, John. [c1704] 1994. *Essay on a Land Bank*. Ed. Antoin Murphy. Dublin: Aeon Publishing.

Leddet, Pierre. 1928. Le journal du sire de Gouberville: Noms de monnaies et évaluations. *Revue numismatique*, 4th ser. 31:187–211.

Leijonhufvud, Axel S. B. 1984. Inflation and Economic Performance. In *Money in Crisis: the Federal Reserve, the Economy, and Monetary Reform*, ed. Barry N. Siegel, 19–36. San Francisco: Pacific Institute for Public Policy Research.

L'Estoile, Pierre de. 1992. *Registre-journal du règne de Henri III*. Ed. Madeleine Lazard and Gilbert Schrenck. Geneva: Droz.

Levasseur, Émile. 1902. *Mémoire sur les monnaies du règne de François Ier*. Paris: Imprimerie nationale.

Li, Ming-Hsun. 1963. *The Great Recoinage of 1696 to 1699*. London: Weidenfeld and Nicolson.

Liautey, André. 1921. *La hausse des prix et la lutte contre la cherté en France au XVIe siècle*. Paris: Jouve et Cie.

Locke, John. 1691. *Some Consideration of the Consequences of the Lowering of Interest and the Raising the Value of Money*. London: Awnsham and John Churchill.

Lotz, Walther. 1893. *Die drei Flugschriften über den Münzstreit der sächsischen Albertiner und Ernestiner um 1530*. Leipzig: Duncker & Humblot.

Lozanne, Claudia de. 1997. *Geldtheorie und Geldpolitik im frühneuzeitlichen Spanien*. Saarbrücken: Verlag für Entwicklungspolitik.

Lucas, Robert E., Jr. 1982. Interest Rates and Currency Prices in a Two-Country World. *Journal of Monetary Economics* 10 (3): 335–60.

Lucas, Robert E., Jr, and Nancy L. Stokey. 1987. Money and Interest in a Cash-in-Advance Economy. *Econometrica* 55 (3): 491–513.

Luschin von Ebengreuth, Arnold. 1926. *Allgemeine Münzkunde und Geldgeschichte des Mittelalters und der neueren Zeit*. Munich: R. Oldenbourg.

Macaulay, Thomas Babington Macaulay, Baron. [1855] 1967. *History of England, from the Accession of James the Second*. Part 2. London: Heron Books.

MacKay, Angus. 1981. *Money, Prices, and Politics in Fifteenth-Century Castile*. London: Royal Historical Society.

Mailliet, Prosper. 1868–73. *Catalogue descriptif des monnaies obsidionales et de nécessité, avec atlas*. Bruxelles: F. Gobbaerts.

Majer, Giovannina. 1933. Una moneta veneziana inedita: Il piccolo di Andrea Contarini. *Archivio Veneto*, 5th ser. 13:229–33.

———. 1953. L'officina monetaria della Repubblica veneziana. *Archivio veneto*, 5th ser. 52–53:28–44.

Mandich, Giulio. 1988. Delle prime valutazioni del ducato d'oro veneziano (1285–1346). *Studi veneziani* n.s. 16:15–31.

Mariana, Juan de. [1609] 1987. *Tratado y discurso sobre la moneda de vellón*. Madrid: Ministerio de economía y hacienda, Instituto de estudios fiscales.

———. [1609] 1994. *De monetae mutatione*. Ed. Josef Falzberger. Heidelberg: Manutius Verlag.

Marimon, Ramon. 1997. Learning from Learning in Economics. In *Advances in Economics and Econometrics: Theory and Applications. Seventh World Congress*, Vol. I, ed. David M. Kreps and Kenneth F. Wallis, 278–315. Cambridge: Cambridge University Press.

Marion, Marcel. 1919. *Histoire financière de la France depuis 1715*. Vol. 2. Paris: Rousseau et Cie.

Mayhew, Nicholas J. 1992. From Regional to Central Minting, 1158–1464. In *A New History of the Royal Mint*, ed. Christopher E. Challis, 83–178. Cambridge: Cambridge University Press.

Mazerolle, Fernand. 1907. *L'hôtel des monnaies*. Paris: H. Laurens.

McCallum, Bennett T. 1989. The Gold-Standard: A Commodity Money System. In *Monetary Economics: Theory and Policy*. New York: Macmillan.

Meyer, Joseph. 1840–55. *Das großes Conversations-Lexicon für die gebildeten Stände*. Hildburghausen: Verlag des bibliographischen Instituts.

Mill, John Stuart. 1857. *Principles of Political Economy*. 4th ed. London: John W. Parker and Son.

Mironov, Boris N. 1992. Consequences of the Price Revolution in Eighteenth-Century Russia. *Economic History Review* 45 (3): 457–78.

Mises, Ludwig von. 1953. *The Theory of Money and Credit*. Trans. H. E. Batson. London: Jonathan Cape.

Mitchell, Brian R. 1988. *British Historical Statistics*. Cambridge: Cambridge University Press.

Mitchiner, Michael. 1988–98. *Jetons, Medalets and Tokens*. London: Hawkins Publications.

Mitchiner, Michael, and Anne Skinner. 1984. English Tokens, c. 1200 to 1425. *Numismatic Journal* 53:29–77.

Monroe, Arthur Eli. 1923. *Monetary Theory before Adam Smith.* Cambridge, MA: Harvard University Press.

Montanari, Geminiano. [1683] 1804. *Della moneta: Trattato mercantile.* In *Scrittori classici italiani di economia politica, parte antica,* vol. 3. Milan: G. G. Destefanis.

Motomura, Akira. 1994. The Best and Worst of Currencies: Seigniorage and Currency Policy in Spain, 1597–1650. *Journal of Economic History* 54 (1): 104–27.

———. 1997. New Data on Minting, Seigniorage, and the Money Supply in Spain (Castile), 1597–1643. *Explorations in Economic History* 34 (3): 331–67.

Mueller, Reinhold C. 1980. L'imperialismo monetario veneziano nel Quattrocento. *Società e Storia* 3 (8): 277–97.

Munro, John H. A. 1972. *Wool, Cloth, and Gold: The Struggle for Bullion in Anglo-Burgundian Trade, 1340–1478.* Toronto: University of Toronto Press.

———. 1974. Billon, Billoen, Billio: From Bullion to Base Coinage. *Belgisch tijdschrift voor filologie en geschiedenis / Revue belge de philologie et d'histoire* 52:293–305.

———. 1988. Deflation and the Petty Coinage Problem in the Late-Medieval Economy: The Case of Flanders, 1334–1484. *Explorations in Economic History* 25 (4): 387–423.

———. forthcoming. The Monetary Origins of the 'Price Revolution' Before the Influx of Spanish-American Treasure: The South German Silver-Copper Trades, Merchant-Banking, and Venetian Commerce, 1470–1540. In *Monetary History in Global Perspective, 1500–1808,* ed. Dennis Flynn. London: Ashgate Publishing.

Nanteuil, Henri de. 1928. *Le frai des monnaies d'or et d'argent.* Paris: H. Rolland.

Newald, Johann. 1885. Das österreichische Münzwesen unter den Kaisern Maximilian II, Rudolf II und Matthias. *Numismatische Zeitschrift* 17:167–416.

Niehans, Jürg. 1978. Commodity Money. In *The Theory of Money.* Baltimore: Johns Hopkins University Press.

North, Douglass C., and Barry R. Weingast. 1989. Constitutions and Commitments: The Evolution of Institutions Governing Public Choice in Seventeenth-Century England. *Journal of Economic History* 49 (4): 803–32.

Nussbaum, Arthur. 1950. *Money in the Law, National and International.* Brooklyn, NY: The Foundation Press.

Pamuk, Şevket. 1997. In the Absence of Domestic Currency: Debased European Coinage in the Seventeenth-Century Ottoman Empire. *Journal of Economic History* 57 (2): 345–66.

Panormitanus (Niccolò de' Tudeschi). 1617. *Commentaria in quinque Decretalium libros.* Venice: Giunta.

Paolozzi Strozzi, Beatrice, Giuseppe Toderi, and Fiorenza Vannel Toderi. 1992. *Monete della Repubblica senese.* Siena: Silvana Editoriale.

Papadopoli, Nicolò. 1893–1909. *Le monete di Venezia.* Venice: Ferdinando Ongania.

Parenti, Giuseppe. 1939. *Prime ricerche sulla revoluzione dei prezzi in Firenze.* Florence: C. Cya.

Peck, C. Wilson. 1960. *English Copper, Tin and Bronze Coins in the British Museum, 1558–1958.* London: The Trustees of the British Museum.

Pegolotti, Francesco Balducci. 1936. *La pratica della mercatura.* Ed. Allan Evans. Cambridge, MA: The Mediaeval Academy of America, Publications, 24.

Pepys, Samuel. 1970–83. *The Diary of Samuel Pepys.* Ed. Robert Latham and William Matthews. Berkeley: University of California Press.

Pérez García, María Pilar. 1990. *La real fábrica de moneda de Valladolid a través de sus registros contables.* Valladolid: Secretariado de publicaciones, Universidad de Valladolid.

Petty, William. 1899. *The Economic Writings of Sir William Petty.* Ed. Charles Henry Hull. Cambridge: Cambridge University Press.

Postan, Michael M. 1973. *Essays on Medieval Agriculture and General Problems of the Medieval Economy.* Cambridge: Cambridge University Press.

Posthumus, Nicolaas W. 1946. *Inquiry into the History of Prices in Holland.* vol. 1. Leiden: E. J. Brill.

Pothier, Robert Joseph. 1824. *Œuvres.* vol. 4. Paris: Béchet aîné.

Poullain, Henri. 1709. *Traitez des monnoyes.* Paris: Frédéric Léonard.

Proctor, Samuel, ed. 1696–98. *Price-Courant: The Price of Merchandise in London.* London.

Promis, Domenico. 1868. *Monete della Repubblica di Siena.* Turin: Stamperia Reale.

Pulgar, Fernando del. 1943. *Crónica de los Reyes católicos.* Madrid: Espasa-Calpe.

Raveau, Paul. 1929. La crise des prix au XVIe siècle en Poitou. *Revue Historique* 162 (September): 1–44, (November): 268–93.

Recueil des anciennes ordonnances des Pays Bas. 1907. 2nd ser., vol. 4. Brussels: J. Goemaere.

Redish, Angela. 1990. The Evolution of the Gold Standard in England. *Journal of Economic History* 50 (4): 789–805.

———. 2000. *Bimetallism: An Economic and Historical Analysis.* Cambridge: Cambridge University Press.

Redlich, Fritz. 1972. *Die deutsche Inflation des frühen 17. Jahrhunderts in der zeitgenössichen Literatur: Die Kipper und Wipper.* Cologne: Böhlau Verlag.

Reekmans, Tony. 1949. Economic and Social Repercussions of the Ptolemaic Copper Inflation. *Chronique d'Égypte* 48 (July): 324–42.

Reher, David S., and Esmeralda Ballesteros. 1993. Precios y salarios en Castilla La Nueva: La construcción de un indice de salarios reales, 1501–1991. *Revista de historia económica* XI (1): 101–151.

Ricardo, David. 1817. *On the Principles of Political Economy and Taxation.* London: John Murray.

Richet, Denis. 1961. Le cours officiel des monnaies étrangères circulant en France au XVIe siècle. *Revue historique* 225:359–96.

Rittmann, Herbert. 1975. *Deutsche Geldgeschichte, 1484–1914.* Munich: Battenberg.

Rogers, James E. Thorold. 1887. *The First Nine Years of Bank of England.* Oxford: Clarendon Press.

Rolnick, Arthur J., and Warren E. Weber. 1986. Gresham's Law or Gresham's Fallacy. *Journal of Political Economy* 94 (1): 185–89.

———. 1997. Money, Inflation, and Output under Fiat and Commodity Standards. *Journal of Political Economy* 105 (6): 1308–21.

de Roover, Raymond A. 1948. *Money, Banking, and Credit in Medieval Bruges.* Cambridge, MA: Mediaeval Academy of America.

———. 1971. *La pensée économique des scholastiques: Doctrines et méthodes.* Montréal: Institut d'Études médievales.

Rouyer, Jules. 1849. Notes pour servir à l'étude des méraux. *Revue numismatique,* 1st ser. 14:356–77.

———. 1858. *Histoire du jeton au Moyen âge.* Paris: Rollin.

———. 1862. Bulletin bibliographique. *Revue numismatique,* 2nd ser. 7:318–22.

Ruding, Rogers. 1840. *Annals of the Coinage of Great Britain and its Dependencies.* London: J. Hearne.

Sahilioğlu, Halil. 1983. The Role of International Monetary and Metal Movements in Ottoman Monetary History: 1300–1750. In *Precious Metals and the Later Medieval and Early Modern Worlds,* ed. J. F. Richards, 269–304. Durham, NC: Carolina Academic Press.

Sapori, Armando, ed. 1934. *I Libri di commercio dei Peruzzi.* Milano: Treves.

Sargent, Thomas J. 1993. *Rational Expectations and Inflation.* New York: HarperCollins College Publishers.

———. 1999. *The Conquest of American Inflation.* Princeton: Princeton University Press.

Sargent, Thomas J., and Bruce D. Smith. 1997. Coinage, Debasements, and Gresham's Laws. *Economic Theory* 10 (2): 197–226.

Sargent, Thomas J., and François R. Velde. 1995. Macroeconomic Features of the French Revolution. *Journal of Political Economy* 103 (3): 474–518.

———. 1999. The Big Problem of Small Change. *Journal of Money, Credit, and Banking* 31 (2): 137–61.

Sargent, Thomas J., and Neil Wallace. 1973. Rational Expectations and the Dynamics of Hyperinflation. *International Economic Review* 14 (2): 328–50.

———. 1982. The Real Bills Doctrine versus the Quantity Theory of Money: A Reconsideration. *Journal of Political Economy* 90 (6): 1212–36.

———. 1983. A Model of Commodity Money. *Journal of Monetary Economics* 12 (1): 163–87.

Saulcy, Louis Félicien Joseph Caignart de. 1879–92. *Recueil de documents relatifs à l'histoire des monnaies.* 4 vols. Paris: Imprimerie nationale.

Say, Jean-Baptiste. 1841. *Traité d'économie politique.* Paris: Guillaumin.

Scaccia, Sigismondo. 1619. *Tractatus de commerciis et cambio.* Rome: Brugiotti.

Schmoller, Gustav. 1900. Über die Ausbildung einer richtigen Scheidemünzenpolitik vom 14. bis 19. Jahrhundert. *Jahrbuch für Gesetzgebung, Verwaltung und Volkswirtschaft im Deutschen Reich* 24 (4): 1–28.

Schnapper, Bernard. 1957. *Les rentes au XVIe siècle: Histoire d'un instrument de crédit.* Paris: S.E.V.P.E.N.

Schönberg, Gustav. 1890. *Handbuch der Politischen Ökonomie.* Tübingen: Laupp'schen Buchhandlung.

Schrötter, Friedrich Freiherr von. 1902. Die letzte städtische Münzprägung in Preußen. *Zeitschrift für Numismatik* 23:209–21.

———. 1906. Über die spanischen Billon- und Kupfermünzen unter den Königen Philipp III. und Philipp IV: Ein Versuch. *Zeitschrift für Numismatik* 25:289–330.

Schumpeter, Joseph A. 1954. *History of Economic Analysis.* New York: Oxford University Press.

Serra, Antonio. [1613] 1804. *Della moneta.* In *Scrittori classici italiani di economia politica, parte antica,* vol. 4. Milan: G. G. Destefanis.

Shaw, William Arthur. 1895. *The History of Currency, 1252 to 1894.* London: Wilsons and Milne.

———. [1896] 1967. *Select Tracts and Documents Illustrative of English Monetary History, 1626–1730.* London: Wilsons & Milne. Reprint, New York: Augustus M. Kelley.

Silva, José Gentil da. 1969. *Banque et crédit en Italie au XVIIe siècle.* Paris: Klincksieck.

Sims, Christopher A. 1989. Solving Nonlinear Stochastic Optimization and Equilibrium Problems Backwards. Institute for Empirical Macroeconomics, Federal Reserve Bank of Minneapolis: Working Paper 15.

———. 1990. Solving the Stochastic Growth Model by Backsolving with a Particular Nonlinear Form for the Decision Rule. *Journal of Business and Economic Statistics* 8 (1): 45–47.

Smith, Adam. [1776] 1937. *An Inquiry into the Nature and Causes of the Wealth of Nations.* New York: Random House.

Soetbeer, Adolf. 1879. *Edelmetall-Produktion und Wertverhältniss zwischen Gold und Silber.* Gotha: Justus Perthes.

Spengler, Joseph J. 1966. Coin Shortage: Modern and Premodern. *National Banking Review* 3:201–16.

Spooner, Frank C. 1956. *L'économie mondiale et les frappes monétaires en France, 1493–1680.* Paris: S.E.V.P.E.N.

———. 1972. *The International Economy and Monetary Movements in France, 1493–1725.* Cambridge, MA: Harvard University Press.

Sprenger, Bernd. 1991. *Das Geld der Deutschen*. Paderborn: Ferdinand Schöningh.

——. 1993. Harmonisierungsbetrebungen im Geldwesen der deutschen Staaten zwischen Wiener Kongreß und Reichsgründung. In *Geld und Währung vom 16. Jahrhundert bis zur Gegenwart*, ed. Eckart Schremmer, 121–42. Stuttgart: Franz Steiner Verlag.

Spufford, Peter. 1970. *Monetary Problems and Policies in the Burgundian Netherlands, 1433–1496*. Leiden: Brill.

——. 1986. *Handbook of Medieval Exchange*. London: Offices of the Royal Historical Society.

——. 1988a. *Money and its Use in Medieval Europe*. Cambridge: Cambridge University Press.

——. 1988b. Mint Organisation in Late Medieval Europe. In *Later Medieval Mints: Organisation, Administration, and Techniques: The Eighth Oxford Symposium on Coinage and Monetary History*, ed. Nicholas J. Mayhew and Peter Spufford, 7–29. Oxford: B.A.R.

Stahl, Alan M. 1985. *The Venetian Tornesello : A Medieval Colonial Coinage*. New York: American Numismatic Society.

——. 2000. *Zecca: The Mint of Venice in the Middle Ages*. Baltimore: Johns Hopkins University Press.

Stampe, Ernst. 1925. *Das deutsche Schuldentilgungsrecht des 17. Jahrhunderts*. Abhandlungen der preußischen Akademie der Wissenschaften, philosophisch-historische Klasse. Berlin: Verlag der Akademie.

——. 1926. *War Carolus Molinaeus Nominalist? Eine Untersuchung über seinen Valor extrinsecus monetae*. Sitzungsberichte der preußischen Akademie der Wissenschaften, philosophisch-historische Klasse, 37–66. Berlin: Verlag der Akademie.

——. 1928. *Das Zahlkraftrecht der Postglossatorenzeit*. Abhandlungen der preußischen Akademie der Wissenschaften, philosophisch-historische Klasse. Berlin: Verlag der Akademie.

——. 1930. *Das Zahlkraftrecht in den Königsgesetzen Frankreichs von 1306 bis 1547*. Abhandlungen der preußischen Akademie der Wissenschaften, philosophisch-historische Klasse. Berlin: Verlag der Akademie.

——. 1932. *Zur Entstehung des Nominalismus: Die Geldgesetzgebung Frankreichs von 1547 bis 1643 und ihre treibenden Kräfte*. Abhandlungen der preußischen Akademie der Wissenschaften, philosophisch-historische Klasse. Berlin: Verlag der Akademie.

Statutes at Large of the United States of America, 1789–1873. 1850–73. Washington, DC.

Sully, Maximilien de Béthune, duc de. 1822. *Mémoires*. Paris: E. Ledoux.

Sussman, Nathan. 1998. The Late Medieval Bullion Famine Reconsidered. *Journal of Economic History* 58 (1): 126–54.

Szlechter, Émile. 1951–52. La monnaie en France au XVIe siècle droit public, droit privé. *Revue historique de droit français et étranger*, 4th ser. 28:500–521, 29:80–116.

Targioni Tozzetti, Giovanni. 1775. Riflessioni sulle cause dell'acrescimento di valuta del fiorino d'oro. In *Nuova raccolta delle monete e zecche d'Italia*, ed. Guido Antonio Zanetti, 1:147–353. Bologna: L. dalla Volpe.

Täuber, Walter. 1928. *Molinaeus' Geldschuldlehre.* Jena: Gustav Fischer.

———. 1933. *Geld und Kredit im Mittelalter.* Berlin: C. Heymann.

Tesauro, Gaspare Antonio. 1609. Tractatus de monetarum augmentus ac variatione. In *Monetarum augmento variatione et diminutione tractatus varii*, 614–738. Turin.

Thireau, Jean-Louis. 1980. *Charles Du Moulin, 1500–1566.* Geneva: Droz.

Thompson, Robert H. 1975. Gloucester Farthings, 1657–1662. *British Numismatic Journal* 45:77–91.

———. 1988. *The Norweb Collection: Tokens of the British Isles, 1575–1750, Part II.* Sylloge of Coins of the British Isles, 38. London: Spink & Son Ltd.

Timbal, Pierre-Clément. 1973. *Les obligations contractuelles d'après la jurisprudence du Parlement (XIIIe–XIVe siècles).* vol. 1. Paris: CNRS.

Trifone, Romualdo. 1962. La variazione del valore della moneta nel pensiero di Bartolo. In *Bartolo di Sassoferrato: Studi e documenti per il VI. centenario*, ed. Danilo Segoloni, 693–704. Milan: Giuffrè Editore.

Twigger, Robert. 1999. Inflation: The Value of the Pound, 1750–1998. House of Commons Library: Working Paper 99/20.

United Kingdom. House of Commons. 1811. *An Account of the Market Prices of Standard Gold in Bars; Foreign (i.e. Portugal) Gold in Coin; Standard Silver in Bars; and Spanish Dollars or Pillar Pieces of Eight . . . .* London.

United Kingdom. Mint. 1914. *Forty-Fifth Annual Report of the Deputy Master and Comptroller.* London: Darling and Son, Ltd.

United States Mint. 1886. *Annual Report of the Director.* Washington, DC: Government Printing Office.

Usher, Abbott Payson. 1943. *The Early History of Deposit Banking in Mediterranean Europe.* Cambridge: Harvard University Press.

Vaissière, Pierre de. 1892. *La découverte à Augsbourg des instruments mécaniques du monnayage moderne et leur importation en France en 1550.* Montpellier: Ricard Frères.

Valencia, Gregorio de. 1598. *Commentaria theologica.* Venice: Fioravante Prati.

Van Gelder, Hendrik Enno, and Marcel Hoc. 1960. *Les monnaies des Pays-Bas bourguignons et espagnols, 1434–1713: Répertoire général.* Amsterdam: J. Schulman.

Van Hove, Leo. 2001. Optimal Denominations for Coins and Bank Notes: In Defense of the Principle of Least Effort. *Journal of Money, Credit, and Banking*, forthcoming.

Van Loon, Gerard. 1732–37. *Histoire métallique des XVII provinces des Pays-Bas, depuis l'abdication de Charles-Quint, jusqu'à la paix de Bade en 1716.* La Haye: P. Gosse.

Velde, François R. 1997. An Anthology of Writings on Money, 12th–17th c. Manuscript. Chicago: Federal Reserve Bank.

Velde, François R., and Warren E. Weber. 2000. A Model of Bimetallism. *Journal of Political Economy* 108 (6): 1210–34.

Velde, François R., Warren E. Weber, and Randall Wright. 1999. A Model of Commodity Money, with Applications to Gresham's Law and the Debasement Puzzle. *Review of Economic Dynamics* 2 (1): 291–323.

Verlinden, Charles, ed. 1959–73. *Dokumenten voor de geschiedenis van prijzen en loonen in Vlaanderen en Brabant.* Brugge: De Tempel.

Vettori, Francesco. 1738. *Il fiorino d'oro antico illustrato.* Florence: Tartini e Franchi.

Wailly, Natalis de. 1857. *Mémoire sur les variations de la livre tournois depuis le règne de Saint Louis jusqu'à l'établissement de la monnaie décimale.* Paris: Imprimerie impériale.

Walras, Léon. [1900] 1977. *Elements of Pure Economics.* Trans. William Jaffé. Fairfield, NJ: Augustus M. Kelley.

Walther, R. 1939. Die Entwicklung der europäischen Münzprägetechnik von der Karolingern bis zur Gegenwart. *Deutsches Jahrbuch für Numismatik* 2:139–58.

Warren, George F., and Frank A. Pearson. 1933. *Prices.* New York: John Wiley & Sons, Inc.

Weber, E. Juerg. 1996. "Imaginary" or "Real" Moneys of Account in Medieval Europe? An Econometric Analysis of the Basle Pound, 1365-1429. *Explorations in Economic History* 33 (4): 479–95.

Wedel, Ernst von. 1960. *Die geschichtliche Entwicklung des Unformens in Gesenken.* Düsseldorf: Verlag des Vereins Deutscher Ingenieure.

Whiston, James, ed. 1696–98. *Merchants Weekly Remembrancer of the Currant Present-Money-Prices of their Goods Ashoar in London.* London.

Willis, Henry Parker. 1901. *A History of the Latin Monetary Union: A Study of International Monetary Action.* Chicago: University of Chicago Press.

Wolontis, Josef. 1936. *Kopparmyntningen i Sverige 1624–1714.* Helgsinfors: Centraltryckeriet.

Wuttke, Robert. 1894. Zur Kipper- und Wipperzeit in Kursachsen. *Neues Archiv für Sächsische Geschichte und Altertumskunde* 15:119–56.

Zarazaga, Carlos E. 1995. Hyperinflations and Moral Hazard in the Appropriation of Seignorage. Federal Reserve Bank of Dallas: Working Paper 95-17.

Legal Citations Index

Corpus Juris Canonici

Decretum Gratiani (D)
  C 32 q. 4 c. 6, 77

Liber Extra (X)
  2.24.18, 81, 88, 91, 92, 106, 219
  3.39.18, 76
  3.39.20, 76

Compilationes (Comp)
  3.25.3, 76

Corpus Juris Civilis

Code (Cod)
  2.40.3, 84

Digest (Dig)
  12.1.2.1, 74, 76, 80, 94, 95
  12.1.3, 75, 77, 81, 84–86, 104, 108
  12.1.5, 85
  12.1.22, 85, 86
  13.7.24.1, 84
  18.1.1, 75 n, 108–110
  18.1.1, 93
  32.78.4, 78
  46.3.99, 76, 79

Institutes (Inst)
  3.14, 75
  4.6.28, 80

Feudal Law

Liber Usus Feudorum (F)
  2.56, 81, 98, 186

Other Law

U.K. Statutes,
  18 Car. II. c. 5, 273
  7 & 8 Will. III c. 10, s. 18, 295
  56 Geo. III c. 68, 303
  57 Geo. III. c. 46, 303

English Reports,
  80 Eng. Rep. 507, 105

United States, Statutes at Large
  1 Stat. 246, 313
  10 Stat. 160, 314
  17 Stat. 427, 3
  21 Stat. 7, 314
  21 Stat. 7, 3
  31 Stat. 45, 319
  48 Stat. 112, 330

Author Index

Following tradition, the names of medieval jurists are alphabetized according to their first names.

Subject Index

Following tradition, the names of medieval jurists are alphabetized according to their first names.